CURRENT LEGAL PROBLEMS 1997

Volume 50

Law and Opinion
at the End of the
Twentieth Century

UNIVERSITY COLLEGE, LONDON
FACULTY OF LAWS

SESSION 1946—1947
(FIRST TERM)

LECTURES ON
CURRENT LEGAL PROBLEMS

On THURSDAYS from 5 to 6 p.m.
in the EUGENICS THEATRE
(Entrance Gower Street) DOORS OPEN AT 4.45 P.M.

October 17th

THE OMNIPOTENCE OF PARLIAMENT
R. O'SULLIVAN, ESQ., K.C., Honorary Lecturer in Laws, U.C.L.

October 24th

THE INDIAN NATIONAL ARMY TRIALS
L. G. GREEN, LL.B., Assistant Lecturer, Faculty of Laws, U.C.L.

October 31st

THE NORTH ATLANTIC FISHERIES ARBITRATION
PROFESSOR G. W. KEETON, M.A., LL.D., Dean, Faculties of Laws,
University of London and U.C.L.

November 7th

LEGAL PROBLEMS OF A SOCIALIST ECONOMY
W. FRIEDMANN, LL.M., Dr.Jur., Quain Lecturer in Laws, U.C.L.

November 14th

THE GERMAN LEGAL SYSTEM UNDER MILITARY
GOVERNMENT
R. H. GRAVESON, LL.M., S.J.D., Ph.D., Reader in English Law in the
University of London

November 21st

LEGAL ASPECTS OF THE NEW INDIAN
CONSTITUTION
M. I. ZAGDAY, Ph.D., Assistant Lecturer in Laws, U.C.L.

November 28th

ADMINISTRATIVE TRIBUNALS
R. FITZGERALD, LL.B., Lecturer in Laws, U.C.L.

December 5th

WAR CRIMES BEFORE INTERNATIONAL AND BRITISH
TRIBUNALS
G. SCHWARZENBERGER, Ph.D., Dr.Jur., Reader in International Law
in the University of London

Admission is free and without ticket

University College, London
(Gower Street, W.C.I)

E. L. TANNER,
Secretary.

LB-DN/6822

A notice for the first series of Current Legal Problems *Lectures*

CURRENT LEGAL PROBLEMS 1997

Volume 50

Law and Opinion at the End of the Twentieth Century

Edited by

M. D. A. FREEMAN

with

A. D. E. LEWIS

as
Assistant Editor

OXFORD UNIVERSITY PRESS
1997

Oxford University Press, Great Clarendon Street, Oxford OX2 6DP
Oxford New York
Athens Auckland Bangkok Bogota Bombay Buenos Aires
Calcutta Cape Town Dar es Salaam Delhi Florence Hong Kong Istanbul
Karachi Kuala Lumpur Madras Madrid Melbourne Mexico City
Nairobi Paris Singapore Taipei Tokyo Toronto Warsaw
and associated companies in
Berlin Ibadan

Oxford is a registered trade mark of Oxford University Press

Published in the United States
by Oxford University Press Inc., New York

British Library Cataloguing in Publication Data
Data available

Library of Congress Cataloging in Publication Data
Data available
ISBN 0–19–826599–9
ISBN 0–19–826787–8 (Pbk)

1 3 5 7 9 10 8 6 4 2

Typeset by Cambrian Typesetters Frimley, Surrey
Printed in Great Britain
on acid-free paper by
Biddles Ltd., Guildford and King's Lynn

PREFACE

This is the fiftieth volume of *Current Legal Problems*. *Current Legal Problems* was established in 1946 as a series of lectures. Only during that year did the idea of producing an annual publication emerge. The first published volume was thus the second series of lectures. Re-reading it now one is struck by its breadth and internationalism. There was a contribution in French by a leading international lawyer, one by the Chinese ambassador (whose son Bin Cheng, a distinguished professor at UCL, subsequently made a number of important *Current Legal Problems* contributions), one on Japan (in the days before UCL had a Professor of Japanese Law), one on Islamic law, one on polygamy. From Georg Schwarzenberger, who with George Keeton, was the founding editor, we get such pearls as 'Britain teaches nations how to live'. Reforming the House of Lords was the agenda of one of the first year's essays. This called for the exclusion of Lords of Appeal in Ordinary and Bishops from sitting in the Lords, and also for the disestablishment of the Church of England. In another contribution, Marshall was critical of the long delays in executing convicted murderers sentenced on Caribbean islands. The first volume sold for 17 shillings and 6 pence!

The second volume contained the first Bentham Club Presidential Address, a regular though not invariable feature of volumes since. It was delivered by Lord du Parcq, who sadly died within two months of giving it. This volume contained the first of many contributions by Dennis (later Lord) Lloyd. His thoughts on codification repay study even today. The volume is also notable for essays by Edwards on mens rea and bigamy and Marshall on the well-known 'findings' cases. From Schwarzenberger we learn that jurisprudence is still pretty much as it was in Kant's day and that 'the jurists seek a concept of law.' A pity that H. L. A. Hart never gave a CLP!

The third volume is the first to contain a contribution from an academic at an English university rather than UCL—Professor Eastwood from Manchester. Lectures pointed to anachronisms in equity like the doctrine of conversion, which only disappeared from English law during the course of this year's lectures, and half secret trusts, and also to the new concept of planning. The volume contained too Lloyd's first foray into landlord and tenant, and an extraordinary piece on the 'colour problem' in South Africa and the U.S.A. This lecture was almost exactly contemporaneous with the arrival of the *Empire Windrush* and its 492 Jamaicans!

The fourth volume contains Glanville Williams's still much-admired 'inaugural' on the 'aims of the law of tort', George Webber on frustration and articles by Ernest Scamell, a future editor, Arthur Goodhart and Wolfgang Friedmann. In the fifth volume, Lord Denning's search for a 'new equity' stands out. In his article, which reproduces a Bentham Club address, he regretted the fusion of law and equity and lamented the then fact that the House of Lords was bound by its own decisions. (He speculated on the consequences had the three/two split in *Donoghue* v. *Stevenson* gone the other way!) He concluded, as only he could, with a ringing call for another Bentham to rise up.

The volumes throughout the fifties reflect the legal climate and political concerns of those times: nationalization (Scamell), compulsory acquisition of land (Fitzgerald), hire purchase (Ivamy), back-street abortions (Glanville Williams), colonialism and the breakup of Empire (Denys Holland, who contributed a remarkable and sustained series on constitutional developments and crises in West Africa, Kenya, Singapore and Cyprus). In volume 7 Lloyd examined the cost of litigation: had his proposals been implemented Lord Woolf's task in recent years would have been rendered a little easier. Volume 8 contains Glanville Williams's much-cited article on the definition of crime, and Ernest Scamell's attack on privity of contract as having outlived its raison d'être. Volume 9 stands out for Raphael Powell's 'good faith in contracts', an essay revisited only last year by Roger Brownsword of the University of Sheffield in an essay which is likely to figure prominently in future thinking in this area. Volume 10 contains Dennis Lloyd's 'Inaugural' on the 'right to work': *Bonsor* v. *Musicians Union* had just been decided.

The first article on tax law (Scamell again) is in volume 11, on an issue of intellectual property in volume 14 (by Lloyd). Bentham gave a lecture in 1962 (only it was R. W. on charity). Roger Rideout, who subsequently edited eighteen volumes, published his first article, on the future of trade union law, in 1965. The first article on a medical law issue was written by Ian Kennedy and published in volume 22. He was then, we read today, a 'Lecturer in Latin American Law': this was long before we went on to 'unmask medicine'— and join the 'opposition'! His essay 'Alive or Dead' still remains a very current legal problem. Whether quasi-delict does—the subject of Peter Birks' first published article in the same volume—is more questionable. What is not in question is that *Current Legal Problems* was first to publish many who went on to distinguished academic careers. Thus, in 1970, the twenty-third volume saw John Baker using legal history to illuminate common law principles (he wrote on non est factum) and Dan Prentice writing on drunken driving.

I heard my first CLP some years earlier in 1962. It was on that very current legal problem in 1834, the Zollverein! This was part of the first series—the only one until this year—to be thematic. Although de Gaulle had just denied the U.K. entry into the Common Market, the already-planned series on the implications of the U.K. joining the E.E.C. went ahead. With characteristic understatement, Dennis Lloyd told us that, if we joined, it would present us with a challenge. Still, some years later, another contributor to CLPs told us that joining Europe would have no impact on our legal system, and another, in 1966, doubted whether European law existed!

The early 1970s saw my baptism (on divorce reform); Bill Butler's (on comradely justice), Tony Oakley's much-acclaimed essay on the constructive trust (subsequently worked into a book), and the first articles by Jim Stephens and Rodney Austin. Jeffrey Jowell's 'Inaugural'—delivered the same day as President Carter's 'Inaugural' but arguably with greater impact—on the limits of law in urban planning is in volume 30. Dawn Oliver's first article, 'The Mistress in Law' (have we come that far?) was in 1978. The same year the volume included the first of Ian Dennis's essays on the criminal law, on this occasion analysing impossibility, and Bill Butler's 'Inaugural' on law reform in the Soviet Union. 1979 (volume 32) saw the first co-authored articles (two, on race relations and on abortion respectively). Stephen Guest's first foray into Dworkin was also included in that volume, offering insights into the contribution that legal theory can make to legal education. Robert Mnookin's 'Bargaining In The Shadow of the Law'—a fuller version in the *Yale Law Journal* being one of the most-cited of law review articles—is also in the 1979 volume.

The 1980s opened with Andrew Lewis's first contribution (exploring liability where there has been improper application of European Community legal provisions), and with essays on the moon treaty (by Bin Cheng), the Benson commission on legal services (by Michael Zander), constitutional solutions to the Irish problem (by Claire Palley), and on children's rights (by myself). Zander and Palley were not at UCL, but since the mid-1970s the lecture series and volumes were opened up by invitation to distinguished outsiders. So the 1975 volume features René Joliet and Aubrey Diamond, the 1976 David Hayton, the 1977 Francis Jacobs, John Hazard and Issac Zamir (revisiting the declaratory judgment) and the 1978 included Karl Olivercrona on Bentham (the first 'Austin Lecture') and John Smith, as well as the Soviet experts G. I. Tunkin and Bernard Rudden.

By 1980 the character of *Current Legal Problems* had changed. The majority of contributions are now from outside contributors. The 1984 volume, for example, contains only three UCL contributors (Parkinson, Freeman and Guest) though two other contributors (Birks and Brown) were former UCL faculty members. Professor Birks' lecture was the first J. A. C. Thomas commemorative: Thomas lectures have been a regular feature of the volumes since and have offered some of the finest scholarship in the series. The excavation by Alan Rodger, now Lord Rodger of Earlsferry, of *Donoghue* v. *Stevenson*, in volume 41 is particularly memorable.

Volume 36, a year earlier, was a particularly strong issue, with Bob Hepple's 'Inaugural' 'Judging Equal Rights', Lord Lloyd's last contribution (his Bentham Club Presidential Address), and contributions by Neil MacCormick, Peter Birks, Francis Reynolds and Norman Palmer. Nicola Lacey's essay on dangerousness and criminal justice, and Paul Matthews's wide-ranging piece on people as property also feature in this volume.

The 1985 volume (volume 38) contains essays on economic theorising about tort (Veljanovski), a critique of Charles Fried's 'Contract As Promise' by Andrew Burrows, then at Manchester and now one of UCL's professors, articles on community involvement in crime control (Nelken) and the 'good administration' of European Community Law (Usher), as well as my 'Inaugural' and Sir Jack Jacob's 'Bentham Address'. A year later the volume examined by use of short research working papers the Miners' strike and the Westland Helicopter Affair. The implications of the 'reproduction revolution' featured for the first time, including a contribution by Baroness Warnock whose report into, what she called, 'a matter of life' had sparked off so much of the debate.

Volume 40 was reached in 1987. There is a potted history of law in the University of London, based on a lecture given at Queen Mary College by William Twining, and there are essays on co-ownership, minority languages, and 'contracts' as a social work technique, as well as Gavin Lightman's intriguingly-entitled 'Scargill Unbound'. In volume 41 there was a clear theme with aspects of criminal justice featuring in no less than seven contributions: three of this year's chairmen also gave lectures (Lords Steyn, Browne-Wilkinson and Rodger). More inaugurals are found in the following year's volume (Mendelson and Dennis) and two first contributions (Gardiner and O'Dair) in the year after this.

Throughout the publishers had been Stevens/Sweet and Maxwell. In 1992 Oxford University Press took over *Current Legal Problems*. As part of this transfer a new venture began: a second subsidiary volume, the 'Annual Review'. During its five years of production the Annual Review offered an up-to-date summary of developments in core areas of law. The Annual Review ceased publication in 1996 and is to be replaced by a sister, rather than subsidiary, volume, 'Current Legal Issues', beginning in 1998. But before looking to the future, a few words must be said about the immediate past.

This volume is the sixth with OUP. The first (volume 45) was published in 1992. Remarkably it contains no contribution by a member of the UCL Law Faculty, though two by members of the Monopolies and Mergers Commission! Essays on aspects of contract law feature prominently in this volume. It was also Roger Rideout's last volume as editor.

This is the fifth volume under my editorship. The first (volume 46) examined institutions (including Elaine Genders on Grendon Underwood), assessed the limitations of concepts such as trusts and unjust enrichment, and explored the relationship of law and social and economic theory. Volume 47, containing Normal Palmer's 'Inaugural' and Jane Holder's first contribution, emphasized civil liberties issues. It also contained Kevin Gray's essay on property and empowerment which is, I believe, one of the best articles to appear in the fifty years of *Current Legal Problems*. Volume 48 has two more 'Inaugurals' (Burrows and Oda) and in general an international and comparative flavour. It also offers an insight into feminist legal theory (Lacey) and the human genome project, neither of which subjects could have been anticipated when *Current Legal Problems* was founded. And so to last year with David O'Keeffe's 'Inaugural' on European Union Citizenship, Roger Rideout exploring the law of unincoporated associations and Helen Reece's baptism challenging the orthodoxy of the paramountcy principle. *Current Legal Problems* began with an international perspective and so it was appropriate that as fifty years approached the subject of globalization should be tackled, and it was, last year, by William Twining.

This year's volume is sub-titled, 'Law and Opinion at the End of the Twentieth Century'. It is based on a series of lectures given between October 1996 and March 1997—and thus completed before the General Election of May 1st—by members of the Faculty of UCL (the only outside contributions hardly come from outside since both Bob Hepple and David Nelken are so closely associated with us). It is the first 'home-based' volume for a very long time. But, if this is to constitute a precedent, it is one only for such commemorative occasions. Perhaps it will be repeated in 25 years!

There are of course precedents for volumes on law and opinion. There is Dicey's masterly study and Morris Ginsberg's *Law and Opinion in England in the Twentieth Century*. This was based on a series of lectures at LSE and published in 1959. Our volume is as different from Ginsberg's, as his was from Dicey's. Unlike the LSE model we do not offer separate chapters on trends of thought or aspects of social policy. In 1959, even at LSE, it was natural to separate law from such branches of knowledge. But current legal problems cannot be so decontextualized and the essays in this volume though legally-focused do not ignore either ideological concerns or considerations of social policy. They are offered as explorations of the state of English law at the end of the century. They look back and to the future.

This preface has offered a retrospective, but a few words about our future are also in order. From next year we will be publishing a sister volume to *Current Legal Problems*. Entitled *Current Legal Issues*, this will be published each spring, with *Current Legal Problems* continuing to be published in the autumn. *Current Legal Issues* will be inter-disciplinary. The basis for each volume will be a two-day colloquium scheduled to take place at the end of June each year. The first colloquium and volume is on law and science, the second on law and literature. Succeeding volumes will explore such disciplines as medicine, history, political science and geography. This, we believe, is an important new venture: we hope it will be welcomed.

Next year's *Current Legal Problems* will celebrate the 250th anniversary of Jeremy Bentham's birth by examining legal theory at the end of the millennium.

It remains to thank those who have assisted with the preparation of this year's volume, in particular my secretary, Rebekah Williams. Once again our series was graced by a number of distinguished chairs (the new Lord Chief Justice, Lord Bingham of Cornhill, the new Master of the Rolls, Lord Woolf of Barnes, Dame Mary Arden, Lord Browne-Wilkinson, Lord Goff, Lord Hoffmann, Lord Mustill, Lord Nicholls of Birkenhead, Lord Rodger of Earlsferry, Lord Slynn of Hadley, Lord Steyn and Lord Justice Ward): to them we express our sincerest thanks for supporting this project.

Michael Freeman
May 1997

CONTENTS

TABLE OF CASES

TABLE OF STATUTES

Foreign Legislation

International Treaties, Conventions etc

THE CHANGING CONSTITUTION IN THE 1990s

Dawn Oliver

More than most subjects, constitutional law tends to be more opinion than law. It is therefore appropriate to look back over the last century of constitutional law and forward to the future in order to identify how both the law and opinion about the constitution have changed and are likely to continue to change.

When Her Majesty the Queen visited UCL in 1985 her attention was drawn to a display containing the then recently published first edition of *The Changing Constitution*.[1] Her Majesty expressed surprise at the idea that the constitution was changing, and asked for a copy to be supplied to the Palace—a request with which we dutifully complied. I do not know whether the Palace now considers that the constitution is changing. On the surface, it is true, the 'dignified' constitution, to use Bagehot's words,[2]— especially viewed from the end of the Mall—may not be changing greatly. But the 'efficient' constitution—the actual working system of government—certainly is changing very radically, and has been changing for at least twenty years.

I have become particularly conscious of how the subject has changed over the years in the course of the work I have been doing, with Lord Lester of Herne Hill and Katya Lester, on the revision of *Halsbury's Laws of England* on *Constitutional Law* (now renamed *Constitutional Law and Human Rights*). The title had not been

---

[1] The collection of essays edited jointly by Professor Jeffrey Jowell and myself.
[2] Walter Bagehot, *The English Constitution* (London, 1865) (Fontana edition, 1963, introduction by R. H. S. Crossman).

replanned since the first edition in 1909,[3] and it gave, as Butterworths' internal reviewer put it, 'a very Victorian outlook on the constitution'. In fact, again as the reviewer put it, it was 'a rag-bag title'. So it was part of our task to remove the Victorian outlook, and to give the subject some coherence.

We can learn something about how the subject has changed by considering what was missing from previous editions, and what was in which is no longer there. In previous editions there were large sections, now removed to a new title, *Crown Lands and Privileges*, on miscellaneous Royal Prerogatives and the Hereditary Revenues of the Crown. In the 1974 edition there was a chapter on Northern Ireland, but nothing on Scotland or Wales. There was nothing on standards of conduct in public life, and almost nothing on human rights or civil liberties. There were a couple of paragraphs on Parliament (though there was a separate Halsbury title, *Parliament*), and a few paragraphs on the Judiciary (though there was a title on *Courts*). In 1974 there was almost nothing on Europe (which we had just joined) and nothing on non-departmental public bodies.

We took the view that the scope of constitutional law must cover our relations with Europe, relations between the countries forming

---

[3] I pay tribute to the excellent scholarship of previous editors, Sir William Holdsworth and Professor Lawson, from whom I learned a great deal in the revision process.

The first edition, 1909, was written, incidentally, by Professor W. S. Holdsworth, who at that time was Fellow and Lecturer in Law at St John's College Oxford, having previously been Professor of Constitutional Law at UCL; by the time of the second edition of Halsbury's *Constitutional Law* in 1932 Holdsworth was Sir William Holdsworth, and held the Vinerian Chair of English Law at Oxford.

In the first footnote to the first paragraph of the first and second editions is the following: 'Dicey defined constitutional law as embracing all rules which directly or indirectly affect the distribution or exercise of the sovereign power in the State (*Law of the Constitution*, 8th edn., 22). But this definition, like Austin's (*Jurisprudence*, i, 73), rests upon theories of sovereignty which had best be kept out of substantive law.' John Austin had been Professor of Jurisprudence at University College London.

In the second edition Holdsworth was assisted by F. H. Lawson, at that time All Souls Reader in Roman Law in the University of Oxford. Lawson later became Professor of Comparative Law in the University of Oxford.

The previous, 1974, edition of Halsbury was completed, by F. H. Lawson, in circumstances of constitutional upheaval which no editor would relish: during the editing process there was a radical rearrangement of government departments and a stalemate general election; Northern Ireland was in a chaotic state (as Butterworths' internal reviewer put it).

the United Kingdom, basic principles including standards of conduct in public life, human rights, Parliament, the judiciary, and non-departmental public bodies—though avoiding undue overlap with other titles has been a problem. All of those subjects are now covered, though of course some are also covered at length in other Halsbury titles. We have tried to overcome the rag-bag effect by increasing our coverage in many respects to reflect the current concepts of what is constitutional and what is not, and by removing material, especially about the monarchy, that is now of only marginal, if any, constitutional relevance. This reflects some of the changes that have taken place in the subject over the last century.

But change is a continuing process and we need to look forwards as well as backwards. I suggest the issues in the subject and the changes in constitutional law that are currently taking place or being mooted revolve around relationships—between institutions, between the nations of the United Kingdom and the centre, between individuals and the community, and with Europe. These link in strongly with changes in the nature of the intellectual discipline of constitutional law.

Relationships I: Institutions

First, relationships between institutions: until about twenty years ago the principles governing relationships between the legislative, executive, and judicial organs of government in the United Kingdom were the rule of law, parliamentary sovereignty, and ministerial responsibility. Constitutional lawyers traditionally regarded the rule of law and the sovereignty of Parliament, which are about relationships between the courts on the one hand and Parliament, government, and individuals on the other, as being the central pillars of the constitution. Political scientists on the other hand paid relatively little attention to these two tenets and were more preoccupied with politics, and in particular with ministerial responsibility—the relationship between government and Parliament—as the central pillar of English constitutional theory. This difference of approach is hardly surprising, given the different intellectual skills the two disciplines require and the different literatures each, until recently, resorted to.

In this period there has been a steady trend to resort to legal measures to secure responsible government, which represents an acknowledgement of the limited effectiveness of ministerial responsibility as a control on government. This trend has drawn the disciplines of law and politics together.

Recognition of the shortcomings of ministerial responsibility to Parliament and the limitations on what Members of Parliament can achieve in imposing responsibility on ministers were highlighted in, for instance, the establishment of the Parliamentary Commissioner for Administration in 1967, and in the recent extensions of his jurisdiction into access to information, the machinery of justice, contracted-out services, and the Citizen's Charter.

Acknowledgement of the powerlessness of Parliament in its relationships with government is also evident in the rapid expansion of the grounds for judicial review and the areas of governmental activity that it covers, and in resort to that jurisdiction by applicants over the last fifteen years or so. In a climate of judicial and public scepticism about the effectiveness of ministerial responsibility as a check on government the courts have been willing to step in and review decisions, for example those exercised as part of the royal prerogative, which would previously have been regarded as inappropriate for judicial review and more suited to parliamentary mechanisms of control. The former judicial deference to ministers and to Parliament, seen in cases such as *Liversidge* v. *Anderson*,[4] has weakened and judges commonly state that they do not regard ministerial responsibility to Parliament as a bar to judicial review.

The centrality of ministerial responsibility in the constitution has also diminished because of a range of modernizing institutional reforms that have been introduced in the last two decades or so. Under the so-called 'Next Steps initiative', there are now over 100 executive agencies within government departments. Examples are the Prison Service, the Child Support Agency, the Highways Agency, the Employment Service, and the Benefits Agency. Ministers do not regard themselves as responsible when operational mistakes are made in these agencies. They accept only a duty to try to put things right or to see that they do not go wrong again. In addition to the 100 true agencies, there are some fifty units in non-ministerial departments—the Board of Inland Revenue and Her Majesty's Customs and Excise, for instance—operating on agency lines. In total some 390,000 people, over 70 per cent of the civil

---

[4] [1942] AC 206.

service, are covered by these arrangements, which dilute ministerial responsibility as we used to understand it in the good old days of Crichel Down.[5]

But beyond these Crown bodies is a huge army of entirely *extra-governmental* organizations, spending about £80 billion a year, well over 35 per cent of all public expenditure. Half of this was formerly controlled or influenced by local authorities.[6] These bodies are not subject to ministerial responsibility at all. They number about 5,500, and include over 350 non-departmental executive public bodies (NDPBs) like the Securities and Investments Board, the Bank of England, the Arts Councils, the BBC, and the Gas Consumers' Council. In addition to the NDPBs there are over 600 National Health Service bodies—trusts and authorities (which are officially regarded as departmental public bodies) and some 4,500 bodies operating at local level but outside local government—grant-maintained schools, housing action trusts, training and enterprise councils, sixth form colleges, colleges of further education, and housing associations. These bodies have come to be known as 'the new magistracy' and their members number some 65,000.

There is thus a vast area of public activity that is not subject to ministerial responsibility to Parliament at all. In view of these developments that doctrine can hardly be regarded any longer as a pillar of the constitution.

The Committee on Standards in Public Life (the Nolan Committee) considered standards of conduct in executive NDPBs and NHS bodies in its first report[7] and a wide range of Local Spending Bodies in its second report.[8] The Government's response was summarized in a White Paper, *The Governance of Public Bodies: A Progress Report*.[9] Broadly, the Government acknowledged the

---

[5] There are now more 'non-ministerial departments' in government than ever before, with the addition of regulatory bodies such as Ofsted, Oftel, Ofgas, and so on to the established non-ministerial departments of the Board of Inland Revenue and Customs and Excise. There is no direct ministerial responsibility for the day-to-day activities of these bodies, though they are Crown bodies and subject to audit by the National Audit Office.

[6] See W. Hall and S. Weir, *The Democratic Audit of the United Kingdom* (London, 1996).   [7] Cm 2850–1, 1995.   [8] Cm 3270, 1996.

[9] Cm 3557, 1997. See also the Chancellor of the Duchy of Lancaster (Mr Roger Freeman) at HC Deb., vol. 290, 12 Feb. 1997, cols. 290–3.

need to extend the jurisdiction of the Parliamentary Commissioner for Administration in this sector as widely as possible, and to appoint external (though not independent) adjudicators to deal with complaints where possible. It promised to codify good practice and standards of conduct in these bodies by introducing a model code for staff of NDPBs and fuller and clearer guidance on codes of practice. It undertook to introduce consultative arrangements to bring together local public bodies and local authorities, and a national consultative forum to bring together key interests in the public sector led by the National Audit Office, the Audit Commission, and the Accounts Commission. The appointment system would be more open: ministers would remain responsible for appointments to NDPBs, and these would be made openly and on merit and subjected to various forms of independent scrutiny, including via the newly appointed Commissioner for Public Appointments. The power of inspection of the Comptroller and Auditor General would be extended to all NDPBs which were not already audited, and audit would cover compliance with codes of conduct as well as financial propriety and value for money issues.

We have here, I suggest, the beginnings of a model of accountability outside ministerial responsibility (save for matters of appointment, discipline, and dismissal of officials) which may, in due course, come to replace individual ministerial responsibility as a pillar of the constitution. The model bears some resemblance to the system operating in Sweden,[10] a parliamentary system without a doctrine of individual ministerial responsibility to Parliament, and yet one with developed and effective accountability mechanisms which operate through a strong system of administrative law. But the Swedish system differs from the proposals in the White Paper and generally from developments in Britain in important ways: it is based on statute, its redress of grievance provisions are independent of government, openness is not voluntary but is secured through a statutory freedom of information regime, and audit is not limited to financial matters and value for money, but extends to administrative practice.

---

[10] On this and the Swedish system generally see O. McDonald, *Swedish Models* (London, 1992) and *The Future of Whitehall* (London, 1992); D. Oliver and G. Drewry, *Public Service Reform. Issues of Accountability and Public Law* (London, 1996).

Since the late 1970s or thereabouts debate about institutional relationships in the United Kingdom has moved away from ministerial responsibility and focused instead on the concept of accountability. The usefulness and versatility of this concept (which dates back to the writings of Aristotle) have proved attractive to both lawyers and political scientists. It serves to highlight the importance attached to duties owed by all public bodies to explain and give an account of the way in which their functions are being discharged, and their duties to accept blame and make amends if it should seem that errors had been made.

Accountability is a process that we can see operating, for instance, in financial and efficiency audits, in judicial review, in the investigations by parliamentary select committees, and through the various ombudsmen in the system. It is a far more flexible and broadly applicable concept than ministerial responsibility. The duty to account is owed not just to Parliament but to a range of bodies. Each 'accountee' body adopts procedures suitable to its particular role, and applies far more explicit criteria than Parliament applies when holding a minister responsible for his or her department. Here the trend to publish codes, criteria, framework documents, charters, and guidelines, to which I shall return, serves to strengthen accountability by spelling out the criteria against which bodies are to be measured.

The relationship between the new concept of accountability and the old concept of responsibility has been an issue in particular in relation to the individual responsibility of ministers to Parliament, and relationships between junior and senior ministers, ministers and civil servants, and civil servants and their seniors[11] (especially civil servants working in 'Next Steps' agencies in their Departments). These were the issues the Scott Report[12] was largely about. The Treasury and Civil Service Committee, now divided into the Public Administration Committee and the Treasury Committee (and other House of Commons select committees including the Defence Committee in the Westland Affair), examined relationships between ministers and civil servants on a number of occasions and

---

[11] See Sir Christopher Foster, 'Reflections on the true significance of the Scott Report for government accountability' (1996) 74 *Public Administration* 567.
[12] Sir Richard Scott, *Inquiry into the Export of Defence Equipment and Dual-Use Goods to Iraq and Related Prosecutions* (London, 1996) (1995–6, HC 115).

expressed concern that ministers claim only to be *accountable* for what happened in their departments but not *responsible* for it.[13]

A major problem is that ministerial responsibility still entails that ministers are permitted to get away with their claim to the *exclusive* right to give an account of what had happened in their departments. The Osmotherly rules (currently entitled *Departmental Evidence and Response to Select Committees*, 1994) state that civil servants give evidence to select committees on behalf of and at the direction of their ministers. When ministers themselves answer questions they commonly refuse the information requested on a number of grounds which ministers have relied on for many years.

The House of Commons is trying to be less compliant than it has been in the past in allowing ministers to set the rules about who answers questions and whether questions may be answered. The Public Service (now Public Administration) Committee reiterated the point that *Questions of Procedure for Ministers*[14] and the Osmotherly rules were the government's own conventions, not Parliament's, and the committee urged that they should not be accepted by Parliament as binding;[15] they recommended that the House of Commons pass a resolution to this effect,[16] and this both Houses did in the last days of the 1992–7 Parliament. The resolution reads:

That, in the opinion of this House, the following principles should govern the conduct of Ministers of the Crown in relation to Parliament: (1) Ministers have a duty to Parliament to account, and be held to account, for the policies, decisions and actions of their Departments and Next Steps Agencies; (2) It is of paramount importance that Ministers give accurate and truthful information to Parliament, correcting any inadvertent error at the earliest opportunity. Ministers who knowingly mislead Parliament will be expected to offer their resignation to the Prime Minister; (3) Ministers should be as open as possible with Parliament, refusing to provide information only when disclosure would not be in the public interest which should be decided in accordance with relevant statute and the Government's Code of Practice on Access to Government Information (Second

---

[13] See for instance the Second Report from the Public Service Committee, *Ministerial Accountability and Responsibility* (1995–6, HC 313); D. Woodhouse, 'Ministerial Responsibility: Something Old, Something New' [1997] *Public Law* 262.   [14] 1992, revised in 1997.
[15] 1995–6 HC 313, paras. 39, 82.   [16] *Ibid.*, para. 60.

Edition, January 1997); (4) Similarly, Ministers should require civil servants who give evidence before Parliamentary Committees on their behalf and under their directions to be as helpful as possible in providing accurate, truthful and full information in accordance with the duties and responsibilities of civil servants as set out in the Civil Service Code (January 1996).[17]

There are other ways in which the House of Commons has been seeking to assert its role in holding ministers to account in recent years. For instance, the Commons' Table Office has in the last couple of years changed its practice, which had been to refuse to accept any questions that ministers had ever previously refused to answer. The new practice is to refuse to accept only questions that Ministers have refused to answer in the current Parliament. But there is still no effective coercive machinery for compelling ministers to answer questions, or for enforcing the attendance of civil servants, or their answering of questions.[18]

Sir Richard Scott stressed in his *Report on the Export of Defence Equipment . . . to Iraq*[19] that information is the key to effective accountability, more important than the expectation that ministers should resign. The Public Service Committee endorsed that view[20] and it is reflected in the House of Commons resolution referred to above. If information is denied it, the House of Commons is denied its role in adjudicating on who is to blame or even whether anything has gone wrong. This is entirely contrary to the theory of ministerial responsibility. Improved access to information is essential, in my view, as long as accountability remains a key concept in British constitutional theory.

---

[17] HC Deb. 19 Mar. 1997, cols. 1046–7; HL Debs., 20 Mar. 1997, cols. 1055–62. And see D. Woodhouse, n. 13 above.

[18] In the Westland Affair in 1986 for instance, the Secretary of State for Trade and Industry refused to allow civil servants to give evidence to select committees, and also refused to discipline civil servants for the wrongful leak of a document. This attitude on the part of government assumes that allocating blame is entirely an internal governmental matter. The Defence Committee was left unable to discover who had done wrong and whether anyone had taken responsibility in the sense of blame for it: Fourth Report from the Defence Committee, *Westland plc: The Government's Decision Making*, 1985–6 HC 519. As a result of this and other incidents in which ministers have refused to accept blame, there has seemed to be a lacuna in our constitutional arrangements: see for instance Seventh Report from the Treasury and Civil Service Committee, *Civil Servants and Ministers: Duties and Responsibilities*, 1985–6, HC 92;.   [19] 1995–6, HC 115.

[20] 1995–6, HC 313, paras. 26, 32, 60.

Relationships II: The Nations of the United Kingdom

Fifty years ago the relations between the nations of the United Kingdom were not matters of controversy. That is no longer the case, and high on the current political agenda is the creation of a whole tier of new nation-based and regional institutions: a new Parliament for Scotland, a Senedd for Wales, settlement of the Northern Ireland question, possibly regional assemblies for England. These reforms might go in step with reform of the House of Lords, starting with the abolition of the voting rights of hereditary peers and possibly the introduction of members representing the nations and regions.

The underlying themes in these reforms may again be linked to accountability: devolution is about securing that governmental bodies are accountable, and therefore responsive, to local electorates by moving power from Westminster and Whitehall to the nations and regions of Britain. Reform of the House of Lords seeks to make the government accountable to parliamentarians chosen on a less unacceptable basis than heredity. But here we confront major problems about the coherence of constitutional reform, for devolution and reform of the second chamber are in truth intimately linked. Most other countries with a second or upper chamber have a subnational tier of government, and the second chamber is where that tier is represented in the national legislature. It is I think typical of the British approach that the political parties have not yet articulated the relationship between devolution and reform of the second chamber: in the next few years we are likely to be faced with ill-thought-out opportunistic reforms which will not produce anything like a coherent system—despite the excellent work of the independent Constitution Unit[21] on just this point.[22]

---

[21] For an account of the Constitution Unit see D. Oliver, 'Constitutional reform moves up the political agenda' [1997] *Public Law* 193.
[22] Its full reports are: *Delivering Constitutional Reform, Reform of the House of Lords, An Assembly for Wales, Scotland's Parliament. Fundamentals for a New Scotland Act, Regional Government in England, Human Rights Legislation*, and *Report of the Commission on the Conduct of Referendums*, all published in London in 1996. In addition they have published a number of briefing papers.

Relationships III: The Individual and the State

A central concern of constitutional law as the twentieth century draws to a close, I suggest, is the relationships between the individual and the state, and between individuals and their communities. Human rights or civil liberties were not of such central interest in constitutional law thirty years ago, much less a 100 years ago.[23]

I hope I may be forgiven at this point for drawing again on *Halsbury's Laws of England* to illustrate the relative lack of interest in civil liberties in English law until the last three decades or so. The first edition of Halsbury's *Constitutional Law* title was published in 1909. There was a short section on 'Relations between the Crown and Subject', which was concerned with the Crown's duties to the subject as expressed in the Coronation oath, the subject's duty of allegiance, and the offence of treason and various treasonable offences. There was nothing on civil liberties, and no other Halsbury title dealt explicitly with civil liberties issues, though they arose incidentally and under other guises in the context of police powers, criminal law, and so on.

An innovation in the third edition of 1954 was the removal of the large section on treason. In the fourth edition, 1974, there were twelve pages of new material on the duties and rights of the subject, which covered—very succinctly—roughly what was taught as civil liberties in constitutional and administrative law courses in universities at that time.

In the latest, fourth edition reissue, there is a substantial chapter of 100 paragraphs on 'Human rights and freedoms', written by Lord Lester and a team from 2 Hare Court. This covers the positions in English law and under the European Convention on Human Rights, and the relations between the two. It fairly indicates the importance of the topic in constitutional law in these late years of the second millennium.

---

[23] Dicey did deal at length with the rights to personal freedom (mainly through habeas corpus), freedom of discussion (mainly to contrast the English position with the Declaration of the Rights of Man in France and express his strong preference for the English approach), and public meeting in his exposition of the Rule of Law: A. V. Dicey, *Introduction to the Study of the Law of the Constitution* (London, 1885) (10th edn., 1959), chaps. V to VII.

In the last ten years or so, the focus in both legal and political debate has broadened to a quest for a definition and concept of citizenship that extends beyond the protection of civil and political rights. Towards the end of the 1980s the word 'citizenship' suddenly became part of the currency: the Speaker of the House of Commons set up a Commission on Citizenship, whose report *Encouraging Citizenship* stressed the importance of active citizenship. In the late 1980s Douglas Hurd[24] and other members of the government also started emphasizing the importance of 'active citizenship', involving participation in neighbourhood watch schemes and the like, and voluntary activity for the community. Derek Heater adopted an historical approach, analysing the history of citizenship theory from Greek and Roman models to the present day,[25] and stressing the importance of civic virtue. David Selbourne in *The Principle of Duty*[26] has focused on the duties and responsibilities of citizens. John Major launched the Citizen's Charter in 1991.[27]

What many of these themes in current citizenship debates have in common is a non-political view of the place of the individual in society. Here, I think, we can tie in the current constitutional reform debates with restiveness about whether there is such a thing as citizenship and what it might involve. Since the 1960s a number of proposals for constitutional reform have been on the agenda of some of the political parties and other interested persons and bodies. Given constraints of space, I can mention only the most prominent: I have already referred to proposals for the reform of the House of Lords, a Parliament for Scotland, a Senedd for Wales, regional government in England, a settlement of the Northern Ireland troubles. In addition there are live proposals for a Bill of Rights for the United Kingdom, electoral reform, freedom of information, and, perhaps most crucially, reform of the reform process itself, including the use of referendums and parliamentary procedures.

---

[24] D. Hurd, 'Citizenship in the Tory Democracy', *New Statesman*, 29 Apr. 1988, and 'Freedom will flourish where citizens accept responsibility', *Independent*, 13 Sep. 1989.
[25] D. Heater, *Citizenship: The Civic Ideal in World History, Politics and Education* (London, 1990).
[26] London, 1994.
[27] See *The Citizen's Charter: Raising the Standard* (London, 1991), Cm 1599.

What many of these reform proposals have in common is the view that individuals should have a greater input into the political processes that most closely affect them: devolution would bring government closer to the people and increase their influence in it, a Bill of Rights would secure the freedoms of speech and association that are essential to protect political activity from government control, reform of the second chamber should make government more representative and thus enhance citizen participation in and access to the political process, and electoral reform—or at least preferential voting—would give individuals a greater voice than they have under the first past the post system. There is here an implicit rejection of the citizen as nothing more than an obedient servant of the state and a market operator. But where many of these reforms are weak, in my view, is in their assumptions that politicians and political activity will be more effective than the market in providing opportunities for citizens to influence the political process and run their own lives. Those assumptions are unduly optimistic about the importance of ministerial responsibility in the constitution.

There is no very explicit concept in our law of what citizenship might involve. However, I believe that the common law, especially in judicial review, but also in some aspects of private law, is gradually developing a concept of the individual as a citizen in a liberal-republican sense[28]—enjoying rights and freedoms, but also closely knitted into civil society as a participating, responsible individual exercising 'civic virtue'. There is not the space to develop this idea here,[29] but, to summarize my argument, I think we can draw from judicial review cases concern to protect the autonomy, dignity, and respect of individuals and—and this is a relatively new development, in my view—acknowledgement of the needs of individuals for protection of their status in society and their security, in their jobs, their memberships of social organizations, their relations with state organizations. The grounds for

[28] See D. Heater, n. 25 above; D. Oliver and D. Heater, *The Foundations of Citizenship* (London, 1994); D. Oliver, 'What is happening to relations between the individual and the state?' in J. Jowell and D. Oliver (eds.) *The Changing Constitution* (3rd. edn.) (Oxford, 1994).

[29] But see D. Oliver, 'The underlying values of public and private law' in M. Taggart (ed.), *The Province of Administrative Law* (Oxford, 1997), 217.

judicial review tacitly acknowledge this, for these are the values protected by procedural propriety, legality, and 'Wednesbury reasonableness'. A large part of the point of procedural propriety, legitimate expectations, and rationality in decision-making is to protect the status and security of applicants for judicial review. These values, especially as protected by requirements of procedural propriety, are also to do with enabling individuals and collective organizations to participate in public decisions. The recent cases extending locus standi in judicial review to voluntary organizations and other concerned individuals or bodies represent an acceptance of the positive contribution that citizens can make to the political process by participating in decision making. This is evident in the Pergau Dam case[30] (in which the World Development Movement successfully applied for judicial review of a decision to give aid to a project in Malaysia), and in a number of other cases.[31] I consider that the courts, by allowing themselves to be used as fora for the resolution of essentially political disputes, are facilitating citizen participation in political decisions and thus tacitly admitting the limitations of parliamentary channels for effective participation.

My sense is that very similar developments, recognizing the needs of individuals for autonomy, dignity, respect, status, and security (what I have called elsewhere the five key values underlying the common law) can also be found in private law, especially where there are power imbalances. In family relationships, in particular, the weaker parties are protected, as they are in employment law. I could extend these ideas into property law, trusts, and obligations, showing that these are in many ways concerned to protect the status and security of those in weak or vulnerable positions—but space does not permit.[32] The point I make is that a concept of liberal-republican citizenship is currently developing and pervades many aspects of law outside, as well as within, constitutional law. It

---

[30] R. v. *Secretary of State for the Foreign and Commonwealth Office, ex parte World Development Movement* [1995] 1 All ER 611.
[31] Including R. v. *Secretary of State for the Home Department, ex parte Fire Brigades Union* [1995] 2 WLR 464 (challenge to a new tariff scheme for criminal injuries compensation); R. v. *Inspectorate of Pollution, ex parte Greenpeace (No 2)* [1994] 4 All ER 329; R. v. *Secretary of State for Social Security, ex parte Child Poverty Action Group* [1990] 1 QB 540.   [32] See n. 29 above.

is filling a gap in the law about what the relations between the individual and the state are or should be.

Relationships IV: Europe

English constitutional law has been slow to come to terms with our membership of the European Community. Accountability, again, is a key in discussions of the constitutional impact of our relations with Europe. Recurring issues are: to whom should public and official bodies be accountable? and against what criteria should they be judged? The transfer to Europe of power by Member States means that much policy is determined by bodies who are not accountable to individual Member States, let alone to regional or national communities within states, but to the Community or Union as a whole; and the criteria against which they are held accountable are to do with the interests of the Community, not of individual Member States or regions. The ability of individuals in each Member State to influence those by whom they are governed is thus reduced.

My own feeling is that the advantages of membership are such that we have to put up with some, I hope short-lived, loss of accountability while new mechanisms and new balances of sub-sidiarity are achieved; and we should not be too starry-eyed about the effectiveness of our home grown accountability mechanisms or the effectiveness of our own institutions to deal with Europe-wide and global problems. But a major pressure point will be finding common concepts or compatible concepts across Europe for solving what we regard as accountability problems, though our European partners may conceive them differently.

The Scope of Constitutional Law

So far, in considering the relationships that are currently central to constitutional law, we have looked at issues and referred to institutions which by any definition of the subject would be regarded as 'constitutional'. But ideas about what is constitutional and what is not have changed radically over the years. By way of example, the first edition of *Halsbury's Laws of England*[33] on

---

[33] London, 1909.

Constitutional Law treated the whole of the subject as being concerned with the powers and position of the monarchy or Crown. In the editions of 1909, 1932, and 1974 the section on the Royal Prerogative included ports and harbours, the coinage, and weights and measures. The enormous section on the Hereditary Revenues of the Crown (which took up nearly 100 pages out of a total of 435 in the 1974 edition) included material on Surrendered Revenues arising from Prerogative Rights, among which were wreck, treasure trove, waifs, estrays, fisheries and royal fish, and royal swans.

These were in the constitutional law section, I suppose, because they were governed principally by the royal prerogative. It was the source of a law that dictated whether it was constitutional or not. That of course is no longer the case and, I am pleased to say, ports and harbours, coinage, and weights and measures have been banished from the latest edition of Halsbury on *Constitutional Law*. They are dealt with instead in other Halsbury titles. The Surrendered Revenues, along with most of the material on the monarchy, are being moved into the new section of Halsbury entitled *Crown Lands and Privileges*. Despite their connections with the monarchy these topics are no longer regarded as of constitutional significance.

A major change in constitutional law in the last fifty years, then, has been a recognition that it is the nature of an institution's power rather than its source that determines whether it is 'constitutional'. This of course is acknowledged in the *CCSU*[34] case, but it is noteworthy that it was not until *ex parte Lain*[35] in 1967 and then the *CCSU* case that the significance of the nature of power as determinative of the legal controls to which it is to be subject was recognized.

It would be misleading to suggest that there was no awareness in the early years of this century, for instance, of the difficulty in deciding whether certain bodies are public authorities or not. For example in the second, 1932, edition of Halsbury there is the comment that '[f]rom the legal point of view, government may be described as the exercise of certain powers and the performance of

---

[34] *Council of Civil Service Unions* v. *Minister for the Civil Service* [1985] AC 374.
[35] *R.* v. *Criminal Injuries Compensation Board, ex parte Lain* [1967] 2 QB 864.

certain duties by public authorities or officers, together with certain private persons or corporations which exercise public functions.'[36] We would all agree wholeheartedly with that perceptive comment even today. And yet, having made these points, the rest of that volume of Halsbury was primarily concerned with central government—the Crown.

Interdisciplinarity and Sources of Constitutional Law

So far I have been concentrating on the content and substance of constitutional law. But the nature of the discipline has changed over the last fifty years or so. In particular it has become increasingly interdisciplinary and the disciplines with which law interacts are less those of history—its closest relative until some thirty years ago—than the disciplines of political science and economics and, if they are disciplines, those of practical politics and public service. The constitutional reform agenda is of increasing interest to constitutional lawyers as well as politicians and political scientists— and, still, historians. A number of charitably-funded initiatives in the field of constitutional reform have brought together people across both academic and practising disciplines in a most fruitful way in the last decade or so. Those working on the Institute for Public Policy Research project to produce a written constitution for the United Kingdom in the 1990s included political scientists and academic and practising lawyers.[37] The contributors to the Democratic Audit[38] have been political scientists, lawyers, journalists. And the team working in UCL's Constitution Unit has included

---

[36] Para. 424. In a footnote to para. 427, in the context of a discussion of which authorities exercise powers and duties, is the following: 'it is indeed often difficult to ascertain whether a body is a public authority or private corporation. . . . Compare . . . universities, which are established by Royal Charter, yet are in the main independent of government control, and are not public authorities. It might also be said that the Inns of Court, The Law Society and the General Medical Council perform public functions, yet they are not public authorities.' That was in 1932, yet the comments are still apposite today.

[37] Institute of Public Policy Research, *The Constitution of the United Kingdom* (London, 1991).

[38] For an account of the Democratic Audit see S. Weir, 'The Democratic Audit of the United Kingdom' [1993] *Public Law* 56. Its first major report is F. Klug, K. Starmer, and S. Weir, *The Three Pillars of Liberty. Political Rights and Freedoms in the United Kingdom* (London, 1996); for the 'democratic criteria' used by the Audit see D. Beetham, *Auditing Democracy in Britain* (London, 1993).

three ex-civil servants. The Unit's advisory board and working groups included academic lawyers, historians and political scientists, practising politicians, civil servants, and journalists. The combination produced work which is of the highest quality for its purpose, that of providing constructive and wise advice to a government that might be committed in principle to reforming the British constitution.

Interdisciplinarity is also evident in much of the current literature on constitutional law, which concerns itself with many issues and sources that are not strictly legal in a positivist or traditional sense. It has of course long been accepted that students of constitutional law should read beyond cases and statutes. Dicey recognized the importance of conventions to constitutional law, though his reason was, partly, that breach of convention will ultimately lead to illegality, an argument which is no longer convincing. But for many years statutes were regarded as interlopers in constitutional law. For instance, Keir and Lawson's[39] *Cases in Constitutional Law* (first edition 1928) managed to give an account of the subject without including any statutory material—not even Magna Carta, the Bill of Rights, the Act of Union, the Act of Settlement—though in later editions extracts from the Crown Proceedings Act 1947 were included.

Students of law and legal academics are seldom concerned today about whether the sources they are considering are 'really' legal. But this is nothing new. From the first edition of Halsbury in 1909 onwards a much broader view of legal sources has been taken than one finds in 'black letter' subjects in Halsbury. There are many references to proceedings in each of the Houses of Parliament in which statements were made about the relationship between the monarch, the government, and parliament: these were taken as

---

[39] F. H. Lawson was joint editor with Sir William Holdsworth of the second edition of Halsbury's *Constitutional Law*, and took responsibility himself for the third and fourth editions. He was Professor of Comparative Law at the University of Oxford at the time of the third edition, and Emeritus Professor at the time of the fourth. We can guess that he was responsible for introducing into the second edition, footnote (a) to the introductory paragraph 423, the comment: 'The distinction which Dicey drew between English Law and the French droit administratif is better expressed as a difference between a legal system which does not and one which does recognise a distinction between public and private law.

authoritative statements of the constitutional position. In the first edition[40] for instance, there is reference to the statement by Lord Glanville to the House of Lords in 1864 that the presence of the monarch at any meetings of his ministers where deliberations or discussions take place is now clearly recognized as being contrary to constitutional practice (it survives in the latest edition![41]). Indeed, the source for the material on the relations between the sovereign and the Cabinet and for ministerial responsibility was almost entirely parliamentary.

There have also been extensive references to authoritative legal textbooks and history books in all the previous editions—Blackstone's *Commentaries*, Todd's *Parliamentary Government*, Hallam's *Constitutional History*, Anson's *Law and Custom of the Constitution*, Harris' *Life of Hardwicke* are examples. This reflects, again, the longstanding interdisciplinary nature of constitutional law. Holdsworth was a legal historian, and the historian in him was very evident in his two editions of Halsbury. So the willingness of constitutional lawyers, even judges, to take into account parliamentary and other non-statutory and non-judicial material is not as new as we might sometimes assume.

But what is new in the last twenty years or so in sources of constitutional law—or norms, as we might fashionably call them now—is the proliferation and publication of non-statutory codes of various kinds. Codes often contain standards of conduct,[42] and this too is a new issue in the discipline, to which relatively little importance was attached until recently. In the last five years codes have attracted the attention of lawyers. The Nolan Committee recommended amendment of *Questions of Procedure for Ministers*, the Cabinet Handbook, to spell out the ethical standards expected of ministers, and also recommended the introduction of a civil service code, a code of conduct for MPs, a code for public

[40] At para. 67; see Parliamentary Debates, 3rd series, Vol. CLXXV., 251.
[41] At para. 411.
[42] *Questions of Procedure for Ministers* was first issued to ministers on a confidential basis by Clement Attlee in 1945, though elements in it are older. It was not officially published until 1992 as part of the Government's Open Government initiative. The Osmotherly rules (or *Departmental Evidence and Response to Select Committees*) provide a further example of the use of codes in government—both are in fact government documents.

appointments: all of these recommendations have been implemented, together with other reforms designed to improve and
clarify standards of conduct.[43] The Scott Report also criticized
Questions of Procedure for Ministers and the Osmotherly rules.
These criticisms were taken up by the Public Service Committee in
its 1996 report on Ministerial Accountability and Responsibility
and led to the amendment of *Questions* (now Ministerial Code).

The upshot of this sort of activity is that in the last two years or
so the number of published codes regulating the conduct of
ministers, civil servants, and Members of Parliament has increased
substantially and their importance to the discipline of constitutional law is growing as the shortcomings of unarticulated
understandings as mechanisms of control have come to be
recognized. They raise intriguing issues as to their legal status or
relevance in the exercise of discretionary powers or judicial review
and their relevance for parliamentary self-regulation.

Conclusion

By way of conclusion let us draw together some unifying threads in
looking at the state of the discipline of constitutional law at the end
of the century. First, the discipline is in a state of flux, reflecting the
changing political—and economic—situation in the United
Kingdom and Europe. Many of its traditions are in doubt and the
authority of state institutions is questioned. The subject is
increasingly interdisciplinary, and its raw materials and the norms
on which it draws are composed to a considerable extent of codes,
statements in Parliament, and other sources, as well as cases and
statutes. And yet these developments represent more of an
evolution than a radical departure from the past—constitutional
law has always drawn on sources other than cases and statutes.

The disciplines with which constitutional law interacts have also
changed, moving away from history towards political science and
practical politics and public service, for instance. But again this is a
matter of evolution, for there has long been an interdisciplinary
tradition in constitutional law.

---

[43] The Scott report, as we saw earlier, dedicated considerable time and space to
Questions of Procedure for Ministers, raising objections to the lists of matters on
which parliamentary questions would be disallowed or not answered.

At the start of the century the law conceived of the individual as a subject owing deference to the Crown and to authority generally. Individual autonomy, respect and dignity, status, and security were not highly regarded, save that the rule of law was designed to protect individuals from having their liberties interfered with by government. The mystique surrounding the Crown and the royal prerogatives shielded them from judicial supervision, and much faith was placed in Parliament and ministerial responsibility as guarantors of good government and the freedoms of the subject. Despite Dicey's strong focus on the rule of law in the early years of this century, ministerial responsibility and political mechanisms for checking government were far more significant checks than the law.

Today the emphasis is on redressing imbalances of power between government and individuals and providing legal, rather than political, mechanisms for redress of grievances. A late entrant in the list of constitutional values has been citizenship, adding opportunities for participation in the community to the traditional civil and political rights. The developing concept of accountability in its varied forms is designed to protect individuals against abuse of state power and to promote the public interest and good government. It is from this set of ideas that we can draw values of individual autonomy, respect and dignity, and acknowledgement of the importance of the individual's status and need for security in the community.[44]

On the institutional front major changes have included the proliferation of extra-governmental organizations which fall outside ministerial responsibility, and the normativization and subjection to legal control of large chunks of the greatly grown state. These developments expose ministerial responsibility as a rather ineffective, unconvincing, and marginalized constitutional check—hardly the pillar of the constitution it once was. This realization opens up alternative forms of accountability, of which the law is an increasingly important example.

Socially, there has been a substantial loss of deference to politicians, due to the weakening of class system, education, the mass media. The demystification of government that this has produced has led to the development of new checks, and in particular to the growth of judicial review.

[44] I have expanded on this thesis elsewhere: see n. 29 above.

There are a number of similarities in the United Kingdom's experience and experience in other countries. There seems to be a lack of faith in politicians in many of the countries of the former Eastern bloc, though they turn to academics rather than judges to solve their problems. This is true in Italy too. That trend has not yet hit the United Kingdom!

Looking ahead to the next fifty years I predict that the concept of accountability will be refined, both in the United Kingdom and the European Community, to produce a more effective set of checks and balances. More attention will be paid to developing the criteria against which public bodies are to be held accountable, the fora in which they are accountable, and the sanctions for error. Inevitably this will lead to increased legal regulation of public functions, increasingly sophisticated auditing techniques, and the development of new institutions akin to ombudsmen and auditors to hold public bodies to account. Ministerial responsibility will decline in importance as it becomes clearer not only that Parliament cannot impose responsibility effectively but also that much activity takes place outside its scope. If, as I predict, legal controls do increase we shall be moving closer to our continental partners, who do not rely as we do on ministerial responsibility to hold government to account. I have little doubt that substantive checks in a Bill of Rights will also be introduced, and that concepts of citizenship will continue to evolve.

As far as the intellectual discipline of constitutional law is concerned, I believe that it will become increasingly interdisciplinary, establishing relationships with economists as well as political scientists and historians—and practitioners. And the sources which its students and practitioners will deal with will extend well beyond cases and statutes and their European equivalents.

I shall conclude by recalling the words used by A. J. P. Taylor in the opening chapter of *English History 1914–1945*. He said, 'Until August 1914 a sensible, law-abiding Englishman could pass through life and hardly notice the existence of the state, beyond the post office and the policeman. . . .' In 1996 I would say, 'A sensible, law-abiding European citizen living in the United Kingdom in the year 2,014 will be able to pass through life and hardly notice Parliament, ministers, or the monarchy; but he will notice another state, consisting of laws and codes and governmental agencies.'

That is the direction in which our constitution is changing. It is right, therefore, that lawyers and political scientists should consider together how, in that climate, the interests of citizens and the general public can be protected against misrule. It is my belief that a strong system of public law based on accountability, and which makes proper provision for independent redress of grievances, consultation, clarification of standards, openness, and audit, has a major role to play here.

ENGLISH CONTRACT LAW
A Rich Past, an Uncertain Future?

Ewan McKendrick *

This article serves a dual function. It is my contribution to the present series of lectures entitled 'Law and Opinion at the End of the Twentieth Century' and it represents my inaugural lecture as Professor of English Law. The Faculty of Laws at University College London has a long and a distinguished history, and it is both an honour and a privilege for me to be associated in this way with the Faculty and the College at what I hope is still a relatively early stage of my career. Nevertheless I feel that I must begin with a confession. My confession is that the title Professor of *English* Law rests somewhat uneasily on my shoulders because I was not trained as an English lawyer. My undergraduate legal education took place north of the border at the University of Edinburgh on a four year undergraduate programme, a luxury unimaginable on this side of the border. During that four-year period I was referred to English law on a number of occasions. Sometimes it was for the purpose of examining a possible answer to an issue which had not been resolved in Scots law or which had been resolved in a manner which was thought to be less than satisfactory. But my recollection, such as it is, is that, more often than not, the references to English law were rather uncomplimentary as they concerned the damage done to Scots law by uncritical borrowing from, or unthinking imposition of, English law. The relationship between Scots law and English law has never been an easy one and it is not my purpose to

* A lightly revised version of an inaugural lecture delivered at University College London on 17 Oct. 1996. I am grateful to Jack Beatson, Hugh Beale, Hugh Collins, William Lucy, Jane Stapleton, James Scott, and Steve Smith for their help in the preparation of this lecture. I remain responsible for the views expressed.

rehearse that history here. Suffice it to say that to date the borrowing has been largely in one direction: from England to Scotland. The ears of many Scots lawyers still ring with the words of Lord Cranworth, spoken in 1858, when he said, '[b]ut if such be the law of England, on what ground can it be argued not to be the law of Scotland?'[1] In so saying he introduced the reviled doctrine of common employment into Scots law, which was to exercise its malign influence until its demise in 1948. But the times are changing. The Scots are fighting back and we are now beginning to infiltrate English law. Soon we shall be able to say 'if such be the law of Scotland, on what ground can it be argued not to be the law of England?'

But, traditional nationalistic rivalries apart, there is a serious point to be made here. We live in an increasingly international and interdependent world. At the same time it is a world which is changing rapidly, and the law must take steps to keep abreast of the changes which are occurring in society. To that end, it is no longer sufficient for a lawyer to have a knowledge only of his or her own legal system. He or she must learn how lawyers in other jurisdictions think. As the Lord Chancellor's Advisory Committee on Legal Education stated in its first report:

Legal transactions are increasingly international in character. An understanding of the different ways that civilian lawyers approach common law problems can no longer be regarded as the preserve of a few specialists. Legal education in England and Wales must be both more European and more international.'[2]

One of my aims is to place the English law of contract in its wider international context. In doing so I shall proceed in four stages. In the first part, I shall give a working definition of 'contract' and an outline of the central characteristics of English contract law. The second, and the major, part will be devoted to a consideration of the development of the law of contract this century. The third section will seek to defend the claim that the English law of contract has a rich past, while the final section is devoted to a consideration of the future of the English law of contract.

---

[1] *Bartonshill Coal Co. v. Reid* (1858) 3 Macq. 266, 285.
[2] The Lord Chancellor's Advisory Committee on Legal Education and Conduct, *First Report on Legal Education and Training* (London, 1996), para. 1.13.

1. Definition

A useful starting point might be to consider, albeit briefly, the meaning which the English lawyer gives to the word 'contract'. While we may all feel that we know a contract when we see one in our everyday lives, the legal definition of a contract is not so straightforward. Indeed, there is no universally agreed definition of a contract in English law. In large part this is because it has never been necessary to produce such a definition. English contract law is unusual in that it did not develop from some underlying theory or conception of a contract but rather developed around a form of action known as the action of assumpsit. What mattered was the procedure, or the form of action, and not the substance of the claim. With the abolition of the forms of action by the Common Law Procedure Act 1852, the grip of procedural considerations over substantive law began to decline. At about the same time the practice of writing treatises on the law of contract began to increase and the authors of these texts sought to rationalize the existing mass of case law in principled terms, and in doing so they relied heavily on the works of continental jurists.[3] The outcome of this process was a number of influential books, most notably by Sir Frederick Pollock and Sir William Anson, which sought to set out the general principles of the law of contract. While these authors succeeded in establishing a series of general principles which commanded almost universal acceptance, it was still not necessary to frame a precise definition of a contract.[4] A system based on case law does not require a definition which commands universal acceptance.

While there is no universally agreed definition of a contract, the basic principles of the law of contract can be set out with a large degree of certainty. To conclude a contract the parties must reach agreement, the agreement must be supported by consideration, and there must be an intention to create legal relations. The scope of the

---

[3] See generally A. W. B. Simpson, 'Innovation in Nineteenth Century Contract Law' (1975) 91 *LQR* 247.

[4] Where definitions were provided they were obviously not intended to be definitive. These definitions tended either to explain a contract as a *promise* for the breach of which the law gives a remedy or as an *agreement* which creates obligations which the law enforces or recognizes.

contract so made is limited in its scope to the parties to it: as a general rule a third party can neither take the benefit of, nor be subject to a burden by, a contract to which he is not a party. This is known as the doctrine of privity of contract. The law also polices the terms of contracts and the procedures by which a contract is concluded. Thus a contract may be set aside where it has been entered into under a fundamental mistake, where it has been procured by a misrepresentation, duress, or undue influence, where its object or method of performance is illegal or contrary to public policy, or where an event occurs after the making of the contract which renders performance impossible, illegal, or something radically different from that which was in the contemplation of the parties at the time of entry into the contract. Assuming that a valid contract has been made, a failure to perform an obligation under the contract without a lawful excuse is a breach of contract. A breach of contract gives to the innocent party a claim for damages, the aim of which is to put the innocent party in the position which he would have been had the contract been performed according to its terms. Where the breach is of an important term of the contract the innocent party may also be entitled to terminate further performance of the contract without incurring any liability for doing so. But the law does not generally require the party in breach to perform his obligations under the contract: specific performance is an exceptional remedy, not the primary remedy. The law is committed to give a money substitute for performance, not performance itself.

Three points should be noted about this brief outline of the law of contract. The first is that it has remained largely unchanged over the last century. Sir William Anson, who published the first edition of his book in 1879, would not have dissented a great deal from this outline. The second is that these propositions are stated to be of general application. They purport to apply to all contracts, not just to some. But the reality today is that many contracts are the subject of specific regulation, so that the general principles of the law of contract are either excluded or of minimal importance. To illustrate the point one needs only to consider the principal contracts to which we are parties. Many of you are married: but the terms of your marriage contract are the subject of distinct regulation and not the general principles which I have set out. Many of you are employees or tenants but the terms of your contracts of employment or your tenancy agreements are heavily regulated by statute and the common law rules simply provide the foundation upon which the statutory rules are built. You may recently have bought an electrical appliance on credit: once again we find that the contract is the subject of detailed regulation by the Consumer Credit Act 1974 so that the common law rules are either displaced or of minimal significance. As Professor Atiyah has stated, the general principles 'remain general only by default, only because they are being superseded by detailed ad hoc rules lacking any principle, or by new principles of narrow scope and application'.[5]

The ever diminishing practical significance of the general principles of the law of contract leads us on to our third point, which is that the general principles are also of marginal importance when it comes to an analysis of the standard terms to be found in modern commercial contracts. Both the standard textbooks and the traditional Contract Law course in English universities focus on the doctrines of the law of contract, not the terms which are habitually included within a modern contract. Take an example. The late Professor Schmitthoff in his book on *Export Trade* states[6] that the following are the 'most important' clauses which an exporter should include in his general terms of business. The first is a general clause stating that every contract of sale is subject to the seller's conditions of sale. Such a clause would fall within our general principles in so far as it gave rise to an offer and acceptance problem where the buyer's terms also contained a clause stating that the contract was subject to its conditions of sale. This would give rise to what contract lawyers call the 'battle of the forms'. The second clause is a retention of title clause, under which the seller, in essence, purports to retain title to (or ownership of) the goods until they are paid for by the buyer. These clauses have been the subject of complex litigation but they do not fall within our general principles and they are not taught in most contract courses in English universities: they belong within the fold of commercial law involving as they do a mix of contract law, personal property law, and the law of securities. Next Schmitthoff lists a price escalation clause, a clause making provision for the payment of interest on

---

[5] P. Atiyah, 'Contracts, Promises and the Law of Obligations' in Atiyah, *Essays on Contract* (Oxford, 1986), 19.
[6] *Schmitthoff's Export Trade* (9th edn.) (London, 1990), 75–6.

monies outstanding, and a *force majeure* clause. A *force majeure* clause is a clause which seeks to regulate the impact which unforseen events (such as wars, strikes, or unexpected increases in prices) may have on the performance of the contract. Yet the contract books and the modern contract courses have little to say about *force majeure* clauses. They focus instead on the doctrine of frustration, according to which a court will, in exceptional circumstances, recognize that a contract, the performance of which has become radically different from what the parties had in contemplation when they entered into the contract, has been discharged. But frustration is the exception, not the rule. Next Schmitthoff lists a choice of law clause. Such clauses are of great practical importance, but they are not part of the contract course: rather, they belong in a third-year option entitled Conflict of Laws. Then, finally, we have an arbitration clause. But arbitration also falls outside the traditional Contract course, being, in the main, a postgraduate course. If the general principles are of marginal importance to the regulation of many important types of contract and are also of marginal significance to the terms of individual contracts, why do we continue to study the general principles of the law of contract and, further, to require all students to pass an examination on the law of contract? The question is a good one and we shall return to it at the end of this article.

2. The Development of the Law of Contract

It is no easy task to chart within short compass the development of the law of contract this century. Such have been the changes in society that it is difficult to know where to begin. It is suggested that a helpful approach is to distinguish four different aspects of the development of the law of contract: contracts in practice or contracts in fact; the doctrines of the law of contract; contract theory; and the teaching of contract law.

A. Contracts in Fact

To my knowledge there has been no attempt to engage in a systematic analysis of contract forms and styles of drafting over the century. One must therefore proceed largely by way of impression. Three issues seem worthy of comment. The first is the growth in the use of standard form contracts. These standard forms may be industry-wide, an example being the JCT contracts which are in wide use within the construction industry. These contract forms perform useful functions in so far as they lay down industry-accepted standards which save valuable negotiation time. And they give rise to few legal problems, apart from difficulties of interpretation which depend largely on the quality of the drafting of the contract form. Standard form contracts produced by individual businesses have given rise to greater legal difficulties. In the case of inter-business transactions, the use of standard terms of business has given rise to 'battles of the forms' as each business seeks to ensure that its standard terms prevail. While a number of cases involving battles of the forms have come before the courts, the judges have not evolved any special set of rules to regulate these battles.[7] Instead, they have applied the traditional mirror image rules of contract formation, albeit with signs of the occasional strain to find the existence of a contract. This failure to devise a new set of rules has been criticized, but it is my belief that this criticism is generally misconceived. New legislative solutions devised in other jurisdictions[8] have not escaped criticism[9] and do not seem to constitute much of an improvement. The source of the problem is the parties' failure to reach agreement and the blame for the difficulties and uncertainties created by these failures to agree should not be visited on the courts: it lies with the parties themselves. Standard form contracts under which businesses seek to impose their terms upon consumers have given rise to greater problems because their terms can be one-sided. A particular problem has been the sweeping exclusion clauses which these contracts contain. The common law failed to deal with this

---

[7] See, e.g., *Butler Machine Tool Co. Ltd.* v. *Ex-cell-O Corporation (England) Ltd.* [1979] 1 WLR 401; *Hitchins (Hatfield) Ltd.* v. *H Butterworth Ltd.*, unreported, Court of Appeal, 25 Feb. 1995; and *Nissan UK Ltd.* v. *Nissan Motor Manufacturing (UK) Ltd.*, unreported, Court of Appeal, 26 Oct. 1995.

[8] See, e.g., sect. 2–207 of the Uniform Commercial Code and Art. 19 of the United Nations Convention on Contracts for the International Sale of Goods (the Vienna Convention).

[9] For criticism of the Uniform Commercial Code see R. Rawlings, 'The Battle of Forms' (1979) 42 *MLR* 715, 719–20, and for criticism of the Vienna Convention see F. Vergne, 'The "Battle of the Forms" Under the 1980 United Nations Convention on Contracts for the International Sale of Goods' (1985) 33 *American Journal of Comparative Law* 233.

problem. Lord Denning did his best,[10] but he could not persuade
his colleagues to give themselves the power to refuse to give effect
to an unreasonable exclusion clause.[11] Although the courts were
sometimes able to protect the weaker party by applying stringent
rules of interpretation[12] or by refusing to incorporate the exclusion
clause into the contract,[13] the general picture is one of the
impotence of the common law. Instead it was left to Parliament to
intervene to control the excesses of these standard form contracts.
Parliament was slow to intervene. It was not until 1977 that it
found the time to enact the Unfair Contract Terms Act 1977, and
even then it was via a private member's Bill. Consumers have
recently been given greater protection courtesy of Europe. The
Unfair Terms in Consumer Contracts Regulations 1994, passed in
response to a European Directive, gives consumers much broader
protection from unfair terms in standard form contracts. The law
has finally adjusted to the existence of these standard form
contracts: but it has done so slowly.[14]

The second point to note is that modern contracts have become
increasingly complicated. Contracts today include a vast array of
clauses which seek to provide for various eventualities which may
have an impact upon contractual performance. Some of these
clauses are designed to take away rights which the law would
otherwise give, as in the case of exclusion and limitation clauses.
Other clauses are a response to the perceived rigidities of the
common law. The common law has generally set its face against
court adjustment of contract terms and is reluctant to conclude that

---

[10] See, e.g., *Thornton* v. *Shoe Lane Parking Ltd.* [1971] 2 QB 163, 170; *Gillespie Bros. & Co. Ltd.* v. *Roy Bowles Transport Ltd.* [1973] QB 400, 416; and *Levison* v. *Patent Steam Carpet Cleaning Co. Ltd.* [1978] QB 68, 79.

[11] *Photo Production Ltd.* v. *Securicor Transport Ltd.* [1980] AC 827, 848. J. Wightman, in his book *Contract A Critical Commentary* (London, 1996), 4–7, highlights the courts' inability to formulate a new set of rules as an example of what he calls 'doctrinal failure' in the modern law of contract.

[12] See, e.g., *Alderslade* v. *Hendon Laundry Ltd.* [1945] KB 189.

[13] See, e.g, *Hollier* v. *Rambler Motor (AMC) Ltd.* [1972] 2 QB 71 and *Thornton* v. *Shoe Lane Parking Ltd.* [1971] 2 QB 163.

[14] Textbooks were slow to adapt to the problem. It was not until the publication of the 21st edition of Anson's *Law of Contract* in 1959 that there was distinct discussion of the subject of standard form contracts, where Professor Guest stated (at 146) that 'one of the most important developments in the sphere of contract during the last 100 years has been the appearance of the standard form contract, or "contract of adhesion" as it is sometimes called'.

hardship can discharge a contract: to meet this problem parties have included within their contracts complex hardship and *force majeure* clauses which enable the contract to be adjusted, suspended, or terminated in the event of hardship or the dislocation of performance. Some clauses are examples of attempts to exploit opportunities which the common law affords, as in the case of retention of title clauses. While there may be a move towards the use of plain English in the drafting of contracts (at least with consumers) the substantive complexity of contracts has not been reduced. In part this may be attributable to the value of the contracts involved and the length of time for which it is intended that they will subsist; thereby requiring more detailed planning.

The third point is that the scope of contract is extending in so far as areas of what we would traditionally call public law are being subjected to the discipline of contract. A classic example is the creation of the internal market in the health service (albeit that, as we shall see,[15] the 'contracts' concluded are not always enforceable in the courts). The emergence of this new form of 'contracting' is likely to raise many issues of interest for the contract lawyer of the future.[16]

B. CONTRACT DOCTRINE

The rules which together make up the law of contract have undergone significant change in the course of the century. Painting with a rather broad brush, it is possible to identify five significant issues. In the time available, it is feasible only to identify the essential changes which have occurred and to assess them briefly.

(i) The Fairness of the Bargain

A feature of the development of English contract law is that the pace of change has been slow: English law favours incremental rather than revolutionary change. Yet the gradual nature of the change should not blind us to the fact that significant changes have occurred in the content of English contract law over the century. The most obvious in my view is that the modern law pays more overt attention to the fairness of the bargain (both in procedural

---

[15] See 66–67 below.
[16] See section D below.

and substantive terms) than did the law in the nineteenth century. Nineteenth-century contract law was built upon the twin foundations of freedom of contract and sanctity of contract. Thus it is commonplace for judges and commentators to state, as I have done, that English law is not concerned with the fairness of the bargain: the adequacy of the consideration is for the parties, not the courts. Yet, to some extent this broad statement was always misleading. In equity the courts have always exercised a jurisdiction to grant relief from unconscionable bargains,[17] particularly those concluded by the poor and ignorant[18] and by expectant heirs.[19] But the equity cases were not always integrated into the textbooks on contract law and so tended to be marginalized. The law in this area thus appeared fragmented and rudimentary. An example, drawn this time from the common law, is provided by the development of the doctrine of duress. At the beginning of the century the courts recognized that a contract concluded as a result of threats of violence could be set aside,[20] but duress of goods did not suffice to set aside a contract,[21] nor did the application of economic pressure.[22] Today it is very different. The courts have now recognized the existence of a doctrine of economic duress,[23] according to which a contract concluded as a result of the application of illegitimate economic pressure can be set aside. It is true that the scope and indeed the basis of the doctrine of duress

---

[17] *Earl of Chesterfield* v. *Janssen* (1751) 2 Ves. Sen. 125.

[18] *Fry* v. *Lane* (1884) 40 Ch.D 312.

[19] *Earl of Aylesford* v. *Morris* (1874) 8 Ch. App. 484.

[20] *Cumming* v. *Ince* (1847) 11 QB 112; *Scott* v. *Sebright* (1886) 12 PD 21.

[21] *Skeate* v. *Beale* (1841) 11 A & E 983. But the courts did also recognize that an action in money had and received could be brought to recover money paid to release goods which had been unlawfully detained (see *Astley* v. *Reynolds* (1731) 2 Str. 915).

[22] At this point in time the extent to which it was permissible to use economic power was the subject of consideration in the economic torts and the courts had taken a laissez-faire approach: see *Mogul Steamship Co. Ltd.* v. *McGregor, Gow & Co* [1892] AC 25 and *Allen* v. *Flood* [1898] AC 1, but contrast *Quinn* v. *Leatham* [1901] AC 495. For the background to these cases see J. A. G. Griffith, *The Politics of the Judiciary* (4th edn.) (London, 1991), 78–80.

[23] The vital first step was taken in *The Siboen and The Sibotre* [1976] 1 Lloyd's Rep. 293 and the doctrine has become as established as a result of cases such as *North Ocean Shipping Co. Ltd.* v. *Hyundai Construction Co. Ltd.* [1979] QB 705; *Pao On* v. *Lau Yiu Long* [1980] AC 614; *Universe Tankships of Monrovia* v. *International Transport Workers Federation* [1983] 1 AC 366 and *Dimskal Shipping Co. Ltd.* v. *International Transport Workers' Federation* [1992] 2 AC 152.

remain unclear, but it seems inevitable that economic duress will play an increasingly important role in future cases.[24] The development of duress has not displaced the old equitable, discretionary jurisdictions: on the contrary, they continue to be utilized by the courts[25] and, in the case of undue influence, may even be said to have flourished.[26] While it must be conceded that English law has refused to bring these discrete doctrines under the umbrella of a doctrine of 'inequality of bargaining power'[27] this may be attributable to English law's aversion to general principles[28] and not its indifference to the fairness of the bargain concluded by the parties. Further evidence of the concern of the modern law with the fairness of the bargain can be found in recent statutory interventions in the field of contract law. For example, the Consumer Credit Act 1974 enacted a complex protective regime for consumers entering into credit transactions, which includes in section 137(1) the power to 'reopen' extortionate credit bargains 'so as to do justice between the parties'. The Unfair Contract Terms Act 1977 regulates unreasonable exclusion, limitation and indemnity clauses in consumer and in some commercial contracts, and the legislation is now beginning to have some bite if reported cases are an accurate guide. The Unfair Terms in Consumer Contracts Regulations 1994 provide a more comprehensive range of protection for consumers from sellers or suppliers who insert into the contract unfair terms which have not been individually negotiated. In essence these regulations seek to regulate the 'small print' in standard form contracts. It is true that much work remains to be done in terms of

---

[24] Especially after the decision of the Court of Appeal in *Williams* v. *Roffey Brothers* [1991] 1 QB 1, in which it became apparent that contract modifications would in future be regulated by the doctrine of duress and not by the doctrine of consideration.

[25] See, e.g., *Boustany* v. *Piggott* (1995) 69 P & CR 298 and *Creswell* v. *Potter* [1978] 1 WLR 255. The courts have refused to put this equitable jurisdiction on a sound, principled basis, insisting that the court in the exercise of this jurisdiction is a 'court of conscience' (see *National Westminster Bank plc* v. *Morgan* [1985] AC 686, 709, *per* Lord Scarman).

[26] Especially in the aftermath of the decisions of the House of Lords in *Barclays Bank plc* v. *O'Brien* [1994] 1 AC 180 and *CIBC Mortgages plc* v. *Pitt* [1994] 1 AC 200, usefully discussed by B. Fehlberg, 'The Husband, the Bank, the Wife and Her Signature—The Sequel' (1996) 59 *MLR* 675.

[27] *National Westminster Bank plc* v. *Morgan* [1985] AC 686, rejecting the need for a general principle previously advocated by Lord Denning in *Lloyd's Bank* v. *Bundy* [1975] QB 326.   [28] On which see text to nn. 64–71 below.

identifying the limits of these doctrines and their basis in principle.[29] It seems clear to me that English contract law is concerned both with the fairness of the procedure by which the contract was concluded and, albeit within narrow limits, the fairness of the bargain concluded by the parties. It is not difficult to provide a sound justification for the law's concern with the fairness of the procedure by which the contract was concluded, but it is more difficult to find the principle which explains why the law is concerned with the fairness of the terms of the contract. Work has begun,[30] but there is much more to be done.

(ii) Freedom from Contract

The commitment to freedom of contract at the turn of the century was matched by a commitment to freedom from contract; that is to say the principle that, as long as a contract has not been concluded, the parties are free to withdraw from negotiations without incurring liability for so doing. This commitment to freedom from contract has also eroded as the century has progressed. At first sight this might not seem obvious. English law still refuses to recognize the existence of a duty to negotiate with reasonable care. While a negotiating party must not tell lies, he does not owe his negotiating party a duty of good faith or a fiduciary duty. But careful examination of recent cases shows that the courts have been able to place not insignificant limits upon the ability of a party to withdraw from negotiations without incurring any liability for doing so. They have done so largely by drawing upon doctrines from outside the law of contract, by, for example, imposing a restitutionary obligation to pay for work done in anticipation of a contract which does not materialize[31] or by protecting 'confidential' information

---

[29] An excellent recent example of this, seeking to put undue influence on a rational basis, is provided by P. Birks and Chin Nyuk Yin, 'On the Nature of Undue Influence' in J. Beatson and D. Friedmann (eds.), *Good Faith and Fault in Contract Law* (Oxford, 1995), 57.

[30] See, e.g., S. A. Smith, 'In Defence of Substantive Fairness' (1996) 112 *LQR* 138.

[31] *British Steel Corporation* v. *Cleveland Bridge and Engineering Ltd.* [1984] 1 All ER 504. But where the negotiations have been entered into on a 'subject to contract' basis this will generally shut out the restitutionary claim: see *Regalian Properties plc* v. *London Docklands Development Corporation* [1995] 1 WLR 212.

which has been disclosed in the negotiation process.[32] Courts overseas have been prepared to go further and hold that a party may be estopped by his conduct from denying the existence of a contract when he has strung the other party along and encouraged him to act to his detriment in the belief that a contract will be concluded.[33] Occasionally the courts have been able, by a benevolent interpretation of the facts, to find that those who appear to be negotiating parties have, in fact, concluded a contract.[34] Via such covert means the courts have been able to give the appearance that formal contract doctrine has not changed. The reality is otherwise. There can be little doubt that freedom from contract has been whittled away to the extent that the law must now consider whether it has reached the point that it should recognize openly what it has been doing surreptitiously: namely recognize that negotiating parties can, in some circumstances, be subject to a duty to exercise reasonable care or to act in good faith.[35]

(iii) The Emancipation of the Law of Restitution

A further notable development this century has been the expulsion from the law of contract of a subject which should never have been there: here I am referring to the law of restitution. For many years lawyers persisted with the idea that the obligation to repay a sum of money which has been paid by mistake (to give but one example) was an obligation which arose from an implied promise by the recipient to repay the money. They even gave the subject the title of 'quasi-contract' which served to emphasize that it was no more than a sub-category of contract, where the contract was implied.

---

[32] *Seager* v. *Copydex (No. 2)* [1969] 1 WLR 809. The potential of this line was reasoning was demonstrated by the Supreme Court of Canada in *Lac Minerals Ltd.* v. *International Corona Resources Ltd.* (1989) 61 DLR (4d) 13.

[33] See, e.g., *Walton's Stores (Interstate) Ltd.* v. *Maher* (1988) 164 CLR 387 and *Hoffman* v. *Red Owl Stores* (1965) 133 NW (2d) 267. English courts have not yet taken this step because estoppel cannot create a cause of action, although there are signs that they might yet do so (see, e.g., *Salvation Army Trustee Co. Ltd.* v. *West Yorkshire Metropolitan City Council* (1980) 41 P & CR 179).

[34] See, e.g., *Blackpool and Fylde Aero Club Ltd.* v. *Blackpool Borough Council* [1990] 1 WLR 1195.

[35] See further H. Collins, *The Law of Contract* (2nd edn.) (London, 1993), 168–206 and P. Atiyah, *An Introduction to the Law of Contract* (5th edn.) (Oxford, 1995), 101–7.

We know better today. The promise to repay was no more than a fiction and the justification for the imposition of an obligation to repay is to reverse an unjust enrichment which would otherwise occur. Thanks largely to the work of Lord Goff, Professor Jones, and Professor Birks, the law of restitution has been emancipated from the shackles of quasi-contract and its independence recognized.[36] Yet from our position today it is easy to forget the difficult struggle for independence. For many years the law of restitution seemed inextricably entangled within the law of contract. For example, it was not until the publication of the 22nd edition of Chitty on Contracts in 1961 that restitution was moved from its prominent position in chapter 3, where it basked under the title 'Implied Contracts and Quasi Contracts', to the end of the first volume in chapter 29 where it was re-titled 'Quasi-Contract and Restitution'. Further, it was not until the publication of the 24th edition in 1977 that the title 'quasi-contract' was dropped and the chapter was simply called 'Restitution'. The emergence of the law of restitution from the shadows of the law of contract has been one of the great intellectual achievements in the law of obligations in the latter part of the century.

(iv) An Increasingly Sophisticated Case Law

It is obviously not possible within this article to chart other developments in case law over the century. I can make only one general observation, which is that many of the rules have become more sophisticated, or complex, as a myriad of cases have worked their way through the system. To a large extent this increased sophistication is simply a product of the case law system as rules have been refined in the fire of litigation.[37] As new fact situations have arisen, existing doctrines have had to be adapted and rules which, at the turn of the century, were of marginal importance have been elevated to a more prominent position. For example, the doctrine of frustration, by which supervening events may discharge a contract, was conceived in the nineteenth century but was very much in its infancy at the turn of the century. But the two World

---

[36] It was formally recognized as an independent subject by the House of Lords in *Lipkin Gorman (a firm)* v. *Karpnale* [1991] 2 AC 548. And see Burrows below, 106.
[37] An example might be the law relating to discharge for breach where the rules have become much more complex as the century has progressed.

Wars were to change that, as the courts were required to consider the impact which these wars had on a wide range of contracts. It was the litigation which the wars generated which brought the doctrine of frustration to its maturity, and it would be no exaggeration to say that frustration is 'very largely a twentieth-century development'.[38] The changes in drafting styles which we have noted[39] have also generated litigation as courts have been asked to rule with increasing frequency on the validity of clauses such as exclusion clauses, limitation clauses, and clauses making provision for the payment of damages on a breach of contract.[40] On other occasions the increased sophistication can be attributed to a change in direction by the courts, adding a new layer of rules to the existing body of law. The best example is perhaps the development of the innominate term in 1962[41] when the Court of Appeal held that it was entitled to have regard to the consequences of the breach in deciding whether or not a party was entitled to terminate the contract on account of the other party's breach. This innovation was not at the expense of the old law, but was an addition to it, and the law has had to grapple ever since with the tension between the supposed[42] certainty of the old rule, where the focus was on the nature of the term broken, and the remedial flexibility of the new approach.

In other areas the sophistication, or complexity, is attributable to underlying difficulties with the existing rules of English law. A classic example here is provided by the doctrine of privity. The courts have, on a number of occasions, expressed disquiet about the

---

[38] A. W. B. Simpson, n. 3 above.

[39] See the text between nn. 14 and 15 above.

[40] It was not until 1915 that the House of Lords was able to rationalize the rules for distinguishing between a liquidated damages clause and a penalty clause: see *Dunlop Pneumatic Tyre Company Ltd. v. New Garage and Motor Co. Ltd.* [1915] AC 79. The rules for distinguishing between the two were still a matter of doubt at the end of the nineteenth century: see, e.g., *Willson v. Love* [1896] 1 QB 626, 633, *per* Rigby LJ.

[41] *Hongkong Fir Shipping Co. Ltd. v. Kawasaki Kisen Kaisha* [1962] 2 QB 26.

[42] I use the word 'supposed' because, once the court has decided whether or not the term broken is a condition or a warranty, it is true that the remedial entitlement is clear, but considerable uncertainty can arise in deciding whether or not the term at issue is a condition or a warranty: a good example of this uncertainty is provided by *Compagnie Commerciale Sucres et Denrées v. C. Czarnikow Ltd. (The Naxos)* where there was a wide divergence of views as to whether the clause at issue was or was not a condition: see [1990] 1 WLR 1337 (HL) and [1989] 2 Lloyd's Rep. 462.

injustice caused by not allowing a third-party beneficiary to bring a claim on a contract concluded for his benefit,[43] but their response has been to increase the bewildering array of exceptions to the doctrine rather than to uproot the doctrine itself. The consequence has been an unnecessarily complex patchwork of rules. The same can be said about the doctrine of consideration. While cases can be found in which the courts have strained to find consideration on the facts,[44] one of the growth areas of the twentieth century has been the resurrection of estoppel, which the courts have employed to give limited effects to gratuitous promises which have induced (detrimental) reliance on the part of the promisee.[45] It is true that the English courts have not been as adventurous as their Australian counterparts in their use of estoppel.[46] They have not sought to use it as a panacea for all ills. But this comparative underdevelopment does not remove the fact that the emergence of estoppel has been one of the most important features of the law of obligations in the twentieth century.[47]

(v) The Role of Parliament

This leads us into a further aspect of the modern law of contract, which is the increasing role that legislation plays within the law of contract. Professor Reynolds has recently drawn attention to two distinct purposes for which statutes have been employed. The first is to 'effect a limited codification'.[48] Statutes were used for this purpose at the beginning of this century, the most notable examples

---

[43] See, e.g., *Beswick* v. *Beswick* [1968] AC 58, 72 (Lord Reid) and *Woodar Investment Development Ltd.* v. *Wimpey Construction UK Ltd.* [1980] 1 WLR 277, 300 (Lord Scarman).

[44] *Williams* v. *Roffey Bros & Nicholls (Contractors) Ltd.* [1991] 1 QB 1.

[45] See, e.g., *Central London Trust Property Ltd.* v. *High Trees House Ltd.* [1947] KB 130; *Crabb* v. *Arun D.C.* [1976] Ch. 179.

[46] See, e.g., *Walton Stores (Interstate) Ltd.* v. *Maher* (1988) 164 CLR 387 and *Commonwealth of Australia* v. *Verwayen* (1990) 170 CLR 394. See, more generally, L. J. Priestley, 'Contract—The Burgeoning Maelstrom' (1988) *JCL* 15.

[47] I use the word 'obligations' rather than contract because it remains to be considered whether estoppel is properly part of the law of contract or whether it belongs in some other area of the law (such as tort). English law now recognizes that contract and tort can co-exist in the same fact situation (see *Henderson* v. *Merrett Syndicates Ltd* [1995] 2 AC 145) but it has yet to work out the precise line of demarcation between the two. And see Hepple below, 69.

[48] F. M. B. Reynolds, 'Contract: Codification, Legislation and Judicial Development' (1995) *JCL* 11, 17.

being, perhaps, the Sale of Goods Act 1893 and the Marine Insurance Act 1906.[49] But interest in codification soon waned, and it was not until the creation of the Law Commission in 1965 that codification of the law of contract came back on to the agenda. The Law Commission worked on the project in earnest for a number of years and a draft code was, in fact, produced,[50] but work on the project was suspended in 1973 after the withdrawal of the Scottish Law Commission. The project has never been resurrected. The Law Commission has since confined itself to an examination of specific issues, of varying degrees of importance, within the law of contract. This leads us on to the second use of statutes identified by Professor Reynolds, namely to effect a 'limited piece of law reform'.[51] There have been a number of examples of this type of intervention. We have already noted[52] that Parliament has intervened on a number of occasions to regulate unfair terms in contracts. Parliament has also intervened to regulate the remedial consequences of the frustration of a contract,[53] minors' contracts,[54] and to regulate the remedies for misrepresentation.[55] While a major reform of privity of contract is in the pipeline, the tinkering with the law of contract has generally been on a minor scale in comparison with jurisdictions such as New Zealand[56] and Australia,[57] where there has been a greater willingness to intervene in the general principles of the law of contract. Although Parliament has generally been unwilling to intervene in the general principles of the law of contract, the same

---

[49] Other examples are the Bills of Exchange Act 1882 and the Partnership Act 1890.

[50] H. McGregor, *Contract Code*, drawn up on behalf of the English Law Commission. The existence of the code was revealed by Dr McGregor at a conference on 'The Future European Code of Contracts' in Pavia in October 1990. His revelation of the Code's existence was described as 'sensational' by Continental jurists and steps were then taken to publish the code. This was done in 1993 when the Code was published by Giuffré Editore of Milan and Sweet and Maxwell.

[51] Reynolds, n. 48 above, 18.   [52] See test to nn. 27–9 above.

[53] Law Reform (Frustrated Contracts) Act 1943.

[54] Minors' Contracts Act 1987.

[55] Misrepresentation Act 1967.

[56] See generally B. Coote, 'The Contracts and Commercial Law Reform Committee and the Contract Statutes' (1988) 13 *NZULR* 160.

[57] See in particular s.52 of the Australian Trade Practices Act 1974 (Cth.) which, it has been claimed, has had a 'quite dramatic impact on the general law of contract': see D. J. Harland, 'The Statutory Prohibition of Misleading or Deceptive Conduct in Australia and its Impact on the Law of Contract' (1995) 111 *LQR* 100.

cannot be said of specific contracts: as I have said, there has been substantial legislative regulation of the employment relationship, consumer credit contracts, landlord and tenant contracts, and contracts for the sale of goods (particularly, but not exclusively, those with consumers). Two consequences flow from limited Parliamentary intervention in the general law of contract. The first is that there is no continuous comprehensive re-examination of the law of contract: we tinker but do not overhaul. The second is that there is no consistent analysis of the relationship between statute law and the common law.[58] Statutes have been used both as a justification for the withdrawal of the courts from the regulation of unfair contract terms[59] and as a 'platform'[60] which the courts can use to regulate unfair terms which do not fall quite within the scope of existing legislation. Both views cannot be right. The issue requires further examination.

(vi) An Assessment

One consequence of the incremental nature of the development of the law of contract is that there appears to have been no fundamental change in the structure of the law of contract. While there have been claims, most notably by Professor Collins,[61] that the law of contract has been transformed this century, this has not been clearly reflected in a transformation of the *doctrines* of the law of contract. Freedom of contract and freedom from contract remain the background norms. Privity and consideration remain as central doctrines in the law of contract. Exceptions may have proliferated but English law has neither recognized new general, guiding principles, nor cast off the general principles which it inherited from its formative era. The explanation for this may lie in nothing more than English law's deep-seated reluctance to embrace general principles. One of the reasons why all law students know about *Donoghue v. Stevenson*[62] is because it is atypical; it is a rare

---

[58] The best analyses in my view are by P. Atiyah, 'Common Law and Statute Law' (1985) 48 MLR 1 and J. Beatson, 'Has the Common Law a Future?' (1997, Cambridge University Press, Inaugural Lecture).

[59] *National Westminster Bank plc v. Morgan* [1985] AC 686, 708.

[60] *Timeload Ltd. v. British Telecommunications plc* [1995] EMLR 459, 468, *per* Sir Thomas Bingham MR.

[61] H. Collins, n. 35, above, esp. chap. 2.   [62] [1932] AC 562.

example of a judge seeking to deduce a new general principle from a wilderness of single instances. This reluctance to embrace change openly makes it more difficult, I think, to evaluate the transformation thesis with any confidence. At a formal level, the law seems to favour the status quo, that is to say, the preservation of the existing doctrines. This can be proved positively (the preservation of existing doctrines) and negatively (no new doctrines).

Take first the refusal of the law to recognize new doctrines. Two examples can be given here. The first is that in 1974 Lord Denning sought to unify a number of hitherto discrete doctrines under the umbrella of 'inequality of bargaining power'[63] but his judgment subsequently received a frosty reception in the House of Lords[64] and it has since been quietly laid to rest. A second, more topical example of the reluctance of English law to embrace general principles is its refusal to countenance the existence of a doctrine of good faith in the making and performance of contracts, a topic admirably discussed by Professor Raphael Powell in his inaugural lecture here at this College almost thirty-one years ago to the day.[65] Many internationally agreed conventions and standard forms include an unexcludable term to the effect that each party must act 'in accordance with good faith and fair dealing'[66] but English law steadfastly refuses to join in. One should, however, be careful when drawing lessons from this refusal. A foreign observer should not conclude that English law is not concerned with the good faith of the parties: it is. Where it deems it necessary, for example, in the context of contracts of insurance, English law recognizes a duty of *utmost* good faith. Specific examples of bad faith, such as telling lies, using illegitimate pressure, and abusing positions of confidence, constitute grounds upon which a contract may be set aside, and the judiciary will think long and hard before reaching a conclusion which is 'counter to the reasonable expectations of

---

[63] *Lloyds Bank* v. *Bundy* [1975] QB 326, 339.
[64] *National Westminster Bank plc* v. *Morgan* [1985] AC 686, 708.
[65] R. Powell, 'Good Faith in Contracts' [1956] *CLP* 16.
[66] Art. 1.7 of the UNIDROIT Principles for International Commercial Contracts. Other examples of the recognition of a duty of good faith can be found in Art. 7(1) of the Vienna Convention on Contracts for the Sale of Goods, Arts. 1–201(19), 1–203, and 2–203(1)(b) of the Uniform Commercial Code and Art. 1.106 of the Principles of European Contract Law.

honest men'.[67] English law may often reach the same result as a civilian lawyer would reach via the doctrine of good faith but do so by a different route[68] namely by the use of more narrowly defined doctrines (for example, English law developed distinct doctrines of impossibility or impracticability, albeit within narrow confines, rather than use the broad notion of good faith). So it may be that the recognition by English law of a duty of good faith and fair dealing would produce little by way of change in the actual results of cases: if this is right then English law would apparently benefit little from the recognition of such a duty because there would be no compensating advantages to set off against the disadvantages which would arise from the uncertainty created while the doctrine bedded down. On the other hand, the express recognition of a duty of good faith and fair dealing would require more searching re-examination of rules which are alleged to be incompatible with such a standard, it would help bring English law into line with many other jurisdictions, and it would make it easier for English law to accede to international conventions. And there are signs that the traditional English hostility to good faith might be abating. The Court of Appeal has adopted a more sympathetic stance on three occasions recently,[69] and the express reference to 'good faith' in the Unfair Terms in Consumer Contracts Regulations 1994 might nudge English law in the direction of the recognition of a duty of good faith and fair dealing. But the House of Lords has recently held that English law does not recognize the existence of a duty to 'carry on negotiations in good faith'[70] so that the formal position remains that English law does not yet recognize the existence of a duty of good faith and fair dealing in the formation and performance of contracts.

[67] *First Energy (UK) Ltd.* v. *Hungarian International Bank Ltd.* [1993] 2 Lloyd's Rep. 194, 196, *per* Steyn LJ.
[68] See, e.g., *Interfoto Picture Library Ltd.* v. *Stiletto Visual Programmes Ltd.* [1989] QB 433 where the Court of Appeal held that an onerous term had not been incorporated into the contract because insufficient steps had been taken to draw it to the attention of the other party (see also *AEG (UK) Ltd.* v. *Logic Resource Ltd.*[1996] CLC 265). A civilian lawyer might have got to the same conclusion through the invocation of good faith and fair dealing.
[69] *Timeload Ltd.* v. *British Telecommunications plc* [1995] EMLR 459; *Philips Electronique Grand Publique SA* v. *British Sky Broadcasting Ltd.* [1995] EMLR 472 and *Balfour Beatty Civil Engineering Ltd.* v. *Docklands Light Railway Ltd.* (1996) 78 BLR 42, 67–8.   [70] *Walford* v. *Miles* [1992] 2 AC 128.

Let us turn now to the inability of the courts to cast out existing general principles. Two of the distinctive doctrines of English contract law which stand out to a foreign observer are consideration and privity. Both have been under great pressure for a large part of the century but they continue to survive. Lord Denning did make several attempts to uproot privity of contract and recognize a limited third party right of action[71] but he failed to command the support of the House of Lords who, albeit reluctantly, re-affirmed the existence of the doctrine.[72] The death-knell for privity has, however, recently been sounded by the Law Commission, and Parliament may soon take the issue out of the hands of the judiciary. Consideration might be harder to shake off because it is of little practical importance, at least in the City. But its continued existence is not attributable to widespread approval of its qualities. Thus we find that Lord Goff stated in a recent case that:

> our law of contract is widely seen as deficient in the sense that it is perceived to be hampered by the presence of an unnecessary doctrine of consideration and (through a strict doctrine of privity of contract) stunted through a failure to recognise a jus quesitum tertio.[73]

In one sense it is remarkable to find at this stage in our legal history a senior and distinguished member of the judiciary openly questioning two of the central doctrines of English contract law. Yet his sentiments would be shared by many academic commentators. Consideration finds no role within international conventions and, indeed, it made no appearance in the Contract Code which Dr Harvey McGregor drafted for the Law Commission in the late 1960s. These criticisms should, however, be seen in their proper perspective. It is not that commentators are arguing that bargain promises should not be enforced: rather it is their contention that consideration draws the net of enforceability too tightly. As

---

[71] See, e.g., *Smith and Snipes Hall Farm Ltd.* v. *River Douglas Catchment Board* [1949] 2 KB 500, 514 and *Beswick* v. *Beswick* [1966] 3 WLR 396, 407.

[72] See, e.g., *Midland Silicones Ltd.* v. *Scruttons Ltd.* [1962] AC 466 and *Beswick* v. *Beswick* [1968] AC 58.

[73] *White* v. *Jones* [1995] 2 AC 207, 262–3. Writing extra-judicially Lord Goff stated that the fact that the doctrine has given rise to very few practical problems has perhaps promoted the survival of a doctrine which is 'generally of little or no value and occasionally harmful' (B. Markesinis (ed.), *The Gradual Convergence* (Oxford, 1993), 129).

Professor Dawson has pointed out, '[e]ven the most embittered critics of bargain consideration do not really object to the enforcement of bargains. The objection has been to its transformation into a formula of denial, a formula that would deny legal effect to most promises for which there is nothing given or received in exchange.'[74] Yet we must proceed carefully here because we cannot simply abolish consideration. As Professor Atiyah has pointed out, talk of the abolition of consideration is 'nonsensical' because there 'will always be a need for rules determining what promises will be legally enforceable unless (which is unthinkable) *all* promises are to become enforceable'.[75] Yet it is a notable feature of academic analyses of consideration that they are stronger on their criticisms of the existing doctrine than they are on suggestions for its replacement.[76] The main competitors seem to be the use of 'intention to create legal relations' as the central control device or the use of a more fluid test of 'enforceability', under which bargain is only one of several alternative conditions of enforceability. The difficulty of formulating an alternative, combined with the fact that consideration gives rise to few practical problems, may combine to preserve consideration for the immediate future.

The reform of privity is more pressing because of the commercial inconvenience to which the present doctrine gives rise. Yet, as the Law Commission has recently discovered, while it is relatively easy to propose the abolition of the existing doctrine of privity, it is much harder to work out the limits of the new third-party enforceable right and to strike the right balance between flexibility and certainty. And in large part this difficulty is attributable to an underlying theoretical vacuum.[77] Here we also encounter a weakness in English academic scholarship. As we shall see, English contract lawyers have tended to focus on exposition of the rules rather than the theoretical foundation of the subject and they have

---

[74] J. Dawson, *Gifts and Promises* (New Haven, Conn., 1980), 3–4. To similar effect see M. Eisenberg, 'The Principles of Consideration' (1982) 67 *Cornell Law Review* 640, 643.

[75] P. Atiyah, n. 36 above, 149.

[76] The most sustained attack on consideration has been provided by Professor Atiyah, 'Consideration: A Restatement' in *Essays on Contract* (Oxford, 1986), 179, a revised version of his inaugural lecture at the Australian National University.

[77] A point neatly illustrated by R. Halson, 'Variation, Privity and Law Reform' in R. Halson (ed.), *Exploring the Boundaries of Contract* (Aldershot, 1996), 83.

tended to be rather better at criticizing existing doctrines than suggesting alternatives.

C. Contract Theory

Professor Atiyah once stated that 'modern contract law probably works well enough in the great mass of circumstances, but its theory today is a mess'.[78] It is unlikely that such a statement would have been made at the beginning of the century. In so far as writers were concerned with the theory of contract, the basis of the obligation created by a binding contract was attributable to the will of the parties. The most influential contract scholars of that time were Sir Frederick Pollock and Sir William Anson, both of whom authored textbooks in the latter half of the nineteenth century. Both books sought to rationalize the existing case law in terms of general principles of contract law. If a feature of the modern law of contract is its unwillingness to embrace general principles, the same could not be said of Pollock and Anson. While Anson was careful to point out to his readers that the origin of consideration as a test of actionability was uncertain and that it had indeed been challenged by Lord Mansfield in 1765,[79] he also maintained that in a system, such as English law, where all promises may be actionable 'it follows that there must be some universal test of actionability, and this test was supplied by the doctrine of consideration'.[80] Consideration was not *a* test of the enforceability of promises: it was *the* test. The same generalizing tendency can be seen in Anson's treatment of the doctrine of privity. As a matter of authority, the hold of the doctrine of privity in English law in 1900 was rather uncertain. But for Anson privity was 'an integral part of our conception of contract'[81] because, for him, a contract was an agreement between two or more persons to which the third party was simply not a party and, of course, it was this view which was to prevail in the House of Lords in 1915.[82] While Anson and Pollock

---

[78] P. Atiyah, *Pragmatism and Theory in English Law* (London, 1986), 173.
[79] *Pillans* v. *Van Mierop* (1765) 3 Burr. 1663.
[80] W. Anson, *Law of Contract* (7th edn.) (Oxford, 1899), 52.
[81] *Ibid.*, at 230.
[82] *Dunlop Pneumatic Tyre Co. Ltd.* v. *Selfridge & Co. Ltd.* [1915] AC 847, esp. 853, *per* Lord Haldane.

were committed to the search for rationality, it is important to note that their search was not confined to English case law. Pollock, in particular, drew on Roman law sources and the writings of prominent civilian jurists, such as Savigny and Pothier. But this emphasis on general principles and the invocation of the writings of civilian jurists was not to the taste of everyone. Thus Philip London in his Preface to the third, and thankfully final edition of Pease and London *Law of Contracts* in 1925 stated:

> The aim of the book, as in previous editions, is to state the principles of the law of contract as they are applied in the Courts today, without attempting to find any juristic foundation for them. It seems to us that there has been a tendency in recent years to overload elementary textbooks on the common law with the theories of continental jurisprudence which, while they are admittedly an essential element in a complete legal education, are often difficult to fit into our own exceedingly empirical system.[83]

As we all know, it was the views of Anson and Pollock which were to prevail, and they are credited, perhaps wrongly,[84] with the creation of the modern law of contract.[85] Anson wrote explicitly for a student audience and new editions of his book appeared at regular intervals in the latter part of the last century and the early part of this century. It was certainly not the only student book on the market, but it is probably true to say that it was the most influential on the minds of future practitioners. The work of Pollock and Anson was reinforced in the minds of students by the appearance of casebooks. Thus in 1886 the first edition of Finch's casebook, *A Selection of Cases on the English Law of Contract*, was published and it was heavily influenced by Langdell's teaching in Harvard and, in its selection of cases, relied heavily upon the 'masterly works' of Pollock and Anson. But it was to take a longer period of time for the influence of Anson and Pollock to spread through to the practitioner works, which continued to be dominated by particular contracts rather than general principles. Indeed, it was not until 1961 that Chitty was to undergo significant revision under the general editorship of Dr Morris. He noted in his Preface

---

[83] Pease and P. London, *Law of Contracts: Student Summary* (3rd. edn.), (London, 1925).

[84] See J. Gordley, *The Philosophical Origins of Modern Contract Doctrine* (Oxford, 1991).   [85] P. Atiyah, n. 35 above, at 170.

the 'extraordinarily haphazard and inconvenient' arrangement of the first volume of the previous edition of Chitty, whereby a number of important topics, such as frustration and discharge by breach, were not to be found in the Table of Contents. He continued: 'we do not agree with the implied suggestion that only students deserve rationally arranged textbooks and that practitioners will put up with anything provided only that it is traditional'[86] He maintained that practitioners brought up on Pollock, Anson, and Cheshire and Fifoot expect to find 'their textbooks arranged in accordance with such a plan'.[87]

The appearance of *Cheshire and Fifoot* in 1945 and *Treitel* in 1962 further enhanced the standing of the expository school, as the general principles of the law of contract were re-stated for readers in a more modern form. During this period Anson was updated by Professor Guest and new life was breathed into what had then become 'a somewhat run-down period piece'.[88] The fate of Pollock was not so fortunate: its final edition was to appear in 1951.[89]

The casebooks produced by Cheshire and Fifoot[90] and Smith and Thomas[91] continued to set out the core cases in a manner which would have been acceptable to Langdell, Pollock, and Anson. While Pollock and Anson would notice that the modern books attached less importance to matters of capacity and form and gave more attention to matters such as frustration, standard form contracts, and remedies for breach of contract, they would, I think, recognize the outline of 'the plan'.

But a gradual change began to occur in English legal scholarship in the late 1960s, the hallmark of which was a more critical approach to the study of contract law. Perhaps the most influential scholar in this respect has been Professor Atiyah. His principal contribution to English contract law has been his assault on the

---

[86] *Chitty on Contract* (22nd edn.) (London, 1961), Preface.
[87] Ibid.
[88] A. W. B. Simpson, 'Contract: The Twitching Corpse' (1981) 1 *OJLS* 265, 266.
[89] F. Pollock, *Principles of Contract* (13th edn.) (London, 1951).
[90] The first edition of Cheshire and Fifoot's *Cases on the Law of Contract* appeared in 1946 as a companion to their textbook which was published in the previous year.
[91] The first edition of J. C. Smith and J. A. C. Thomas, *A Casebook on Contract* appeared in 1957. The book is now in its 10th edition.

classical law of contract[92] and its central doctrines, such as consideration[93] and the commitment to the protection of the expectation interest when awarding damages for breach of contract.[94] His concern was to challenge the existing legal framework and to erect in its place a general law of obligations based on benefit-based and reliance-based liabilities. It is important to note that his aim was not to construct a new model of contract law. But Atiyah was only the first of many to offer a more critical approach to the study of contract law. Today the literature on the law of contract is more diverse than it has ever been. Alongside the traditional, established textbooks and a growing range of monographs,[95] there has emerged a steady stream of new texts which seek to study the law of contract 'in context'[96] or from a particular theoretical perspective.[97] Modern casebooks encourage their readers to go beyond the study of the central doctrines of classical contract law by including a broader range of materials within their pages.[98] There have been some notable collections of essays published recently[99] and the periodical literature is beginning to blossom again.[100]

---

[92] See in particular *The Rise and Fall of Freedom of Contract* (Oxford, 1979). See also the successive editions of *An Introduction to the Law of Contract*, now in its 5th edition, which has stimulated generations of law students since its first appearance in 1961.

[93] See, in particular, P. Atiyah, 'Consideration: A Re-statement', n. 5 above, 179.

[94] See, e.g., 'Contracts, Promises and the Law of Obligations', n. 5 above, 10, and 'Executory Contracts, Expectation Damages and the Economic Analysis of Contract', *ibid*, 150.

[95] See, e.g., B. Coote, *Exception Clauses* (London, 1964) (which, although now rather dated, is still an outstanding example of its type); G. Treitel, *Remedies for Breach of Contract* (Oxford, 1988); J. Cartwright, *Unequal Bargaining* (Oxford, 1991); and G. Treitel *Frustration and Force Majeure* (London, 1995).

[96] H. Collins, n. 35 above.

[97] See, e.g., J. Adams and R. Brownsword, *Key Issues in Contract* (London, 1995), and J. Wightman, n. 11, above.

[98] Pride of place must be given to H. Beale, W. Bishop, and M. Furmston, *Contract Cases and Materials* (3rd edn.) (London, 1995). A more radical approach has also been taken by S. Wheeler and J. Shaw, *Contract Law Cases, Materials and Commentary* (Oxford, 1994).

[99] See, e.g., J. Beatson and D. Friedmann, *Good Faith and Fault in Contract Law* (Oxford, 1995); R. Brownsword, G. Howells, and T. Wilhelmsson (eds.), *Welfarism in Contract Law* (Aldershot, 1994); and D. Campbell and P. Vincent-Jones (eds.), *Contract and Economic Organisation* (Aldershot, 1996).

[100] A notable contribution here has been made by the *Journal of Contract Law*, under the editorship of Professor Carter. But there have also been significant

So how then should we sum up English contract law scholarship? Let me start with some negatives. It has not been particularly inter-disciplinary: there has, it is true, been some flirtation with economics, in which this Faculty has participated, but, I venture to suggest, the return has been modest. With one or two notable exceptions,[101] contract law scholarship has not been empirical. Textbooks writers have not followed Pollock's example and drawn on civilian sources: the focus is almost exclusively on the English law of contract, leaving comparative analysis to the specialist texts[102] or the occasional contribution to the periodical liter-ature.[103] Nor has the scholarship been particularly rich in its theoretical content:[104] although it is still in its infancy, much of this new scholarship is based on ideas which originated in North America[105] and is negative in nature, that is to say it seeks to attack the classical model of contract law rather than build up an alternative conception of contract law.[106] Turning to the positive side of contract scholarship, it has had an impact on the evolution

---

contributions elsewhere in the leading periodicals: see, e.g., the notable contribu-tions made by my former colleague Steve Smith: see 'Reconstructing Restraint of Trade' (1995) 15 *OJLS* 565; 'In Defence of Substantive Fairness' (1996) 112 *LQR* 138; and 'Future Freedom and Freedom of Contract' (1996) 59 *MLR* 167.

[101] The exceptions being H. Beale and A. Dugdale, 'Contracts between Businessmen' (1975) 2 *Brit. J Law & Society* 45; P. Vincent-Jones, 'Contract Litigation in England and Wales 1975–1991: A Transformation in Business Disputing' [1993] *CJQ* 337; and some of the work which is currently being done on 'contracts' in the National Health Service, of which D. Hughes, J. McHale, and D. Griffiths 'Contracts in the NHS: Searching for a Model?' in Campbell and Vincent-Jones (eds.), n. 99 above, 155, is an excellent example.

[102] There have, however, been some outstanding contributions to comparative contract law scholarship, of which G. Treitel, *Remedies for Breach of Contract* (Oxford, 1988), and the work of Professor B. Nicholas are examples. Comparative lawyers have also provided scholarly accounts of contract law in other jurisdictions (see, e.g., B. Nicholas, *The French Law of Contract* (2nd edn.) (Oxford, 1992).

[103] An excellent recent example being S. Whittaker, 'Privity of Contract and the Law of Tort: The French Experience' (1995) 15 *OJLS* 327.

[104] e.g., H. Beale, W. Bishop, and M. Furmston, n. 98 above, include a section in their book entitled 'Contract Theory' (see 655–723). Only two of the 16 extracts in the section are written by English contract scholars (Atiyah and Collins). A similar result is obtained if one looks at a book such as D. Craswell and R. Schwartz, *Foundations of Contract Law* (Oxford, 1994).

[105] On which see text to nn. 109–21 below.

[106] A point recognized by Professor Campbell in 'The Undeath of Contract: A Study in the Degeneration of a Research Programme' (1992) 22 *HKLJ* 20, 21, when he stated that the 'classical law can be placed finally to undisturbed rest only by a better contract research programme conducted along non-classical lines'.

of some modern contract doctrines, duress.[107] But it is suggested that its particular strength lies in the quality of its exposition of the law. Treatise-writing still occupies a considerable proportion of the time of contract scholars. And there have been some outstanding examples of this genre. Particular mention must be made in this connection of the work of Professor Treitel. His textbook on the *Law of Contract*, now in its ninth edition, has in a short period of time established itself as an authoritative text of the highest standing. Its careful and accurate account of the law of contract has no equal. His textbook and his comparative work, particularly his monograph *Remedies for Breach of Contract* and his recent authoritative account of the law relating to *Frustration and Force Majeure*, mark him out as a great contract scholar of our time. Professor Treitel has recently retired as Vinerian Professor of English Law in the University of Oxford, a chair which, through his writings, he has held with great distinction. It is only right that his enormous contribution to our understanding of the law of contract should be formally acknowledged and I would like to wish him a long and happy retirement. Mention must also be made in this context of the work of Professor Guest who, as editor of Chitty and the editor responsible for the re-casting of Anson, has had a considerable role to play in the formulation and presentation of modern contract doctrine.

This emphasis on treatise-writing stands in stark contrast to modern scholarship in North America where it has been stated that 'the great days of treatise writing are now over'.[108]

The emphasis there is on theory and not on the exposition of the rules of law. It is therefore no surprise to find that the major theoretical contributions to contract scholarship have emerged from the other side of the Atlantic.[109] The most frequently cited article has been Fuller and Perdue's 'The Reliance Interest in

---

[107] See, e.g., the influence of Professor Beatson's article, 'Duress as a Vitiating Factor in Contract' (1974) 33 *CLJ* 97, on the development of economic duress, as evidenced by the judgment of Mocatta J in *North Ocean Shipping Co. Ltd.* v. *Hyundai Construction Co. Ltd.* [1979] QB 705, 719.

[108] A. W. B. Simpson, n. 88 above, 270.

[109] See generally R. Hillman, 'The Crisis in Modern Contract Theory' (1988) 67 *Texas Law Review* 103.

Contract Damages'.[110] The article has been hailed as a classic and its influence on a number of contract scholars has been immense,[111] but its major impact has been on the terminology which we all use when discussing the different measures of damages that can be recovered on a breach of contract, rather than on the substantive law of contract where the courts have not shown great inclination to abandon their commitment to the protection of the expectation or performance interest in favour of protection of the reliance interest.[112] Other influential writers include Professor Macneil, who has argued that the classical account of the law of contract, with its emphasis on discrete transactions, is gravely deficient in that it fails to take account of the 'relational' aspects of modern contracting.[113] There are signs that his analysis is beginning to have an influence here,[114] although I personally am not convinced that there is a case for a separate category of relational contracts.[115] Professor Macaulay has written extensively on contract law in action and has highlighted the limited role which the law of contract actually plays in the governance of contractual

[110] It is the ninth most cited article published in the *Yale Law Journal* with 236 citations by 1990: see E. Shapiro, 'Most Cited Articles from the Yale Law Journal' (1990) 100 *Yale LJ* 1449 where it is stated that 'few law review articles have affected legal thinking so powerfully'.

[111] e.g., Professor Atiyah in *The Rise and Fall of Freedom of Contract*, acknowledges his 'great indebtedness' to the article by Fuller and Perdue. For a wider survey of the significance of the article see T. Rakoff, 'Fuller and Perdue's The Reliance Interest as a Work of Legal Scholarship' [1991] *Wisc. L Rev.* 203.

[112] See S. Macaulay, 'The Reliance Interest and the World Outside the Law Schools' Doors' [1991] *Wisc. L Rev.* 247, esp. 266–87 and D. Friedmann, 'The Performance Interest in Contract Damages' (1995) 111 *LQR* 628.

[113] See, e.g., I. R. Macneil, 'The Many Futures of Contracts' (1974) 47 *S Cal. L Rev.* 691; I. R. Macneil, 'Contracts: Adjustments of Long-Term Economic Relations Under Classical, Neoclassical, and Relational Contract Law' (1978) 72 *Northwestern Univ. L Rev.* 854; I. R. Macneil, 'Economic Analysis of Contractual Relations: Its Shortfalls and the Need for a "Rich Classificatory Apparatus" ' (1981) 75 *Northwestern Univ. L Rev.* 1018; and C. J. Goetz and R. E. Scott, 'Principles of Relational Contracts' (1981) 67 *Virg. LR* 1089.

[114] See, e.g., D. Campbell, 'The Social Theory of Relational Contract: Macneil as the Modern Proudhon' (1990) 18 *International Journal of the Sociology of Law* 75 and D. Campbell and D. Harris, 'Flexibility in Long-term Contractual Relationships: The Role of Co-operation' (1983) 20 *Journal of Law and Society* 166.

[115] E. McKendrick, 'The Regulation of Long-term Contracts in English Law' in J. Beatson and D. Friedmann (eds.), n. 29 above, 305.

relations.[116] Thus he has pointed out that businessmen often do not plan or draft their agreements with the precision which classical law expects and that they often prefer to preserve their relationship than insist upon the enforcement of their rights under the contracts which they have concluded. The 1970s witnessed a surge in interest in the economic analysis of law as Judge Posner and others sought to explain the rules of contract law in terms of the promotion of economic efficiency and so gave birth to a huge volume of law-and-economics literature.[117] Critical legal studies scholars have offered their own distinctive analysis of contract law,[118] Professor Fried has elegantly attempted to restate a modern liberal conception of the law of contract based on the promise principle,[119] Professor Gilmore, in a series of lectures, held what has been called 'a rather riotous wake'[120] in which he pronounced the death of contract and its 'reabsorption into the mainstream of tort'.[121] American scholars also appear to be better versed in philosophy[122] and more willing to search for solutions to contract problems in other disciplines such as psychology.[123]

Why is it that the major theoretical writings have emerged from the Law Schools of North America and not from English law schools? One answer may be that law is a graduate subject in America, whereas here it is a predominantly undergraduate subject of study. American law students and their law professors therefore have a background in another discipline, such as economics, sociology, or politics, which is not generally shared by their English counterparts and English law schools have not traditionally

---

[116] See, e.g., S. Macaulay, 'Non-contractual Relations in Business: A Preliminary Study' (1963) 28 *American Sociological Review* 55 and 'An Empirical View of Contract' [1985] *Wisc. L Rev.* 465.

[117] See, e.g., A. Kronman and R. Posner, *Economics of Contract Law*, (Boston, Mass., 1979) and R. Posner, *Economic Analysis of Law* (4th edn., Boston, Mass., 1992) chap. 4.

[118] See, e.g., X. Feinman, 'Critical Approaches to Contract Law' (1983) 30 *UCLA L Rev.* 829 and C. Dalton, 'An Essay in the Deconstruction of Contract Doctrine' (1985) 94 *Yale LJ* 997.

[119] C. Fried, *Contract as Promise* (Cambridge, Mass., 1981).

[120] Campbell, n. 106, 20.

[121] G. Gilmore, *The Death of Contract* (Columbus, Ohio, 1974), 87.

[122] See, e.g., J. Gordley, n. 84 above.

[123] See, e.g., M. Eisenberg, 'The Limits of Cognition and the Limits of Contract' (1995) 47 *Stanford L Rev.* 211.

encouraged their students to venture far beyond the doors of the law school. The second point is that much of English legal scholarship has traditionally been tied to legal education and the needs of future practitioners of the law.[124] American legal scholarship, by contrast, has become much more inter-disciplinary, to the extent that it has been claimed that articles 'about private law ... have essentially disappeared today'.[125] I am not myself convinced that we want to go down the American road. We must retain our traditional expository skills but at the same time increase our empirical and theoretical content. Textbooks, such as *Chitty*, should be encouraged to mould the future development of the law rather than simply reflect existing practice. I have already drawn attention to the increasing diversity of English contract scholarship and so there are reasons for optimism on this front.

D. CONTRACT TEACHING

It is difficult to chart the development of the teaching of the law of contract over the past century, largely because the explosion in the number of law schools is a relatively modern phenomenon.[126] Contract law remains one of the core subjects on the law curriculum, which must be studied by all students who wish to practise law in this country and it is also usually compulsory even for those law students who have no intention of practising whatsoever. My own belief is that contract law is an important foundation subject for a wide range of subjects and that its present status as a core subject should be maintained. Yet there is a danger that university law schools today place insufficient attention on the core subjects. The enormous growth in postgraduate legal education at a time when resources are diminishing has placed a great

---

[124] See generally G. Wilson, 'English Legal Scholarship' (1987) 50 *MLR* 818.

[125] M. Tushnet, 'Legal Scholarship in the United States: An Overview' (1987) 50 *MLR* 804, 805. Although contract scholars such as Professors Eisenberg, Gordley, and Rakoff continue to make regular appearances in the pages of the law reviews: see, e.g., M. Eisenberg, 'The Principle of Hadley v Baxendale' (1992) 80 *Calif. L Rev.* 563 and J. Gordley, 'Enforcing Promises' (1995) 82 *Calif. L Rev.* 547.

[126] For a discussion of different approaches to the teaching of contract see P. Birks (ed.), *Examining the Law Syllabus: The Core* (Oxford, 1991), in particular the essays by Collins, Brownsword, Wightman, and Hepple.

strain on the undergraduate programme. The teaching of post-graduate courses is held out as having greater intellectual appeal; it enables the teacher to engage in what is styled 'research-led teaching'. Even within the undergraduate degree, there is a trend towards the development of third-year options and academics are encouraged to develop their own areas of specialization, apart from the core. The result of all of this is that senior and junior members of staff are increasingly been drawn away from the core, giving an ever greater role to former students who have just left university and who are sometimes only one step ahead of the students. The teaching of core subjects is, in my view, too important to be left in the hands of students of such limited experience, however gifted many of them are. It has been fashionable for legal academics to decry the Common Professional Examinations as an inadequate foundation for the practice of law. This may well be so but universities must tread carefully here. The relative neglect of the core may, sadly, result in students receiving a better grounding in the core subjects on the CPE than on the regular LLB courses in universities.

A further fact which is worth pointing out is that contract law is generally a first-year subject. At this stage students are still learning how to read cases and statutes and the course must be designed with these limits in mind. There are few, if any, postgraduate courses on the general principles of the law of contract. Most masters' courses examine specific contracts in detail and in an intensely practical way. The result is that the basic foundational principles of the law of contract escape searching examination in the classroom: to the detriment both of future practitioners and of university teachers themselves. The superficial nature of the study of the general principles of the law of contract may itself be a major contributory cause of the relative absence of critical analysis of major contract doctrines.

3. A Rich Past

My argument to date may seem to make it very difficult for me to defend the claim that English contract law has had a rich past. To some extent I would agree. English contract law has not been rich in its theoretical content: one would not commend English law for its conceptual elegance. At the same time its base in case law rather than legislation has made it difficult to export to other jurisdictions (although it has, of course, had a significant influence on other common law systems, particularly in the Commonwealth). It cannot be transplanted in the way that Articles of the American Uniform Commercial Code can be. One is not aware of legal systems falling over themselves in their desire to import the doctrine of consideration, privity, or frustration. Yet there is a very real sense in which English contract law has had a rich past and that relates to the volume of trade which has been done on contracts governed by English law. English contract law has exerted an enormous influence on international trade. A glance at the law reports will tell you that some of the leading contract cases have been litigated between parties who have no connection with England other than the fact that their contract is governed by English law. The explanation for this undoubtedly lies in this country's great trading history, which has been of great profit to the City of London and English law, if not to other parts of the United Kingdom. Some commodities markets have had their centres in England and many contracts for the sale of commodities are governed by English law. London has also been an important arbitration centre and a number of our great contract cases started life as stated cases referred to arbitration, before the stated case system fell into disrepute and was abolished in the Arbitration Act 1979. While English contract law may never have been pretty, it has had the great merit of providing clear, practical answers to a wide range of contract problems. In this sense English contract law has undoubtedly had a rich past.

4. An Uncertain Future?

(A) A European or International Law of Contract?

We now come to the final section of this article: the future of the English law of contract. In a number of respects it might be thought that English contract law has an uncertain future ahead of it. The most pressing problem is created by the present momentum towards the creation of an international or a European law of contract. Developments are occurring at a number of different levels. In the first place there is the impact of our membership of the European Union. European law has had a significant impact on certain specific types of contract,[127] but its impact on the general principles of the law of contract has been almost non-existent. This may be about to change. The Unfair Terms in Consumer Contracts Regulations 1994, enacted in implementation of a Directive on Unfair Terms in Consumer Contracts,[128] is the first major European encroachment upon the heartland of English contract law. Further, the Council of the European Community has the power to adopt measures which have as their 'object the establishment and functioning of the internal market'[129] and the creation and development of the Single Market is surely likely to fuel demands for a single European contract law. At the second level we have internationally agreed conventions which can be incorporated into domestic law, such as the United Nations Convention on Contracts for the International Sale of Goods. While English lawyers participated in the drafting of the Convention, the United Kingdom has still not ratified it, despite the fact that a number of major trading nations have done so. At another level there have been attempts to draft principles of the law of contract which are not intended for incorporation into domestic law (at least not initially) but which are available for express adoption by contracting parties as a modern *lex mercatoria*. UNIDROIT has already produced a statement of Principles for International Commercial Contracts and work is under way to produce a statement of Principles of European Contract Law. Part I of the European Principles has been completed, dealing with Performance, Non-Performance, and Remedies, and publication of the remaining parts is anticipated in the near future. In the long run, these Principles are likely to form the foundation for an attempt to create a European or even an international contract law.[130] English lawyers are tempted to adopt their traditional stance: participate in the drafting of the document but then decline to sign up to the finished product. After all, why should English law sign up to these international agreements? Contracting parties from all over the world presently

---

[127] See, e.g., the extensive regulation of public procurement.
[128] 93/13 EEC [1993] OJ L95/29.
[129] Art. 100A of the Treaty of Rome.
[130] That this is so can be seen from the Introduction to O. Lando and H. Beale (eds.), *The Principles of European Contract Law Part I: Performance, Non-Performance and Remedies* (Dordrecht, 1995), esp. pp. xvii–xix.

agree that their contracts should be governed by English law precisely because it is English law which they want, not some new-fangled international creation. But there is no empirical evidence one way or the other. It is probably safe to assume that businesses wish to avoid unnecessary upheaval and uncertainty in the law of contract, but are they really interested in the finer points of English contract law? The experience with the recent Arbitration Act 1996 suggests that they might not be. The thrust of this legislation is to give greater autonomy to the parties to arbitration and to free English arbitration law from some of its self-imposed limitations. One of these limitations was that English law did not recognize the validity of a clause giving the arbitrator the power to decide *ex aequo et bono* or to act as an *amiable compositeur*.[131] The function of the arbitrator was to decide the case in accordance with the law and not simply according to notions of equity and fairness. But the Arbitration Act 1996 has changed all that and has recognized the validity of these clauses.[132] A clause empowering an arbitrator to apply 'internationally accepted principles of law governing contractual relations' would now appear to be valid. And if international parties are happy to have an arbitrator in London apply a modern *lex mercatoria* in the resolution of their dispute, why should they be so appalled at the prospect of a judge in the Commercial Court doing the same?

Like it or not, the pressure to produce a European or international code of contract law is unlikely to go away. Such a Code could have great advantages in terms of encouraging international trade by eliminating national differences in legal systems which may act as a barrier to trade. These conventions and Principles should be incorporated into our teaching of contract law for both academic and practical reasons because they are likely to be the contract law of the future in the sense that the Vienna Convention or UNIDROIT will govern an increasing range of contracts and they will also give the English law student of the future a greater insight into the way that civilian lawyers approach similar problems. The traditional hostility of the English lawyer to good

---

[131] See *Orion Compania Espanola de Seguros* v. *Belford Maatschappij voor Algemene Verzekgringeen* [1962] 2 Lloyd's Rep. 257, 264, *per* Megaw J.
[132] See ss. 1(1)(b), 33(1), and 46(1)(b).

faith might weaken after reading these conventions and a consideration of the Civilian experience of good faith. Civilian lawyers can in turn learn from the English lawyer and the pragmatic genius of English law: the relative simplicity of the English remedial regime for breach of contract might be thought to contrast rather well with the more flexible but rather uncertain regime contained in the Vienna Convention. Through the study of these conventions we can begin to appreciate our different legal cultures and perhaps begin to move towards a common solution to common problems. Professor Rose has done us all a great service in including both the UNIDROIT Principles and Principles of European Contract Law in the most recent edition of his Blackstone's Collection of Statutes on Contract, Tort and Restitution.[133] The materials are now accessible to students and they should be used.

This commitment to the study of contract law in its international context should not be taken to imply that the creation of an international contract law is inevitably a good thing. It is not. There are powerful counter-arguments.[134] One relates to the quality of the drafting of these international conventions. For example, the drafting of the Directive on Unfair Terms in Consumer Contracts has been the subject of trenchant criticism[135] and the statutory instrument which has implemented the Directive has done nothing to clarify its ambiguities.[136] Perhaps the most outspoken attack on the quality of drafting of these conventions has been launched by Sir John Hobhouse writing extra-judicially. Sir John argued that modern international conventions 'are inevitably and confessedly drafted as multi-cultural compromises between different schemes of law'[137] and that the pursuit of uniformity 'inevitably results in the production of an inadequate legal tool without compensating

---

[133] F. D. Rose (ed.), *Blackstone's Statutes on Contract, Tort and Restitution 1996–7* (7th edn., London, 1997).

[134] See, e.g., P. Legrand, 'Against a European Civil Code' (1997) 60 *MLR* 44.

[135] See T. Hartley, 'Five Forms of Uncertainty in European Community Law' [1996] *CLJ* 265, esp. 266–73.

[136] The draftsman having employed the 'copy-out' technique of implementation, on which see C. Bright and S. Bright, 'Unfair Terms in Land Contracts: Copy Out or Cop Out?' (1995) 111 *LQR* 655.

[137] J. Hobhouse, 'International Conventions and Commercial Law: The Pursuit of Uniformity' (1990) 106 *LQR* 530, 533.

gain'.[138] In his view 'international commerce is best served not by imposing deficient legal schemes upon it but by encouraging the development of the best schemes in a climate of free competition and choice. . . . What should no longer be tolerated is the unthinking acceptance of a goal of uniformity and its doctrinaire imposition on the commercial community.'[139] It is true that this is a view which is not universally held[140] and it is a card which has been played by English lawyers in the past without foundation.[141] But it is a view which must be carefully considered because the need to compromise in an effort to reach agreement on the uniform law may result in a final product which lacks the advantages of all the different systems put together. Other problems are likely to arise. How should an international law of contract be interpreted and who should do the interpreting? National courts may well interpret them differently and so uniformity will be lost. Some internationally agreed forum for the resolution of disputes is still a long way off. And how would these conventions, once agreed, be amended? The difficulties involved in reaching agreement are likely to inhibit regular renegotiation. But international trade is constantly changing and the law must adapt to these changes: an international or European code might not be able to do so. Professor Goode has stated that the Uniform Customs and Practice for Documentary Credits is 'the most successful of the Codes'[142] by which the mercantile community has created its own law. Yet the most notable feature of letters of credit is that they are autonomous obligations which stand free from other obligations. It is much easier to secure agreement because the focus is on a narrow issue and a relatively small group of players. The law of contract is much more diverse and thus harder to regulate at a European or international level. We are therefore some way away from a European or international law of contract. Domestic contract law is safe for the short to medium term future.

---

[138] *Ibid.*, at 534.   [139] *Ibid.*, at 535.

[140] For a reply see J. Steyn, 'A Kind of Esperanto?' in P. Birks (ed.), *The Frontiers of Liability*, Vol. 2 (Oxford, 1994), 11.

[141] See Lord Roskill's account of the objections of Scrutton LJ and MacKinnon LJ to the enactment of the Hague Rules into English law (1992) 108 *LQR* 501.

[142] R. Goode, *Commercial Law* (London, 1995), 40.

(B) A LAW OF CONTRACT OR A LAW OF CONTRACTS?

A further cause of uncertainty relates to the future of a general law of contract. Will it be superseded by laws of particular contracts to the extent that there will no longer be any point in expounding or teaching the general principles of the law of contract? It seems certain that we are likely to witness a greater fragmentation of the legal regulation of contracts. A further division which is likely to emerge in English law is between consumer contracts and commercial contracts as the former become the subject of regulation to which the latter are exempt. The Unfair Terms in Consumer Contracts Regulations 1994 is the latest piece of legislation to draw a clear line between consumer and commercial contracts. Fragmentation is increasing in other directions as emerging industries, such as information technology, claim to be the new battleground where contract principles will be developed.[143] Keeping abreast of the latest developments in contract law has become an increasingly difficult task simply because the cases on the law of contract are increasingly difficult to find as they are spread across a vast range of specialist law reports.[144] Yet, while the fragmentation may have increased in recent years, I refuse to believe that contract law has descended to a wilderness of individual instances with no unifying thread or threads. The difficulty which lies ahead is to discern the fundamental principles of the modern law of contract and to work out the relationship between these general principles and the host of specific legislation which regulates particular types of contracts.

(C) THE SHAPE OF THE MODERN LAW OF CONTRACT

Bargains are likely to remain at the core of the modern law of contract and the courts can be expected to continue to protect the expectations generated by a binding promise in the absence of an

---

[143] See, e.g., S. Stokes, 'Shaping the Next Wave of Case Law', *The Lawyer* 28 Nov. 1995, 15.

[144] Such as the Entertainment and Media Law Reports, Lloyd's Law Reports, Trading Law Reports, Building Law Reports, and almost any set of law reports other than the official law reports.

overwhelming countervailing policy. The difficult question which will have to be faced relates to the extent to which the law will protect expectations engendered by, or detrimental reliance induced by, a non-bargain promise. Rather than set the threshhold for enforceability relatively high, as was the case with the traditional doctrine of consideration, and then provide full protection for the expectation engendered by that binding promise, the courts may choose to 'set the threshold for enforceability relatively low, but to carefully scrutinise enforceable promises for violation of discrete unconscionability norms, and to tailor the extent of enforcement to the substantive interest that enforcement is designed to protect'.[145] Such a formulation would enable the courts, for example, to protect only the reliance interest in a case in which expenditure is incurred in reliance upon a non-bargain promise. This is neither the time nor the place to seek to sketch out the limits of such a principle but it seems to me that contract scholarship in the future will have to place more emphasis on the scope of, and the justifications for, such a principle and less emphasis upon the deficiencies of the existing system. More difficult still is the need to sketch out the countervailing policies which will deny the enforcement of an otherwise binding promise.

In my view, two issues stand out for the future. The first is whether the undoubted concern of the modern law of contract with the fairness of the bargain should be openly recognized by the creation of a general doctrine of unconscionability and the second is whether the law should develop a principle of good faith and fair dealing. Once again the acceptability of these principles depends in large part upon the scope of these principles. What impact would a good faith doctrine have on the existing rules of English law? Does good faith simply mean the absence of bad faith; does it require subjective good faith or objective good faith? These questions have to be answered with greater precision before we can sensibly decide whether or not to recognize such a duty. The recognition of a duty of good faith and fair dealing in the Second Restatement of Contracts adopted by the American Law Institute in 1981 has been hailed as a reflection of 'one of the truly major advances in

---

[145] M. Eisenberg, 'The Principles of Consideration' (1982) 67 *Cornell L Rev.* 640, 665.

American contract law during the past fifty years'.[146] Professor Reynolds has recently pointed out that 'the more informal Restatement technique may be a more practical way forward[147] than codification but the difficulty, of course, is that we have no equivalent to the American Restatement. Perhaps we should have. It is unlikely that the Law Commission will play the role of the American Law Institute and oversee such a general project. Yet who will do so? Pollock and Anson did not refrain from the task of seeking to deduce principles of general application from the existing mass of case law. Is there therefore any justification for the present generation of academic lawyers holding back from the task of deducing new principles of general application suitable for the new millennium? Perhaps the editors of influential works such as *Chitty*, of whom I happen to be one, should assume a more proactive role and begin the task of moulding the present fragmented doctrines into a more coherent whole from which a general doctrine of good faith and fair dealing might emerge. Whatever the outcome of this process, the thrust of my message is that academic lawyers of the future must spend more of their time constructing and testing the limits of new models of contract and less on the deficiencies of the existing system.

(D) PUBLIC SECTOR 'CONTRACTS'

While the law of contract may work tolerably well in the case of commercial contracts, it is not so clear that it is well-suited to contracts which are entered into with a view other than one to make a profit. Some illustrations will demonstrate the point. For example, I enter into a contract with a builder to have a swimming pool built in my garden and I stipulate that it must be built to a depth of seven feet six inches. Now I do not enter into the contract to make a profit: I enter into the contract because I want to be able to swim in the comfort of my own house and to be able to dive into the pool in safety. In breach of contract, I am supplied with a swimming pool which is only six foot six inches deep. How is the law to measure the damages to which I am entitled? Alternatively, I

---

[146] R. Summers, 'The General Duty of Good Faith—Its Recognition and Conceptualization' (1982) 67 *Cornell L Rev.* 810.

[147] Reynolds, n. 48 above, 27.

enter into a contract with a builder under which he agrees to repair the roof of my parents' house. He does the job defectively and so I call in another builder to do the job properly. How is the law to measure the damages to which I am entitled? Or suppose that a local authority enters into a contract with a contractor for the provision of a fire service and the contractor in breach of contract supplies the local authority with fewer men and fewer fire engines than those contracted for and in doing so it saves a substantial sum of money. The local authority does not enter into such a contract with a view to profit: it is seeking to provide a service for its residents. Once again the question arises: how is the law to measure the damages for this breach of contract? The underlying difficulty with all three cases lies in identifying and measuring the loss which has been occasioned by the breach. The law's commitment to the protection of the plaintiff's expectation interest is generally understood to be a reference to the *financial* situation of the plaintiff had the contract been performed.[148] But the difficulty with all three cases I have outlined is that the plaintiff never entered into the contract with a view to enhancing his financial position. As Lord Mustill recently remarked, 'the law must cater for those occasions where the value of the promise to the promisee exceeds the financial enhancement of his position which full performance will secure'.[149] Yet it is not at all clear that the law has yet catered for these occasions. English law would appear to allow the plaintiff in the first case to recover the cost of curing the deficiency in the swimming pool where it is reasonable for him to do this, but where it would be unreasonable for him to do so, for example because the cost of doing the work substantially outweighs the benefit obtained by the carrying out of the work, the plaintiff will be confined to a claim for any diminution in the value of his property (which is likely to be very small or nothing at all) and loss of amenity damages for the disappointment suffered at not getting the pool which he was promised (which again is likely to be small).[150] The answer to the second case is not at all clear. Lord Griffiths was of the opinion that I would be entitled to recover the cost of 'securing the performance of the bargain by completing the roof repairs

---

[148] See, e.g., *Ford v. White* [1964] 1 WLR 885.
[149] *Ruxley Electronics and Construction Ltd. v. Forsyth* [1996] 1 AC 344, 360.
[150] *Ibid.*

properly by the second builder'[151] but the other members of the House of Lords expressly left the point open. In the third case it is likely that the local authority would be entitled to recover only nominal damages.[152] These cases suggest that the commitment of the law to the protection of the plaintiff's interest in performance is rather weak[153] and that English contract law must develop a more expansive conception of loss to embrace these cases. But why do these cases matter? It could be said that they are insignificant aberrations which should not be of great concern to us. In my opinion such a view is profoundly mistaken because we are on the verge of a huge increase in local authority contracting where these problems are likely to emerge. Local authorities do not generally contract out services with a view to profit, there are great difficulties involved in drafting the specifications of performance in these contracts and therefore difficulties must inevitably arise in terms of identifying and measuring the loss occasioned by any non-performance or defective performance. How is the law going to respond to this explosion of public sector contracting?

It might be objected that these agreements are not truly contracts because they are not enforceable in the courts. While this is true of some 'public sector' contracts it is certainly not true of them all. And, even in the case of contracts declared not to be enforceable in the courts, it raises fascinating issues for the contract lawyer. The most interesting example by far is the creation of the internal market in the National Health Service, where section 4(3) of the National Health and Community Care Act 1990 expressly states that these agreements 'shall not be regarded for any purpose as giving rise to contractual rights or liabilities, but if any dispute arises with respect to such an arrangement, either party may refer

---

[151] *Linden Gardens Trust Ltd.* v. *Lenesta Sludge Disposals Ltd.* [1994] 1 AC 85, 97.

[152] This example is based on the American case of *City of New Orleans* v. *Fireman's Charitable Association*, 9 So. 486 (1891) but in the light of the decision of the Court of Appeal in *Surrey County Council* v. *Bredero Homes Ltd.* [1993] 1 WLR 1361 it is suggested that an English court would reach the same conclusion.

[153] Contrast the view of Professor D. Friedmann 'The Performance Interest in Contract Damages' (1995) 111 *LQR* 628, 650, who maintains that *Ruxley* is a decision 'predicated on the approach that pacta sunt servanda and that the plaintiff's performance interest should be respected', but this claim is hard to defend because protection of his performance inter .t would surely have given him the money which he required to obtain a swimming ; ool constructed to the agreed depth.

the matter to the Secretary of State for determination under the following provisions of this section'. The aim here is presumably to obtain the greater choice, quality, and efficiency which it is alleged that contracts can bring without triggering the expense of litigation which a formal contract can generate: we want the discipline of contract but not its associated costs. Empirical studies have demonstrated that there is considerable uncertainty within the NHS as to the way in which these new agreements should be drafted.[154] Should they follow standard commercial contracts and make provision for liquidated damages, exclusion, and limitation of liability and the vast array of techniques at the disposal of the commercial lawyer, or should they develop a more co-operative model of contracting with greater emphasis on co-operation and partnership and less emphasis on strict adherence to the letter of the agreement? What standards will be applied by those required to adjudicate when disagreements arise under these agreements? Will they apply a standard derived from commercial law or will they develop their own adjudicative standards? A number of empirical studies are up and running, but it is still too early to say which model of 'contracting' will prevail, although early signs are that a more co-operative style of contracting is emerging. This will prove to be a fascinating and fruitful area of study for contract lawyers in the future and it may call into question some of our traditional thinking about the scope of the law of contract and the remedial regime which it currently employs.[155] A law formed with commodities markets in mind may not be entirely suited to local authority contracting.

Finally, what is the future of the Professor of English Law who has a particular interest in contract law? In the current state of university finances, I suppose that it will not be rich in a pecuniary sense, but I am optimistic that it will be rich in other respects. I suspect that future generations of contract scholars will adopt an increasingly European and international perspective as the importance of a purely domestic study of the law of contract declines in

---

[154] See, e.g., P. Allen 'Contracts in the National Health Service Internal Market' (1995) 58 *MLR* 321 and D. Hughes, J. McHale, and D. Griffiths, n. 101 above.

[155] For example it could be argued that the present law attaches too much importance to termination as a remedy which, while appropriate in the context of a commodities contract, is not appropriate for a long-term relationship where the parties may wish to keep the agreement alive albeit under new terms.

significance. At the same time I suspect that the contract lawyer of the future will have to expand his or her own horizons beyond the cases and the statutes and engage in more empirical and theoretical analysis. The links with the world of legal practice will become closer as more work is done on the use of the law in drafting contracts and in litigating claims. The field of contract law will extend beyond commercial law and into areas which we currently call public law. All in all I am confident that, should I be spared, there is enough here to keep me gainfully employed until my retirement in some thirty years time.

NEGLIGENCE: THE SEARCH FOR COHERENCE

Bob Hepple

Introduction

Negligence has triumphed in the twentieth century. Liberated by *Donoghue* v. *Stevenson*[1] from the confines of specific categories of duties of care into a fluid principle of civil liability, the independent wrong of Negligence has overshadowed all other torts, encroached on their territory, and sometimes entirely overwhelmed them.

This development has continued unabated since it was first brilliantly described by Maurice Millner thirty years ago.[2] Recent examples are the *Cambridge Water Co.* case[3] in which the House of Lords held that only foreseeable damage is compensable under the so-called strict liability rule in *Rylands* v. *Fletcher*, and the even more radical decision of the High Court of Australia effectively abolishing that rule by holding that it has been absorbed by general principles of negligence.[4] Another example is *Spring* v. *Guardian Assurance plc*[5] in which a majority in the House of Lords held that an employer could be liable to a former employee in negligence for providing an inaccurate reference. This conclusion by-passed the limitations of the tort of malicious falsehood where proof of mere negligence is insufficient, and also those of the tort of defamation, where the defence of qualified privilege would have been available to the defendant because the false statement was made without malice to a person with an interest in receiving it.

Even more significant is that negligence has expanded its reach

---

[1] [1932] AC 562.
[2] M. A. Millner, *Negligence in Modern Law* (London, 1967).
[3] *Cambridge Water Co.* v. *Eastern Counties Leather plc* [1994] 2 AC 264.
[4] *Burns Port Authority* v. *General Jones Pty. Ltd.* (1994) 20 ALR 42; R. F. V. Heuston and R. A. Buckley (1994) 110 *LQR* 506.
[5] [1995] 2 AC 296.

into what was once seen as the exclusive sphere of contract in respect of recovery for economic loss. In his book *The Death of Contract*[6] Grant Gilmore noted the absorption of contract into tort in the United States. A similar, although more subtle, development has occurred in England. *Hedley Byrne and Co. Ltd.* v. *Heller & Partners*[7] recognized that the assumption of responsibility to make an accurate statement could give rise to a duty of care to a plaintiff who suffered economic loss by relying on that assumption of responsibility. In *Henderson* v. *Merrett Syndicates Ltd.*[8] (the Lloyds' 'Names' case) it was made clear after years of vacillation that the *Hedley Byrne* principle is not limited to statements but applies to any assumption of responsibility to provide professional or quasi-professional services. Moreover, the House of Lords unanimously held that a contractual duty of care between the parties does not preclude the concurrence of a tort duty in the same respect. Lord Goff's speech is particularly important because he rejects the argument that the law of tort can be used only to fill the gaps left by the law of contract. His approach was to treat 'the law of tort [as] the general law out of which the parties can, if they wish, contract'.[9] In *White* v. *Jones*[10] (the case of the disappointed beneficiaries who successfully sued the solicitor who had carelessly failed to act on their father's instructions to amend his will before his death), a further step was taken by applying the *Hedley Byrne* principle, or a radical interpretation of it, to a situation where there was no reliance on an assumption of responsibility by those whose expectations were disappointed. We thus appear towards the end of the century to be close to a law of civil wrongs in which the breach of a duty of care causing harm is the determining and integrative element. One may include among civil wrongs those which are redressed in equity, such as breach of trust, knowing assistance in fraud, and abuse of confidence.[11]

Yet at the very moment of its ascendancy, the law of negligence is almost universally criticized for its lack of coherence. The shifting

---

[6] G. Gilmore, *The Death of Contract* (Columbus, Ohio, 1974), 90.

[7] [1964] AC 465.   [8] [1995] 2 AC 145.

[9] [1995] 2 AC at 193.   [10] [1995] 2 AC 207.

[11] On the justifications for this, see Peter Birks, 'The Concept of a Civil Wrong' in David G. Owen (ed.), *Philosophical Foundations of Tort Law* (Oxford, 1996), 31 at 34–5; and Sir Robin Cooke, 'The Condition of the Law of Tort' in P. Birks (ed.), *The Frontiers of Liability*, vol. 2 (Oxford, 1994), 49 at 61–2.

emphasis of different judges in the analysis of the duty of care has been said to lead to 'confusion, complexity and high levels of litigation'.[12] The critics are not limited to academics. Lord Cooke of Thorndon has said extra-judicially that 'the debilitated condition of the law of tort may be seen as partly due to judicial failure to take sufficient exercise in discharging the judicial function for looking after the development of the common law'.[13] Lord Lloyd of Berwick has expressed alarm that the law of negligence is disintegrating 'into a series of isolated decisions without any coherent principes at all'.[14]

The criticisms deserve to be taken seriously because coherence is generally regarded as an important value in its own right. However we need to distinguish formal coherence from coherence of purpose. Formal coherence is concerned with the internal intelligibility of legal rules. The rules relating to obligations in general and to tort in particular must make sense when taken together.[15]

The second approach to coherence is functionalist or purposive. This recognizes that the law of negligence pursues a variety of goals. In 1951 Glanville Williams identified four such aims of the law of tort: appeasement, justice, deterrence, and compensation and he concluded that there was a lack of coherence with the law of tort trying to serve a multiplicity of purposes but succeeding in none.[16]

The argument of this article is that the lack of both formal and functional coherence in the law of negligence arises because the law is pulling in two ways at once. On the one hand, there is the belief in *individual responsibility* for making good the harm caused by one's fault. This may be said to reflect notions of corrective justice, that is the need to maintain a balance between the wrongful injurer

---

[12] J. Stapleton, 'Duty of Care and Economic Loss: A Wider Agenda' (1991) 107 *LQR* 249 at 295.

[13] Sir Robin Cooke, n. 11 above, at 51. See, too, Lord Cooke of Thorndon, 'The Temptation of Elegance Revisited' in *Turning Points in the Common Law* (Hamlyn Lectures, 1996) (forthcoming).

[14] *Marc Rich & Co. AG v. Bishop Rock Marine Co. Ltd. (The Nicholas H.)* [1996] 2 AC 211 at 230.

[15] Neil MacCormick, *Legal Reasoning and Legal Theory* (Oxford, 1978), 179. There are dissenters, see *e.g.* Tony Weir, 'Errare Humanum Est' in *The Frontiers of Liability*, n. 11 above, 13, 103 at 109–10.

[16] Glanville Williams, 'The Aims of the Law of Tort' (1951) 4 *CLP* 137.

and the victim for moral reasons. It belongs to the two-dimensional world of loss shifting between the wrongdoer and the victim. On the other hand, there is the belief in *social responsibility*, namely that losses which are an inevitable consequence of modern life should be borne by those who benefit from the activities which cause them, or even more widely by society at large. This rests on notions of distributive justice which seeks to spread losses according to the goal of maximizing social welfare.

These ideas of individual and social responsibility are powerful currents in twentieth-century opinion. It is therefore not surprising that they have created an inner tension and lack of coherence in judicial attempts to formulate a theory of liability for civil wrongs. Many years ago, Oliver Wendell Holmes said that the general purpose of the law of tort is 'to reconcile the policy of letting accidents lie where they fall, and the reasonable freedom of others with the protection of the individual from injury'.[17] In striking a balance between these conflicting interests in freedom of action and in security, the law obviously reflects changing social and moral opinions about individual and social responsibility.

I shall argue that a more coherent framework of negligence law will not be achieved until the conceptual straitjacket imposed by the notion of a 'duty of care' is discarded and replaced by a broad principle of fault. Within that framework policy considerations would be paramount and would lead to 'a pattern of liability as diversified as befits the complex society which [negligence law] serves'.[18]

Nineteenth-century Individualism

The starting point of this argument is to recognize the many and not always consistent strands in nineteenth-century individualism. A mixture of Kantian moral philosophy and the economic dogma of laissez-faire provided an intellectual climate sympathetic to the notion of 'no liability without fault'. The question of liability was increasingly resolved in the nineteenth century by asking not the traditional question 'Who caused the accident?', but rather 'Who

---

[17] O. W. Holmes, *The Common Law* (Boston, Mass., 1881), 144–5.
[18] Millner, n. 2 above, at 237.

was at fault?'. Horwitz,[19] who studied this transformation from strict liability to fault liability in the United States between 1780 and 1860, claimed that the judges applied the law in a way which effectively subsidized entrepreneurial activity by protecting industry from the claims of workers, consumers, and railway passengers. While the development of fault liability was undoubtedly influenced by the needs of the industrial revolution, it is too reductionist an analysis to see economic forces as a decisive element in the transformation of tort law in England. Here we have to place at the centre of the stage the conflict between Benthamite principles of liberalism or individualism and what Dicey, in *Law and Public Opinion in England in the Nineteenth Century*, described as 'collectivism'. By collectivism he meant 'the school of public opinion often termed (and generally by more or less hostile critics) socialism, which favours the intervention of the state, even at some sacrifice of individual freedom, for the purpose of conferring benefit upon the mass of the people'.[20]

As a 'salient example' of the decline of Benthamite individualism, he cited the 'effort lasting over many years to amend the law with regard to employer's liability for damage done to his workmen in the course of their employment'.[21] During most of the nineteenth century, employees were thwarted in their attempts to make their employers pay for injuries caused by fault through a trilogy of defences: common employment (which prevented the employee from making the employer vicariously liable for an injury caused by the negligence of a fellow-employee); *volenti non fit injuria* (the employee was deemed to have consented to all obvious dangers of the job; and contributory negligence, which at that time was a complete bar to action. The aim of the Benthamite liberals was to remove these defences which were regarded as a defect in the common law. By doing so, they hoped to clear the path for self-help. When their attempts to do so failed, there was 'some sort of historical watershed'.[22] Joseph Chamberlain introduced what Dicey described as the 'thoroughly collective legislation embodied

---

[19] M. Horwitz, *The Transformation of American Law 1780–1860* (Cambridge, Mass., 1977).

[20] A. V. Dicey, *Lectures on the Relation Between Law and Public Opinion in England in the Nineteenth Century* (2nd edn.) (London, 1914), 64.

[21] *Ibid.* 68.

[22] David G. Hanes, *The First British Workmen's Compensation Act 1897* (New Haven, Conn., 1968), 105.

in the Workmen's Compensation Acts 1897 and 1990'.[23] In effect, Chamberlain's Act was at odds with the common law of negligence because it made compensation payable by the employer for injuries arising out of and in the course of employment without proof of fault, fixed compensation not on an indemnity basis but on the principle of division of loss between employer and employee, and left the employer free to spread the cost by taking out liability insurance. Employees had to elect between their tort remedy and workmen's compensation claim but the great majority claimed under the scheme because it had the advantage of compensating for basic economic losses with relative speed. This led to a growth of liability insurance (although this was never made compulsory except in coal-mining from 1934), and the consequent loss-spreading which enables us to characterize the Act as embodying a notion of social rather than individual responsibility.

Another crucial feature of liberalism was a belief in contractual freedom. I am heavily indebted to Patrick Atiyah's study of the *Rise and Fall of Freedom of Contract* for the following brief account of this phenomenon. In the nineteenth century the law of negligence operated largely within a contractual context, with actions between strangers being the exception rather than the rule. Negligence might cause injury to a railway passenger or to a visitor on dangerous premises or to an employee. As Atiyah points out,[24] all these sorts of accident presented a contractual flavour to the nineteenth-century lawyer.

When Baron Bramwell, a strong supporter of the defences of common employment and *volenti* and an opponent of the loss-spreading device of vicarious liability, was asked by the House of Commons select committee on employer's liability in 1876 why a passenger who was injured through the negligence of the railway company was entitled to damages when the injured workman was not, his reply was that a passenger was entitled to compensation by virtue of his contractual right to be carried safely. When he was pressed to explain why the worker did not have a right to be safely employed, his answer was in effect that the worker was paid to take the risk of injury and so to compensate him would undermine the

---

[23] The original Act was limited in scope but it was generalized in 1906, and was amended on a number of occasions.

[24] P. S. Atiyah, *The Rise and Fall of Freedom of Contract* (Oxford, 1979), 502.

bargain he had made with his employer.[25] The question-begging nature of this argument, which assumes that the worker knew when he took the job that he had no right to compensation, is apparent to us today, but it is a powerful example of the influence of individualism and contractualism.

The same adherence to classical contract theory lies behind *Winterbottom v. Wright*[26] in which it was held in 1842 that the manufacturer of a carriage with a defective wheel was not liable to an employee of the purchaser who was injured as a result of the defect. The case was argued as one in tort. The action failed, not, as was later suggested in *Donoghue v. Stevenson*, because of the 'privity of contract' fallacy, but essentially on the policy ground that to allow an action in tort for negligence would open the floodgates. In effect, Lord Abinger was concerned that the manufacturer's contract with the purchaser, bargained on the (assumed) basis of being liable only to the purchaser and not to the purchaser's employees, would be 'ripped open'.[27] The court failed to recognize that if manufacturers were made liable to the ultimate consumer or user of their products, their potential liability could in future be taken into account through insurance and higher prices, thus spreading the losses.

In the nineteenth century, then, the coherence of the law of negligence rested largely within a contractual matrix and it was confined to protection against physical harm and personal injuries. After *Lumley v. Gye*,[28] tort also became important for the protection of contractual interests against intentional interference particularly in the context of trade disputes: hence Dicey's fury at the Trade Disputes Act 1906 which gave trade unions an immunity in tort. But a fundamental distinction was drawn in the second half of the nineteenth century between intentionally and negligently caused economic loss. In *Derry v. Peek*,[29] an attempt to extend the tort of deceit to cover negligently made statements failed, and in *Cattle v. Stockton Waterworks*[30] it was held that there could be no liability for negligently interfering with a contract between the

---

[25] HC Parliamentary Papers (1876), ix, 669; x, 551, 628 ff.; Atiyah, n. 24 above, 378.　　[26] (1842) 10 M & W 109.
[27] (1842) 10 M & W 109 at 115; Atiyah, n. 24 above, 503.
[28] (1853) 2 E & B 216.　　[29] (1889) 14 App. Cas. 337.
[30] (1875) LR 10 QB 453.

plaintiff and a third party. Even in the sphere of physical harm and personal injury the idea of using the law of negligence to compensate relational losses—that is, losses suffered as a result of a relationship with another person who has also suffered loss—was anathema to liberal ideas. It took the utilitarian arguments of Edwin Chadwick—that it was in the self-interest of the railway companies to alleviate the dreadful conditions of the railway navvies—and the political subtlety of Lord Campbell to achieve the obscure and limited Fatal Accidents Act of 1846, which gave spouses, parents, and children the right to sue for the loss of a breadwinner.[31]

The Separation of Law from Policy in the Twentieth Century

By 1900, utilitarianism had ceased to be influential in British legal thinking. It was the Austinian positivist tradition which the judges absorbed as part of their legal training in the universities and Inns of Court, a theory which gave comfort to legal conservatives. One characteristic of this thinking was the separation of law from morals and politics. The judges tended to avoid explicit questions of policy, although in reality these were never far from the surface. Another feature was an obsession with conceptual classification of the myriad of decided cases, a legal parallel to the then popular Darwinian scientific classifications of plant and animal life. The problem was how to classify those situations in which legal liability for fault had been recognized without a contract. Once liability for negligence was separated from its origins in consensual arrangements, there was the risk of collectivism or state interference of the kind seen in the Workmen's Compensation Acts.

In the first edition of Pollock's *Law of Torts* published in 1887, the author stated dogmatically that 'duties imposed in tort are fixed by the law and independent of the will of the parties'. From this it was a short step to his formulation that 'all members of a civilised commonwealth are under a general duty towards their neighbours to do them no hurt without lawful cause or excuse'.[32] As a proposition of law, this was certainly wrong in 1887, since duties of

---

[31] W. R. Cornish and G. de N. Clark, *Law and Society in England 1750–1950* (London, 1989), 513, 515.
[32] *Pollock's Law of Torts* (London, 1887), 3.

care were recognized only in specific situations, most of them involving direct relations between the parties. The attempt of Sir Baliol Brett MR in *Heaven* v. *Pender*[33] to lay down a general principle of liability for fault in the sense of foreseeable harm judged by the standards of the 'person of ordinary sense', was rejected by his fellow judges because of their fears that people would be held responsible for indeterminate consequences. So Brett MR himself (as Lord Esher) was forced to qualify his general principle ten years later in *Le Lievre* v. *Gould*,[34] in which liability for negligent statements was denied, by prescribing a criterion of 'nearness' which as 'proximity' has confused the issue of duty of care ever since.

In *Donoghue* v. *Stevenson* Lord Atkin revived the idea of 'some general conception of relations giving rise to a duty of care' and formulated his famous 'neighbour' principle, which encapsulated both of Lord Esher's requirements, namely reasonable foreseeability and proximity. This caused consternation among the conceptualists who were quick to point out the inconsistency with previous House of Lords decisions such as *Derry* v. *Peek*. Even so great a commercial judge as Scutton LJ strongly dissented from Lord Atkin's principle,[35] and as late as 1939 Landon, Pollock's editor, denied any general principle.[36] The predictability and certainty which seemed possible so long as negligence remained in a contractual framework or within the limits of a number of specific categories had been threatened by Lord Atkin. While the rule that the manufacturer was liable for negligence was readily espoused, possibly because it thwarted the extension of contractual warranties to the ultimate purchaser of defective products, the neighbour principle had little impact before the 1950s. In 1951, however, Landon had to record that 'wherever the Court wishes to find for the plaintiff that doctrine will be used, just as it will be disregarded where the defendant is the favoured party'. As a result, complained Landon, 'much uncertainty now prevails throughout the whole law of Negligence'.[37]

---

[33] (1883) 11 QBD 503 at 509.   [34] [1893] 1 QB 491 at 499.
[35] *Farr* v. *Butters & Co.* [1932] 1 KB 146 at 168.
[36] *Pollock's Law of Torts* (14th edn., by P. A. Landon) (London, 1939), Chap. 11.
[37] *Pollock's Law of Torts* (15th edn., by P. A. Landon) (London, 1951), 329.

The confusion was a product of the conceptualist approach, which demanded a specific 'duty of care' as a precondition of liability. Had a general notion of liability for fault been adopted (as in Articles 1382 and 1383 of the French Civil Code, or even the more limited level of abstraction of paragraph 823(1) of the German Code) then proximity could have been confined to its proper role as a test of remoteness of damage. Indeed, it has been persuasively argued by David Howarth that what Lord Atkin was saying in *Donoghue* was simply that negligence requires both fault (including foreseeability) and an absence of remoteness.[38] This is why Lord Atkin stressed the importance of inquiring whether inspection by the person using a defective product or someone else could reasonably be contemplated.

However, Lord Atkin himself was a prisoner of the conceptual categories. He had inherited a way of thinking of 'duty', not simply as exercise by a reasonable person of a standard of care, a question of fact for a jury, but as a question of law for the judge to decide. This was echoed in Lord Macmillan's statement in *Donoghue* that the law 'concerns itself with carelessness only where there is a duty to take care'.[39] These judges were in effect asserting the judicial power to limit the scope given to the jury to determine liability based on fault. Whatever its justification in 1932, this control is unnecessary now that jury trials in civil cases for negligence have disappeared. Instead of laying down a general principle that all damage which is caused by defendant's fault and is not too remote gives rise to liability unless there is a lawful justification, the requirement of 'reasonable foreseeability' came to be thrice incanted: as a test of the notional duty, as a test of carelessness, and as a test for remoteness. 'Proximity' was invoked twice, both in relation to the notional duty and to remoteness.

It was as if the judges believed that by repetition of the formulae of 'reasonable foreseeability' and 'proximity', one could ward off the dangers of limitless liability outside the sphere of contract. Behind this lay the contradiction between the moral promise of nineteenth-century individualism and the social reality of modern society with its increasing risks of harm through inadvertent

---

[38] D. Howarth, *Textbook on Tort* (London, 1995), 265.
[39] [1932] AC at 618.

negligence. This is a society in which 'negligence without fault'—those momentary lapses which every one of us is bound to commit in the course of motoring[40] or operating machinery—is commonplace. The judges have tried to recognize this by modifying the notion of negligence itself. Even in the nineteenth century, *Rylands* v. *Fletcher* made the controller of things brought on to land 'likely to do mischief if they escape' strictly responsible. The opportunity was missed to extend this rule to the control of motor vehicles.[41] Instead, a so-called 'objective' standard of care has been applied to all motorists including even learner drivers who are doing their best, but who are not up to the standards of the reasonably skilled driver.[42] The maxim *res ipsa loquitur* is readily invoked to shift the evidential burden of proof in circumstances where an untoward event requires a satisfactory explanation by the defendant. Such developments reflect the changing function of negligence law from a means of specific deterrence to one of compensation. As late as 1924, Sir John Salmond's fundamental thesis in the sixth edition of his *Law of Torts* was that negligence was essentially a subjective fact and that with certain exceptions, wrongful intent or a negligent state of mind was essential for civil liability in tort. In this we can detect the still powerful grip of nineteenth-century Kantian moral philosophy and its corollary of 'no liability without fault'. Like Bentham and Austin, Salmond believed that 'pecuniary compensation is not in itself the ultimate justification of legal liability. It is simply the instrument by which the law fulfils its purpose of penal coercion.'[43]

This theory of deterrence had to be abandoned by Salmond's editor after *Donoghue* v. *Stevenson*.[44] However, despite the underlying rationale in *Donoghue* v. *Stevenson* of compensating consumers, English law lay trapped within the conceptual framework of the 'duty of care'. One might instructively compare the more robust approach of common lawyers in the United States. There the legal reformers of the early twentieth century considered

---

[40] According to a recent survey, the average motorist makes 50 serious mistakes a week: *The Times*, 2 Dec. 1996, reporting a study commissioned by Autoglass.

[41] See J. R. Spencer, 'Motor Cars and the Rule in *Rylands* v. *Fletcher*—A Chapter of Accidents in the History of Law and Motoring' [1983] *CLJ* 65.

[42] *Nettleship* v. *Weston* [1971] 2 QB 691.

[43] *Salmond on Torts* (6th edn.) (London, 1924), 12.

[44] *Salmond on Torts* (8th edn. by W. T. S. Stallybrass) (London, 1934), p. vii.

conceptualist modes of thought reactionary and incapable of solving modern problems. Perhaps the greatest of all common law judges this century was Benjamin Cardozo. He wrote in 1920:

> I was much troubled in spirit in my first years on the bench, to find how trackless was the ocean on which I had embarked. I sought for certainty . . . I was trying to reach land, the solid land of fixed and settled rules.[45]

But he recorded that he became 'reconciled to the uncertainty' by seeing judging as 'not discovery but creation', and understanding that when 'principles that had served their day expire' new principles could be 'born' at the hands of judges. In *The Nature of the Judicial Process* he described the four methods of 'logic', 'custom', 'tradition', or 'sociology' as justifications for the decisions which he made. Although he cited Cardozo's judgment in *Macpherson* v. *Buick Motor Co.*[46] where the negligence liability of an automobile manufacturer was extended beyond car dealers to consumers, Lord Atkin did not employ Cardozo's judicial method, which required a detailed evaluation of the relationship between all the protagonists.

The lack of coherence of English law has stemmed from its over-reliance on vague concepts like 'reasonable foreseeability' and 'proximity'. This confusion is particularly evident in the cases about psychiatric damage (what lawyers still quaintly call 'nervous shock'): witness the different definitions of the area of foreseeability ('impact' or 'shock') of Lord Macmillan and Lord Wright in *Bourhill* v. *Young*,[47] the denial by Lord Scarman in *McLoughlin* v. *O'Brian*[48] that policy has a role to play in these cases contrary to the powerful assertion by Lord Edmund-Davies in the same case that it does; and the profoundly unsatisfactory result in *Alcock* v. *Chief Constable of South Yorskhire*[49] (the Hillsborough disaster) that the relationship of brothers-in-law, grandparents, uncles, and friends with the deceased or injured were too distant and a brother, who was present in another part of the stadium, lost simply because he had offered no proof that he had a close relationship with his brother who was a victim of the disaster. Recent attempts to

---

[45] B. Cardozo, *The Nature of the Judicial Process* (New York, 1921), 166–7; see generally, G. Edward White, *Tort Law in America* (New York, 1980), Chap. 4.
[46] 217 NY 382 (1916).
[47] [1943] AC 42.   [48] [1983] 1 AC 410.   [49] [1992] 1 AC 310.

reinvent the distinction between those within the area of physical danger (primary victims) from those outside this area (secondary victims)[50] have not led to practical justice: most commentators find it appalling that the plaintiff who witnessed the horrific death of his brother in the Hillsborough stadium was denied damages for his post-traumatic stress, while police constables performing their professional duty in the stadium were compensated.[51]

Once the requirements of fault (would a reasonable person have taken the risks into account?), factual causation (did the relationship make any difference?), and remoteness (was the accident the most important cause of the nervous shock?) are satisfied then the question of which relationships ought to be protected is essentially a matter of policy.[52] The tests of 'foreseeability' or 'proximity' are incapable of resolving such questions. As Lord Oliver recognized in *Alcock*,[53] *Murphy*,[54] and *Caparo*[55] and Lord Nicholls did in *Stovin* v. *Wise*,[56] 'proximity' is essentially a question of policy—of 'fairness and reasonableness'—when applied to the construction of a notional duty of care. The confusion between the concepts of fault, factual causation, remoteness, and the notional duty of care lie at the heart of the formal incoherence of negligence law.

Insurance and Social Responsibility

Another product of English conceptualism was for a long time the pretence that insurance does not exist. The courts behaved as if their function was simply loss-shifting and not loss-spreading. They refused to take account of the fact that one party is better able to bear the burden than the other, because that party carries, or is more likely to carry, insurance. As late as 1959, the House of Lords, when deciding that an employer was not liable for providing defective equipment to a worker, took no account of the existence of employer's liability insurance.[57] Viscount Simonds said: 'It is not the function of a court of law to fasten upon the fortuitous

---

[50] *Page* v. *Smith* [1996] 1 AC 155.
[51] *Frost* v. *Chief Constable of South Yorkshire* [1997] 1 All ER 540, CA.
[52] Howarth, n. 38 above, 259.
[53] [1992] 1 AC at 416–19.   [54] [1991] AC at 488.
[55] [1990] 2 AC at 651.   [56] [1996] AC 923 at 932.
[57] *Davie* v. *New Merton Board Mills Ltd* [1959] AC 604.

circumstances of insurance to impose a greater burden on the employer than would otherwise lie upon him.'[58] It needed legislation ten years later to overcome the effect of that decision.[59] In 1978 Lord Diplock said extra-judicially: 'It is not the function of a law of negligence to allocate the cost of compensating individual cases of personal injury caused by accident in such a way as to spread the burden over a wide section of the public by imposing it, irrespective of fault, on whoever can most easily cover the risk by liability insurance.'[60] He regarded this as 'welfare legislation', outside the province of the law of tort.

However, Lord Denning MR,[61] followed by judges in New Zealand and Australia,[62] recognized the importance of insurance, and in *Smith* v. *Eric S. Bush*, Lord Griffiths stated unequivocally that the 'cost of insurance must be a relevant factor when considering which of two parties should be required to ᵥear the risk of a loss'.[63] Information about the availability of insurance enables the court to place the costs of the accident on the person best able to distribute the loss and best able to avoid the accident, i.e. to allocate or internalize the costs. By allocating the cost of risk bearing, the court is fulfilling an ideal of social responsibility.[64] Courts are now slow to extend negligence liability unless they believe that affordable insurance can be found to cover it.

A recent and important example is the decision of the House of Lords in *The Nicholas H.*[65] The House (Lord Lloyd dissenting) in deciding on policy grounds that a classification society was not liable to cargo owners for damage they had allegedly suffered as a

---

[58] At 626–7.

[59] Employer's Liability (Defective Equipment) Act 1969.

[60] Lord Diplock, 'Judicial Developments in the Law of the Commonwealth' [1978] 1 *MLJ* p. cviii.

[61] See *e.g. Nettleship* v. *Weston* [1971] 2 QB 691; *Launchbury* v. *Morgans* [1971] 2 QB 245, but *cf*. Lord Wilberforce when this reached the House of Lords; *Morris* v. *Ford Motor Co. Ltd.* [1973] QB 792 at 798; *Spartan Steel and Alloys Ltd.* v. *Martin & Co. (Contractors) Ltd.* [1973] QB 27.

[62] *Bowen* v. *Paramount Buildings (Hamilton) Ltd.* [1977] 1 NZLR 394 at 419, *per* Woodhouse J; and cases noted by Luntz, Hambly, and Hayes, *Torts: Cases and Commentary* (4th edn.) (Sydney, 1995), 1.1.21.

[63] [1990] 1 AC 831 at 858.

[64] *e.g.* in *Stovin* v. *Wise* [1996] AC 923 at 955, Lord Hoffmann saw as an argument against liability of a public authority that this would simply be 'compensating insurance companies out of public funds'.

[65] *Marc Rich & Co. AG* v. *Bishop Rock Marine Co. Ltd.* [1996] 2 AC 211.

result of negligence by a surveyor acting for the classification society, took insurance factors into account. One could not look for a better illustration of my theme than the contrast between the speeches of Lord Lloyd (dissenting) and Lord Steyn (with whom Lord Keith, Lord Jauncey, and Lord Browne-Wilkinson agreed). Lord Lloyd said that 'it cannot be right that the courts should reach conclusions on the availability of insurance or the impact of imposing a fresh liability on the insurance market generally without proper material'.[66] Instead, he relied on precedent and the conceptual classification of this as a case of 'property' damage, to conclude that there should be a straightforward application of *Donoghue* v. *Stevenson* so as to impose liability. Only this, he believed, could avoid a 'risk that the law of negligence could disintegrate into a series of isolated decisions without any coherent principles at all'.[67] Lord Steyn, on the other hand, took the view that the case 'can only be decided on the basis of an intense and particular focus on all its distinctive features, and then applying established legal principles to it'.[68] This led him to take account of the fact that classification societies act for the collective welfare which in their absence would have to be fulfilled by states. If a duty of care was held to exist, the cost of insuring against potential claims would ultimately be passed on to the shipowners, thereby outflanking the contractual structure governing dealings between shipowners and cargo owners, which was based on a system of double or overlapping insurance of cargo and the limitation of shipowners' liability to cargo owners under the Hague Rules and Hague Visby Rules and tonnage limitation provisions. He said that an extra layer of insurance would become involved with the attendant litigation and arbitration. There was a risk that classification societies would adopt, to the detriment of their traditional role, a more defensive position and might be unwilling to survey the very vessels which most urgently require independent examination. Those who argued that liability should be imposed on the classification societies in order to deter negligence must have been surprised by the fact that, even without a finding of liability, the societies have since this decision acted to impose tighter regulations on shipowners to ensure that their ships are well designed and built,

---

[66] At 228–9.   [67] At 230.   [68] At 236.

and properly maintained.[69] This suggests that regulation rather than compensation, and prevention rather than cure, can be achieved without the imposition of tortious duties.

It was the belief that the law of negligence is primarily a system for compensation for harm that led many tort scholars from the 1950s onwards to argue that the law of negligence has never conformed fully to the requirements of a moral system of corrective justice.[70] They pointed out the failure of negligence law to compensate more than 12 per cent of all traffic and work accident victims and the manifest unfairness and inefficiency of the tort system as a means of distributing tort losses for personal injuries and death.[71] This led them to campaign for the abolition of tort law in the sphere of personal injuries and its replacement by a comprehensive system of social security, based on ideas of community responsibility for all disability and misfortune. However, New Zealand was the only common law country in which liability for negligence was abolished in respect of accidental injury or death, and replaced by a no-fault compensation scheme. The scheme was never applied to all industrial diseases, nor to medical misadventure. It has now been significantly scaled down, leading to mounting pressures for the reintroduction of tort law.[72]. In Britain, the Pearson Report[73] disappointed those who had expected some rationalization of the various statutory and common law compensation schemes, and only about twenty of its 158 modest proposals have ever been implemented.

In a period in which the welfare state is shrinking and being privatized, a comprehensive state-run social security scheme in

[69] *Financial Times*, 21 July 1995.

[70] See *e.g.* Glanville Williams, 'The Aims of the Law of Tort' (1951) 4 *CLP* 137; D. W. Elliott and Harry Street, *Road Accidents* (Harmondsworth, 1968), 283–6 (advocating a state-funded road accidents scheme); Terence Ison, *The Forensic Lottery* (London, 1967) (advocating diversion of tort revenues into a national insurance scheme for sick and disabled persons); Patrick Atiyah, *Accidents, Compensation and the Law* (London, 1970) (single comprehensive compensation system).

[71] Donald R. Harris *et al.*, *Compensation and Support for Illness and Injury* (Oxford, 1984) provided the fullest and most well-researched evidence of this, and made detailed proposals for the integration of the various compensation systems.

[72] Accident Rehabilitation and Compensation Act 1992 (NZ); see Joanna Morny [1995] *NZ L Rev.* 156.

[73] *Report of the Royal Commission on Civil Liability and Compensation for Personal Injury* (London, 1978), Cmnd. 7054.

place of negligence law is no longer on the political agenda. Even Professor Atiyah, who, until the third edition of his path-breaking book on *Accidents Compensation and the Law*, advocated a single comprehensive system for assisting disabled persons, has recently made the once unthinkable suggestion that tort liability for personal injury and death should be abolished and replaced by the 'free market'.[74] This would mean leaving individuals to arrange their own private first-party insurance against the risks of accident and disease. It presages a return to notions of self-help and personal responsibility which would have been familiar to our Victorian forefathers, but operating in the vastly more technological and dangerous society of the twenty-first century.

It is not my purpose here to discuss the complex question whether compensation for personal injuries should simply be left to the free market, as Atiyah contends. I have to say, however, that when I hear the words 'free market' I reach for my begging bowl. Would low income earners be able to afford first-party insurance? How would unemployed people or unwaged women at home be protected? How would the private insurance market react to the abolition of tort? It would be more realistic to speak of limited reforms, such as first-party no-fault road insurance on a compulsory basis for pecuniary losses up to a fixed limit, and no-fault employer's liability for work-related injuries and diseases backed by compulsory liability insurance.

The real relevance of Atiyah's proposal for the theme of this lecture is that it compels us once again to recognize the inadequacy of the law of negligence as a vehicle of distributive justice in the area of personal injuries. Dr Stapleton has asked whether 'we have coherent reasons, moral or economic, for shifting the burden of misfortune from victims to the class of injurers?'[75] I respectfully agree with Atiyah that within the confines of the negligence system, particularly in the higher courts when new areas of liability are being explored, it is right that detailed consideration should be given to the claims of the plaintiff against the defendant and the general class to which the defendant belongs, who may be expected

---

[74] P. S. Atiyah, 'Personal Injuries in the Twenty-First Century: Thinking the Unthinkable', in P. Birks (ed.), *Wrongs and Remedies of the Twenty-First Century* (Oxford, 1996), 1.
[75] J. Stapleton, 'Tort, Insurance and Ideology' (1995) 48 *MLR* 820.

to pay the costs of liability through insurance. However, as soon as we start discussing law reform, or broader moral arguments about social responsibility, then we cannot limit our inquiry to the distributive effects between the class of victims and the class of wrongdoers. Why should the accident victim who is able to prove fault on the part of an identified defendant be so much better compensated than the victim who cannot prove fault? And how can we justify large lump sum awards or structured settlements for victims of fault when those who suffer illness or disability for other causes have to survive on low levels of social security? In other words, as Atiyah contends, many tort claimants have much weaker claims to be compensated than many of those who fall right outside the system. By its very nature, the tort process does not allow for considerations such as this. The subject of compensation for personal injuries and death is, in a word, too important a subject to be left to the courts. Sooner or later Parliament, instead of tinkering with the tort system, as in the recent limited reforms relating to damages[76] and in the procedural changes proposed by the Woolf Report,[77] will have to return to the question of community responsibility for the disabled, including the victims of accidents.

The Problem of Professional Responsibility

While the shadow of abolition still hangs over the negligence law in its most important social sphere, that of compensation for personal injuries and death, the greatest commercial and intellectual challenges come from the field of professional responsibility. The growing division of labour, and the crucial role of professional advice and services in an 'information society', has led to an awareness of the responsibility of professionals not only to their clients in the context of contractual duties, but also to others who are affected by their activities. Here, negligence law serves two main functions. The first is compensation and risk allocation. In the world of commercial and professional relationships, the starting point, as Lord Steyn has said, 'must be that prima facie the loss must lie where it falls. Sound and cogent reasons must be

---

[76] Damages Act 1996, c. 48.
[77] *Access to Justice, Final Report* (London, HMSO, 1996).

demonstrated for the common law to intervene by decreeing that the losses to be borne by another person.'[78] This can be said to reflect the notion of individual responsibility. The general principle should be to determine the allocation of risks and insurance coverage that the professional and his client would have agreed to had they bargained over the matter, and to treat this as an implicit term of the contract for professional services. In practice, coverage will not be complete, either because insurance at an affordable cost is not available or because of the differing 'tastes' for risk of the parties. This in turn may justify either an immunity from liability or limited liability.[79]

The second aim, which reflects the public or social interest, is to improve the quality of professional services. Civil liability for negligence is a fairly unobtrusive form of regulation, and it offers the possibility of some judicial control on professional conduct. It provides the professionals with a financial incentive to exercise greater care.[80] Private actions for negligence may sometimes be more effective than professional self-regulation; indeed, in *White* v. *Jones* the court was told in argument that for 'mere negligence' in failing to draw up a new will in accordance with the testator's instructions, the solicitor could not even be censured in disciplinary proceedings.[81] (It may be noted that the Office for the Supervision of Solicitors, set up by the Law Society from 1 September 1996, has not been given the power to investigate allegations of negligence as such.) This provided a strong argument for the imposition of tort liability to the disappointed beneficiaries. The new procedure, adopted by the Bar Council in 1996, for complaints against barristers does not deal specifically with complaints of negligence but only of 'professional misconduct' or 'inadequate professional services'. This would provide an argument for tort liability, possibly even to third parties, where the immunity of advocates from civil suit does not apply.

---

[78] *White* v. *Jones* [1995] 2 AC 207 at 236, *per* Lord Steyn.
[79] See C. G. Veljanowski and C. J. Whelan, 'Professional Negligence and the Quality of Legal Services—An Economic Perspective' (1983) 46 *MLR* 700.
[80] This argument based on general deterrence has also been invoked in the context of personal injuries: e.g. *Stovin* v. *Wise* [1996] AC 923, *per* Lord Hoffmann, and *Frost* v. *Chief Constable of South Yorkshire* [1997] 1 All ER 540 at 567, *per* Henry LJ.   [81] [1995] 2 AC 207 at 236.

The fulfillment of the objectives of risk allocation and deterrence (i.e. improving the quality of services) has been severely hampered by the arid conceptualism of English law, in particular the inadequacy of contractual theory. The limitations on the doctrine of consideration led to the elaborate yet ultimately unsatisfactory doctrine of 'assumption of responsibility' in *Hedley Byrne*. The way to create liability in situations 'equivalent to contract' was surely to broaden the conception of contract. The defendant's undertaking in *Hedley Byrne* to do something for the plaintiff and then either not doing it at all or doing it badly, thus causing damage, would be regarded as sufficient to constitute a breach of contract in a system unencumbered by the doctrine of consideration.[82] Instead of confronting the arguments so powerfully made by Atiyah for regarding reliance as a ground which justifies the enforcement of a promise, English lawyers have been bound by the strict conceptual classification of contract and tort and have expanded tort to meet the inadequacies of contract. The *Hedley Byrne* doctrine has been heavily criticized by academic commentators[83] and was effectively demolished by Lord Griffith's speech in *Smith* v. *Eric S. Bush* where he described 'the voluntary assumption of responsibility' as not a 'helpful or realistic test of liability'.[84] There will rarely be an express assumption and, as Lord Griffiths said, the assumption can be seen to rest upon a fiction which expresses a conclusion that a duty of care is to be imposed. It does not tell us how to reach that conclusion or the circumstances which will support a 'voluntary assumption of responsibility'. However, in *Henderson*[85] Lord Goff revived this discredited fiction, and used it to extend liability to all cases of economic loss flowing from the negligent performance of professional services. Moreover, he went even further by saying that once a case is identified as falling within the *Hedley Byrne* principle, there is no need to embark on any further inquiry, whether it is 'fair, just and reasonable' to impose liability for economic loss. A legal fiction was used to avoid explicit discussion of the problems of risk allocation and deterrence.

[82] Cf. *De la Bere* v. *Pearson* [1908] 1 KB 280, where the CA managed to devise an artificial consideration in a case of negligent advice.

[83] e.g. by K. Barker, 'Unreliable Assumptions in the Modern Law of Negligence' (1993) 109 *LQR* 461.

[84] [1990] 1 AC 831.

[85] [1995] 2 AC 145 at 180–1.

The later decision of the House of Lords in *White* v. *Jones* shows just how questionable the 'assumption of responsibility' argument can be. Lord Goff acknowledged that it would be difficult to treat the solicitor as having assumed responsibility under the *Hedley Byrne* principle to a third-party beneficiary of a will, since his direct assumption of responsibility was to his client. It was therefore necessary to invoke the needs of justice in order to take the incremental step of extending liability in favour of the beneficiaries.[86] Lord Browne-Wilkinson regarded the crucial factor as being the solicitor's knowledge that the intended beneficiary's economic well-being depended upon his careful execution of the task assumed.[87] But, as Lord Mustill responded in his dissenting speech,[88] this is quite different from undertaking the task *for* the beneficiaries.[89] Lord Nolan equated the assumption of responsibility to other road users by driving a car with the assumption of responsibility by a professional person to those who, to his knowledge, may suffer loss through careless performance of his skills.[90] This comparison makes a nonsense of treating 'assumption of responsibility' as a concept distinct from the *Donoghue* v. *Stevenson* duty of care. Indeed, it would have been more intellectually coherent to base liability on the now unpopular two-stage test enunciated by Lord Wilberforce in *Anns* v. *Merton London Borough Council*,[91] than by this 'incremental' extension of Hedley Byrne through a fictional assumption of responsibility. The notion of an 'assumption of responsibility' which can be applied 'incrementally' suffers from the very defects of ambiguity and uncertainty which led to the rejection of the *Anns* principle.

The real problem in this context, as in others such as *Junior Books* v. *Veitchi & Sons*,[92] and *The Aliakmon*,[93] is the rigidity of the privity of contract rule. Had the disappointed beneficiaries been

---

[86] [1995] 2 AC 207 at 259–60.   [87] At 275.

[88] At 279.   [89] At 294.   [90] At 294.

[91] [1978] AC 728 at 751–2; compare *Gartside* v. *Sheffield, Young and Ellis* [1983] NZLR 37, esp. at 46, where the New Zealand CA anticipated the result in *White* v. *Jones* simply on the basis of the general professional duty of a solicitor.

[92] [1983] 1 AC 520, a case where the facts might have supported a collateral contract, but this point was never argued.

[93] *Leigh and Sillavan Ltd.* v. *Aliakmon Shipping Co.* [1985] QB 350 at 396–400, for Robert Goff LJ's theory of transferred loss rejected by Lord Brandon in the House of Lords [1986] AC 785 at 819.

able to seek a remedy on the analogy of a contract for the benefit of a third party, as is allowed in Germany and the United States, it would have been unnecessary to resort to the conceptual contortions of tort law.[94]

Undoubtedly, the courts have recently made a good deal of progress in breaking down some of the conceptual barriers to professional responsibility, such as the distinction between negligent statements and the negligent provision of services, the recognition that a failure to act is rarely simply a case of nonfeasance (the solicitor's failure to revise the will was no more an omission than a driver's failure to stop at a halt sign),[95] and by permitting concurrent liability in tort and contract for negligence.

Another barrier which has recently been severely dented is that between property damage and economic loss. In *The Nicholas H* it had been argued for the cargo owners that in cases of physical damage to property in which the plaintiff has a proprietary or possessory interest, the only requirement is proof of reasonable foreseeability. While acknowledging the 'qualitative difference between cases of direct physical damage and indirect economic loss', Lord Steyn stated that 'the elements of foreseeability and proximity as well as considerations of fairness, justice and reasonableness are relevant to all cases, whatever the nature of the harm sustained by the plaintiff'.[96]

Commonwealth judges have also had misgiving about ring-fencing indirect economic loss. For example, Stephenson J said in *Canadian National Railway* v. *Norsk Pacific SS Co.*, 'although I am prepared to recognise that a human being is more important than property and lost expectations of profit, I fail to see how property and economic losses can be distinguished'.[97] The weakening of the distinction between economic loss and property damage, so far as the duty of care is concerned, does not mean an increasing

---

[94] See B. S. Markesinis, *The German Law of Torts* (3rd edn.) (Oxford, 1994), 305–12; and note also his observations in *Five Days in the House of Lords: Some Comparative Reflections on White* v. *Jones* (Rome, 1995), 16.

[95] However, leading judges differ on where the draw the line between acts and omissions: compare Lord Hoffmann in *Stovin* v. *Wise* (above) with Lord Nicholls (dissenting) in the same case.

[96] [1996] 1 AC 211 at 235.

[97] (1992) 91 DLR (4th) 289 at 383. For a critical review of the cases see Howarth, n. 38 above, 296–300.

recognition of liability for economic loss; on the contrary, it means that contrary to the view of Lord Goff in *Henderson*, both property loss and economic loss cases must be subjected to overriding considerations of 'fairness, justice and reasonableness'.

The central point is that the concepts of 'reasonable foreseeability', 'proximity', 'assumption of responsibility', and 'reliance' have been asked to do too much. If reasonable foreseeability were confined to its proper role of determining whether there has been fault, and proximity were used as a test of whether the damage suffered by the particular plaintiff was too remote ('risk imports relation' said Cardozo in the famous *Palsgraf* v. *Long Island Railroad* case[98]), then it would be possible to make the kind of 'intense and particular focus' on all the distinctive features of each professional relationship, which Lord Steyn pursued in *The Nicholas H.* Instead of expressing surprise that the surveyors in *Smith* v. *Bush* and the solicitors in *White* v. *Jones* were held liable, while the auditors in *Caparo* and the classification societies in *The Nicholas H.* went scot free, we need to examine the purpose for which particular professional functions are performed. For example, it has been said that the work of building inspectors is to protect the health and safety of the occupiers, while the role of a company's auditors is to provide the members with the information which they can rely upon when exercising their rights as shareholders. As Keith Stanton has recently argued, we have to 'face the obvious (but rarely stated) truth that a wide range of professional skills exist in our society which are exercised to protect a variety of different interests'.[99]

We also have to recognize the wider social responsibilities of particular professions: hence the immunity of advocates in respect of litigation,[100] the absence of a duty of care by the Crown Prosecution Service to those whom it prosecutes,[101] or by the police

---

[98] 248 NY 339 (1928).

[99] K. M. Stanton, 'Professional Negligence in Tort: The Search for a Theory' in P. Birks (ed.), n. 74 above, 67 at 87.

[100] *Rondel* v. *Worsley* [1969] 1 AC 191; *Saif Ali* v. *Sydney Mitchell & Co.* [1980] AC 198; Courts and Legal Services Act 1990, s. 62 (non-barristers have same immunity).

[101] *Elgouszli-Daf* v. *Comr. of Police of the Metropolis* [1995] 1 All ER 833; but cf. *Welsh* v. *Chief Constable of Merseyside Police* [1993] 1 All ER 692 where there was said to be an assumption of responsibility.

to the victims of crime.[102] The fact that a defendant acts for the collective welfare is a matter to be taken into consideration in considering whether it is 'fair, just and reasonable' to impose a duty of care.

We should abandon the attempt to place civil liability for professional negligence within a single conceptual formula. Once fault and proximity are established, it is necessary to concentrate on the specific features of each professional relationship in order to determine whether the *prima facie* rule that loss lies where it falls should be displaced in order to meet the aims of efficient risk allocation and the improvement of the quality of professional services.

Conclusion

Thirty years ago, Millner said that 'ironically, in the very moment of its triumph, the shadow of its decline is upon [negligence law]'.[103] Millner commented that 'fostered by the individualism of the nineteenth century whose needs and spirit it accurately reflects, negligence is in some ways basically unsuited to the paternalistic society of the twentieth'. Thirty years later, when the dominant ethos is one of individual self-interest rather than collective welfare, negligence law once again seems to have come into its own. However, I have tried to show that its conceptual apparatus, which still seeks to draw artificial lines between law and policy, produces the incoherence of which this subject is justly accused.

In seeking a new framework for negligence law, we need to start with a proper assessment of the nature of individualism in present-day society. Contemporary neo-liberalism contrasts individualism with the discredited 'collectivism' of the first part of the twentieth century. However, 'individualism' has many meanings, only one of which is the profit-maximizing behaviour of self-seeking individuals in 'free markets'. There is a different kind of individualism which may help us to reconcile individual and social responsibility. This can be best understood in Anthony Giddens's concept of 'social

---

[102] *Hill* v. *Chief Constable of West Yorkshire* [1989] AC 53; *Alexandrou* v. *Oxford* [1993] 4 All ER 328; compare *Capital and Counties plc* v. *Hampshire CC* [1996] 4 All ER 336 (fire services are liable).
[103] Millner, n. 2 above, at 234–5.

reflexivity'.[104] This is the idea that individuals must achieve a certain degree of autonomy of action in order to filter all sorts of information relevant to their life situations and routinely act on the basis of that filtering process. Individuals need information and knowledge and must have the ability to control their circumstances in order to survive and forge a life. Individual responsibility in this sense does not mean self-interest, but it implies reciprocity and inter-dependence. The task of many areas of law in the twenty-first century will be to provide a means of securing for individuals the information and knowledge which they need to act autonomously.

This will, in my view, entail removing from the sphere of negligence law those aspects which are solely concerned with the compensation for personal injury and death, because the tort process is an inadequate vehicle for reconciling individual and social responsibility for disability and illness. Eventually, the sheer cost of liability insurance for motorists will, I believe, lead to the replacement of fault liability by compulsory first-party insurance schemes to cover basic pecuniary losses. Moreover it is difficult to believe that the National Health Service can continue to support the costs of a fault-based system. The disappearance of the industrial injuries preference in respect of work accidents may be expected to lead to pressure for the abolition of tort and the reintroduction of some kind of strict liability workers' compensation scheme, as exists in many other countries.

This will leave negligence law with a crucial role in respect of professional responsibility and also environmental damage (a subject which I have not had time to consider). Another area where negligence law is likely to grow in significance is that of civil liability for defective public services, particularly in the context of privatization and contracting-out, a topic which I have discussed elsewhere.[105]

I have advocated a new framework of principle in which the redundant and incoherent concept of a notional duty of care is abandoned. In the ordinary negligence action only three questions have to be asked: (1) was the defendant entitled to take the risk? (the fault issue); (2) if not, would the damage have occurred had the

---

[104] Anthony Giddens, *Beyond Left and Right* (London, 1994), 13.
[105] 'Tort Law in the Contract State' in P. Birks (ed.), *The Frontiers of Liability*, vol. 2, 71.

defendant acted without fault? (the factual causation issue); and (3) was the kind of damage to this class of plaintiff within the scope of the risk? (the remoteness issue). When it is sought to extend liability into new areas not covered by precedent, the starting point should be that loss lies where it falls, unless it can be shown that liability for negligence will empower individuals to acquire the information and knowledge which they need to control their situations, while at the same time distributing losses effectively and deterring harmful conduct.

In many cases the best way of deciding on an extension or modification of liability in negligence will be by legislation after careful research and consultation by the Law Commission. But there will always be a residuary role for the higher judiciary, who need to be properly assisted not only by counsel, but also by the academic legal profession and others, when considering the complex issues of 'fairness, justice and reasonableness'.[106] For it is only through the overt and detailed examination of the policy issues that the law can help to reconcile individual and social responsibility in a coherent way.

---

[106] See M. A. Clarke (1996) 7 *Insurance LJ* 173 at 191–6; and [1977] *LMCLQ* 1 at 4–6.

RESTITUTION
Where Do We Go From Here?

Andrew Burrows

This article is divided into three unequal parts. The first asks the question, where have we got to with the law of restitution? The second asks the question, how have we got to here? The third reflecting the title, asks, where do we go from here?

1. Where Have We Got To?

On one level, there is a very straightforward description of where we have got to. We now have a law of restitution founded on the principle against unjust enrichment whereas 100 years ago, and indeed until the decision of the House of Lords in *Lipkin Gorman* v. *Karpnale Ltd.*[1] in 1991, England had no such subject or category of law. But what does it actually mean to say that we now have a law of restitution whereas previously we did not?

Clearly, what it does not mean is that there is suddenly a whole new body of law that did not previously exist. In that sense the law of restitution is not like, for example, social security law, European Community law, or even, perhaps, administrative law. They are new because they deal with a large body of new law that did not previously exist. Nor is the position quite the same as with, for example, family law which has become a new subject in the latter part of the twentieth century only in the limited sense that books,[2] and law school courses, started to study all the law relating to the same *factual* subject matter, namely the family.

What it means to say that we now recognize a law of restitution, whereas previously we did not, is that we now recognize that there

---

[1] [1991] 2 AC 548.
[2] The pioneer was Peter Bromley's *Family Law* (London, 1957). See also 318 below.

is a principle, namely the principle against unjust enrichment, that underpins a wide body of law that was previously regarded as a hotch-potch of different unconnected areas. Restitution is a new subject in that we now recognize that there is a body of law based not so much on the same factual subject matter but rather on the same legal principle. In this sense the law of restitution is as fundamental as, for example, the law of contract or the law of tort, which are similarly, in my view, categories of law based on underpinning principles.

In recognizing the principle against unjust enrichment there were two main barriers that had to be overcome in the law as it stood at the start of the century.

The first was the implied contract theory. If, for example, a plaintiff paid a defendant £1,000 under a mistake of fact, his common law remedy to recover the £1,000 was said to rest on the defendant's implied promise to pay it back. Yet such a promise plainly did not rest on the defendant's actual intention to repay and was a fiction which served merely to obscure the real basis of the remedy. Yet, until the latter part of the twentieth century, the implied contract theory held sway. It was this fiction that accounted for the law on mistaken payments and payments made under duress, on failure of consideration, on necessitous intervention, and on discharge of another's debt under legal compulsion, being seen as an off shoot of contract law—hence the label quasi-contract. It is also why the two classic contract books in existence at the end of the nineteenth century—*Chitty*, the practitioners' work first published in 1828, and *Anson*, the classic student text, first published in 1879—each had separate sections dealing with implied contracts or quasi-contract. Despite the recognition of an independent law of restitution, the current editions of those books still have those sections, albeit that the editors have felt duty-bound to change the title of the offending chapters from quasi-contract to restitution.[3]

---

[3] The relevant chapter in *Chitty* was renamed 'Restitution and Quasi-Contract' in the 23rd edn. in 1968. Quasi-Contract was entirely removed from the title in the 24th edn. in 1977. The relevant chapter in *Anson* was renamed 'Restitution' in the 25th edn. in 1975. In the previous edition in 1975 it had still been called Quasi-Contract. Cf. Cheshire and Fifoot, *Law of Contract* (London: first published in 1945) in which Quasi-Contract is still the title of the relevant chapter in the 13th edn. in 1996.

The second main barrier was the division between common law and equity. The principle against unjust enrichment underpins and draws on areas of common law and equity. It is a principle that fuses those historical divisions. Although the common law courts and the Court of Chancery had been fused in the 1870s, it is not surprising that at the turn of the century a fusion of the substantive rules of law and equity would have been thought to be a long way off. Even today the single greatest battle faced by the law of restitution is to integrate and fuse the areas of common law and equity that are based on the principle against unjust enrichment. It is a battle that has by no means been won and certainly in, for example, Australia, where the dominance of great equity lawyers such as Justice Gummow and Judge Finn is all pervasive, and Justice Deane and Chief Justice Mason have recently retired, one fears that the battle in the short term may be lost and that unjust enrichment thinking may be confined to areas of the common law only.

But what difference does the recognition of this new subject make? Mr Hedley has recently argued that recognition of the principle against unjust enrichment, and the refinement of it by commentators, serves no useful goal.[4] Is he correct?

I would immediately concede that recognition of unjust enrichment does not mean that, in a wide range of cases, the courts will suddenly reach different decisions than before. On the contrary, as the 'implied contract' theory was a fiction, deeper reasoning must always have been guiding the courts; and it is my view that the courts have throughout been applying the principle of unjust enrichment, albeit at times in an unadventurous and stunted way. This is why the law of restitution legitimately draws on case law and indeed is largely comprised of case law pre-*Lipkin Gorman*.

But, with respect, Mr Hedley is making a serious mistake in suggesting that recognition of unjust enrichment makes no practical difference. He is wrong for at least two reasons.

First, it is a good in its own right that the judges, the legislature,

---

[4] S. Hedley, 'Restitution: Contract's Twin?' (Paper presented to SPTL Annual Conference, Cambridge, 1996). He has been making similar claims for over a decade. See S. Hedley, 'Unjust Enrichment as the Basis of Restitution—An Overworked Concept' (1985) 5 *Legal Studies* 56, and 'Unjust Enrichment' (1995) 54 *CLJ* 578.

and commentators use language that is accurate, simple, and clear.
The rule of law demands this. Fictions and obscure jargon in the
law are an abomination and must be sought out and excised. The
law cannot fulfil its role of guiding behaviour if fictions, like the
'implied contract' theory, survive. Much of the modern writing on
restitution is an attempt to explain legal concepts in precise and
modern terminology. A criticism can be made that the new
language of 'unjust factors', 'incontrovertible benefit', 'free acceptance', 'unjust enrichment by subtraction', 'restitutionary damages'
is not simple enough. But it is a bit rich when some lawyers accuse
restitution commentators of using incomprehensible jargon. They
would no doubt prefer to stick with the language of the club,
nonsensical to outsiders: actions for money had and received to the
plaintiff's use, money paid to the defendant's use, quantum meruit,
liability as a constructive trustee, subrogation, 'waiver of tort', and
so on. This is the language of the late nineteenth century. It should
not be the language at the end of the twentieth century.

There is a linked footnote point here. In the shrinking world of
the global economy, and with talk of harmonizing the laws of the
European Union, civil law becomes ever more important to the
development of the common law. Civil law systems have long
recognized a category of law based on unjust enrichment, and it
would therefore only have served to hamper meaningful dialogue—
and to undermine this opportunity to enrich our own law—if we
had failed overtly to recognize the unjust enrichment principle.

The second, and perhaps more important, reason why Mr
Hedley is wrong is that the acceptance of the unjust enrichment
principle can be expected to lead to some differences in the results
of cases. While in most cases the judges would have got to the same
result anyway, however obscurely, clarity of concept does have
practical consequences. This is an important point and I want to
give six examples of it.

(1) MONEY PAID UNDER VOID CONTRACTS

In *Sinclair* v. *Brougham*,[5] decided by the House of Lords in 1914, a
building society acted *ultra vires* by carrying on a banking business.

---

[5] [1914] AC 398.

On the winding up of the society, one question was whether those who had loaned money under the *ultra vires* banking facilities (the 'depositors') could recover their money in a personal restitutionary remedy, that is, in an action for money had and received. The House of Lords held that they could not. In reaching that decision their Lordships were heavily influenced by the 'implied contract' theory. As an express contract to repay the loans would have been void as being *ultra vires* the building society, so necessarily, it was argued, must be an implied contract. And as an action for money had and received was conceived as being based on an implied contract, the claim failed.

But once one recognizes that the basis of the action for money had and received is unjust enrichment, not implied contract, the way is open to reach a different decision. *Prima facie* the building society was unjustly enriched by receiving the depositors' money for a purpose that could not be carried through. And there is no convincing reason why the fact that the contract of borrowing was unenforceable should mean that the building society was left unjustly enriched at the depositors' expense. So it is that, in applying unjust enrichment reasoning, the House of Lords in 1996 in *Westdeutsche Landesbank Girozentrale* v. *Islington London BC*[6] overruled *Sinclair* v. *Brougham*. Lord Browne-Wilkinson said:

> The common law restitutionary claim is based not on implied contract but unjust enrichment: in the circumstances, the law imposes an obligation to repay rather than implying an entirely fictitious agreement to repay. In my judgment, your Lordships should now unequivocally and finally reject the concept that the claim for moneys had and received is based on an implied contract. I would overrule *Sinclair* v. *Brougham* on this point. It follows that ... the depositors should have had a personal claim to recover the moneys at law based on a total failure of consideration.[7]

(2) Change of Position

In *Lipkin Gorman* v. *Karpnale Ltd.*[8] the House of Lords accepted for the first time that it is a general defence to restitutionary claims that the defendant has changed its position. Lord Goff said, '[T]he defence is available to a person whose position is so changed that it would be inequitable in all the circumstances to require him to

---

[6] [1996] 2 AC 669.   [7] *Ibid.*, at 710.   [8] [1991] 2 AC 548.

make restitution, or alternatively to make restitution in full'.[9] What is basically in mind is the situation where the recipient of an unjust enrichment, in good faith, spends or loses that enrichment or incurs a detriment in reliance on it. The defence responds to the fact that, while once unjustly enriched, the defendant is no longer so. Indeed one simply cannot explain this defence without recognizing that the law is based on a principle against unjust enrichment.

Although there was a limited all or nothing form of change of position recognized pre-*Lipkin Gorman* in the defence of estoppel, acceptance of change of position cannot but alter decisions. If we again turn to the early part of this century, in 1913 in *Baylis* v. *Bishop of London*[10] the plaintiffs had mistakenly paid to a bishop (who was acting as sequestrator for a parish on the bankruptcy of its rector) tithe rent-charges on certain property in which their leasehold interest had already expired. The bishop in good faith applied some of the money in providing for the needs of the parish and paid over the surplus to the rector's trustee in bankruptcy. It was held by the Court of Appeal that the bishop had no defence to the plaintiffs' restitutionary claim for money paid by the mistake of fact. Today the bishop would have a defence of change of position and restitution would be denied on the same facts.

(3) Restitution of Money Paid by Mistake of Law and Restitution of Money Paid on a Partial, but not Total, Failure of Consideration

It remains the general law that money paid under a mistake of law, rather than of fact, or for a consideration that has failed partially rather than totally, is irrecoverable.[11] While it is possible to expose the weaknesses in those bars to restitution without relying on a theory of unjust enrichment, recognition that these areas are based on the unjust enrichment principle makes it all the easier to see that those bars lack justification.

If an insurer pays £10,000 to his assured because he mistakenly

---

[9] [1991] 2 AC 580. [10] [1913] 1 Ch. 127.
[11] See, e.g., R. Goff and G. Jones, *The Law of Restitution* (4th edn., London, 1993), chap. 4, 400–4; P. Birks, *An Introduction to the Law of Restitution* (Oxford, 1985), 164–7, 242–8; A. Burrows, *The Law of Restitution* (London, 1993), 109–20, chap. 9.

believes that the policy between them is valid, it cannot make any difference to the injustice of the assured's enrichment that the insurer's mistake rests on his false belief that the assured has kept up all his premiums—a mistake of fact—or on his false belief that he is not entitled to avoid the policy for the assured's non payment of premiums—a mistake of law.

As Dickson J said in his dissenting judgment in the Canadian case of *Hydro-Electric Commission of Nepean* v. *Ontario Hydro*,[12] which was later approved by the Supreme Court of Canada in *Air Canada* v. *Pacific Airlines*[13] in removing the mistake of law bar in Canada, 'Once a doctrine of restitution or unjust enrichment is recognised, the distinction as to mistake of law and mistake of fact becomes simply meaningless.' And in the words of the majority of the High Court of Australia, led by Mason CJ, in *David Securities Property Ltd.* v. *Commonwealth Bank of Australia*,[14] which abrogated the mistake of law rule in Australia, 'If the ground for ordering recovery is that the defendant has been unjustly enriched, there is no justification for drawing distinctions on the basis of how the enrichment was gained, except insofar as the manner of gaining the enrichment bears upon the justice of the case.'

Similarly if a bank has paid £100,000 up front to a local authority under a void interest rate swap transaction[15] can it possibly make sense to allow restitution to the bank where the local authority has made no counter-payment but to deny restitution to the bank where the local authority has made one counter-payment of £10 so that the consideration for the payment has not totally failed?[16] The injustice of the local authority's enrichment is the same in both cases and the difference between them can be easily dealt with by allowing the local authority counter-restitution of £10.

The principle against unjust enrichment provides a strong *prima facie* justification for allowing restitution for mistakes of law, as well as fact: and for allowing restitution for partial as well as total

---

[12] (1982) 132 DLR (3d) 193, 209.
[13] (1989) 59 DLR (4th) 161.   [14] (1992) 175 CLR 353.
[15] For this type of situation, see *Westdeutsche Landesbank Girozentrale* v. *Islington London BC* [1996] 2 AC 669.
[16] The notion of 'total failure' may be distorted to avoid this result: see, e.g., the *Westdeutsche* case [1996] AC 669, 710. Cf. *Goss* v. *Chilcott* [1996] AC 788.

failure of consideration. With respect to Mr Hedley it seems to me indisputable that such glaring defects in the law can be exposed more easily—and hence can be eradicated more quickly—once one sees the law as being based on unjust enrichment.

(4) Restitution for Ignorance and Restitution for Wrongs

My fifth and sixth examples are again connected. These are restitution for ignorance and restitution for wrongs. Here the unjust enrichment principle has the important consequence of linking together for the first time areas of common law and equity and thereby exposing inconsistencies between them. Although the picture I am about to paint remains controversial, I am confident that it will ultimately emerge as the way forward.

If we first take restitution for ignorance, there are a number of cases in which money has been recovered from a defendant in an action for money had and received at common law where the ground for restitution was that the plaintiff's money was transferred to the defendant without the plaintiff's knowledge; and the defendant has been held strictly liable to repay the money, subject to a change of position or *bona fide* purchase defence. A classic example is *Lipkin Gorman* v. *Karpnale Ltd.*[17] itself. Cass, without the knowledge of his co-partners, had drawn on the partnership account at Lloyds Bank to pay for his gambling at the Playboy Club. The partners had thereby suffered the loss of some £220,000. The club had overall won £154,695 from the money stolen and used for gambling by Cass: that is, although the stolen money staked by Cass was a lot higher, the club had changed its position by paying out winnings to Cass thereby reducing its net gain. The solicitors succeeded before the House of Lords in being awarded £150,960 in an action for money had and received against the club (plus £3,735 damages for conversion of a banker's draft that on one occasion had been used for gambling by Cass instead of cash). Here one has strict liability applied at common law, subject to the successful partial defence of change of position and the unsuccessful, on the facts, although carefully discussed, defence of *bona fide* purchase.

---

[17] [1991] 2 AC 548.

This model (strict liability subject to defences) is exactly in line with the well accepted standard case of payment by a mistake of fact, the only differences being that, first, the plaintiff's intention is vitiated not by a mistake but by a complete lack of knowledge and consent to the payments (that is, ignorance); and, secondly, that the payment is made to the defendant by a third party rather than by the plaintiff itself.

Stripped down to its bare essentials the same elements are present in the equity cases discussed conventionally under the heading of 'knowing receipt and dealing'.[18] Here the plaintiff's money is paid away in breach of fiduciary duty—without the plaintiff's knowledge or consent—to the defendant. In principle, applying unjust enrichment, the position ought to be that, as at common law, the defendant is strictly liable to repay the money, subject to defences such as change of position and *bona fide* purchase. And although mysteriously and irrationally hived off as being concerned with the administration of estates, this is very close to the position actually reached on the personal equitable claim in *Ministry of Health* v. *Simpson (sub nom. Re Diplock)*.[19] Yet in the vast bulk of equity cases, the approach has been to insist on the recipient being at fault—and in some cases even dishonest—before a personal liability to account for the money received has been imposed.

We therefore have needless irrationality and inconsistency between the strict common law and the fault based equitable approaches to what is essentially the same fact situation. The importance of recognizing the unjust enrichment principle is that it enables us suddenly to see that inconsistency and to question its validity and to argue for its eradication.[20] Contrary to Mr Hedley, I do not believe that that inconsistency would have been exposed without reliance on the principle against unjust enrichment.

The same applies as regards restitution for wrongs. We have long been used to the equitable restitutionary remedy of an account of profits being awarded to strip away gains made by an equitable wrong, such as breach of fiduciary duty or breach of confidence.

---

[18] e.g., *Carl Zeiss Stiftung* v. *Herbert Smith & Co. (No. 2)* [1969] 2 Ch. 276; *Belmont Finance Corp.* v. *Williams Furniture Ltd. (No. 2)* [1980] 1 All ER 393; *Re Montagu's Settlement Trusts* [1987] Ch. 264.

[19] [1951] AC 251.

[20] The inconsistency was first exposed by Peter Birks, 'Misdirected Funds: Restitution from the Recipient' [1989] *LMCLQ* 296.

Yet when it comes to common law wrongs, for example, torts, we are initially surprised that the courts are sometimes concerned to strip away the wrongdoer's gains rather than to compensate the victim for its loss. As late as 1988 we find the Court of Appeal in *Stoke-on-Trent CC* v. *Wass*[21] suggesting that it is outside the powers of a court below the House of Lords to award a restitutionary, rather than a compensatory, remedy for a proprietary tort. Again the unjust enrichment principle enables one to cut through the confusion and inconsistency. It reveals that through different personal remedies—that is through an action for money had and received in 'waiver of tort' cases, through damages assessed according to the gains made by a tortfeasor rather than the loss to the victim, and even through an account of profits awarded for intellectual property torts—there are examples of the courts awarding restitution for torts as they have been standardly doing for equitable wrongs.[22] Indeed the real dilemma is not so much whether restitution is a possible remedial measure for a tort but whether restitution should be effected by a proprietary rather than a personal remedy as the equitable wrong cases, such as *Boardman* v. *Phipps*[23] and *Attorney General for Hong Kong* v. *Reid*[24] would suggest.

As with restitution for ignorance, the essential point is that the recognition of the principle against unjust enrichment has for the first time exposed the inconsistency (or, at least, the initial apparent inconsistency) between the treatment in common law and equity of what, stripped down to essentials, is the same phenomenon. The way has been paved for these like cases of gains made by wrongdoing to be treated alike in the future.

2. How Have We Got to Here?

Here I ask, what influences have brought about the recognition and present shape of the law of restitution? I divide this into two sections. The first looks at the critical events in the growth of

---

[21] [1988] 1 WLR 1406.
[22] See, e.g., Goff and Jones, n. 11, above, chap. 38; Birks, n. 11, above, chap. X; Burrows, n. 11, above, chap. 14.
[23] [1967] 2 AC 46.   [24] [1994] 1 AC 324.

restitution in the twentieth century and the most influential individuals involved; and the second looks at the general philosophies and ideas in society that have shaped the law.

(1) Events and People

This is a story, I am sorry to say it at UCL, which largely involves an interplay between Harvard, Oxford, and Cambridge. I would argue that there have been four key events in the growth of restitution in this century, involving five main players.

The first was the publication in 1937 of the US Restatement of Restitution by the American Law Institute. The Chief Reporters for that Restatement, and the first two individuals I wish to name, were the Harvard Professors Austin Scott and Warren Seavey: the former a specialist in trusts and equity; the latter a common lawyer, whose other main interest was torts. Pooling their talents, they were able to pull together the operation of the unjust enrichment principle in common law and equity. And for better or for worse, it was they who christened the subject 'Restitution'.[25]

It is of interest and significance to appreciate the *raison d'être* and working methods of the American Law Institute.

First, the *raison d'être*. The preface to the Restatement of Restitution includes the following passage:

The Institute recognises that the ever increasing volume of the decisions of the courts, establishing new rules or precedents, and the numerous instances in which the decisions are irreconcilable, taken in connection with the growing complication of economic and other conditions of modern life, are increasing the law's uncertainty and lack of clarity. It also recognises that this will force the abandonment of our common law system of expressing and developing law through judicial application of existing rules to new fact combinations and the adoption in its place of rigid legislative codes, unless a new factor promoting certainty and clarity can be found. The careful restatement of our common law by the legal profession as represented in the Institute is an attempt to supply this needed factor.

The working methods of the American Law Institute in relation to the Restatement of Restitution were as follows. The Institute at the time (and still today) comprised a large body of senior judges,

---

[25] See W. Seavey and A. Scott, 'Restitution' (1938) 54 *LQR* 29.

practitioners, and academics. An executive committee of thirty three drawn from those ranks then chose two reporters (both academics), aided by an advisory committee (largely academics), to draw up the Restatement. We are told that the work took approximately three years, that the advisory committee held twenty-eight conferences lasting three to four days each, and that the Council put forward a tentative draft at the annual meetings of the Institute in 1935 and 1936. The point I wish to emphasize is that this is a superb working methodology. Academic lawyers had primary responsibility for the drafting but their draft was then scrutinized and commented on not only by other academics but also by judges and practitioners. The process exemplified the academic and practising branches of the legal profession working together to a common goal.

The second key event was the publication in 1966 of Goff and Jones' *The Law of Restitution* (now in its fourth edition, published in 1993). This was to do for England what the Restatement did for the United States. The third and fourth individuals I want to mention therefore are Robert Goff and Gareth Jones. There are three points of interest here. First, we again have the combination of the common lawyer, Robert Goff, and the equity lawyer, Gareth Jones. Secondly, when the work was started both were academics, the former a don at Lincoln College, Oxford, the latter at Cambridge, although by the time the work was finished Robert Goff had left academia for the Bar. Thirdly, it is perhaps of some relevance that, while I know not where Robert Goff's interest in the subject started, Gareth Jones studied at Harvard under Professors Austin Scott and Warren Seavey.

The third critical event was the publication in 1985 of Peter Birks' *An Introduction to the Law of Restitution*. If *Goff and Jones* was a masterly bringing together of the raw English material, it was Birks who rigorously exposed its structures and underlying themes in a way that fired the imagination of students, fellow academics, and judges alike. So Peter Birks is my fifth main player.

The fourth and crowning key event was the recognition of unjust enrichment by the House of Lords, led by Lord Goff, in *Lipkin Gorman* in 1991. So Robert Goff comes in again here, but now in his role as judge rather than as author. I would also mention in passing his other earlier important judgments, which paved the way for *Lipkin Gorman*, in for example *Barclays Bank Ltd. v. W. J.*

Simms,[26] *BP (Exploration) Co. Libya Ltd.* v. *Hunt (No. 2),*[27] and *Attorney General* v. *Guardian Newspapers Ltd. (No. 2)*;[28] and his rousing speech, following *Lipkin Gorman,* in *Woolwich Equitable Building Society* v. *Inland Revenue Commissioners,*[29] in which it was held, following Peter Birks' thesis,[30] that a payment demanded *ultra vires* by a public authority is recoverable as of right without any need to show mistake or duress.

(2) PHILOSOPHIES AND IDEAS

I now turn to examine the general philosophies and ideas in society that have shaped the law of restitution since the end of the nineteenth century.

At least until the 1880s,[31] the ruling political philosophy was still one of laissez-faire individualism. The law of obligations reflected this. The law of contract was pre-eminent as a source of obligation. Imposed obligations through the law of tort and, as we would now say, the law of restitution were relatively restricted. And even where obligations were imposed on the basis of unjust enrichment this was forced into the mould of voluntarily undertaken obligations either by being seen as an adjunct to contract—through the quasi-contract implied contract fiction—or by being seen as an adjunct to intention-based or express trusts, through the language of constructive trusts.

In line with the gradual dilution of laissez-faire individualism and the growth of the welfare state during the twentieth century, there has been an increase in the imposed obligations of tort and restitution. So much so that by the end of this century, tort and restitution can be regarded as equal partners with contract as a source of obligation. As the quantity of imposed obligations has increased, so the artificiality of regarding them as voluntarily undertaken has been heightened leading inevitably to the shattering of the implied contract theory. It is also possible to argue (although

---

[26] [1980] QB 677.   [27] [1979] 1 WLR 783.
[28] [1990] 1 AC 109.   [29] [1993] AC 70.
[30] P. Birks, 'Restitution from the Executive: A Tercentenary Footnote to the Bill of Rights' in P. Finn (ed.), *Essays on Restitution* (Sydney, 1900), chap. 6.
[31] See P. Atiyah, *The Rise and Fall of Freedom of Contract* (Oxford, 1979), 587.

this is a much more difficult matter)[32] that an analogous
development was Lord Browne-Wilkinson's suggestion in the
Westdeutsche Landesbank Girozentrale case in 1996[33] that the law
might develop the constructive trust as a restitutionary remedial
device wholly divorced from the intention-based express trust.

It can be seen from this that tort and restitution have a close
affinity with each other as imposed, rather than voluntarily
undertaken, obligations. There is a further parallel that I want to
draw. At the turn of the century, the tort of negligence was not
identified as such. One rather had a range of individual instances of
liability for negligence. It took Lord Atkin to draw them together
into a tort of negligence based on the neighbourhood principle—the
duty to use reasonable care not to harm one's neighbour—in 1932
in *Donoghue* v. *Stevenson*.[34] The tort of negligence continued to
develop incrementally, underpinned by Lord Atkin's principle, until
the late 1970s when Lord Wilberforce in *Anns* v. *Merton London
Borough Council*[35] thought that the time had come to abandon
incrementalism and to move instead to a *prima facie* or generalized
negligence principle, restricted only by clearly articulated policy
constraints. We know that ten years later in *Murphy* v. *Brentwood
DC*[36] the House of Lords abandoned Lord Wilberforce's scheme
and reverted to incrementalism for fear that otherwise the scope of
the tort of negligence would be too far-reaching. One can see
parallel trends and tensions in the law of restitution. One can say
that for much of this century it developed as a mass of individual
instances of liability until finally, as per Lord Atkin, it was drawn
together by Goff and Jones and by the House of Lords in *Lipkin
Gorman* into a law of restitution based on the unjust enrichment
principle. The equivalent to Lord Wilberforce's 'general principle'
approach was Goff and Jones' call, in the second and third editions
of their work,[37] for there to be a generalized right to restitution,
wherever there is an unjust enrichment, qualified only by clearly
articulated policy constraints. But as with the tort of negligence this
idea has not found favour. Incrementalism remains the name of the

---

[32] See Burrows, n. 11 above, 39.

[33] [1996] 2 AC 669, 716.   [34] [1932] AC 562.

[35] [1978] AC 728.   [36] [1991] 1 AC 398.

[37] See R. Goff and G. Jones, *The Law of Restitution* (2nd edn., London, 1978),
23–5 (3rd. edn., 1986), 29–30.

game at the end of the twentieth century and, in line with the demise of *Anns* v. *Merton*, Goff and Jones in their fourth edition in 1993 have abandoned all reference to a generalized right to restitution.

I finish the second part of this article with some comments on the role of law schools in the development of restitution and, more generally, on what law schools can learn from the development of the law of restitution. The recognition of the law of restitution in the last third of the twentieth century can be regarded as a triumph for a close working relationship between academia and the judiciary. Just as the two bodies came together in the work of the American Law Institute, so in this country the two have worked together to mould and create new law. If we focus on the interests and activities of the now numerous academic 'restitution lawyers' involved in this collaborative enterprise we can see that, while academics, they nevertheless regard their role as being to grapple with, and unravel, difficult practical problems; we see that they are concerned to analyse carefully the latest reported decisions; that they regard precision in analysis and language to be essential; that they seek to influence the judiciary and aspire to, and can expect to, be cited in judgments; that they regard the primary purpose of their work as being to ensure consistency and rationality in decision making, based on shared political and moral values in society, rather than the introduction of new social policies; and that they tend to have close contact with practitioners, especially at the Bar.

And yet in many law schools today—especially in the United States and Australia but, perhaps, increasingly here—we find that this type of academic lawyer is derided as a 'black-letter lawyer' or a 'formalist', or a 'rule fetishist'. The praise is often lavished on those who stand outside the enterprise, who analyse the law from an economic or feminist or philosophical perspective, and who tend to dismiss case analysis and all practitioners' works as far too boring and straightforward for them.

I do not seek for one moment to deny the fascination and significance of jurisprudence, law and economics, law and litera-ture, and the like. I have long been fascinated by them myself. Without question they have a role to play in a modern law school. But to regard those studies as 'what proper legal academics should be doing' seems to me unacceptable. How on any true scale of values can one regard theorizing about, say, philosophy as somehow more worthy and more of an intellectual challenge than the (academic) lawyer's task of shaping practical decisions affecting the workings of society in general.

In this respect I have been intrigued by the ongoing debate in the United States sparked by Harry T. Edwards' 1992 article in the *Michigan Law Review* entitled, 'The Growing Disjunction between Legal Education and the Legal Profession'.[38] In that article, Edwards criticizes the 'law and something else' movements; he calls for legal academics to concentrate on 'practical scholarship' that can be of direct use to judges, legislatures, and practitioners, rather than 'impractical scholarship' which has no direct relevance to decision-making; he calls for theory to be woven into arguments that affect practical decisions rather than theory being exposed for its own sake; and he articulates the view that, for example, the economic analysis or philosophical analysis of law should be carried out by those who are first-rate economists and first-rate philosophers rather than by first-rate lawyers who are second-rate economists and second-rate philosophers and are in danger of ending up being jacks of all trades and masters of none. In short, the article is a call for law to be treated essentially as an autonomous discipline. While not denying the insights that other disciplines can offer—and the value therefore of studying those subjects at law school—the primary concentration in law schools and in legal scholarship should, in Edwards' view, be on practical decision-making and not on deep theory.

If one wanted an example of the sort of scholarship of which Edwards would approve, then one could do no better than to point to the bulk of English scholarship on the law of restitution over the last thirty years. Indeed it is a sad fact, and directly supports Edwards' criticism of the position in his homeland, that in the

---

[38] (1992) 91 *Mich. LR* 34. See also R. Zimmermann, 'Savigny's Legacy: History, Comparative Law, and the Emergency of a European Legal Science' (1996) 112 *LQR* 576; John H. Langbein, 'Scholarly and Professional Objectives in Legal Education: American Trends and English Comparisons' in P. Birks (ed.), *Pressing Problems in the Law, Volume 2, What are Law Schools For?* (Oxford, 1996), 1–7. Edwards' article stimulated eighteen responses in a symposium in the (1993) 91 *Mich. LR* of which perhaps the most important was R. Posner, 'The Deprofessionalisation of Legal Teaching and Scholarship' (1993) 91 *Mich. LR* 1921. See generally William Twining, *Blackstone's Tower: The English Law School* (London, 1994), chap. 6.

United States equivalent scholarship on the law of restitution has virtually died a death. While in this country Goff and Jones and Birks have inspired a large number of books and articles and indeed the subject's own law review, George Palmer's excellent four-volume treatise on restitution in the United States published in 1978 has had comparatively little impact. A course on restitution or unjust enrichment is not to be found in any of the major law schools in the United States and a student learns his or her restitution, if at all, in remedies courses. In line with this the American Law Institute has shelved a second Restatement of Restitution (although I understand that Professor Andrew Kull of Emory University is attempting to persuade the Institute to take it up again).

But on this side of the Atlantic such is the practical utility of English scholarship on restitution that in 1997—in sharp contrast of course to 1897—few judges deciding a restitution case, or practitioners arguing a restitution case, would think it sensible to proceed without knowing what the restitution scholars have to say. Long may this close and productive working relationship between academics and practitioners continue.

(3) Where Do We Go From Here?

So I come to the third and final part of this article, the future. Where do we go from here? Gazing into my crystal ball, I would anticipate six significant developments in the next few decades.

First, I believe that defences, in particular change of position, will play an increasingly important role in the development of the law of restitution. Until recently, the courts have tended to restrict the ambit of restitution by limiting the grounds for restitution. In particular, we have seen above the artificial restrictions imposed on restitution for mistakes and for failure of consideration.[39] But the new strategy is likely to be to cast off old restrictions on the grounds for restitution and to rely instead on defences to control the ambit of the unjust enrichment principle. A clear signal that this will be the way forward was given by Lord Goff in *Lipkin Gorman* where he said that one beneficial effect of recognizing the defence of

---

[39] See 100–102 above.

change of position was that 'it will enable a more generous approach to be taken to the recognition of the right to restitution, in the knowledge that the defence is, in appropriate cases, available'.[40]

Secondly, I think that we will see a continued assimilation of common law and equitable rules on restitution. To use Jack Beatson's phrase,[41] 'integrating equity' is the law of restitution's 'unfinished business'. Relating back to the examples given earlier,[42] I would expect to see strict liability subject to defences, such as change of position and *bona fide* purchase, taking over 'knowing receipt and dealing'. I would expect personal restitutionary remedies for wrongs, stripping away gains made by wrongdoers, to become widely accepted in respect of torts as well as equitable wrongs. And I would expect the other great area where English law at present irrationally divides common law and equitable rules, namely tracing, to be reformed so that, for example, the apparent common law rule that one cannot trace into a mixed fund will be emasculated.[43]

Thirdly, I anticipate that within the near future there will be a solution to the continuing mystery of the relationship between property law and unjust enrichment. This is obviously not an appropriate place for me to attempt to solve that mystery, but I would like to make three observations that may be of assistance.

The first is that, while in the past I thought it helpful to treat a proprietary remedy given because the plaintiff owned particular property before and after it was received by the defendant as restitutionary based on an unjust factor of 'the retention of property belonging to the plaintiff',[44] I now accept that it is more helpful to draw a clear distinction between that case (which Goff and Jones call a 'pure proprietary claim' and civil lawyers would call a *vindicatio* claim) and other cases where the proprietary remedy is given because the law is creating a new proprietary right in response to the defendant's unjust enrichment at the plaintiff's expense (what Goff and Jones call a 'restitutionary proprietary

---

[40] [1991] 2 AC 548, 581.

[41] *The Use and Abuse of Unjust Enrichment* (Oxford, 1991), 244.

[42] See 102–103 above.

[43] See, in particular, the observations of Millett LJ in *Trustee of the Property of F. C. Jones* v. *Jones* [1996] 3 WLR 703.

[44] N. 11 above, chap. 13.

claim').[45] An important consequence of recognizing this distinction is that change of position ought to be a defence to a proprietary restitutionary claim but not to a pure proprietary claim (for example, a delivery up of one's property).

The second observation is that, as the work of Peter Birks and Lionel Smith has emphasized,[46] one needs to distinguish between the process of tracing and the decision whether to award a personal or proprietary restitutionary remedy. I would argue that tracing is a technique that goes to the 'at the expense of' element of subtractive unjust enrichment. That is, a plaintiff will need to rely on the technique of tracing where establishing that the defendant's enrichment was 'subtracted from' the plaintiff is problematic because of a change in the form of the property subtracted and/or because the property in question has been received by the defendant from a third party rather than directly from the plaintiff. While, no doubt, tracing is normally invoked by a plaintiff with the aim of obtaining a proprietary restitutionary remedy over property retained by the defendant, tracing may also be invoked with the aim of seeking a personal restitutionary remedy (for example, an award of money had and received or an equitable accounting) in respect of property *received* by the defendant where property has reached the defendant from a third party (so that establishing that the enrichment was subtracted from the plaintiff is problematic) as, for example, in *Lipkin Gorman* itself.

The third observation is that any attempt to confine the unjust enrichment principle to the law of obligations, by denying that proprietary (as opposed to personal) remedies are ever restitutionary, flies in the face of a wide range of situations where, in my view, the law already creates new proprietary rights in response to unjust enrichment. Examples include constructive trusts imposed on gains made by equitable wrongs (as in *Boardman* v. *Phipps*,[47] and *Attorney General for Hong Kong* v. *Reid*);[48] examples of subrogation (for example, as provided for in section 5 of the Mercantile Law Amendment Act 1856, and as illustrated in the

---

[45] N. 11 above (4th edn.), 73–4.

[46] P. Birks, 'Mixing and Tracing: Property and Restitution' (1992) 45(2) *CLP* 69; L. D. Smith, 'Tracing into The Payment of a Debt' (1995) 54 *CLJ* 290. See also Millett LJ's observations in *Boscawen* v. *Bajwa* [1996] 1 WLR 328.

[47] For discussion of this, see P. Birks, 'Unjust Enrichment—a Reply to Mr Hedley' (1985) 5 *Legal Studies* 67–8.   [48] [1994] 1 AC 324.

cases of *Boscawen* v. *Bajwa*,[49] and *Lord Napier* v. *Hunter*[50]); equitable liens that have been imposed on land because it has been mistakenly improved;[51] the rescission of an executed contract which has revested the proprietary rights to goods or land transferred under the contract (as in, for example, *Car and Universal Finance Company Ltd.* v. *Caldwell*[52]); and equitable proprietary remedies awarded following equitable tracing,[53] where it is important to see that it is fictional to say that one's entitlement to the property is based on one's pre-existing equitable ownership of it. That is, if one is entitled to trace from a pig to a horse to a car one cannot say, without invoking fiction, that one is entitled to proprietary restitution of the car because one already owns it. The truth is that one's ownership of the pig which has been substituted by the car entitles one to claim for the first time ownership of the car because the owner of the car is unjustly enriched at one's expense (the tracing rules being invoked to show that the subtraction of one's pig has become the defendant's enrichment in the form of the car). On the other hand (running contrary to the above examples), after *Westdeutsche Landesbank* we now know that a defendant who is unjustly enriched by a mistaken payment or a payment under a void contract is normally susceptible to only a personal and not a proprietary restitutionary remedy. It has to be conceded, it seems to me, that this picture of the law as to when unjust enrichment will and will not trigger new proprietary rights lacks all coherence. The judges must and, I am sure will, move the law, with the assistance of academics, to a more coherent position on this most difficult of issues.

Fourthly, I expect legislation to have a greater impact on the law of restitution than hitherto. My recent work on a cases and materials book on restitution with Ewan McKendrick has made it startlingly apparent to me just how limited has been the role of statute in this sphere. One hardly gets beyond the Law Reform (Frustrated Contracts) Act 1943, the Civil Liability (Contribution) Act 1978, the Minors' Contracts Act 1987, and a few minor

---

[49] [1996] 1 WLR 328.   [50] [1993] AC 713.
[51] *Unity Joint Stock Mutual Banking Assoc.* v. *King* (1858) 25 Beav. 72; *Cooper* v. *Phibbs* (1867) LR 2 HL 149.
[52] [1965] 1 QB 525.
[53] See e.g., *Re Hallett's Estate* (1880) 13 Ch. D 696; *Re Diplock* [1948] Ch. 465.

sections in the Torts (Wrongful Interference with Goods Act) 1977 and intellectual property statutes. Yet, as Dean Calabresi has emphasized, we are in the age of the statutes.[54] Certainly within three of the projects with which I am concerned at the Law Commission—namely, limitation periods, non-compensatory damages, and illegal transactions—it is essential that we deal legislatively with aspects of restitution. I would expect that the nonsense of the decision in *Friends Provident Life Office* v. *Hillier Parker May & Rowden*,[55] where existing wording designed for compensation in the Civil Liability (Contribution) Act 1978 was forced to fit restitution, will increasingly be rendered unnecessary as the legislature, following on *Lipkin Gorman*, and with the assistance of the Law Commission, comes to terms with the language and ideas of the law of restitution.

Fifthly, I expect to see comparative European law having an increased influence over the English law of restitution. This expectation is a reflection of, first, the increased recognition by our judiciary of comparative material; and, secondly, of the fact that the United Kingdom's membership of the European Union has brought us closer to European thinking. Certainly in the area of unjust enrichment there is an enormous amount that we can learn from, for example, German law. Perhaps, as with Olé Lando and Hugh Beale's, *The Principles of European Contract Law*,[56] we will see in the future a publication entitled 'Principles of European Unjust Enrichment Law'. In this respect Dr Eric Clive's superb Scottish Code of Unjust Enrichment Law produced in 1996 for the Scottish Law Commission may be of great significance.[57]

Finally, for better or worse, I think academic literature on restitution will tend to become more theoretical and to move further away from Harry Edwards' 'practical scholarship'. Kit Barker, in an excellent recent review article of English literature on restitution entitled, 'Unjust Enrichment: Containing the Beast',[58] writes that we should now

---

[54] Guido Calabresi, *A Common Law for the Age of the Statutes* (Princeton, NJ, 1982). See also J. Beatson, 'Has the Common Law A Future?' (Inaugural lecture, 29 Apr. 1996, Cambridge).   [55] [1996] 2 WLR 123.

[56] 'Part 1: Performance, Non-Performance and Remedies' (Dordrecht, 1995).

[57] *Scottish Law Commission Draft Rules on Unjustified Enrichment and Commentary* (Appendix to Scot. Law. Com. Discussion Paper No 99) (Edinburgh, 1996).   [58] (1995) 15 *OJLS* 457.

look more closely at [the subject's] internal 'philosophical foundations' or 'ground-theory'. If there is a general flaw in the recent literature, it is the failure to excavate this deeper level of enquiry. Authors tend to engage in lively arguments about what the beast should look like . . . They have tended to fight shy of the logically prior (and governing) question of why it exists.[59]

I agree that there is scope for more theory, but the challenge facing Kit Barker, and others who have embarked on the same enterprise, is to ensure that their theories link directly and intelligibly to practical decision-making. The danger of the next generation of restitution scholars crossing the line from practical to impractical scholarship—and thereby losing the influence we have over decision-makers in the area—is very great indeed.[60]

This leads me to leave you with a question that has long troubled me. Does my predicted trend towards deeper theory indicate that the practical legal academic has a limited role? Put another way, does a particular field become so saturated with practical scholarship that one has to move to deeper theoretical analysis to say anything original? If we take Contract as an example, is the explosion in deep theoretical analysis, the United States style of scholarship, inevitable?

It is true that, once Goff and Jones or Birks has been written, one cannot write another 'path-breaking' book in the same style. My own firm view, however, is that the law is so rich that at any one time there are numerous path-breaking articles and books of practical legal scholarship that cry out to be written. At this moment in time unjust enrichment is still far from saturated but, even if it were, there are other areas where the possibilities seem endless, most especially I would suggest in the field of commercial law (one thinks for example of our poor understanding of the law on guarantees or assignment or agency). The work of the practical legal scholar is never complete. As lawyers, while there may be a need for us to switch specialist horses, there is no need for us to abandon our subject in order to find opportunities for intellectually challenging, creative, and path-breaking work. At the end of the

---

[59] (1995) 15 *OJLS* at 463.

[60] I recognize that views may differ as to where the line should be drawn between practical and impractical scholarship and that the distinction is one of degree rather than of kind.

twentieth century the work of the practical legal scholar—and our working relationship with the judiciary—is too important to society for us to sell out to the departments of philosophy, history or economics. If there are no heirs to Scott and Seavey in the United States, I am confident that in England there will be heirs aplenty to Robert Goff, Gareth Jones, and Peter Birks.

PROPERTY LAW
Re-establishing Diversity

Alison Clarke

As far as property law is concerned, the key events marking the opening of this century (if one can allow the latitude of a decade or so) are the passing of the 1925 property legislation and the codification of mercantile sales rules by the Sale of Goods Act 1893. These two events can be seen as signalling the culmination of a process of rationalization that had been taking place in various areas of property law over a number of years, accelerating towards the end of the nineteenth century. This spirit of rationalization set the tone for the start of this century and has had a significant influence on the thinking of judges and legislators throughout this century, particularly the first half of it.

However, perhaps inevitably, the rationalized structures erected at the start of the century are now beginning to break down. This is not necessarily because of any inherent weakness in the structures themselves, more because times have changed. Commercial, social and domestic relationships now are of course very different from what they were at the start of the century, but it is not just that they are different—they are also very much more diverse. It is this last factor—the increased diversity of commercial, social, and domestic relationships—that is now prompting a growing awareness of a need to recognize a wider range of property interests than those envisaged at the start of the century.

More specifically, the key change that has taken place over this century is our view of things as commodities. By 'things' I mean here all stuff—land, goods, ideas, debts, shares—anything, whether tangible or intangible, in which we recognize property interests. At the start of the century, the major concern of property lawyers was to facilitate the 'commercial' use of things, using the word commercial here in the very narrow sense, meaning simply buying and selling. Buying and selling things is facilitated by narrowing down the range of property interests that can exist in relation to the thing in question, and ensuring that each interest is clearly defined, easily discoverable by third parties, and readily convertible into money—the classic mid-twentieth century criteria for acceptance of an interest as proprietary.[1] The following description given in 1937 in the fourth edition of *Cheshire's Modern Real Property* demonstrates this view of the objectives of the 1925 property legislation:

[The] legislation . . . introduced changes of so fundamental a character that, despite its claim to be evolutionary and not revolutionary, it undoubtedly marked the opening of a new epoch in the history of real property law, and was a further stage, it may be a definitive stage, in the modernisation of the one department of English law that still abounded in anachronisms which belonged to an extinct social system. . . . Whether the draftsmen of the 1925 Statutes succeeded in their design is a debatable question with which we are not concerned, but there was at any rate ample justification for their attempt. Their vindication was the necessity of casting off those shackles, relics of a feudal age, which prevented land from being as saleable a commodity as an industrial society demands. Dismal as the view may be, trade is the means by which man now attains the goal of his ambitions. Buying and selling, whether it be of goods, stocks, land, skill or brains, is the daily occupation of all the world, and in most departments of life a sale involving sums of great magnitude can be effectively transacted in a few moments. But when we examine the case of land we find that even as late as 1925 feudalism in some measure still governed us from its grave, for many of its rules, though introduced to meet the needs of a society which had passed away centuries before, continued to lay a retarding hand upon that facility of disposition which should be the object of any system of land law.[2]

So, for Dr Cheshire in the 1930s, the revolution brought about by the 1925 property legislation, the radical excision of the skeleton of feudalism, was necessary so that land could be bought and sold as freely as any other commodity, in recognition of what he saw as the dismal truth, that 'buying and selling . . . is the daily occupation of all the world'.

---

[1] See in particular *National Provincial Bank Ltd.* v. *Ainsworth* [1965] AC 1175, *per* Lord Wilberforce at 1247–8 and *Milirrpum* v. *Nabalco Pty. Ltd.* (1971) 17 FLR 141, *per* Blackburn J at 272.

[2] G. C. Cheshire, *Modern Law of Real Property* 4th edn. (London, 1937), 67–8. See also M. Chalmers, 'Codification of Mercantile Law' (1903) 19 *LQR* 10 in relation to the Sale of Goods Act 1894.

However, as we now approach the end of this century, it begins to look as if things are not quite as dismal as Dr Cheshire thought—or maybe just dismal in a different sort of way. It is increasingly apparent that there *is* more to life than buying and selling, and that this is just as true of commercial life as it is of social and domestic life. A wide variety of people now have a broad and diverse range of legitimate expectations in relation to things—real, tangible things and intangible things—and it is the job of property law to accommodate their expectations. In order to do so it is having to disinter—or, where necessary, reinvent—some if its forgotten diversity of property interests, and to accept that the mid twentieth century template for a property interest—well established, clearly defined, and readily convertible into money—is too rigid and simplistic.

Before looking in more detail at this pressure towards diversity, however, there are some preliminary points to be made.

First, the argument about diversity is not precisely the political or philosophical one about the role of alienability and the free market in the allocation of resources. One of the most striking developments in legal theory over the latter half of this century has been the revival of interest in property as an institution,[3] and it is certainly easier to argue now than it was at the beginning of this century that free alienability of resources does not necessarily lead to their optimific distribution, if we take the view that for a distribution to be optimific it must also be just and in the interests of the community. However, the argument here is that even apart from all that, ordinary mundane social and commercial pressures may in some circumstances require a recognition of a more diverse range of property interests, even if this means that resources are less freely alienable, because both social life and commercial life have themselves become more complex and more diverse. Put simply,

---

[3] See e.g. the following major works, all produced within the last twenty years: J. Waldron, *The Right to Private Property* (Oxford, 1988), A. Ryan, *Property* (Milton Keynes, 1987) and *Property and Political Theory* (Oxford, 1986), J. W. Harris, *Property and Justice* (Oxford, 1996), Stephen Buckle, *Natural Law and the Theory of Property: Grotius to Hume* (Oxford, 1991), L. Becker, *Property Rights: Philosophical Foundations* (Boston, Mass., 1977), J. O. Grunebaum, *Private Ownership* (London, 1987), S. R. Munzer, *A Theory of Property* (Cambridge, 1990), J. Christman, *The Myth of Property: Towards an Egalitarian Theory of Ownership* (New York, 1994).

commerce does sometimes require things simply to be bought and sold as commodities, in which case the first priority is free alienability, but at other times it requires us to do more complex things with them, and in those cases alienability is relatively unimportant.[4]

Secondly, and this is really linked to the previous point, a key development that has taken place over this century is a recognition that it is not appropriate to treat a thing as a commodity if the holder of an interest in that thing values the thing for its own particular qualities rather than simply for the monetary value it represents. This distinction, which Bernard Rudden has described as the difference between things viewed as thing and things viewed as wealth,[5] is close to, but not precisely the same as, the civil law distinction between fungible and non-fungible things. Adopting Bernard Rudden's terminology, I value a picture or a mass-produced but well-designed chair as 'thing' rather than as 'wealth' if I would not consider payment of its monetary value in the open market to be an adequate substitute for it. This may be simply because I rate its artistic merits higher than the market does, but it may also be because it is an integral part of the overall design of my flat, or because it was a present from an old friend who is coming to dinner tomorrow and will be offended not to see it on display. Similarly, either a sentimental attachment I have towards an old sweater, or a disinclination to waste time shopping for a replacement for it, might make me value the sweater as thing rather than as wealth. Even something as entirely fungible as an electric light bulb can be valuable to me as thing rather than wealth if it is the working light bulb in my reading lamp late at night when I want to go on reading. Margaret Jane Radin has developed the same idea as part of an analysis of the relationship between property and personhood. As she argues:

One's expectations crystallise around certain 'things', the loss of which causes more disruption and disorientation than does a simple decrease in aggregate wealth. For example, if someone returns home to find her sofa has disappeared, that is more disorienting than to discover that her house has decreased in market value by 5%. If, by magic, her white sofa were

---

[4] For a full consideration of the issues see S. Rose Ackerman, 'Inalienability and the Theory of Property Rights' (1985) 85 *Columbia LRev.* 931.

[5] B. Rudden, 'Things as Thing and Things as Wealth' (1994) 14 *OJLS* 81.

instantly replaced by a blue one of equal market value, it would cause no loss in net worth but would still cause some disruption in her life.[6]

This distinction was as valid at the beginning of this century as it is now, and in fact Radin's analysis is explicitly derived from Hegel's *Philosophy of Right*.[7] Whilst it may be doubted whether many English property lawyers at the turn of this century read Hegel late into the night, they are hardly likely to have found the distinction made either novel or difficult to grasp. The difference is rather one of emphasis: their overriding consideration was to devise legal structures which would allow things to be treated as wealth rather than as thing, whereas by the end of this century we are developing a greater concern to protect the interests of those who value things as thing rather than as wealth.

The Re-emergence of Communal Property

This time last century the future for communal property in this country must have seemed bleak, to land lawyers at least. The period marked the end of one movement and the beginning of another—the final tailing off of the enclosure movement, which involved the conversion of communal property rights in land to private property, and the emergence of the campaign for the preservation of public open spaces. It is generally agreed that it was the second which finally killed off the first,[8] but for present purposes the important point is that they were each, in their own way, equally inimical to communal property.

Over the last few decades there has been considerable debate, particularly in the law and economics and political philosophy fields, about the efficiency or otherwise of private property,[9] but much of the debate has been obscured by uncertainties in the categorization of the alternatives. Private property is usually considered in apposition to state property and communal property.

---

[6] M. J. Radin, 'Property and Personhood' (1982) 34 *Stan. LR* 957 at 1004.
[7] T. Knox's translation of which was published in 1821.
[8] A. W. B. Simpson, *A History of Land Law* 2nd edn. (Oxford, 1986), 261 ff.
[9] The classic economist analysis is H. Demsetz, 'Towards a Theory of Property Rights' (1967) 57 *Am. Econ. Rev.* 347; see also R. A. Posner, *Economic Analysis of Law*, 4th edn. (Boston, Mass., 1992), chap. 3; J. O. Grunebaum *Private Ownership*, n. 3 above, and R. C. Ellickson, 'Property in Land' (1993) 102 *Yale LJ* 1315.

State property can be said, reasonably uncontroversially, to mean resources vested in the state and allocated by the state amongst its citizens according to some policy such as need, or central efficiency, but not on the basis of, or by a process which confers, an entitlement that can be asserted against the state.[10] About the term 'communal property', however, there is little consensus. It has been used to mean everything from what might be described as 'no-property' (resources such as sunlight, or air, or wild animals, which are available for use by everyone, but in which property rights are not recognized, whether because of non-scarcity or because of difficulty in exclusion) through what is best described as 'open-access' commons (resources which every person has a right to use, such as public open spaces and public rights of way[11]) to what will be referred to here as 'limited access' commons (resources which every member of a group has a right to use).

The term 'communal property' is used here in this last sense, to describe the communal use of a resource by a group of people who are defined by reference to a status. The use they make of the resource may be communal (for example, inhabitants of a village using the village hall for village meetings, or members of a commune grazing their communally owned stock on their pasture land) but it need not be: each member of the community may have the right to make use of the resource for her own private benefit. So, for example, any person who is a free inhabitant of ancient tenements in the borough of Saltash in Cornwall has the right to dredge for oysters in the River Tamar from 2 February to Easter Saturday in each year.[12] Similarly, the inhabitants of a particular

---

[10] Not to be confused with resources which the state uses for carrying out its bureaucratic purposes (e.g. the premises of government departments) which it owns in much the same way as a private individual owns private property, nor with resources that the state owns but makes available to everyone on an as of right basis, such as public highways.

[11] Some theorists, particularly those writing in the law and economics tradition, appear to envisage a type of 'pure' open access commons where a resource—communal land, for example—is available for use by any person, as of right and for any purpose. It is difficult to think of any real-life example of such a resource: in most open access commons, although every person might have a right to use the resource, the *purpose* for which it may be used (e.g. for grazing, or for recreation, or as a footpath) is regulated.

[12] Assuming there have been no further developments since the validity of the right was confirmed by the House of Lords in *Goodman* v. *The Mayor and Burgesses of the Borough of Saltash* (1892) 7 App. Cas. 623: see further 126 below.

area might each have the right to pasture their privately owned sheep on land owned either by themselves communally or by someone else.[13]

Adopting this definition of communal property—the communal use of a resource by a group of people defined by reference to status—the essential element is that individuals within the group have whatever rights they have only by virtue of their membership of the community in question. The community can be any group of people who have a common interest in a thing—it may be by virtue of being inhabitants of a particular locality, but it could also be any other common interest group, for example parents of children who attend a particular school. The distinguishing feature, however, is that power over the communal resource is intended by the community to remain in the community, so that it can exclude outsiders and decide for itself how the resource should be managed, exploited, conserved, or alienated. It follows therefore that the interest of each person in the community lasts only for so long as she remains a member—in other words, no individual within the community can dispose of her interest in the communal resource to anyone outside the community, nor can she retain her interest when she leaves the community.

By the late nineteenth century the courts seemed to be having great difficulties with these communal property rights. The rights that were then coming before them were the last vestiges of a widespread communal land-holding and land-exploiting system that had been virtually wiped out over the past two centuries by the combined effect of approvement and enclosure (approvement being the process by which the lord of the manor could convert communal grazing land to his own private ownership, and enclosure the process, carried out initially by Private Acts of Parliament but subsequently by a series of statutory procedures, by which land was discharged from communal rights and parcelled out in private ownership between the landholder and the commoners).[14] These surviving rights were extremely old: at one time

---

[13] e.g. the stintholders of Burnhope Moor, held by the House of Lords in *Brackenbank Lodge Ltd.* v. *Peart* (1996) *The Times*, 26 July (reversing the decision of the Court of Appeal reported at (1994) 67 P & CR 249, CA) not to hold the underlying fee simple in the Moor: see further 132 below.

[14] A. W. B. Simpson, n. 8 above, 107–14.

historians viewed them as vestiges of the feudal system, but the later and better view, current by the beginning of this century, was that these communal rights almost certainly pre-dated feudalism, originating in the Anglo-Saxon open field system.[15]

Since these rights were so long established it might be thought that the courts would have had little difficulty in accommodating them within their conceptual framework. In fact their general view appears decidedly ambivalent. On the one hand there was a strong impulse to presume that long-established usages were of lawful origin and therefore enjoyable as of right.[16] On the other hand, the courts appeared to have developed severe reservations about acknowledging as proprietary any possessory or usage right that vested in a community rather than in a legal person.

Some of the reservations that the courts articulated about communal property rights at this time were to become very familiar in law and economics literature over the rest of the twentieth century. Essentially, there were two concerns. The first was that because these communal rights were held by a fluctuating class of persons they could never be surrendered, varied, or extinguished. The second was the tragedy of the commons argument considered in more detail below—the argument that a communally used resource was likely to be exhausted by over-exploitation—a perhaps surprising argument to deploy in relation to communal resources such as the Tamar oyster beds in *Goodman* v. *Saltash*,[17] which had demonstrably avoided this fate for more than 1600 years.

Other arguments accepted by the courts at this period seem rather to derive from a difficulty in conceiving of property rights in anything other than private property terms. A concern about certainty first expressed in a case in 1607 but cited at this period betrays profound misgivings about the very idea of a status right, where the interest of any individual within the group necessarily arises and disappears automatically as and when the individual

---

[15] T. E. Scrutton, 'The Origin of Rights of Common' (1887) XII *LQR* 373 and see also Cheshire, *Modern Law of Real Property*, 4th edn. n. 2 above, 273.

[16] See e.g. *Lord Chesterfield* v. *Harris* [1908] 2 Ch. 397, *per* Cozens-Hardy MR at 407, and *Goodman* v. *Saltash*, n. 12 above, at 639, *per* Lord Selbourne LC.

[17] (1892) 7 App. Cas. 623; the argument was successfully deployed in *Lord Chesterfield* v. *Harris* [1908] 2 Ch. 397.

acquires and loses the status in question. Such rights were thought to be objectionable on the ground that

> such common will be transitory and altogether uncertain, for it will follow the person, and for no certain time or estate, but during his inhabitancy, and such manner of interest the law will not suffer, for custom ought to extend to that which hath certainty and continuance.[18]

In much the same vein, in other cases where the courts wanted to uphold ancient rights they would resort to fictions, presuming a long lost grant of corporate status on the commoners, so that the rights in question could be treated as private property rights inhering in a legal person, rather than as communal rights enjoyed by a group defined by virtue of status. The success of this device was, however, unpredictable, if only because of uncertainty over precisely how fictitious the fiction could be. So, for example, in *Lord Rivers* v. *Adams*[19] the claimants (who had long exercised what they thought of as rights to cut timber and furze on Tollard Common in Cranbourne Chase) lost because, understandably as one might think, they were unable to produce evidence that the fictitious corporation had ever held meetings or appointed officers.

Those communal rights that managed to avoid the attentions of the courts at the turn of the century then had to be brought within the rationalized land holding structure created by the 1925 property legislation. One of the main objects of the Law of Property Act 1925 was to secure that in relation to all land, there should be an owner of full age able to deal with the legal fee simple or leasehold interest in favour of a purchaser, and one of the ways of achieving this object was by imposing a trust whenever a legal estate was held by more than one person, so that the legal title (and consequently the capacity and power to deal with purchasers) was vested in trustees holding on trust for the beneficial owners.[20] Both the objective and the means of achieving it are inappropriate for communally held land: dealing in the land as a commodity becomes

---

[18] *Gateward's Case* (1607) 6 Co. Rep. 59b, cited by Kelly CB in *Lord Rivers* v. *Adams* (1878) 3 Ex. D 361, 364.

[19] (1878) LR 3 Ex.D 361.

[20] *Wolstenholme and Cherry's Conveyancing Statutes* (13th edn. by J. T. Farrand) (London, 1972), Vol. 1, 32–3.

the dominant purpose, and the relationship of trust replaces that of communal ownership. Nevertheless, an attempt was made to bring existing communally held land within this structure by paragraph 2 of Part V of Schedule 1 to the Law of Property Act 1925, which vested ownership of at least some of this land in the Public Trustee to hold on trust for sale, with the proviso however that there should be no sale without leave of the court and that pending sale pre-existing rights of access and user should continue. Because of the rather curious drafting of the provision[21] it is not clear how much common land it actually affected. More significantly, however, the effect (although not necessarily the intention) of the Law of Property Act 1925 was to make it impossible for any new land to come into communal ownership. From 1926 until 1 January 1997, when the land holding structure was modified by the coming into force of the Trusts of Land and Appointment of Trustees Act 1996, any attempt to put land into communal ownership would necessarily result in the fee simple becoming vested in the first four named communal owners as trustees, and the trustees coming under a duty to sell the land with only a power to postpone the sale, leaving the other intended communal owners with no rights of user as against the trustees, merely with interests as beneficiaries in the potential proceeds of sale. Although as developed by the courts this became a surprisingly efficient means of running and preserving some limited access commons,[22] nevertheless the enforced trust structure represents an impoverishment of the land-holding system and distorts the relationship between the parties. The 1996 Act allows for more diversification by removing the automatic duty to sell and making provision for occupation rights for beneficiaries,[23] but nevertheless the inappropriate trust structure remains.

---

[21] It is cast in private property terms, applying only to 'an open space of land (with or without any building used in common for the purposes of any adjoining land) . . . held in undivided shares, in right whereof each owner has rights of access and user of the open space'; 'open space' is not defined. For the difficulties posed by this definition see the cases cited in the annotation to para. 2 in *Wolstenholme and Cherry's Conveyancing Statutes*, n. 20 above, Vol. 1, 371.

[22] The collateral purpose doctrine, which enabled the court to use their jurisdiction under s. 30 of the 1925 Act to prevent a sale of land held on trust for sale where a collateral purpose of the trust still subsisted, originated in *Re Buchanan-Woolaston's Conveyance* [1939] Ch. 217, where the CA refused to order sale of open land bought by owners of four neighbouring properties to preserve their view of the sea.   [23] See further 147 below.

Further inroads into the integrity of existing commons were made by section 193 of the Law of Property Act 1925, which by creating public rights of access 'for air and exercise' over all commons within areas formerly covered by metropolitan and urban district councils, further advanced the process started towards the end of the last century of converting limited access commons to open access commons.[24] However, whilst communally held land was, in theory at least, transformed by the 1925 property legislation, communal use rights over land in private ownership[25] were left relatively untouched, and were expressly stated to be overriding interests in registered land, and so enforceable against purchasers of the land although not required (or indeed permitted) to be entered on the land register.[26]

The only major reassessment of communal land rights since 1925 was made by the Royal Commission on Common Land, the Jennings Commission, appointed in 1955. It reported to Parliament in 1958[27] that much of the land then subject to rights of common was, or was in danger of becoming, derelict, largely because of changes in the pattern of agriculture and the disruption caused by the Second World War. Many of the systems which had evolved for administering communal resources had broken down, and traditional patterns of usage had been interrupted by widespread requisition of communal land by the government for war use. Consequently, when pieces of communal land were finally derequisitioned piecemeal there was often considerable uncertainty as to who it should be vested in, and precisely who had what rights in it and powers of management over it.[28]

The Royal Commission was convinced that the decline in common land ought to be reversed and made wide ranging recommendations for setting up systems for the long-term management and improvement of common land.[29] These were never

---

[24] For other legislation providing piecemeal public access to commons in various areas see A. Sydenham, 'Right to Roam' [1996] *Estates Gazette*, 6 July 116.

[25] Including for these purposes land held by public or quasi-public bodies, most notably local authorities and charities such as the National Trust.

[26] Land Registration Act 1925, s. 70(1)(a). See also Law of Property Act 1922, Sched. 12, para. 4, preserving the rights of common over copyhold land converted to freehold by the 1922 Act.   [27] Cmnd 462.

[28] *Ibid.*, paras. 120 and 131–9.   [29] Summarized at paras. 163–4.

implemented. They also proposed as a preparatory step the setting up of a public register for common land, on which would be registered all rights of common, all land subject to rights of common, all town and village greens, and all owners of common land. These registration recommendations *were* implemented, by the Commons Registration Act 1965. The drafting of the 1965 Act and the registration system set up by it have attracted sustained and deserved criticism,[30] but for present purposes the most interesting aspect of the recommendations is the restrictive and essentially preservationalist attitude towards communal property underlying them, an attitude typical of the mid-twentieth century and only now beginning to dissipate.

From this perspective the most notable feature of the Jennings Report is that communal property was clearly not seen as a viable alternative to private property. There is no suggestion that it might provide a useful mechanism for conserving or exploiting natural resources: instead, communal use rights were seen as picturesque relics of our past that ought to be preserved for sentimental/ historical reasons. So, for example, it was recommended that all rights of common (apart from pasture rights and 'rights of the owner of the soil') should be appurtenant to other land, and that the use should be limited to the needs of the commoner's household or farm, as the case may be. It was simply stated, without any discussion, that 'there should be no possibility of commercial exploitation'.[31]

The fundamental issues were therefore not addressed. Why should communal rights be exercisable only for personal private benefit and not for a communal benefit? Whether for private or

---

[30] See, e.g. *New Windsor Corporation* v. *Mellor* [1975] 1 Ch. 380, *per* Lord Denning MR at 391–2; *Corpus Christi College* v. *Gloucester County Council* [1983] 1 QB 360 (CA), *per* Lord Denning MR at 369–70 and Oliver LJ at 371 and 378–9; and *R* v. *Suffolk County Council, ex parte Steed* (1996) *The Times* 2 Aug. (CA), where Pill LJ diagnosed the central difficulty as uncertainty whether the Act was intended merely to provide a mechanism for registering rights or whether it also has the potential to destroy existing rights and permit the creation of new ones; the CA in that case did however reverse the decision of the judge at first instance to deprive the Secretary of State of half his costs in the action on the basis that 'part of the problem is due to the failure of successive Secretaries of State to implement legislation'; some of the more minor criticisms have been met by amendments made by the Common Land (Rectification of Registers) Act 1989, but the fundamental problems remain.   [31] Para. 270.

communal purposes, why should they not be profit-making? If private individuals can make profits, why not communities? There is nothing inherently irrational or self-defeating in exploiting communal use rights to provide a service for the community—for example, generating water or electricity for the neighbourhood—or to maintain local industries. It is not difficult to envisage the benefits to the community that might accrue if, for example, holders of communal fishing rights were to sell their fish in local markets to provide a supply of fresh fish for the neighbourhood, or even simply a tourist attraction.

Another striking feature of the Jennings Report is the confusion, already noted earlier, between communal and public purposes. Common land—i.e. open land subject to communal use rights or used as a town or village green—was seen to be valuable primarily because it provided open spaces for public exercise and recreation, a sort of public health amenity. It was not seen as particularly important that it provided a specific resource for the commoners. Consequently, it was recommended that the process noted earlier of creating rights of public access over common land should be completed, so that it would apply to *all* common land (subject to regulation to ensure that the public use did not interfere with the exercise of the commoner's rights) regardless of its nature and regardless of the nature of the commoners' rights.[32] No reference was made to the considerable (and still continuing) debate over the proper extent of public access over land in private ownership,[33] and whilst the Commission would no doubt have taken the view that a case has to be made for public access over private land, it appeared to find no such justification necessary in the case of public access over communal land. The strong impression conveyed is that the

---

[32] Paras. 314 and 318–9.

[33] See e.g. John Stuart Mill's strongly expressed views in *Principles of Political Economy* (London, 1848), Book II, chap. II, para. 6 that 'the pretension of two Dukes to shut up a part of the Highlands, and exclude the rest of mankind from many square miles of mountain scenery to prevent disturbance to wild animals, is an abuse; it exceeds the legitimate bounds of the right to landed property, particularly in relation to uncultivated land'; the Access to the Countryside Bill published by the Ramblers Association in Dec. 1995 and the subsequent negotiations between them and the Labour party and other interested organizations mark the continuation of the debate.

Royal Commission thought of communal property and public property as one and the same.

The final point to be noted about the Jennings Report is the underlying, unarticulated assumption that communal property is in some way isolated from private property. Although the Report contains long and very useful analyses by the geographer and by the historian on the Commission, it is almost wholly devoid of any legal analysis on any level.[34] This may have been a wise move on the Commission's part, to avoid getting bogged down in a morass of detail, but it does mean that they never addressed the fundamental question of how communal property rights and private property rights inter-relate. This is most strikingly apparent in the registration recommendations. Registration of rights of commons, and of land over which there are communal rights, was obviously a sensible first step, but it is difficult to see why it was thought necessary or desirable to set up a *separate* register for these purposes rather than to incorporate the information into the existing land registration system. As it was, the task of setting up and administering the Commons Registration system was given to local authorities: had it been given initially to the Land Registry, who at least had experience of running a register of land interests, some of the defects in the registration machinery might have been avoided.

However, whatever criticisms one might have of the Jennings Report of 1958 and the resulting Commons Registration Act 1965, one effect they have had is to prompt litigation, and hence judicial analysis. So, for example, in *Brackenbank Lodge Ltd. v. Peart*[35] although the issue was the fee simple ownership of Burnhope Moor in County Durham, the central question was the nature of the grazing rights over the Moor which all parties agreed were held by local farmers. The grazing rights enjoyed by the farmers were rights known as 'stints'; the stintholders claimed they were entitled to the fee simple in the Moor by virtue of the stintage rights they had over it, whereas their opponents Brackenbank Lodge (who had shooting

---

[34] The only lawyer on the Commission appears to have been Sir Ivor Jennings himself, better known as a public lawyer than as a property lawyer.

[35] (1996) *The Times*, 26 July (HL), on appeal from the decision of the CA reported at (1994) 67 P & CR 249.

rights over the Moor and claimed to be entitled to the fee simple by conveyance or adverse possession) claimed that stintage rights gave the holders no rights in the underlying fee simple.

The Court of Appeal adopted the definition of 'stint' given in the Jennings Report. There it was stated that there are two types of stint. The first is the sole or exclusive right to graze a specified number of animals on someone else's land. The second is the right to graze a specified number of animals on a piece of land which the holder of the right owns in common with the possessors of other like rights. Stints of the first type are just like any other profit or grazing right and are thoroughly orthodox in modern property law. However, the Court of Appeal held that these were stints of the second type—what they called proprietary stints—and these are very much more interesting for present purposes. In any orthodox tenancy in common, the tenants in common have as against each other unlimited rights to use the subject matter of the tenancy in common in whatever way they please. In a proprietary stint, however, the *only* user right the stintholding tenants in common have as against each other is the right to graze the designated number and species of animal.[36] This makes the stint a very unusual proprietary right in modern times. Whilst it is commonplace in private property for the ambit or exercise of co-owners' user rights to be limited by contract or waiver or estoppel, such a limitation operates *in personam* only.[37] In the case of a stint, on the other hand, the limitation is proprietary. In principle, the proprietary incidents of property interests are fixed and non-negotiable between the parties, and toleration of sub-species with slightly different incidents is unusual, to say the least,[38] because of the fear that variety will prejudice marketability. But this is precisely what a

---

[36] And, presumably, anything else provided it does not interfere with the grazing rights of the others.

[37] So, e.g. tenants in common of a house agreeing between themselves that each should be allocated their own bedroom nevertheless each retain a proprietary right to use every part of the house, including the bedrooms of the others, which is transmissible to third parties *prima facie* unfettered by the contractual restriction: *Greenfield* v. *Greenfield* (1979) 38 P & CR 570.

[38] *Keppell* v. *Bailey* (1834) 2 My & K 517; *Hill* v. *Tupper* (1863) 2 H & C 121. For a more modern example, see the HL decision in *Prudential Assurance Co. Ltd.* v. *London Residuary Body* [1992] 2 AC 386, reasserting the strict rules on certainty of duration of leases.

proprietary stint is—a tenancy in common with incidents slightly different from those of any other tenancy in common.[39]

This provides a useful reminder that no sharp distinction can be drawn between communal and private property interests. When economic analysis demonstrates the superiority of private property over communal property it takes as paradigms extremes at the opposite ends of a continuum. Whilst this has the merit of underlining essential distinctions, nevertheless it should not be allowed to obscure the fact that there *is* a continuum, not two distinct concepts. The proprietary stint is a good example of an interest which falls almost exactly half way along the continuum, right on the borderline between private and communal property.

This leads on to a further issue, which is the validity of the tragedy of the commons argument referred to earlier. Put crudely, the tragedy of the commons is said to be this: communal ownership is not only economically inefficient but doomed to failure, because no one member of the community will voluntarily restrict the exercise of her unlimited user rights over the communally held property, even if it is clear that over-use is exhausting the property, because she has no way of ensuring that all other members of the community will observe a similar restriction. So, she and the other nine people in her community might know (and care) that the fishing stock in their communal lake will be exhausted if more than 3,650 fish are taken from it in any year, and that if each of them therefore limits their catch to one fish per person per day they will all enjoy a perpetual supply of free fish. Nevertheless, there is no point in her observing this limit because she cannot impose it on the other nine people, and if any one of them exceeds the limit, the stock will be exhausted anyway. So she might as well (and in practice will) go out tomorrow and catch as many as she can. Thus, lakes and pastures are doomed to destruction by over-fishing and over-grazing unless saved by being reduced into private ownership,

---

[39] In the HL, counsel for Brackenbank was prepared to argue that, contrary to the view of the Jennings Committee, there was no such thing in English law as a proprietary stint. In the event the HL was unable to consider the argument because further last-minute research by counsel for Brackenbank revealed that the issue of the ownership of the fee simple in the Moor had already been adjudicated between the predecessors of the parties to this action and resolved in Brackenbank's favour (by a strong Court of Queen's Bench sitting *in banco* in 1867). The HL declined to depart from this earlier decision.

which alone provides the incentive to develop property without exhausting it. The obvious common-sense response to this—that surely the ten of them would get together and sort something out— is demonstrated by the economists to be unrealistic: transaction costs, freeloaders, and hold-outs all conspire to make it unlikely that agreements will be successfully concluded.[40]

The Burnhope Moor stint confounds the economic theorists in two ways. First, it provides a salutary reminder that what nearly annihilated communal ownership in England and Scotland was not the tragedy of the commons so much as the advance of the Enclosure movement. Common land was not exhausted by over-grazing: it was converted to private ownership by Private Acts of Parliament. The same truth has been demonstrated by the native land rights movements in Australia and elsewhere: communal land use, whether nomadic use of scarce resources in the Gove Peninsula,[41] or the cultivation of gardens in the Murray Islands,[42] continued virtually unchanged for centuries until disrupted by colonialism.

Secondly, the stint provides an illustration of how communal ownership must surely always work: by strict regulation. The judgments in the Court of Appeal decision in *Brackenbank* v. *Peart*[43] give extracts from an Enclosure Award made in this case in 1815 which very precisely prescribed the number and type of animal constituting a stint, laid out rules 'for preventing all Disputes as to what may be Deemed the Nature of a Stint . . . and of what the same shall consist' and established what appears to be a comprehensive and eminently workable self-regulatory system. In fact, all the evidence suggests that in this country, as in many others (a) there has always been an acute awareness of the common pool problem inherent in communal ownership and (b) it is invariably met by tight regulation of the communal use. The economists' communal property paradigm—the open access unregulated

---

[40] The classic account is G. Hardin, 'The Tragedy of the Commons' (1968) 162 *Science* 1243; of the many objections made to Hardin's thesis, see in particular R. Ellickson, 'Property in Land', n. 9 above, *passim*; G. G Stevenson, *Common Property Economics* (Cambridge, 1991); and C. J. Dahlman, *The Open-field System and Beyond: A Property Rights Analysis of an Economic Institution* (Cambridge, 1980). [41] *Milirrpum* v. *Nabalco Pty. Co.* (1971) 17 FLR 141.
[42] *Mabo* v. *Queensland (No. 2)* (1992) 175 C.L.R. 1.
[43] (1994) 67 P & CR 249.

common—simply does not exist.[44] Closer to the historical reality is the stint-type right, where the real problem is that the close regulation of use stultifies development and adaptation to changed circumstances.[45] If, however, the object is to conserve rather than to exploit a resource, communal property has rather a good record. Burnhope Moor survived as a sheep grazing resource *because* it was communal property, not in spite of it.

However, communal property has a much wider significance than this. First, there is now a growing scepticism about the desirability, or even viability, of a society wholly dominated by private property. Whilst private property might provide the most appropriate means of developing and exploiting some resources in some circumstances, a sophisticated society will also need to utilize other systems of property-holding to ensure that minority, community, and state needs are also taken into account.[46] Secondly, even on a private law level, in real life we organize ourselves into communities for all sorts of purposes apart from grazing sheep on moors, and we acquire and use resources in our group capacity. As long as we think only in private property terms, we have no satisfactory legal mechanisms for this group-holding of property. Private ownership does not provide a convincing analysis of property holding by unincorporated associations,[47] nor does it satisfactorily allocate control over property held for charitable

---

[44] R. C. Elickson, 'Property in Land', n. 9 above, surveys the extensive literature (historical and anthropological, as well as theoretical) on communal land holding systems that have existed all over the world throughout recorded history; he notes that 'as far as one can determine, no group in human history has ever treated cultivated crops as an open access resource that any passerby could harvest. A human group is as likely to use its hands for walking as it is to put its members' farm products up for grabs' (at 1399); see also his comment, at 1386, that even on an open access public beach, we hesitate to move a beach towel left marking someone's 'place'.

[45] Much the same can be said of the Australian land usages referred to in the previous para.

[46] R. C. Ellickson, 'Property in Land', n. 9 above, K. Gray, 'Property in Thin Air' (1991) 50 *CLJ* 252 and 'Equitable Property' (1994) 47 *Current Legal Problems* 157; W. N. R. Lucy and C. Mitchell, 'Replacing Private Property: The Case for Stewardship' [1996] *CLJ* 566.

[47] See R. W. Rideout, 'The Limited Liability of Unincorporated Associations' (1996) 49 *Current Legal Problems* 187 demonstrating the more startling implications of the private property analysis of unincorporated associations.

purposes,[48] nor does it provide a wholly adequate mechanism for dedicating resources to group purposes, whether using unincorporated association analysis or *Denley*-type purpose trusts.[49] The private property solutions to these group problems are all fundamentally unsatisfactory because they fail to recognize the reality of the group, the community, as the central focus. And in societies where communal land use patterns are still common, an analysis of them in purely private property terms is liable to lead to a denial of rights, as the High Court of Australia recognized in *Mabo* v. *Queensland* (*No. 2*).[50]

We do have collective communal interests in things, and if we try to analyse our collective property expectations solely in terms of individual rights there is a danger that the picture will be distorted. On a more practical level, failure to accept the communal property interest as a legal tool for use in such cases means that we fail to develop and refine it. Communal property interests would be very much more useful to us if we could devise ways of terminating, varying and developing them. We are never likely to do that if we keep them in a separate little box reserved for sheep grazers and Australian aborigines.

The Fall and Rise of Family Property

The community which is perhaps least regarded by property law is the family unit or household. Most people tend to organize themselves into family communities for the purposes of property holding. They regard their debts as their communal responsibility, and their income and capital assets as their communal assets. For the vast majority of people this was probably as true at the start of the century as it is now. The difference is in the pattern of rules that family communities adopt for self-government. Whereas at the start of the century the most likely pattern was a hierarchical structure with a male head as the decision-maker—the person who decided

---

[48] For the anomalous position of members of a charitable organization see J. Warburton, 'Charities, Members, Accountability and Control' (1997) 61 *Conv.* 106.

[49] *Re Denley's Trust Deed* [1969] 1 Ch. 373.

[50] (1992) 175 C.L.R. 1; the High Court rejected the private property approach adopted by Blackburn J in *Milirrpum* v. *Nabalco Pty. Co.* (1971) 17 FLR 141.

how family wealth should be allocated—it is now more likely that the family will be a looser confederation of people, perhaps with more complicated inter-relationships, with each member having some say in wealth allocation decisions. The male-headed hierarchical structure still exists, but is now just one of many possible patterns.

It is not easy to find the appropriate legal mechanisms to reflect these realities. The preoccupation of law reformers in the nineteenth century was to dismantle the old family property regime under which husbands acquired ownership or control over all their wives' assets on marriage. The law reformers were successful,[51] but the result was that at the start of this century family members were treated as autonomous individuals in property law terms. Each person had his or her own personal wealth, and dealings between family members with their personal wealth were governed by the same legal rules as those that governed dealings with strangers. Whilst this undoubtedly caused less positive harm than the regime it replaced, it was no better a reflection of the way society actually organized itself, and most of this century has been spent in trying to construct a property law regime that will respect the autonomy of individuals within a family whilst also recognizing that, because of the interdependence of family members, the family must to some extent be treated as a unit, rather than as a collection of discrete individuals.

So far, these efforts to come up with a new family property regime have had only limited success. On the plus side, matrimonial legislation enables the private wealth of spouses to be re-distributed between them on divorce or judicial separation.[52] Freedom to leave property outside the family by testamentary disposition is curtailed by the Inheritance (Provision for Family and Dependants) Act 1975, to the extent that spouses, ex-spouses, children, and other dependants can apply to the court to have reasonable financial provision made for them out of their estate. Some of the statutory

---

[51] See W. R. Cornish and G. de N. Clark, *Law and Society in England 1750–1950* (London, 1989), 401; the decisive events were the passing of the Married Women's Property Acts of 1882 and 1893. See also 327 below.

[52] Matrimonial Causes Act 1973 as amended by the Matrimonial and Family Proceedings Act 1984; see also s. 37 of the Matrimonial Proceedings and Property Act 1970 as to acquiring a share in real or personal property by making substantial contribution in money or money's worth to its improvement.

rights that residential tenants have against their landlords are, in effect, pooled between members of a family,[53] and on bankruptcy the law gives some (albeit very limited) recognition to the financial interdependence of families, principally by providing that (a) the bankrupt's exempt property, not available to creditors, includes 'such clothing, bedding, furniture, household equipment and provisions as are necessary for satisfying the basic domestic needs of the bankrupt *and his family*'[54] and (b) debts owed to a spouse rank for payment after those owed to any other unsecured creditor.[55]

However, on the minus side, the fact remains that despite creative efforts of the Court of Appeal in the 1960s and 1970s[56] and repeated Law Commission initiatives[57] we still do not have a doctrine of family assets, in the sense of a principle of law that members of a family have, by virtue of that status, a proprietary interest of some kind in assets designed or used for family purposes.

The only proprietary interests that can at present exist in assets that are used for family purposes are those that can exist in any other kind of property, and, in theory at least, the rules for

---

[53] See e.g. the Rent Act 1977, Sched. 1, conferring rights on members of the original tenant's family to claim a statutory tenancy by succession on death of a protected or statutory tenant (now however greatly curtailed by amendments made the Housing Act 1988); Housing Act 1988, s. 17(4) and Housing Act 1985, s. 87 conferring succession rights in respect of assured and secure tenancies; Matrimonial Homes Act 1983, s. 1 as amended (occupation by tenant's spouse treated as occupation by tenant, even if spouses separated); Leasehold Reform Act 1967, s. 7 (calculation of period tenant occupied as residence).

[54] Insolvency Act 1986, s. 283(2)(b) (emphasis added).

[55] Insolvency Act 1986, s. 329; there is no equivalent in corporate insolvency—debts owed to parent, subsidiary, or sibling companies are treated in the same way as debts owed to outsiders. In relation to individual bankrupts see also s. 310(2) (needs of the family to be taken into consideration in making an income payments order) and ss. 339–42 (wider powers to adjust transactions at an undervalue or preferring creditors where the recipient is an 'associate') of the 1986 Act, and also S. M. Cretney, 'Insolvency and Family Law', in H. Rajak (ed.), *Insolvency Law: Theory and Practice* (London, 1994), chap. 4.

[56] Brought to a close by the HL in *Gissing* v. *Gissing* [1971] AC 886.

[57] Chronicled in Law Commission Report, *Family Law: Matrimonial Property* (London, 1988), Law Com. No. 175 at paras. 3.3–3.6. The Law Commission put forward modified proposals in that Report, having decided not to recommend again the wholesale introduction of community of property largely because 'we see very little likelihood of any such complex scheme being brought into effect in the near future'; these modified recommendations were not implemented either.

ascertaining whether any particular member of a family has such an interest are precisely the same as those used as between strangers.[58]

In practice, of course, the courts have found it almost impossible to apply these rules in family situations. Private law demands that legal title in family assets be vested in one or another of the members of the family, or (in the case of interests in land) if in two or more of them then as trustees for themselves and/or others. The location of the beneficial interest then depends on application of trust principles. *Prima facie*, the beneficial interests follow the legal interest, so those members of the family who do not have legal title have no property interest in the asset unless there has been a declaration of trust in their favour. If there has been no declaration of trust, the most that the courts have been able to do is to develop the doctrines of resulting and constructive trusts up to a point where they can award beneficial interests in an asset to a family member who has either (a) made some financial contribution towards its acquisition cost (unless there is evidence that the contributor did not intend thereby to acquire an interest) or (b) acted to their detriment in some way, provided that there is sufficient evidence that the parties—i.e. the legal title holder and the person claiming an interest—positively agreed that the claimant should have an interest.[59]

There are enormous difficulties with this approach. The first is that it requires the courts to discover—whether by direct evidence or by inference[60]—what it was that each party actually intended

---

[58] With the exception of the presumption of advancement, now generally regarded as a relic of a past social era, whereby gratuitous transfers by husbands to wives or by fathers (or others *in loco parentis*) to children are presumed to be made by way of gift; the presumption, which is now easily rebutted, was described by Nourse LJ in *McGrath* v. *Wallis* [1995] 2 FLR 114 at 115 as 're-classified' ever since the HL decision in *Pettitt* v. *Pettitt* [1970] AC 777 'as a judicial instrument of last resort, its subordinate status comparable to that of the contra proferentum rule in the construction of deeds and contracts.'

[59] This brief summary inadequately conveys the indigestibly rich complexity of the law on this point, as will be apparent on reference to any of the excellent commentaries on it, most notably K. Gray, *Elements of Land Law*, 2nd edn. (London, 1993), 371–461 and *Hayton & Marshall's Commentary and Cases on the Law of Trusts and Equitable Doctrines* (London, 1996), (10th edn. by D. J. Hayton), 305–30 and 364–402.

[60] Imputation was ruled out by the HL in *Pettitt* v. *Pettitt* [1970] AC 777 and *Gissing* v. *Gissing* [1971] AC 887, although appears poised to return in the CA, albeit in a more limited role: *Midland Bank plc* v. *Cooke* [1995] 4 All ER 562, considered further 142 below.

from the time when the property was acquired onwards, and (at least in cases falling within (b) above) whether they had communicated these intentions to each other.[61] In most cases this can only be done by dredging through the whole of the family's past life together. As Waite J, as he then was, complained in *Hammond* v. *Mitchell*:[62]

The primary emphasis accorded by the law in cases of this kind to express discussions between the parties ('however imperfectly remembered and however imprecise their terms') means that the tenderest exchanges of a common law courtship may assume an unforeseen significance many years later when they are brought under equity's microscope and subjected to an analysis under which many thousands of pounds of value may be liable to turn on fine questions as to whether the relevant words were spoken in earnest or in dalliance and with or without representational intent. This requires that the express discussions to which the court's initial inquiries will be addressed should be pleaded in the greatest detail, both as to language and as to circumstance.[63]

This process, as he pointed out, is necessarily 'detailed, time-consuming and laborious', occupying in the case before him nineteen days of High Court time at a cost to the parties (one of whom was legally aided) of £125,000.[64] And this was a case of an unmarried couple whose relationship lasted for little more than ten years.

This is bad enough where the dispute is between the two family members in question. Where, as often happens, the dispute is between the person claiming an interest and an outsider who is a creditor of the legal title holder, the search for evidence borders on the farcical.[65]

---

[61] It is implicit in *Lloyds Bank plc* v. *Rosset* [1991] AC 107, the leading case on the constructive trust principle summarized in (b) above, and expressly confirmed by the CA in *Springette* v. *Defoe* (1992) 24 HLR 552, that two people cannot be said to have a common intention for these purposes if it is known that they never expressly communicated their intentions to each other, even if they both intend the same thing and assume their intention is shared by the other. Family members who talk to each other are thus favoured over those who fail to discuss things openly.

[62] [1991] 1 WLR 1127.

[63] *Ibid.*, at 1139; the quotation he gives is from the classic statement of principle given by Lord Bridge in *Lloyd's Bank plc* v. *Rosset*, referred to in n. 61 above.

[64] *Ibid.*, at 1130.

[65] See e.g. the extract from the transcript of the hearing at first instance in *Midland Bank plc* v. *Cooke*, quoted by Waite LJ in the decision of the CA reported

A second and worse difficulty with this approach is that it works least well in the hardest cases—for example, the long-standing partner who has given up her whole life to looking after the legal title holder and their children, and is now facing eviction from her home by her younger and more glamorous successor, or the person who gave up, or never took up, paid employment in order to act as unpaid carer and housekeeper for a sick or infirm relative or partner. These people are least likely to be able to make a successful claim to a property interest in the house they have lived in and in the goods in the household they have run: because they are not wage earners they are unlikely to have made any financial contribution to the cost of acquiring the assets; the fact that the assets were not put in their names suggests that they were not regarded as the dominant partner in their relationship with the legal title holder, which makes it even less likely that there was a specific point at which there were clear and conclusive discussions about their rights in the family assets; and, of course, the longer the relationship, the less likely it is that there will now exist adequate evidence from which the courts can draw an inference that such discussions did take place. In these cases the temptation is there for the courts to cross over the forbidden line between inferring an agreement they suspect the parties never actually articulated— which is legitimate—to imputing an agreement, regardless of whether such an agreement ever in fact existed. Once the courts do that, however, they short-circuit the whole process, and in effect create the doctrine of family assets that Parliament has so far refused to create, as the House of Lords acknowledged in *Pettitt* v. *Pettitt*[66] and *Gissing* v. *Gissing*.[67] Nevertheless, the courts are continually being nudged up to and over the line—at present, with the decision in *Midland Bank* v. *Cooke*,[68] arguably going over it.

at [1995] 4 All ER 565, where counsel for Mrs Cooke is seeking to elicit from Mr Cooke precisely what was in the minds of his parents when they provided the money for a deposit on the newly wedded couple's house, her parents having paid for the wedding and reception.

[66] [1970] AC 777.   [67] [1971] AC 887.

[68] [1995] 4 All ER 565; the wife was awarded a half share in the beneficial interest in the house, even though she had made no actual financial contribution towards the cost of its acquisition (the deposit paid by her husband's parents was treated as a gift to them both, thus allowing the court to treat half of it as effectively contributed by her) and even though the evidence failed to establish an agreement between them as to her share, if any.

So, the price for refusing to accept the reality of family interests in family resources has been a law of an unacceptable uncertainty and complexity. It frequently frustrates the legitimate expectations of those whose contributions to the family community are non-financial, and what is worse is that it does so unpredictably. Consequently, we now have all the disadvantages of the increased diversity of interest that would follow from the adoption of a doctrine of family assets—the present uncertainty as to who has what interests makes the asset less marketable and less desirable as security, in much the same way as if a complex but known pattern of interests existed—with none of the advantages.

Consideration so far has been given primarily to interests in land, but in fact the situation is as bad, if not worse, in relation to chattels. In the case of land there is usually some historic reason why the legal title was vested in one member of the family rather than another, even if no-one can quite remember what it was. But in the case of chattels it is not only more difficult to locate where the legal title is, it is also probably quite fortuitous that it ended up held by one person rather than another—it is largely a question of who does the shopping.[69] It is also rather difficult to make an effective transfer of chattels between members of a family, because of the legal rule that an effective gift of chattels requires either a deed or an intentional delivery of possession from the donor to the donee—an operation not easy to perform successfully when both parties are living in the same house, as the cases testify.[70] As so often happens in the case of chattels, the costs of litigating these issues is usually prohibitive, but that does not make the problems any less real. In *Hammond* v. *Mitchell*[71] Waite J warned all warring

---

[69] And, of course, on whose money is spent: for the uncertainties arising out of payments by one spouse out of a joint bank account see e.g. *Re Bishop* [1965] Ch. 450 (*prima facie* rule that even where joint account belongs to both spouses jointly, chattels bought by one spouse for that spouse's own benefit belong to that spouse), *Heseltine* v. *Heseltine* [1971] 1 WLR 342 (presumption that spouses' joint account belongs to them jointly rebutted by presumption of resulting trust where wife sole contributor); and *Re Figgis* [1969] 1 Ch. 123 (joint account originally opened by one spouse for convenience only, and therefore belonging solely to that spouse, may nevertheless become jointly owned beneficially as the intentions of the parties change); see also Married Women's Property Act 1964 s. 1 (unless agreed otherwise, property bought by wife out of housekeeping allowance provided by husband belongs to husband and wife in equal shares).

[70] e.g., *Re Cole* [1964] Ch. 175.   [71] [1991] 1 WLR 1127.

families that they must accept that the law in its present state is simply not able to deal with disputes about chattels between family members who are not married to each other:

I would wish to express my support for the recent comments in the Chancery Division of Millett J. in *Windeler* v. *Whitehall* [1990] 1 F.C.R. 268, 279, to the effect that sorting out the ownership of chattels bought by parties who have been living together, is something that the parties should be expected to achieve by agreement for themselves without the necessity of a court hearing. I would add, in the light of experience in the present case, that agreement is strongly preferable to crude acts of self-help by removing chattels from the home on the break-up of the association . . . While no one suggests that English law recognises or should develop a doctrine of community of property regarding the household goods of those who settle for an unmarried union, the parties must expect the court in ordinary cases to adopt a robust allegiance to the maxim that 'equality is equity', if only in the interests of fulfilling the equally salutary maxim 'sit finis litis.' If it is really necessary to bring issues of disputed ownership of household chattels to adjudication, the proper way of doing it is a claim for a declaration or inquiry as to the beneficial interest, supported with appropriate affidavit evidence, on lines similar to the procedure for resolving disputes under section 17 of the Married Women's Property Act 1882. It is not normally appropriate to proceed by actions framed in conversion or detinue.

In the case of both land and chattels, there seems little prospect of any improvement in the situation within the foreseeable future. If anything, the current political concern for family values makes the prospect of a legislative solution even less likely. The problem is that the family unit now comes in a variety of different patterns, only one of which is the nuclear family of married couple with children and no other dependants, and yet any reform that is seen to confer family-type benefits outside the magic circle of the married nuclear family is, in the current climate, very likely to be rejected as subversive of the family.[72] But even if there was the political will to extend family property rights outside the nuclear married family, we would still need to give some serious thought to what we think the family is. It is not just a question of treating those who live together as if married as if they *were* married, whether opposite sex or same sex. The more difficult question is how to deal

---

[72] See e.g. the abortive attempts to extend s. 17 of the 1882 Act to cohabiting couples, noted at 347 below.

with extended families, particularly those which are not pivotal on a single couple, whether because for cultural reasons different generations and adult siblings and cousins regard themselves as all forming part of a single unit or a series of interconnected units, or because of family breakdown followed by the creation of new relationships.[73]

However, there is another aspect of family property relevant here, where the transition from rationalization at the start of the century to a revived diversity has been more successful. By the start of this century the transformation of the strict family settlement from a land-holding device into a wealth-holding device had already begun.[74] The process was completed by the 1925 property legislation, which also established the trust for sale as the only other permissible land-holding device that could be used where ownership was fragmented between successive generations and/or shared between concurrent interest holders. The end result was that, not only did we not have a doctrine of family assets, but when families as a matter of choice tried to ensure that their family property was kept under the control of the family, their choice was frustrated by legislation, which had determined that family property (with one minor exception, noted below[75]) should be as freely tradable as any other commodity.

Taken on its own terms, the legislative scheme was remarkably successful. Legal ownership was concentrated in the hands of one person—in the case of a Settled Land Act settlement the tenant for life, who would usually be the current head of the family,[76] and in the case of a trust for sale, two or more trustees—who had full

---

[73] In 1995 the Law Commission announced that it was starting work on a project on the property rights of home-sharers: (1995) Law Com. No. 232, para. 2.78; they received the results of a specially commissioned research project at the end of 1995 (Law Commission, *Thirtieth Annual Report* (1995) Law Com. No. 239, para. 6.12) and a consultation paper is promised for 1997 (*Thirty-first Annual Report* (1996) Law Com. No. 244, para. 5.8).

[74] For excellent analyses see G. R. Rubin and D. Sugarman (eds.), *Law, Economy & Society 1750–1914: Essays in the History of English Law* (Abingdon, 1984), especially at 23–43 (G. R. Rubin and D. Sugarman, 'Towards a New History of Law and Material Society in England, 1750–1914'), 124–67 (M. R. Chesterman, 'Family Settlements on Trust: Landowners and the Rising Bourgeoisie'), 168–91 (E. Spring, 'The Family, Strict Settlements and Historians'), and 209–39 (B. English, 'The Family Settlements of the Sykes of Sledmere, 1792–1900').

[75] See text to n. 78 below.   [76] Settled Land Act 1925, s. 19.

powers to dispose of the land free from the property interests of other family members.[77] As against outsiders, the legal owners were put in the same position as absolute private owners, which meant that outsiders could deal in family assets just as easily and just as safely as in any other commodity. The interests of the other interest-holders were safeguarded by requiring the proceeds of dealings with outsiders to be paid to trustees, and to be held by the trustees on the same trusts as those on which the family assets were held: in other words, the beneficiaries' interests in the land or other asset were simply transferred to the wealth now representing it. In fact, in the trust for sale, commoditization was taken to its extreme by putting the trustees under a *prima facie* duty of immediate sale, with only a power to postpone sale, and by the doctrine of conversion which treated the beneficiaries as having, even before sale had taken place, an interest only in the notional proceeds of sale rather than in the as yet unsold land itself.

This system has broken down over the last few decades for reasons whch probably could not have been foreseen in 1925. It was in fact recognized in the 1925 legislation that family property is not always a commodity—the legislation recognized that there are circumstances in which an interest-holder's interest in a family asset is not adequately represented by its monetary value in the market place. The 1925 legislation drew a distinction between family assets that were just commodities, and should therefore be as freely alienable as any other commodity, and those which were not, where it was legitimate for restrictions to be imposed on dealings with the assets. However, the only family assets that were put in the non-commodity category were the principal mansion house and heirlooms in settled land[78]—not a particularly significant category today. Whether or not the legislators were right at that time to categorize all other interests as simply interests in wealth, the rise of owner occupation quickly made the categorization wholly inappropriate. Most of the second half of this century has been spent in trying to safeguard the interests of beneficiaries under a trust for sale who are, and wish to remain, in occupation of the co-owned

---

[77] By s. 106(1) of the Settled Land Act 1925 any purported restriction of the tenant for life's power of sale was void; for the overreaching effect of a sale under the Settled Land Act 1925 or by trustees for sale see Law of Property Act 1925, ss. 2 and 27.   [78] Settled Land Act 1925, ss. 65 and 67.

property—the paradigm of the person whose interest is valued as thing rather than as wealth. The protection that the courts have been able to provide within the confines of the 1925 legislative scheme has inevitably been bought at the price of some uncertainty in the law, and some weakening of the land registration system.[79]

However, finally this year, in implementation of recommendations of the Law Commission,[80] the Trusts of Land and Appointment of Trustees Act 1996 has, in effect, formally reversed the 1925 policy of treating family property as a commodity.[81] The Settled Land Act settlement and the doctrine of conversion are abolished[82] and trustees of land are no longer under an overriding duty to sell the land. Instead there is a new trust of land usable in all cases where there are successive and/or concurrent interests in land. And in this new trust of land it is for the settlor and the beneficiaries to decide whether the trust property is wealth (in other words, simply an investment) or thing (somewhere to work or live). In particular, beneficiaries with an interest in possession will thereby have a right to occupy the land if it is available for occupation, and the purposes of the trust include making the land available for occupation.[83] In other words, it will be perfectly possible to recreate by express provision in the trust deed an old strict trust for sale, if that is what the parties want, but it will equally be possible to create the type of trust where the primary purpose is occupation, and the rights of occupation are safeguarded. So the Act will actually increase the range of family interests that are recognized and protected by the law, whilst at the same time simplifying the law by removing what had become anachronistic technicalities.[84]

---

[79] For a detailed account of the central cases, *Williams and Glyn's Bank Ltd.* v. *Boland* [1981] AC 487 and *City of London Building Society* v. *Flegg* [1988] AC 54, and their effect on the land registration system, see K. Gray, *Elements of Land Law*, n. 59 above, at 541–83 and 197–229; Law Commission, *Property Law: Third Report on Land Registration* (1987), Law Com. No. 158; and *Emmet on Title*, 19th edn. by J. T. Farrand and A. C. Clarke (London, 1997), paras. 5.130–5.133.

[80] Primarily contained in Law Com. No. 181 (1989) but including also some recommendations as to overreaching and bare trusts made in Law Com. No. 188 (1989).

[81] The Act was brought into force on 1 Jan. 1997 by SI 1997/2974.

[82] Although, as pointed out by P. H. Pettit, 'Demise of Trusts for Sale and the Doctrine of Conversion?' (1997) 113 *LQR* 207, the references to abolition of the doctrine of conversion in the Preamble to the Act and in the side-note to s. 3 promise more than the Act delivers.

[83] Trusts of Land and Appointment of Trustees Act 1996, ss. 12 and 13.

[84] For full details see *Emmet on Title*, n. 97 above, ch. 22.

Expanding the Range of Property Interests in Goods

Until relatively recently, almost no-one studied, practised, or wrote about the law relating to property in goods, as opposed to property in land or in intangible things. The buying and selling of goods as commodities was traditionally studied as part of commercial law but, again until fairly recently, very little consideration was given— in commercial law or elsewhere—to the other things one regularly does with goods, like keeping them, sharing them, using them as security, mixing them with other things, and allowing others to use them.[85] The fact that the only usable word we have for goods is 'goods', is a tell-tale sign: 'goods' has no acceptable singular form— 'goods' are always plural, interchangeable commodities, always things as wealth, never things as thing.

This traditional legal distaste for the law of goods has often been ascribed to the fact that goods, except when traded *en masse*, are relatively low in value compared to land and intangibles. The fact that there is a long-established and sophisticated law of ships would tend to bear this out. However, a more accurate way of putting it might be to say that, except where goods are treated as commodities, the law of goods is poor people's law. Goods probably do form only a small proportion of the wealth of rich people, who tend to have land and money and investments as well: you have to be quite poor to have the major proportion of your wealth in goods.

However, for whatever reason, until the middle of this century the only 'modern' law relating to property in goods was the Sale of Goods Act 1893. The great strength of the 1893 Act was that it set out relatively simple, clear and logical rules to govern the millions of simple, straightforward sales of things that, then as now, take place every day. As one commentator has remarked: '[i]f the economically active part of the community made but three sales or

---

[85] As far as academic attention is concerned, the position has changed dramatically in the last few years: see e.g. A. P. Bell, *Modern Law of Personal Property in England and Ireland* (London, 1989), N. E. Palmer, *Bailment*, 2nd edn. (London, 1991); M. Bridge, 'Form, Substance and Innovation in Personal Property Security Law' [1992] *JBL* 1; N. E. Palmer and E. McKendrick (eds.), *Interests in Goods* (London, 1993); S. Worthington, *Proprietary Interests in Commercial Transactions* (Oxford, 1996), and other works cited here.

purchases a day, the daily number of transactions governed by the legislation would be of the order of 100 million.'[86] What the 1893 Act did not do, and did not set out to do, was to deal with the less straightforward case. In particular, it said nothing about the *kinds* of property interest that can exist in relation to goods, a point that will be considered in more detail below. Also, it covered no dealings in goods apart from sales,[87] leaving commercially important transactions such as bailments and security transactions largely covered by the common law. And finally, it drew no distinction between different kinds of goods (apart from to distinguish ascertained from unascertained goods). In so far as sale is concerned, the Act treats a pet cat or a work of art in precisely the same way as a lump of concrete, a point that will be returned to very briefly at the end.

However, the only one of these problems to be considered here is the limited range of property interests recognized. The main problem is that English law has shown a marked reluctance to allow a full range of property interests in goods to develop. This reluctance is typified by the repeated endorsement by the courts of the rule, originating in a dictum of Lord Atkin in *Re Wait*,[88] that a person with a contractual right to buy goods has no property interest in those goods—a rule that sets goods apart from all other types of property, and sits uneasily with the principles, applicable to goods as to all other property, on which equitable mortgages and floating charges work. In Lord Atkin's view, it was in the interests of commerce that the Sale of Goods Act 1893 should be treated as a comprehensive code governing all legal and equitable proprietary rights arising on a sale of goods:

The total sum of legal relations (meaning by the word 'legal' existing in equity as well as in common law) arising out of the contract for the sale of goods may well be regarded as defined by the Code. It would have been futile in a code intended for commercial men to have created an elaborate structure of rules dealing with rights at law, if at the same time it was intended to leave, subsisting with the legal rights, equitable rights

---

[86] M. Blair, *Sale of Goods Act 1979* (London, 1980), at 1.

[87] By s. 61, the Act specifically did not apply to transactions in the form of a contract for sale which are intended to operate by way of security.

[88] [1927] 1 Ch. 606.

inconsistent with, more extensive, and coming into existence earlier than the rights so carefully set out in the various sections of the Code.[89]

Consequently, since the 1893 Act conferred no such rights on contractual purchasers, no such rights could exist. In relation to sales of a type not envisaged by the Act—most notably where the purchaser, whether because the goods are unique or for whatever other reason, prizes the goods to be purchased as thing rather than as wealth—this is an unfortunate and unnecessary impoverishment of the property rights system.[90] But even in the case of commodity sales for which the 1893 Act was clearly intended, it has become apparent that, in some contexts, a more complex split of property interests between buyer and seller is commercially desirable. So, for example, sellers supplying materials to manufacturers on standard credit terms have had to devise elaborate reservation of title provisions to ensure that they retain some proprietary interest in the goods supplied as security for any amounts left unpaid by the buyer on the buyer's insolvency.[91] And similarly, after sustained criticism of the then existing state of the law from judges, the Law Commission, and academic commentators, the Sale of Goods legislation has now been amended to give contractual purchasers of unascertained goods forming part of an identified bulk (for

[89] N. 88 above, at 635–6; Lord Atkin's dictum was approved by Lord Brandon in *Leigh and Sillavan Ltd.* v. *Aliakmon Ltd. (The Aliakmon)* (1986) 1 AC 785, and subsequently by the PC in *Re Goldcorp Exchange* [1995] 1 AC 74: the rule has since been stated to be apparently 'settled beyond doubt': P. S. Atiyah, *The Sale of Goods*, 9th edn. by J. Adams (London, 1995), 299m and see also R. M. Goode, *Commercial Law*, 2nd edn, (London, 1995), 32 and 224 to similar effect.

[90] A view that has some support in other jurisdictions: see e.g. Hammond J in the High Court of Auckland in *Butler* v. *Countrywide Finance Ltd.* [1993] 3 NZLR 623 at 636, emphasizing the need, in this context, for the further development of 'the notion of commercial uniqueness' to recognize that a contractual purchaser might have a 'thing' interest in goods rather than a 'wealth' interest not only on account of the æsthetic quality of the goods in question, but because they are 'in some sense essential to [his] business and for which the procurement of substitutes would cause disruption to that business for some reason or other. Severe delay would be one such reason; lack of expertise would be another; or high transaction costs.' For a useful review of the Commonwealth authorities see N. E. Palmer, n. 85 above, 1666–7.

[91] See R. M. Goode, *Proprietary Rights and Insolvency in Sales Transactions*, 2nd edn. (London, 1989), chap. V for a definitive analysis of the present state of the law on reservation of title provisions and its development since they were first upheld by the CA in *Aluminium Industrie Vaassen BV* v. *Romalpa Aluminium Ltd.* [1976] 1 WLR 676, a decision described by Prof. Goode at 84 as having 'a greater impact on commercial law than almost any other case decided this century'.

example, the person who contracts to buy ten sheep out of the seller's flock) co-ownership interests in the bulk pending the passing of title in the particular goods to be purchased.[92]

There is a similar reluctance by English lawyers to recognize that when ownership and possession of goods are split, there can be something proprietary about the relationship between owner, possessor, and goods. The inclination of English lawyers has been to analyse problems arising out of ownership/possession splits in goods in terms of contract and obligation rather than in terms of property.[93] This is partly because of the failure of property law to develop a remedy for the owner of a thing who wishes to claim it back from the person in possession of it, leaving her at the mercy of the law of tort.[94] In addition, however, there has been considerable disagreement as to the proper ambit of the over-arching concept of bailment.

The argument that bailment does gives rise to a form of property, in at least some sense,[95] is however now gaining ground. In *Bristol Airport plc* v. *Powdrill*[96] the Court of Appeal held that the interest of a lessee of an aircraft under a chattel lease constituted 'property' for the purposes of section 436 of the Insolvency Act 1986. As Browne-Wilkinson VC, as he then was, pointed out:

It is true that, to date, concepts of concurrent interests in personal property have not been developed in the same way as they over the centuries in relation to real property. But modern commercial methods have introduced chattel leasing. . . . Although a chattel lease is a contract, it does not follow that no property interest is created in the chattel.[97]

Further, in *The Pioneer Container*[98] the Privy Council confirmed that the true basis of the bailment relationship is a voluntary taking

---

[92] Ss. 20A and 20B of the Sale of Goods Act 1979, as added by the Sale of Goods (Amendment) Act 1995, implementing the Law Commission Report, *Sale of Goods Forming Part of a Bulk* (Law Com. No. 215, 1993). For criticisms of the previous law see P. S. Atiyah, n. 89 above, 293–7 and R. M. Goode, n. 91 above, 21–6.

[93] See S. J. Stoljar (1955) 7 *Res Judicatae* 160; W. J. Swadling, 'The Proprietary Effect of a Hire of Goods', in Palmer and McKendrick's *Interests in Goods*, n. 85 above, chap. 1.

[94] See T. Weir, *A Casebook on Tort*, 7th edn. (London, 1992), 473–8, prefaced by his observation that 'If England had a rational system of law there would be no need for a special section on torts to chattels and this chapter could be entirely suppressed'.

[95] Most persuasively put by N. E. Palmer, n. 85 above, 81–99 and F. H. Lawson and B. Rudden, *The Law of Property*, 2nd edn. (Oxford, 1982), 81–2, 96–7 and 147–150.   [96] [1990] 1 Ch. 744.   [97] *Ibid.*, at 755.

[98] [1994] 2 AC 324.

of another's goods into one's possession, rather than a consensual transfer of possession.[99] Consequently, there is a direct bailment relationship between a bailor and a sub-bailee who has taken the bailor's goods into his possession without the knowledge of the bailor, even though there is necessarily no contractual nexus between them. This lends strong support to the argument that the relationship is founded in property, arising out of the fact of possession, rather than in contract, although as the decision in *The Pioneer Container* itself demonstrates, this still leaves considerable scope for development in the analysis of the attributes of the relationship.[100]

As a concluding comment, however, it is worth noting that the greatest potential for development by diversification in property law now lies in the attempts to construct new philosophical and legal frameworks for two categories of thing whose social and commercial importance is only now beginning to be appreciated—human tissue (and the intellectual property derived from it), and cultural property. As far as human tissue is concerned, at the start of this century the courts were reluctant to recognize that property rights might exist in human bodies, live or dead, or in parts or products of them,[101] and viewed the treatment of human bodies as articles of commerce with revulsion.[102] However, because of scientific advances the commercial potential of human tissue can no longer be ignored, and it is increasingly apparent that the legal and moral issues arising out of the exploitation of this potential are complex and difficult to resolve within our existing legal frame-

---

[99] N. 98 above, at 341–2, preferring the views expressed in N. E. Palmer, n. 85 above, 31 ff. and A. Tay, 'The Essence of Bailment: Contract, Agreement or Possession?' (1966) 5 *Sydney Law Review* 239, to that put by A. Bell, *Modern Law of Personal Property in England and Wales*, n. 85 above, 88–9.

[100] For detailed consideration of the uncertainties in the law in a different but equally specialized type of bailment relationship see N. E. Palmer, 'Art Loans' [1995] *University of British Columbia Law Review* 287.

[101] For a review of the English cases at this period see P. Matthews (1983) 36 *Current Legal Problems* 193 and R. Magnusson, 'Proprietary Rights in Human Tissue' in *Palmer and McKendrick's Interests in Goods*, n. 85 above, 237.

[102] See e.g. the wide-ranging analysis of the judges in the High Court of Australia in *Doodeward* v. *Spence* (1908) 6 CLR 406, where an exhibitor of a preserved two-headed human fœtus was nevertheless held entitled to possession of it as against the police officer who had confiscated it when the exhibitor was prosecuted for indecent exhibition.

work.[103] As for cultural property, at the start of the century no English lawyer would have understood what was meant by the term,[104] and it is doubtful whether many would have recognized the concept it embodies (that articles of artistic, historical, or other cultural significance may require special treatment in law).[105] Now, however, the increased importance of the art market, and perhaps also a heightened sensitivity towards the cultural sensibilities of racial and ethnic groups, have prompted legal initiatives at a national and international level,[106] and an ever-expanding legal literature on the wide variety of issues raised.[107] Whilst it remains to be seen how these two expanding areas will be accommodated within our existing property structures, it can be predicted with reasonable confidence that something very much more sophisticated than conventional sale of goods law will emerge.

---

[103] See the decision of the Sup. Ct. of California in *Moore* v. *Regents of the University of California* 793 P 2d 479 (1990) for the classic contemporary analysis of the issues; also S. R. Munzer, 'Kant and Property Rights in Body Parts' (1993) VI *Canadian Journal of Law and Jurisprudence* 319.

[104] It was reportedly first used in the 1954 Hague Convention for the Protection of Cultural Property in the Event of Armed Conflict: see L. P. Prott and P. J. O'Keefe, ' "Cultural Heritage" or "Cultural Property"?' (1992) 1 *IJCP* 307, where the writers advocate its replacement by the term 'cultural heritage'.

[105] The ancient law of treasure trove, finally abolished by the Treasure Act 1996, was concerned more with claiming buried hoards for the Crown than with securing the preservation of culturally important objects: compare the objects covered by, and the general approach of, the 1996 Act (for which see further the Department of National Heritage *Portable Antiquities: A Discussion Document*, Feb. 1996 and 'Response from The Standing Conference on Portable Antiquities', published in (1996) 1 *Art Antiquities and Law* 179, and N. E. Palmer, 'Treasure Trove and Title to Discovered Antiquities' in Palmer and McKendrick's *Interests in Goods*, n. 85 above, 305).

[106] See e.g. the Unidroit Convention on Stolen or Illegally Exported Cultural Objects 1995 (discussed by P. Jenkins in (1996) 1 *Art Antiquity and Law* 163); the ICMOS Charter for the Protection and Management of the Underwater Cultural Heritage (5 Feb. 1995); and the Department of National Heritage Discussion Paper DNH 51/96, 1 Mar. 1996, *Should Works by Living Artists be Subject to Export Controls?*, also set out in (1996) 1 *Art Antiquity and Law* 197 and 191.

[107] For an overview see N. E. Palmer, 'Recovering Stolen Art' (1994) 47 *Current Legal Problems* 215; for a demonstration of the breadth of the issues, and the interdisciplinary approach required, reference can be made to the contents of the two specialized journals started under the general editorship of Professor Palmer, the *International Journal of Cultural Property*, and *Art Antiquity and Law*.

UNDERSTANDING CIVIL JUSTICE

Hazel Genn

Introduction

This chapter focuses on the need to achieve a better empirical understanding of civil justice and to conduct debates about civil justice policy within a broader theoretical framework that addresses the social functions of law and the role and responsibility of the state in civil justice. The discussion draws on socio-legal research in the civil justice field to explore questions about behaviour in and around the civil law and to consider what the system delivers in practice. Against this background recent policy trends in the civil justice field are considered and the contemporary enthusiasm for private dispute resolution explored. The chapter concludes by suggesting that in developing a vision of the civil justice system of the future, there is a need to articulate what and whom the civil justice system is for in a way that takes into account the interests of citizens in having access to public dispute resolution forums with coercive powers and the value of the civil justice system to the social structure.

This discussion is timely. Concern about the 'failure' of the civil justice system is everywhere. It is argued that the courts are too slow, too expensive, too complicated, and too adversarial to provide litigants with what they want. As a result of an apparent consensus about these matters we stand at the end of the twentieth century on the threshold of substantial changes in the civil justice system. The Master of the Rolls, Lord Woolf, has recently concluded a comprehensive review of civil justice procedure. There are proposals for radical changes to the delivery of legal aid and the imposition of budgetary constraints. The Lord Chancellor's Department appears to be committed to policies which involve making litigants bear more of the costs of court services,[1] control of what lawyers can charge, and encouraging a shift away from the courts and towards the cluster of private activities that come under the umbrella of 'Alternative Dispute Resolution'. Perhaps for the first time, policy-makers are looking strategically at the civil justice system. They are becoming less reactive and seeking to exert greater influence over the volume and type of cases that come to court.[2]

Some of the proposals currently being debated can be viewed as the continuation of policies that have been evident since the nineteenth century, while others reflect a more contemporary trend—the contracting-out of the core functions of the State as we have known them in the post-war period. The new role envisaged for the State involves the regulation of markets rather than the direct provision of services.

Arguments about change to litigation procedures and government concerns about the resources devoted to the civil courts have a tendency to be conducted outside any wider context. The framework within which such debates should be set comprises theories about the social function of law, and about the function of the civil justice system as the means by which the law is mobilized by the citizen. Such theories, were they to be considered by policy-makers, would not necessarily help in choosing, for example, between block-contracts or other means of delivering legal aid. They might not determine exactly how much should be charged for court fees. However, without a sense of what the civil justice system is for, we run the risk of adopting short-term presumed solutions while creating new problems and possibly jettisoning aspects of the system that are valuable in social terms.

In the context of current policy developments then, it is important to consider the following questions: what and whom is the civil justice system for? What social functions does it serve?

---

[1] The recent successful challenge to this policy in the High Court is unlikely to change the basic thrust of the policy: *R. v. Lord Chancellor, ex p. Witham* [1997] 2 All E.R. 779.

[2] The basic principles were amplified in a speech given by the Lord Chancellor at All Souls, Oxford, in June 1996 entitled 'Civil Justice: Choice and Responsibility'. The 'twin pillars of policy' were described first as the removal of restrictive practices and the development of alternatives to lawyers and courts; and, secondly, increasing information about alternatives to courts, making costs more predictable, court fees more closely related to the cost of the service, and limiting subsidy by the taxpayer to those instances where there is a 'clear social policy objective'.

Why does the state accept responsibility for providing the means of adjudicating civil disputes and rights claims? It is important to consider some of these fundamental issues even if we do not reach any particular conclusion. We need to lift our eyes occasionally from our preoccupation with policy detail, to gaze on the horizon in order to check in which direction we are moving.

There are proper and important questions to be asked about the future role and interest of the state in protecting rights, resolving disputes, and channelling conflict. However, our ability to engage in such discussions is limited because we lack a convincing description of what the civil justice system *is* doing, and more importantly we lack any normative arguments about what the civil justice system *should be* doing. In recent debates about the 'crisis' in civil justice Lord Woolf has argued repeatedly that the civil justice system is an anachronistic legacy of the nineteenth century; its traditions, procedures, and protection of vested interests are not suited to the late twentieth century, let alone the next millennium. This conclusion may be correct and we may be moving into a transitional period during which we substantially reconsider what the appropriate civil justice system of the future might be. Unfortunately, although there may be some agreement about what we do not want from the civil justice system, there does not seem to be any clear articulation of what we do want—other than for things to be easier and cost less. As I will argue later, however, it is not even clear that we want that. We may think we want access to the courts to be easy and cheap, but do we want it to be so easy and so cheap that litigation becomes a national past-time? If we are not sure what we want—in the broadest sense—from our civil justice system, how can we decide what the appropriate policies or long-term strategy should be?

It is arguable that there is currently no coherent modern vision of the ideal civil justice system. The somewhat contradictory vision of the Lord Chancellor's Department and the judiciary is for the courts to be simpler, cheaper, and more accessible, but at the same time to play a much reduced role in the resolution of civil claims and disputes. The vision of the legal profession is to be left alone to make a living. The vision of pressure groups for the poor often seems to go little further than the objective of maintaining legal aid at current levels. The vision of pressure groups for commercial interests is a world in which law and lawyers could be ignored, but if resort must be had to the courts it should cost as little as possible and be over with quickly, so that business can be got on with and relationships preserved.

The vision of the middle class, as represented by those who presume to speak for them (since there is no obvious pressure group to speak for them), is apparently a world in which access to the courts is simple and cheap, and in which lawyers charge less than plumbers for their services and secure a positive outcome in no longer than it takes to repair a central heating system.[3]

Why, then, do we have no comprehensive understanding of the civil justice system of the present, and no vision of a civil justice system of the future? I would suggest that the difficulty of achieving an understanding of civil justice arises from three factors: an historic lack of interest about how the civil justice system operates; the scope and variety within the civil justice field; and the difficulty of disentangling cause and effect in civil justice behaviour and policy.

Lack of Interest in the Civil Justice System

Civil justice, by comparison with criminal justice, has attracted relatively little interest or attention either by scholars or policy-makers which leaves us with a field that is under-researched and under-theorized. Black-letter scholars have displayed only a peripheral interest in how the law operates in practice, and even less in theoretical questions about what law is for and its relationship, at the broadest level, with society. Civil procedure has never been regarded as a respectable academic subject in English law schools, and the institutions and processes of the legal system, if taught at all, are taught to impatient first years who want to get on and do some real law, like crime. Even socio-legal researchers—who are interested in asking questions about what law is for and how it is used—have found the criminal justice system a more fascinating

---

[3] Even socio-legal researchers who have explored the system empirically have sometimes been criticized for unquestioningly adopting the agenda and rhetoric of policy-makers, and for conducting research with only the limited objective of discovering how the system could all work better within its own terms, rather than challenging more fundamental assumptions and offering an alternative agenda. Cf. Austin Sarat and Susan Silbey, 'The Pull of the Policy Audience' (1988) 10 *Law and Policy* 85.

site for their enquiries. Criminal justice may be easier to comprehend, it is more dramatic, and politically it is more sexy.

There are few votes in civil justice and it therefore does not feature prominently on the agenda of either of the main political parties. An important side-effect of this is that the kind of statistical information that would help us to understand behaviour in relation to the civil courts has never been collected on a national or even a local basis. Despite any possible limitations, the annual statistics published by the Home Office provide the raw material with which analysts can describe and seek to explain patterns and trends in the criminal justice system. Regular crime surveys carried out by the Home Office tell us about victimization rates, reporting behaviour, exposure to risk of crime. We know something about recidivism rates, and we know about sentencing behaviour.[4] By comparison, when the Woolf Inquiry team were carrying out their review of civil justice, the most basic descriptive information was unavailable and currently remains unavailable. Apparently simple questions such as who is using the courts, for what kinds of cases, with what value, at what cost, and with what rate of success are currently unanswerable.[5]

This relative lack of knowledge and enthusiasm for the civil justice field is important and reflects a wider indifference at the political and social level. Representations of law in popular culture focus almost exclusively on the drama of criminal law. For many people the law *is* the criminal law. Ordinary people do not routinely carry a distinction in their head. But lack of interest may also be a direct result of the second problem, which is that of scope.

Scope of the Civil Justice System

A fundamental problem that has dogged theorizing in the civil justice area is the sheer complexity of the task. Theorizing about

---

[4] Examples of published series are: Home Office Statistical Bulletins, *The Criminal Justice System in England and Wales* (Digest 2); Annual Reports from Crown Prosecution Service; Report of Chief Inspector of Constabulary; British Crime Surveys (1982, 1984, 1988, 1992, and 1994, with samples ranging from 10,000 to 14,500).

[5] See the comments of David Sugarman and G. R. Rubin on the paucity of civil judicial statistics as compared with criminal statistics in *Law Economy and Society 1750–1914: Essays in the History of English Law* (Abingdon, 1984), 'Introduction', 55.

behaviour in and around civil justice lags behind criminal justice, not simply because the civil justice system has been a less seductive site for socio-legal researchers, but arguably because it lacks the coherence of the criminal justice system. There is an infinite pool of potential cases. Trouble, conflict, and misfortune are endemic. The possibilities for legal redress are myriad, and the avenues of redress diverse.

Although it is a mistake to think of the civil justice system as a seamless whole there is a tendency to do so. We talk of 'litigants' as if there could be the kind of shared interests and commonalities that we think of in relation to 'the accused' in the criminal courts. However, a moment's reflection will reveal the weakness of such an approach. The parts of the legal system that are not concerned with criminal law comprise a rag-bag of matters and participants. There are disputes relating to the performance or non-performance of contracts involving businessmen suing each other, individuals suing businesses, and businesses suing individuals. There are claims for compensation resulting from accidental injury in which individuals sue institutions. There is the use of the courts by lenders who realize their security by evicting individual mortgage defaulters. Civil justice also involves attempts by citizens to challenge decisions of central and local government bureaucrats, a rapidly growing field that includes immigration, housing, mental health, child welfare, and the like. In these situations individuals and groups confront agencies of the state which can bring to bear apparently unlimited resources to ward off claims. Finally, there are the acrimonious and often heartbreaking struggles between men and women following the breakdown of family relationships as property and children become the subject of legal dispute. All of these matters come within the ambit of the civil justice system.

There is also the question whether we can accurately describe all of this activity as constituting a 'system'. Unlike the criminal justice system, which is mobilized by an extremely narrow class of prosecutors and has limited fora for the disposal of cases, the civil justice system is available to be mobilized by an assortment of litigators and incorporates a collection of fora for dispute resolution with widely differing processes. These fora include the various divisions of the High Court, courts with specialist jurisdiction, the county courts and small claims arbitrations, statutory tribunals, and a growing proliferation of ombudsmen.

The difficulty of adequately theorizing the activities around the civil law among this potential army of litigants with all its different configurations, and the way in which different parts of the system work together or bump against each other, seems to render the possibility of meaningful generalization delusional. The fact that researchers have had limited success in theorizing behaviour across the boundaries of different legal fields is unsurprising. It may be less a failure of imagination than too much imagination, too clear an appreciation of the enormity of the difficulties.

The Problem of Cause and Effect in Civil Justice

The final and perhaps most intractable problem that besets the attempt to understand civil justice is that of disentangling cause and effect in the system. The work of the courts represents the cumulative choices of thousands of decision-makers who have their own personal, group, and cultural impulses towards and against law. These impulses are sensitive, in unknown ways, to procedural and substantive changes *within* the system. We do not know which are stable factors and which are the more volatile. Theoretically, the courts are passive. They do not create cases, but wait for them to arrive. However, we know that courts are in a position to influence behaviour, that they can operate autonomously, and that they do so. We are also aware that other factors influence what comes to court: for example, the availability of remedies, the costs of actions, litigation procedures, the profitability of different areas of legal practice, the certainty of the substantive law, the creation of new regulation. Until we more fully understand the drives, needs, and decision-making processes of users and potential users of the system, and until we understand how changes in structure, procedure, and substantive law interact with these decision-making processes, we will not understand the civil justice system. We will not be able to anticipate the social impact of policy change or the extent to which fluctuation in demand for the courts reflects change in underlying social and economic processes, or is merely a natural reaction to procedural change.

Despite these obstacles to comprehension it is important to begin the project of unravelling the conundrums of civil justice, because arguably civil law provides as important an underpinning to social and economic stability as the criminal law. Civil law fulfils significant practical and symbolic functions. We cannot develop a vision of the civil justice system of the future that serves the wider interests of society unless we have some understanding about the functions of law that we wish to promote.

Functions of Law

It is necessary to reflect on the theoretical functions of law in order to think about what the civil justice system should be delivering in terms of social and economic good. An understanding of the functions of law may also help to explain some of the anxiety expressed about the social impact of lack of access to the courts.

What, then, are the practical and symbolic functions performed by the civil law? Unfortunately, theorists provide no simple answer to the question. What you believe the law is for depends largely upon your politics, your conception of how individuals and society operate, your view about the nature of conflict within civil society, and your view about the relationship between law and state power. Despite the various formulations of argument, there are, however, some broad areas of agreement among theorists. Many of the jobs of law can be reduced to the over-arching necessity of maintaining social order. Although laws and courts that are backed by the coercive power of the state do not have a monopoly over social control,[6] there can be little dispute about their importance. Whether one subscribes to a structural/functionalist view, in which law represents a lubricant between the gently turning cogs of the social machine, or whether one subscribes to the crude Marxist view that law is the tool by which capitalists protect their property and contain revolt—law provides the answer to the central problem of the maintenance of order.

The second area about which there is little disagreement is that a primary function of law is dispute settlement. Almost all societies have fora for the peaceful resolution of disputes. This objective, arguably, offers individual litigants the possibility of remedies for grievances and claims, as well as a sense of justice, and also delivers

---

[6] The communication of social norms and rules of behaviour and the sanctioning of deviant behaviour are also conducted, for example, through the family, religion, and employers. Indeed in the view of some scholars the most important structures of social control have little to do with the coercive power of the State. See E. Ehrlich, *Fundamental Principles of the Sociology of Law* (Cambridge, Mass., 1936).

the collective benefit of stability. It has been frequently observed that societies without lawyers are common; societies without judges and courts are much more rare. Institutions that resolve, or help to resolve, disputes peacefully are ubiquitous, and all but the very simplest societies have them.[7]

An equally important function of state law, and one that is seen by some to be of increasing significance in modern, developed democracies, is that of checking executive power. Although some are sceptical of the extent to which the law is capable of controlling as well as expressing power, there are compelling arguments that it does. Even Marxist theorists suspicious of law as a tool of the powerful accept that the law cannot *seem* to be just without, on occasion, *being* just. As E. P. Thompson memorably observed:

The law may be rhetoric but it need not be empty rhetoric. . . . The rhetoric and rules of a society . . . in the same moment . . . may modify the behaviour of the powerful and mystify the powerless. They may disguise the true realities of power, but, at the same time, they may curb that power and check its intrusions.[8]

There is a difference between arbitrary power and the rule of law. Thus law can serve to maintain the legitimacy of the system of domination while at the same time restraining those with power from acting solely in their own self-interest.[9]

As an instrument of state policy, law can also perform redistributive or innovative functions. It can be used for social engineering to change social conditions, and to regulate economic and social behaviour. It has also been suggested that law has a facilitative function, as an 'enterprise for facilitating voluntary arrangements'. As Lon Fuller pointed out, law fulfils many functions: 'Law is a living process of allocating rights and duties, resolving conflicts, creating channels of co-operation.'[10]

In addition to these primary functions state law also operates as a 'secondary' means of social control. Lawrence Friedman suggests

---

[7] Lawrence M. Friedman, *Law and Society* (Englewood Cliffs, NJ, 1977); Peter Stein, *Legal Institutions* (London, 1984); Simon Roberts, *Order and Dispute* (Harmondsworth, 1979); E. Evans-Pritchard, *The Nuer*, (Oxford, 1940).

[8] *Whigs and Hunters: The Origins of The Black Act* (Harmondsworth, 1975).

[9] Richard O. Lempert, 'Grievances and Legitimacy: The Beginnings and End of Dispute Settlement' (1981) 15 *Law and Society Review* 707, 712.

[10] Lon L. Fuller, 'The Forms and Limits of Adjudication'(1979) 92 *Harvard Law Review* 353.

that 'legal process can act as a teacher, reformer or parent. The law does more than state the norms; it tries to spread the word, explain the norms, convince its public to follow them.'[11] The public nature of trials is important here. Courts make authoritative declarations of what the law is, which obligations must be performed, and which responsibilities must be discharged—in sum courts reflect, communicate, and reinforce society's dominant social and economic values. To this extent the law is a statement of values.[12]

One cannot, however, focus on the facilitative and conflict-reducing potential of law to the exclusion of its other potential. Unfortunately for the project of trying to create a vision of what the civil justice system should be doing, it is accepted that there are also profound dysfunctional effects of legal process. Law can create and reinforce inequalities in society. Litigation can exacerbate and prolong conflict. Litigation can simply offer an outlet for vindictiveness rather than an opportunity for vindication. Regulation can be seen as burdensome and law can distort and even cripple, rather than facilitate, social and economic processes. Laws can be unjust in both design and effect.[13]

The fact that law reflects only certain values, that it attempts to achieve conflicting objectives, and the fact that it can be used by different people and groups to secure both desirable and undesirable ends may account for the ambivalence that we detect in policies regarding the involvement of the state in civil claims and disputes, and the contradictions in access to justice rhetoric, which I will discuss below. However, if we accept that law has important social functions, then there are questions to be asked about the extent to which in our modern, complex, democracy, the State is responsible for providing the conditions within which the theoretical primary and secondary objectives of law can be achieved, and the extent to which they can be safely left to other mechanisms.

[11] Friedman, n. 7 above.

[12] Owen M. Fiss, 'Against Settlement' (1984) 93 *Yale Law Journal* 1073; Marc Galanter, 'The Radiating Effects of Courts' in Keith Boyum and Lynn Mather (eds.), *Empirical Theories About Courts* (New York, 1983), 117.

[13] Cf. William Holdsworth, *A History of English Law*, Vol. 3 (London, 1923), observing quarrelsome lawsuits of medieval England, felt that law had been substituted for private war. He suggested that the sick court system was a kind of tumour. 'Manipulative and hostile use of litigation is widespread. Where law is technical and detached from everyday ideas of right and wrong, it can serve as a weapon of revenge or attack; as a source of unreasonable defence; as a means for delay and frustration of legitimate claims.'

Pattern of Civil Justice Policy

Before focusing on how some aspects of the civil justice system operate in practice, it is useful to set current concerns about the civil justice system in an historical context. The history of policy, in what Sir Jack Jacob has referred to as the 'wretched waters of civil justice',[14] has been characterized by repeated efforts at reform in order better to achieve the objectives of justice. Such reforming activity has always occurred against a background of complaint about the sorry state of the civil courts. On this issue it is important to be clear: the cost and torpor of the civil courts has been a persistent complaint throughout the nineteenth and twentieth centuries,[15] and the pattern of policy and the arguments surrounding proposals for reform during the nineteenth century make extremely familiar reading. For example, the stated objectives of the major court reforms in the nineteenth century were to make law more affordable, accessible, and available to rich and poor alike.[16] The Common Law Procedure Amendment Act of 1838 simplified procedure, reduced legal fees, and cut the length of proceedings. Despite these reforms, business litigants turned in increasing numbers to arbitration as a means of resolving disputes. The establishment of the County Court in 1846 provided a means by which tradesmen could recover credit without an excessive investment of time and money.[17] Reforms continued throughout the latter part of the last century, and the effect, apparently, was to increase the work of both the superior courts and the county courts. In 1854 the *Law Times* informed its readers that court reforms promote the pecuniary interest of lawyers.[18]

At the turn of the century there is evidence of continuing complaint about delays in the civil courts and the cost of litigation, and in 1930 the London Chamber of Commerce reported that although English legal procedure was the most perfect of its kind in the world it had become an expensive luxury and beyond the means

---

[14] Sir Jack I. H. Jacob, *The Fabric of English Civil Justice* (London, 1987), 246.

[15] The *Interim Report* of the Woolf Inquiry into civil justice noted that since 1851 there had been some 60 reports on aspects of civil procedure and the organization of the civil and criminal courts in England and Wales.

[16] Brian Abel-Smith and Robert Stevens, *Lawyers and the Courts* (London, 1967), 29.   [17] *Ibid.*, 34–5.   [18] *Ibid.*, 41.

of the majority of people. The Report recommended simplification of procedure, fixed trial dates, and acceptance of documents unless challenged. Further Commissions and Committees of Inquiry met, considered, and reported on a fairly regular basis.

After the Second World War, during the rush of social legislation, the failings of the legal system were again brought into relief. In 1947 two committees, including both lawyers and laymen, were established to consider what reforms could be introduced to reduce the cost of litigation. The conclusion was that the answer to the problem of the civil courts was not to reduce charges for work done by the profession, but to avoid the necessity of doing the work.

The problem of access to the civil courts by the poor, as opposed to commerce and the middle class, which has been a dominant issue in the twentieth century, has been recognized at least since the time of Henry VII,[19] although the foundations of the modern legal aid system were not established until 1949. Since its introduction citizens have become more assertive and the role of individually enforceable rights has become more central.[20] New rights and entitlements have been created in the fields of housing, education, child care, and mental health, and the public are showing themselves to be prepared to pursue these rights, contributing to the rise in legal aid expenditure. As Goriely and Paterson have recently pointed out, the English legal aid scheme was established at a time of collectivist provision, but now operates within an individually oriented society. It has become one of the most extensive and expensive in the world.[21] During the last decade expenditure has risen faster than the rate of inflation, and the policy response has been to reduce eligibility, increase contributions, and limit the scope of the scheme. The official policy is that, although the rule of law is dependent on the legal system being reasonably accessible, the government cannot keep funding access through legal aid. The answer to the problem of access is, in the Lord Chancellor's view

---

[19] The *in forma pauperis* procedure was given statutory recognition during the reign of Henry VII. See n. 16 above, 12.

[20] Tamara Goriely, 'Rushcliffe 50 Years On: The Changing Role of Civil Legal Aid Within the Welfare State' (1994) 21 *JLS* 545.

[21] Tamara Goriely and Alan Paterson, *Resourcing Civil Justice* (Oxford, 1996), 15.

and yet again, a reduction in the cost and complexity of legal systems.[22]

The true underlying causes of the enduring problems of cost and delay remain somewhat obscure. The fault is frequently laid at the door of the legal profession, with its 'unreformability' being seen as the chief cause.[23] However, the presumed failure of previous reforms may have less to do with the unreformability of the profession than its fascinating capacity to adapt itself to change and to prosper from that change.

We see, then, that complaint about the civil courts is by no means a new phenomenon. However, current concern about the apparent impossibility of making the civil justice system responsive to the presumed needs of citizens seems to be providing the justification for a rather different approach to reform. Hand in hand with the traditional simplification of court procedure and regulation of costs, there is also a state-sponsored retreat from court-based dispute resolution. Although this is not particularly novel in commercial matters, since businessmen have generally been willing to buy private arbitration when it was in their interests, the Alternative Dispute Resolution bandwagon is being propelled towards a wide range of civil disputes by an interesting alliance between ADR providers, the judiciary, and policy-makers eager to find legitimate ways of saving public money. What is being offered is a new solution to old problems and, as always, the new product bears the familiar 'Access to Justice' label.

In the remainder of the chapter I reflect on several key issues that arise out of current policy within the context of what we do know about the way in which the civil justice system is used, and how it operates. I want to consider: why we are worrying about access to justice and for whom and what purpose we want to make the courts more accessible; what people want from the civil justice system as litigants, and what they want as citizens. Finally, I consider what litigants are currently getting from the system and how proposals for change might affect that for better or for worse. In the course of this discussion I consider several aspects of the tired problem of access to justice.

---

[22] Speech to Consumers' Association 1996.

[23] Adrian Zuckerman has argued that the problem has always been and remains the basis upon which lawyers are paid: 'Lord Woolf's Access to Justice: Plus a ça change . . .' (1996) 59 *Modern Law Review* 773.

Access to Justice Revisited . . . Again

In 1978 Sir Jack Jacob wrote:

We must enable legal disputes, conflicts and complaints which inevitably
arise in society to be resolved in an orderly way according to the justice of
the case, so as to promote harmony and peace in society, lest they fester
and breed discontent and disturbance. In truth, the phrase itself, 'access to
justice', is a profound and powerful expression of a social need which is
imperative, urgent and more widespread than is generally acknowledged.[24]

This quotation encapsulates many of the underlying assumptions in
access to justice arguments, and reflects ideas about the functions of
law to which I referred earlier. The role of law and the rule of law
are fundamental to liberal democratic ideology which emphasizes
individualism and liberty, and promises justice and equality before
the law. Moreover, it has been persuasively argued that access to
legal services is a fundamental prerequisite of access to justice.
Luban suggests that in order to participate effectively in the civil
justice system, citizens require legal representation. '[T]he principle
of equal access to the legal system is part of our framework of
political legitimacy . . . to deny a person legal assistance is to deny
her equality before the law, and . . . to deny someone equality
before the law delegitimizes our form of government.'[25]

I argued earlier that concern about use of law and access, or lack
of access, to justice has a long pedigree, but despite Sir Jack's
formulation of the issue, the messages have been, and continue to
be, mixed, not to say confused. We hear of too much use of law; we
hear of too little use of law; we hear that the civil courts are too
slow, too complicated, and too expensive. We also hear that the
availability of legal aid leads to inappropriate use of the courts.
Civil litigation has been described at different times and at the same

---

[24] I. H. Jacob, 'Access to Justice in England' in Mauro Cappelletti and Bryant
Garth (eds.), *Access to Justice, vol. 1 A World Survey* (Milan, 1978), 417.

[25] David Luban, *Lawyers and Justice* (Princeton, NJ, 1988), 251. For an
alternative view and implicit criticism of this basic assumption, see also Christine B.
Harrington, 'The Politics of Participation and Nonparticipation in Dispute
Processes' (1984) 6 *Law and Policy* 203: 'Expanding legal participation is one way
the state seeks to mediate social relations in a liberal democracy. The judiciary plays
an important role in structuring dispute processes to absorb demands for social
justice on the one hand, and maintain social order and stability on the other hand.'

time as an evil, and as necessary to participation in democracy. It has been seen as a manifestation of weakening social solidarity, and as an expression and reinforcement of fundamental societal values.[26] There is a pervasive schizoid element running through policy pronouncements and scholarly analyses of civil justice that simultaneously proclaims the importance of courts and access to them as fundamental to liberal democratic values, while condemning litigants and their lawyers as aggressive troublemakers who ought to be capable of sorting out their problems without resort to the courts. This contradiction, similarly, runs through the discussion and current proposals that underpin the revolution in civil justice promised in Lord Woolf's reforms.[27]

Discourse about access to justice proceeds largely without knowledge of, and without reference to the impulses, interests, strategies, and needs of the community which the system is there to serve. The discourse is anti-empirical. It does not need information, although it does incorporate atrocity stories that support any particular matter under discussion. What is discussed becomes what is known. The mythology is developed and elaborated on the basis of war stories told and repeated. This discourse is conducted among policy-makers, the judiciary, and the profession with contributions by representatives of sectional interests who are sufficiently well organized to be able to communicate their views and sufficiently moderate to be taken seriously. It is inevitable that the participants in this discourse speak on the basis of a partial

---

[26] Carol J. Greenhouse, 'Nature is to Culture as Praying is to Suing: Legal Pluralism in an American Suburb' (1982) 20 *Journal of Legal Pluralism* 17: '[I]t is possible to imagine circumstances under which rising rates of litigation would indicate the increasing integration of society, not the reverse. When law-aversion stems from a rejection of judicial institutions and the state that they represent, rising law use may signal a positive accommodation to or acceptance of the social system. The law is a basis and means of social participation.'

[27] 'A system of civil justice is essential to the maintenance of a civilised society. The law itself provides the basic structure within which commerce and industry operate. It safeguards the rights of individuals, regulates their dealings with others and enforces the duties of government': *Interim Report of the Woolf Inquiry* (London: 1995) at 2. 'The new landscape will have the following features: Litigation will be avoided wherever possible. (a) People will be encouraged to start court proceedings to resolve disputes only as a last resort, and after using other more appropriate means when these are available. (b) Information on sources of alternative dispute resolution will be provided at all civil courts': *Final Report of the Woolf Inquiry*, at 4.

view, derived from experience of dealing with some users of the system. Little is known about the silent majority, both private and business, who deliberately avoid the legal system, the processes that occur outwith the courts, and the everyday strategies adopted to contain and resolve conflict. The absence of reliable, large-scale data relating to the operation of the civil justice system provides the conditions in which such discourse can flourish.

Discussion about the importance of civil justice is often accompanied by dark references to the implications of a civil justice system that is unresponsive to the uncharted needs of the community, but little consideration is given to the reality of the situation. What do we know quantitatively about access or lack of access to justice? What kind of access do litigants and potential litigants need and want? What do citizens mean when they say that they want justice? What would citizens want if they could design their own system, and what kind of access to civil justice does society need in broader social theoretical terms? What is the social impact of the lack of access to the courts?

Although I have said that we lack information that would provide us with a comprehensive understanding of the use of the civil justice system, there is some information available from socio-legal research about the propensity to resort to the courts. The conclusions of several studies tell us, first, that resort to the courts is the exception, not the rule.[28] Our everyday perception of litigation is distorted by media representation of extreme and novel cases where the boundaries of the law are being pushed and where the public are likely to react. A recent example is the attempt by disappointed schoolchildren to sue their schools for failure to deliver an appropriate quality of education. These cases should

---

[28] Donald Harris *et al.*, *Compensation and Support for Illness and Injury* (Oxford, 1984); J. Jenkins *et al.*, *Survey of Use of Legal Services* (London, 1989); MVA Consultancy, *Consumer Study of Knowledge and Use of Legal Services* (London, 1994); National Consumer Council, *Seeking Civil Justice* (London, 1995); Royal Commission on Legal Services, Chairman, Sir Henry Benson GBE (London, 1979), Cmnd. 7648; Herbert M. Kritzer, 'Propensity to Sue in England and the United States of America: Blaming and Claiming' (1991) 18 *Journal of Law and Society* 400; S. M. Lloyd-Bostock, 'Propensity to Sue in England and the United States of America: A Reply' (1991) 18 *Journal of Law and Society* 428. See also Deborah A. Hensler *et al.*, *Compensation for Accidental Injuries in the United States* (New York, 1991); RAND Institute for Civil Justice, *Patients, Doctors and Lawyers: Medical Injury, Malpractice Litigation, and Patient Compensation in New York* (Santa Monica, Cal., 1990).

serve to remind us of the ability of the law to reach into the furthest recesses of our social, family, working, and other relationships. They are examples of the capacity of law, with the assistance of lawyers, to intrude, to control, and to seek to adjust relationships. What the cases do not tell us anything about is the propensity of the *average* citizen to resort to law when trouble strikes, the ability of the law to provide a realistic remedy for the majority of life's vicissitudes, or the value of the existence of the courts, no matter how remote, to the average person's sense of stability and perception that there is order in the world.

Empirical research on the propensity to litigate, then, suggests that most people do not (even when faced with obviously justiciable events). The range of factors that might, in theory, influence decisions about how to deal with life's problems includes: individual psychology; education; religion; belief about the value of the available remedy; resources; attitudes towards the courts and judges; alternative means of securing objectives; relationship with the defendant; the response of the defendant to a complaint; sense of injustices and so on. It is also likely that decisions are influenced by structural factors such as raising or lowering costs; availability of funding for litigation; changes in the law; and changes in the behaviour of lawyers. In his analysis of the 'litigation explosion' in the United States Galanter suggests that the most powerful explanatory factor for the transformation of grievances into disputes in different cultures is, in fact, the different 'institutional-ized ways of handling different kinds of disputes, not on broader cultural propensities to dispute'.[29]

Thus actual litigation rates reflect costs and the ability to pay, versus opportunities to succeed and assessments of what will be gained. Costs include both direct and indirect costs—including psychological costs. The cost-benefit analysis consists of something like this: what does the potential litigant want? What can he get? How much will it cost? How long will it take? How much trouble and discomfort will be involved? How likely is it that he will get what he wants in the end? Although we have a rough idea of the kinds of cases that end up in court, we do not know how court

---

[29] Marc Galanter, 'Reading the Landscape of Disputes: What We Know and Don't Know (And Think We Know) About Our Allegedly Contentious and Litigious Society' (1983) 31 *UCLA Law Review* 51, at 61.

actions relate to the universe of potential claims. We have little information about how these rough cost-benefit analyses are worked out on a daily basis among different groups in society.

Evidence from two current studies provides some insights into these issues. One is a national programme of research seeking to establish the range and prevalence of justiciable events faced by the public and to map responses to such events.[30] In identifying the factors that influence the strategies adopted to deal with these events, we hope to provide a picture of the way in which people seek to resolve conflict, to enforce rights, and to press claims—and the extent to which trouble and injustice is simply *absorbed*. We hope to achieve a better understanding of the factors that deter people from using the law, those that propel people towards the law, and the real motives for bringing civil actions. Is it a sense of an injustice that cannot be supported? Is it that the legal system offers the only possibility of redress? Are there circumstances in which the law is invoked without any particular sense of grievance or injustice, but opportunistically where money may be available with only the investment of time and trouble, but at no risk of cost?

Early developmental work has involved group discussions with members of the public who had experienced a range of events for which legal remedies are available. In talking about how these problems had been managed and the strategies adopted for obtaining remedies, respondents expressed profound disenchantment with lawyers and the legal system. The perception is that the legal system is costly, time-consuming, frustrating, and unlikely to deliver the desired objective. These perceptions were based partly on experience but also on received wisdom. The overwhelming view across the spectrum of social groups was that the law was to be used only as a last resort, when ordinary attempts to gain redress had failed and where the need for redress justified the costs risk. Examples of views are as follows:

'They are the last resort. You have to be very desperate, very desperate and very frustrated to go and see a lawyer, because generally you equate

---

[30] Access to Justice In England and Wales and Access to Justice in Scotland, both funded by the Nuffield Foundation being conducted by Hazel Genn, Patten Smith, and Sarah Beinart of Social and Community Planning Research. The research will be completed in Summer 1998.

whether it is worth the time and effort. You try to sort it out yourself and if you can't sort it out yourself, you then have to equate the cost. And if the cost is there and at the end of the day you can get a result out of it and you can afford it. . . . Basically at the end of the day what happens is when you go and see a solicitor you say "Can I afford it? and is it worth what it is going to cost me?" And that is how you equate it. And it would have to be something very, very serious for you to say "well I don't care what it costs" and that is ultimately how it works.'

'There is no possibility that I would ever go to a solicitor for anything medium range because I am not going to get it paid for. It's just not worth it. It's going to have to be so big an issue that basically I'm going to go bust either way before it's going to be worth going to a solicitor. It just costs too much.'

'I think it's a balance . . Sometimes I feel it is so unjust, it feels so unjust that this should happen, but in terms of how much financially it is going to cost, it is probably just better to forget about it because if you continue you are going to feel more hard done by in the end. You know—if I don't get anywhere and then I have to pay money on top of it, that would make you feel worse at the end of it.'

The cost-benefit analysis, which so often comes out against taking action, is strongly influenced by beliefs about the likelihood of achieving the desired outcome. Scepticism on this count derives from a perception of a disjunction between the law and ideas of justice and fairness. For example:

I went to court a few years ago . . . and the judge said 'well I can see you have been treated unfairly but unfortunately the law is that the housing society can make whatever decision it likes if it makes it in the correct way and followed its own procedures.' So it's not to do with fairness, it's to do with law—which is different.

Scepticism also derives from negative perceptions of the key decision-makers in the legal system. The average citizen has no direct knowledge of the judiciary and perceptions are based on media representation: what they know comes from the generally negative reporting that they read and what they see on the television. As a result, there is a sense, again across social groups, that judges are out of touch and that they are inconsistent. No distinction is made between criminal and civil cases, and accounts of crass remarks by judges and apparently inconsistent sentencing has a considerable impact:

'It just seems a very old system. The people at the top are just very old and I don't think they can understand technical problems. Generally they may not understand your situation. Like a District Judge or something. You know they are going to be much older, and they are not going to be the same age as a younger disputant, and you think this person is going to have completely different ideas to where this dispute is coming from because he comes from a different generation.'

'The top judges are not living in the real world with the kind of comments and kind of sentences they give out.'

'The thing with the judges you get the same case come up and one will get a suspended sentence and someone else will go to a different court with another judge and they will get 10 years. They are not consistent.'

'The people who are up there who are making decisions are some fuddy old judge. He might have lived in the real world 40 years ago but now he is living in a mansion in the middle of Berkshire and when was the last time he went down Soho late at night and got mugged because he didn't have anyone with him? They are not in touch with reality.'

Despite the general negativity of tone, a different reading at least of the earlier quotations reveals the *importance* of the existence of the courts as available for that 'last resort' case. There is no suggestion that the courts would never be used—only that the stimulus for mobilizing the courts would have to be serious and make the expenditure worthwhile. This underlines the sense in which courts contribute to a more generalized sense of stability and order and, in the end, to the faith that justice is achievable. It is not a rejection of the courts. It is an everyday appreciation that courts are there for special and serious events—but that they *are there* and that they are available to be used. As Galanter has argued, the courts, no matter how remote and expensive, provide citizens with 'symbols of entitlement'.[31] They heighten consciousness of rights and expectations of vindication.

Motivations: What do People Want from the Civil Justice System

Available evidence about what people want when they *do* use the courts suggests only a weak linkage with what the system is capable

[31] N. 29 above, 510.

of offering and what in most cases it actually delivers. Interestingly, although the chief remedy offered by the courts is financial compensation, research has shown that litigants frequently state that their primary motivation for taking legal action is something else: for example, achieving an apology, an acknowledgement of having been wronged, preventing the same misfortune from occurring to another, a proper investigation, making sure that people observe their legal obligations in the future[32]—all of these things, which in truth the courts could rarely offer, are, apparently, at least as important as financial recompense. Although respondents to surveys rarely cite punishment as a prime motivation, one should not underestimate the desire to punish and the desire to be publicly vindicated. Recent extended interviews with county court litigants[33] have provided some insights into what drives private and business people into litigation and what keeps them litigating. Accounts of the genesis of disputes and the motivations driving litigation are presented as 'principles' in which reparation, punishment, and vindication are prominent. For example:

'Even if I don't get any money out of this guy I just want to get justice. To get him out of this business so that he can't do this to other people. The law needs to be changed.' [Private Plaintiff]

'I have a slim chance of winning and it will cost my firm a lot of time. His offer of £1,000 is less than he and his wife will spend in a weekend if they choose to go away. The money doesn't matter to him. He says it's the principle—but his principle is that it's for him to decide what was in the contract. We would only go to law on principle, not for money. He has withheld money from us and it puts me in debt. The principle is that even though he is economically more powerful, we will not cave in.' [Business Plaintiff]

'I'm not trying to be unreasonable. I'm happy to make allowances on all the items but frankly I also believe there should be proper reparation. I am

[32] See e.g., National Consumer Council, *Seeking Civil Justice* (London, 1995); C. Vincent, M. Young, and A. Phillips, 'Why do People Sue Doctors? A Study of Patients and Relatives Taking Legal Action' (1994) 343 *The Lancet* 1609; H. Genn, 'Supporting Staff Involved in Litigation' in C. Vincent (ed.), *Clinical Risk Management* (London, 1996).

[33] Interviews have been conducted in the course of an evaluation of an experimental mediation scheme in the Central London County Court. The research, commissioned by the Lord Chancellor's Department, will be completed in Spring 1998.

prepared to spend £10K to get this money from him. The law is there to see that people honour their obligations.' [Business Plaintiff]

These sentiments are what propel some plaintiffs into litigation and they are what provide the resistance to compromise that prevents disputes from resolving themselves *before* litigation is commenced. These principles are felt powerfully—at least until the wear and tear of litigation channels anger, frustration, and a sense of injustice about the *initial event* into anger, frustration, and a sense of injustice about the *legal system* and the inability of legal representatives to deliver what the litigants see as 'justice'.

This leads to the question of what kind of justice the civil justice system delivers.

Justice

It has been widely accepted that the full meaning of access to justice involves more than access to advice and legal services or courts for those who seek such assistance. There is an implicit, and sometimes an explicit, acknowledgement that access involves access to just outcomes. The Woolf Report stressed that the basic principle of the civil justice system is that it should be just in the results it delivers and it should be fair (i.e. comply with principles of natural justice). The new rules of procedure have an overriding objective which is 'to enable the court to deal with cases justly', which includes but does not necessarily comprise: ensuring parties are on an equal footing; saving expense; dealing with cases in a proportionate way (value, importance, complexity, parties' financial position); speed; balancing court resources.

This is a simpler formulation than has been achieved by scholars faced with the problem of defining and articulating the relationship between law and justice, and contains probably one or two items that neither Plato nor Aristotle might have envisaged. The extent to which the law is involved in delivering justice is a vexed question among philosophers and legal theorists. Theorists have struggled with the issue, but a lucid account of the meaning of justice, particularly one that is empirically grounded in everyday concepts of justice, continues to elude us. It has recently been suggested that 'like liberty and equality, justice is yet another notion at the very center of Western political, social, and legal thought whose boundaries are notoriously indistinct, ill-defined and incessantly contested'.[34] The problem has been well put by Jack Balkin who suggests that:

Laws apportion responsibility, create rights and duties, and provide rules for conduct and social ordering. . . . Law is always, to some extent and to some degree, unjust. At the same time, our notion of justice can only be articulated and enforced through human laws and conventions. We may have a notion of justice that always escapes law and convention, but the only tools we have to express and enforce our idea are human laws and human conventions.[35]

There is, however, a commonplace conviction that justice and law are inextricably linked.[36] In the lawyer's conception, justice is to be found in the substantive legal rules and in the rules of procedure. Justice is seen in the impartial, unbiased, and accurate application of substantive laws, the content of which embody justice. Thus, for example, where the driver of a car owes a duty of care to a pedestrian, and the behaviour of the driver falls below the appropriate standard, and the pedestrian suffers damage as a result, it is *just* that the driver pays compensation to the pedestrian.

What, then, does the civil justice system actually deliver in the way of justice? What do users of the system get and what influences what they get? It is important to consider what we know about the kind of justice delivered by the civil justice system, and to assess what an increased emphasis on forcing settlement both within court litigation procedures and outwith the courts might mean for our concept of justice.

Settlement and the Notion of Justice

The idea that the outcome of litigation is necessarily *just*—even in narrow lawyer's terms—presupposes that cases are *decided* in court, on the basis of their merits in relation to the law. This view, however, fails to acknowledge the realities of litigation, the

[34] Austin Sarat and Thomas Kearns, *Justice and Injustice in Law and Legal Theory* (Ann Arbor, Mich., 1996).

[35] 'Being Just with Deconstruction' (1994) 3 *Social and Legal Studies* 393, 401.

[36] 'Though there can be law without justice, justice is realized only through good law.' It has been further argued that law's central link to justice is via the concept of impartiality. See Samuel Weber, 'In the Name of the Law', in chap. 6 in Druscilla Cornell, Michel Rosenfeld, and David Gray Carlson (eds.), *Deconstruction and the Possibility of Justice* (New York, 1992), 232.

pervasiveness of settlement, and the effects of the power relations of
the parties on outcomes.

An important area in which socio-legal research has achieved
success in theorizing across legal boundaries in the civil justice field
is in relation to the factors affecting outcomes in civil litigation.
Several studies highlight the sources of power in litigation and the
ways in which power influences the outcome of settlement
negotiations and, to a lesser extent, the outcome of trial. Factors
which are important are: legal intelligence—getting the right
lawyers and experts; financial resources—paying for the right
lawyers and experts; and having the psychological, social, and
economic ability to endure litigation.

UK studies have shown how in the fields of divorce litigation,[37]
personal injury litigation,[38] and litigation over the retention of
goods following winding-up,[39] the extent to which the resources
available to the parties to investigate and construct claims, and
their ability to withstand the pressures of litigation, influence the
outcome of cases, independent of their legal merits. Legal merits
may exist in objective ether somewhere, but in real life legal merits
depend on storytelling by the parties, by experts, and by advocates.
The facts of legal claims are socially constructed. Settlement
negotiations take place in a climate of uncertainty in which the
balance of evidence is important, but so is the ability to wait for an
outcome, to endure exhaustion, and to withstand costs pressures.
There is rarely a level playing field in litigation. As Davis comments
on divorce settlements, 'Adjudication is a leveller. The real
unfairnesses arise in the context of settlement. Inequality in terms
of the ability and commitment of legal advisers . . is paralleled by
an inequality of bargaining power between the parties—principally
reflected in their ability to tolerate a postponed resolution.'
Similarly, in negotiations over reservation of title clauses Wheeler
concludes that 'the requirements of the formal law form only one of
several planks in the negotiation process. Others of more import-

---

[37] Gwynn Davis, Stephen Cretney, and Jean Collins, *Simple Quarrels* (Oxford, 1994); Richard Ingleby, *Solicitors and Divorce* (Oxford, 1992).
[38] Hazel Genn, *Hard Bargaining: Out of Court Settlement in Personal Injury Actions* (Oxford, 1988).
[39] Sally Wheeler, *Reservation of Title Clauses—Impact and Implications* (Oxford, 1991).

ance are the power of the repeat players and the extent of their control of the process.'[40]

In this context the link between procedure and outcome is crucial. Changes in court procedure and other policies affect not only the question of access to the courts, but also the outcome of cases, by affecting the balance of power in litigation. One of the most important elements of power is insulation from legal costs. Subsidization of parties influences and distorts bargaining and outcomes. The development of conditional fees, informal contingency arrangements, legal expenses insurance, and insurance against failure will theoretically provide more opportunity for potential litigants to use courts. Capping the cost of litigation will also influence power relations, as illustrated by an insurance company claims negotiator talking about the anticipated character of personal injury litigation after Lord Woolf's changes are introduced:

Unfortunately a lot of the time, because of legal aid and legal expenses insurance the cost pressure is more on us than on the actual plaintiff . . . We are really up against the wall. I've never seen a claim where legal expenses insurance has withdrawn funding. Unfortunately not. I think that's where you get a lot of these actions taking up court time. They run the distance. I think fixed costs will really concentrate the mind on that— then these cases will go a lot faster. [Insurance Company Claims Negotiator]

The message is that plaintiffs will settle for less because solicitors will not be inclined to press cases so hard when the amount they can earn is limited under the rules. Thus the balance of power shifts.

In focusing on power relations in litigation, however, we must remember that there are two sides to costs pressures. All defendants—not just institutional defenders—can benefit to some extent from delay and heavy litigation costs. Disadvantaged and poor defendants use the cost and delay of the litigation system as a shield

---

[40] See also on the question of power relations in settlement negotiations: Marc Galanter, 'Why the "Haves" Come Out Ahead: Speculations on the Limits of Legal Change' (1974) 9 *Law and Society Review* 95; Robert Mnookin and Lewis Kornhauser, 'Bargaining in the Shadow of the Law: The Case of Divorce' (1979) 88 *Yale Law Journal* 950.

against claims. Will they be pursued or will they escape because the plaintiff makes a commercial decision? The same is true for rational calculator business defendants who regard payment of the contract price as a game, and gamble on the plaintiff's unwillingness to enter a lose/lose situation by litigating. The disadvantages of an expensive, inaccessible civil justice system create opportunities for potential defendants to escape litigation, and also for *lack* of access to be used as a dispute resolution strategy in itself. For example:

That really is the most powerful remedy. It doesn't really matter what the legal niceties are—if you haven't paid somebody you are in the driving seat and that is your most immediate remedy. Recently I was dealing with some architects . . . they completely failed to deliver either what I'd asked for or on time . . . so I offered them half the fee—which I thought was reasonable. I didn't want to take advantage of the situation, but I also knew that in a way I was exploiting the lack of access to justice myself by knowing that it just wouldn't be worth their while pursuing me even if they were right. So you were in the driving seat from that point of view. Although everybody has the same problem of actually being able to afford to go to law, you can sometimes use that against your opponent.

Structural changes to the courts and expanded opportunities to litigate will affect these decisions. Not everyone is currently unhappy with the cost and delay of the current system, and making the courts quicker, cheaper, and easier to use will not please all litigants or potential litigants, as cases currently unpursued for commercial reasons get sucked into the system.

The Cost of 'Justice': How Cheap is Cheap Enough?

Before considering the future I want to pause briefly on the issue of legal costs and consider how cheap would legal costs have to become before they were cheap enough to satisfy consumers of legal services? Losers in litigation currently face large bills for legal costs, and a disproportionate amount when the sums in issue are small. Current concern about the courts is driven largely by the costs issue. The argument is that if costs could be reduced, more people would be able to engage in litigation (presumably a social good) and people would complain less about legal aid withering away, because more people could afford to pay for themselves. The extent of legal costs is related to the requirements of the substantive law and the procedures for proof. So the argument runs that if we cut down on procedures, costs will fall and potential litigants, currently denied access to the system, will flock to the courts.

However, something that has never been investigated, but is worth considering, is the attitude of ordinary people to the cost of legal services. What is the perception of the value of legal knowledge and skills? Why are people shocked at having to pay £40 for a solicitor's letter or £550 to read a lease when they will pay £2.50 for a glass of fizzy water, £40 for a workman to inspect a faulty appliance, or £5,000 to an estate agent, with relatively little complaint? Is it the sheer scale of legal costs? Is it the uncertainty about the extent of risk as a result of the costs indemnity rule and the fact that costs liability is open-ended? Or is it also something to do with a lack of value in the good that is being purchased? That what people seek from legal assistance is what they believe they are entitled to? They are not *gaining* something—they will not have slaked their thirst, sold their house, or fixed the washing machine. They will simply have avoided some theoretical future problem, or they will have been returned to a position of equity[41]—to have been given back what they feel they have lost. It is just possible that one could almost never reduce legal costs to a level that individual and business litigants found acceptable, because they do not value the service supplied. The following view is typical of the public's perception of the cost and value of legal skills:

At work we recently had a bill from a solicitor who read our lease and he charged £550. He read the lease—that's all he did. If it cost £550 to read a lease God help you if you wanted them to fight your case. If that's a sign of how much solicitors charge! And the sting in the tail was a letter came with the bill saying 'I've tried to reduce my costs as much as I can bearing in mind your situation at the moment and I've reduced the bill to £550.' And all he did was read through four sheets of paper!

The Future

Where does all of this leave us, and what of the future? We cannot conclude a turn of the twenty-first century discussion of civil justice without considering Alternative Dispute Resolution. I

---

[41] For a discussion of the psychological literature see Sally Lloyd-Bostock, 'Fault and Liability for Accidents: The Accident Victim's Perspective' in Donald Harris *et al.*, n. 28 above.

remarked earlier that one of the main planks of civil justice policy is the promotion of alternative, private forms of dispute resolution, and I want to consider the current apparent enthusiasm for ADR in the context of my comments about the functions of law and the role of the state in the settlement of disputes.

The first point is that, although the ADR bandwagon has really started to roll in this country, it is well behind developments elsewhere. Debate and disagreement about the value of ADR has been continuing in the United States for more than a decade and the North American scholarly literature is awash with theoretical discussion and empirical research on ADR schemes. These debates incorporate struggles between competing visions of justice and competing claims about who should control dispute processing. In 1989 Sarat and Silbey convincingly dissected the politics of dispute processing, arguing that the contemporary ADR movement was held together by a critique of courts, and a desire to recast the market for dispute resolution services by different interests attempting to advance their own professional projects.[42] Their analysis, however, shows that the character of the movement in the United States was somewhat different from developments here. In the United States an important stimulus was the desire to save judicial resources for the resolution of business and commercial disputes and the removal of other matters from the courts and possibly the legal field itself. This tendency caused substantial criticism on the ground that the problems of the poor were being downgraded and relegated to inferior courts and inferior forms of justice. The problems of the poor could be jettisoned because they were less important than the problems of business. Similar arguments were made in this country following the Courts and Legal Services Act 1990 and the expansion of the jurisdiction of the county courts.[43]

This is, I think, an occasion when extrapolation from the United States is unhelpful. The current passion for ADR can hardly be a response to court congestion. *Judicial Statistics for England and Wales* show that, for the last two or three years, litigation has been declining. In fact, the promotion of ADR, at least on the part of the

---

[42] Susan Silbey and Austin Sarat, 'Dispute Processsing in Law and Legal Scholarship: From Institutional Critique to the Reconstruction of the Juridical Subject' (1989) 66 *Denver University Law Review* 437.

[43] Stephen Sedley, 'Improving Civil Justice' (1990) 9 *Civil Justice Quarterly* 348.

Lord Chancellor's Department, may simply be another instance in which the state is seeking to withdraw from responsibility for core functions while maintaining overall control—what has been referred to by political scientists as the 'hollowing-out' of the state. This trend, together with the new interest in innovation among the judiciary stimulated by the Woolf Inquiry, means that the energetic lobbying of ADR providers, which has been in progress for several years,[44] is producing an uncritical fervour for ADR at the highest levels. The result is a growth in mediation experiments in civil cases[45] and increasing judicial pressure on litigants to resolve disputes outside court.[46] These developments are running ahead of any systematic evaluation of the presumed benefits or possible disadvantages of private dispute resolution systems.

The evaluation in progress of the mediation scheme in the Central London County Court raises a number of questions that require consideration. First, in common with other experimental schemes, the take-up rate has been low because of the widespread failure of the legal profession to recommend mediation to their clients. Suspicion of mediation among practising lawyers arises from: ignorance about what mediation involves; entrenched views about how litigation should be conducted; a genuine belief that mediation is inappropriate in ordinary litigation; and a lack of any obvious financial incentive to cut cases short.

Those cases that have been mediated in the Central London County Court to date largely concern recovery of money for goods delivered or services rendered, involving small and medium sized businesses suing each other over relatively modest sums of money. The prime motivation for accepting mediation is to alight from the runaway litigation train, and the chief benefit of mediation is seen by litigants as being the avoidance of legal costs and cutting short

---

[44] The leading organization, the Centre for Dispute Resolution, was established in 1990.

[45] Experimental scheme in Bristol county courts; experimental scheme promoted by the Department of Health for medical negligence cases; mediation experiment in the Central London County Court; mediation experiment in the Patents County Court.

[46] Lord Chief Justice's and Vice-Chancellor's Practice Direction of 24 Jan. 1995; Commercial Court Practice Statements in Dec. 1993 and June 1996. A booklet, 'Resolving Disputes without Going to Court', published by the LCD, was distributed to members of the judiciary in Jan. 1997.

litigation time. To that extent the interest of the parties is primarily in *outcome* not in the *process*.

The mediations appear to be capable of producing compromise at an early stage through skilful management and compression of settlement negotiations. Mediations seemed to work well when parties had had legal advice and where there was some rough equality of representation. Legal advice is important because the context is legal. Although parties are urged at the commencement of the mediation to ignore their legal rights and focus on their *interests* in the context of the litigation nightmare, perceptions of legal merits, strength of evidence, and chances of winning at trial provide the foundations for discussions and the impetus that propels the parties toward compromise.

What then are the questions raised by these mediations in the context of a growing pressure towards mandatory use of Alternative Dispute Resolution for much of the current business of the civil justice system?

First, that whether the mediators are lawyers or non-lawyers, the mediations are controlled by the *mediator* and *not* by the parties. Despite the rhetoric of the mediation organizations and despite the conventional introduction given by mediators at the outset of mediations stressing their facilitative role and the parties' control of the proceedings, it is invariably the case that the mediator decides the rules by which the mediation will proceed: for example, who will be permitted to speak and when; what evidence is relevant and what can be produced and discussed. *The mediator sets the criteria of relevance and shapes expectations.* There is thus considerable scope for the exercise of covert power. The evidence, so far, strongly indicates that evaluation is not absent from mediation; it is simply communicated with more or less subtlety depending on the personality and individual philosophy of the mediator. The role of the mediator therefore requires close examination since the activities of mediators are currently unregulated. Mediators are unaccountable, the nature and extent of their responsibility to the parties is unclear, and their ethical standards are unarticulated.

Finally, it seems to me that the current justification for mediation in civil cases derives primarily from the deficiencies of litigation, and *if it is* succeeding it does so within the context of an expensive and stressful litigation system. Without the pressure of mounting legal costs the stimulus for compromise may be lacking. The parties' 'interests today' largely comprise the interest in avoiding further litigation. Absent the disadvantages of the litigation system—what are the parties' interests? We are left with their desire for *full* reparation, for vindication, and for punishment. Litigants are prepared to forgo these things *only* because the financial and psychic costs of litigating in the end are too great.

There is also the question of enforcement. In all cases, the enforceability of mediated agreements is crucial. The first question that many parties ask at mediation is whether any agreement reached will be enforceable and the possibility of coercion through the civil courts to enforce mediated agreements is regarded as essential. It is therefore possible to argue that mediation works, in the context in which I have been observing it, on the one hand because of the disadvantages of the current litigation system, but also because of the continuing shadow cast by the courts. To steal a phrase,[47] mediation in the absence of courts would be the sound of one hand clapping.

Conclusion

It should be a fundamental aim of civil justice to open wide the gates of the Halls of Justice and to provide adequate and effective methods and measures, practices and procedures, reliefs and remedies, to deal with all justiciable claims and complaints. Such an aim would produce greater harmony and concord in society and increase the understanding and respect of the community for law and the system of civil justice.[48]

There are some important, and possibly intractable, problems bundled up in the questions about what the civil courts are for and in arguments about access to justice. But I also think that access to justice concerns reflect deeper anxieties which reform of the civil courts is unlikely to solve. The truth is that even if Sir Jack Jacob's vision of open access to the courts for the widest range of grievances were realized, it is by no means certain that we would be happier, more equal, or more secure. Conflict would not be reduced

[47] Used by Marc Galanter in relation to out of court settlement in the absence of the possibility of litigation, in 'Worlds of Deals' (1984) 34 *Journal of Legal Education* 268.
[48] Sir Jack Jacob, 'Justice Between Man and Man' (1985) 37 *Current Legal Problems* 211, at 230.

and we would certainly not be more prosperous. It is arguable that our future prosperity has more to do with what is going on in offices and factories in the Far East than with whether Lord Woolf's fast track will achieve its objectives.

But on the other hand, the future role of the courts *is* important. The state's responsibility in the provision of courts is about more than the interests of litigants. It is not simply a question of whether people have access to triadic modes of dispute settlement. In addition to adjudicating on disputes the courts develop the law, they can reflect and influence public policy at a broad level, and they communicate and reinforce dominant values. As Sarat and Silbey point out, 'law works quietly and unobtrusively, to shape both attitudes and behaviour . . . and communicating particular visions of order, justice, goodness, property, family, health, education'.[49] Citizens do not routinely perform their duties because they fear the threat of adjudication or compulsion by the state, but because the values of the law—publicly expounded in courts—have been absorbed.

Moreover there are questions about whether the current emphasis on dispute settlement outside court is necessarily to be regarded as intrinsically desirable. Critics of settlement point to the influence of resources and incentives on outcome,[50] the dangers in the loss of the influence of courts in articulating and developing public norms of justice,[51] and the loss of public knowledge about law.[52] Private justice has other potential weaknesses: for example, the creation of the suspicion that in addition to purchasing a process, the content of the decision can also be bought.[53]

Economists have argued for a long time that private arbitration and full-cost sharing by the parties should be totally substituted for

---

[49] Sarat and Silbey, n. 3 above, 138.

[50] See for an example Janet Cooper Alexander, 'Do the Merits Matter? A Study of Settlements in Securities Class Actions' (1991) 43 Stanford Law Review 497 *at* 574–7.　　　　　　　　　　　　　　　　　　　[51] *Owen M. Fiss, n. 12 above.*

[52] *David Luban, 'Settlements and the Erosion of the Public Realm' (1995) 83 Georgetown Law Journal 2619.* See also Judith Resnick, 'Judging Consent' [1987] *University of Chicago Legal Forum* 43; Marc Galanter and Mia Cahill, ' "Most Cases Settle": Judicial Promotion and Regulation of Settlements' (1994) 46 *Stanford Law Review* 1339.

[53] Cf. Samuel Krislov, 'Theoretical Perspectives on Case Load Studies: A Critique and a Beginning' in K. Boyum and L. Mather, n. 12 above, at 169.

present court arrangements.[54] But there is a public purpose in courts, and there are compelling arguments for accountable and universalized justice. Moreover, at a time when family structures are changing, when religious authority is vestigial, the emphasis on self-reliance and the growth of individualism may lead to an increasing judicialization of misfortune and conflict and a greater desire to pursue rights and redress through the courts. The court system is something more than the provision of a consumer service like dry cleaning or motor repairs; it is an essential part of a properly functioning democratic society—as is reflected within the Magna Carta's promise that 'To no one will we sell, to no one deny or delay right or justice'.

If we cannot afford to provide at public expense sufficient courts or judges to decide cases expeditiously and if we believe that certain classes of litigants would do better to take their disputes elsewhere, it is necessary to debate and decide which kinds of cases should have priority in terms of court resources and why. Access to the public dispute resolution system is already rationed through cost and delay, but a *strategy* for the civil justice system of the future requires clearly articulated rationing principles that take account of the social function of the civil justice system and the interests of *citizens* in the structures of civil justice.

[54] William M. Landes and Richard A. Posner, 'The Private Enforcement of Law' (1975) 4 *Journal of Legal Studies* 1.

RESTRAINING THE STATE
Politics, Principle and Judicial Review

*Jeffrey Jowell**

Some journalists I know have collectively resolved, when writing about America, never to quote de Tocqueville's reactions to that country. For different reasons, I have often been tempted to found a club based around a resolution no longer to quote Dicey when beginning a lecture on English public law. How could the views of a nineteenth-century Whig be relevant at the end of the twentieth century? When he wrote in 1885 more than two thirds of members of Parliament were peers or their sons. Far less than half the adult population had the right to vote. There was a heavy property qualification. No woman had the vote. And Dicey passionately opposed female franchise until the end of his life.[1]

You will understand why I want to form my club. But I have already broken the club's prime injunction because there is another side to Dicey. His abiding contribution was his insight that public law (as we call it today) consists not only of positive rules, but also of principle. In addition to his primary enabling principle, Parliamentary supremacy, there was a disabling or restraining principle, the rule of law.[2]

The recognition of principle as a constitutional source and as a possible restraint on governmental action allows the constitution to

* The author would like to thank Gavin Drewry, Stephen Guest, Andrew Le Sueur, and David Sugarman for their helpful discussions about parts of this paper.
[1] See generally R. A. Cosgrove, *The Rule of Law; Albert Venn Dicey, Victorian Jurist* (London, 1980).
[2] A. V. Dicey, *The Law of the Constitution* (London, 1885).

evolve in response to changing understandings about the proper limits of governmental power. Constitutional evolution over this century has been significant, and spearheaded by judicial review. However, as Dicey recognized, the sources of constitutional arrangements are wider than the case law and the statutes. The fact that a statute has *failed* to be passed may be as much a relevant indicator of constitutional principle as the actual passing of a statute into effect.

For example, recently the principle that private property should not be invaded by the state without judicial authorization (based on the notion that an Englishman's Home is his Castle) was threatened in a Parliamentary bill.[3] The *failure* to enact the legislation as planned in that bill is as good an indication of constitutional principle as a piece of enacted legislation or a decided case. The proposal was unable to withstand the principle's moral strictures, even in the absence of any pronouncement upon the question by any court of law.

I shall return to the question of principle and its sources later, but for the moment let me indulge in some court-centred analysis, juridicocentricity if you like, through a very rapid and necessarily selective survey of judicial review this century.

The century divides into four phases. At its beginning courts were freely willing to invoke the 'justice of the common law' to guide the exercise of apparently infinite discretionary power.[4] Even where a statute was silent, the decision-maker was required to provide a hearing, natural justice, to an applicant. Lord Loreburn said in 1915 that the duty to provide natural justice is a duty resting upon 'anyone who decides anything'.[5] That was Phase One.

Phase Two begins with the First World War and continues to the mid-1960s. This was a period of judicial restraint. Artificial barriers were erected by the courts to justify their lack of interference with official decisions. The right to natural justice was cut down in situations that were considered to be 'administrative' in character, as opposed to 'judicial', or where a 'privilege' was in issue rather than a 'right'.[6] Broad discretionary powers were to be

---

[3] The Police Bill 1997.

[4] A phrase used in *Cooper* v. *Wandsworth Board of Works* [1863] 14 CB (NS) 180.   [5] *Board of Education* v. *Rice* [1911] AC 179.

[6] See e.g., *Local Government Board* v. *Arlidge* [1915] AC 120; *Nakkuda Ali* v. *Jarayatne* [1951] AC 66.

construed literally so as to allow the decision-maker to decide on subjective grounds. The classic example is the interpretation by the House of Lords that regulations made at the beginning of the Second World War requiring the Home Secretary to have 'reasonable cause to believe' a person to have hostile associations empowered the Home Secretary to detain Jack Perlzweig, alias Robert Liversidge, indefinitely and merely on the minister's suspicion. Lord Atkin bravely dissented, a dissent which provoked one of his fellow judges openly to question Lord Atkin's patriotism in a letter to *The Times*, and Lord Atkin to be ostracized by the other Law Lords until his death three years later.[7]

In another case during the Second World War a seven-judge House of Lords refused to challenge the privilege of the Crown not to reveal evidence sought by victims of a tragic submarine accident.[8] After the end of the war, clauses ousting the courts' jurisdiction were upheld without judicial resistance.[9] During all of this period the judiciary were at pains to ensure that the executive were largely unconfined in their exercise of power.

From the mid-1960s, the third phase, judicial deference ceased, almost abruptly. Judges grew increasingly willing to restrain official power at all levels of government. In 1964 the House of Lords, in *Ridge* v. *Baldwin*,[10] dismantled the artificial barriers to natural justice. In 1967, in *Conway* v. *Rimmer*,[11] the Lords held that documents for which the Crown claimed privilege should be produced for inspection for the courts to decide. In 1968, in *Padfield*[12] the Lords held that a statute which appeared, on a literal interpretation, to give an unfettered discretion to the minister of agriculture to hold an inquiry into a complaint from farmers, should be interpreted so as to give effect to its objects and purposes, rather than its literal meaning. In 1969, in *Anisminic*,[13] the House of Lords barged through a clause in a statute purporting to oust their jurisdiction to challenge a determination of the Foreign Compensation Commission.

---

[7] The case was *Liversidge* v. *Anderson* [1942] AC 206. See generally, R. Stevens, *Law and Politics* (London, 1979), 287.
[8] *Duncan* v. *Cammell Laird & Co.* [1942] AC 624.
[9] *Smith* v. *East Elloe RDC* [1956] AC 736. [10] [1964] AC 40.
[11] [1968] AC 910. [12] [1968] AC 997. [13] [1969] 2 AC 147.

In the space of a mere five years, a large number of technical barriers to judicial intervention collapsed and a purposive approach to the interpretation of statutes broke through the barricade of the literal. 'The minister may', could mean 'the minister must'; power granted in the form of broad discretion was no longer read as a conferral of unconstrained fiat.

During the 1970s this trend continued, with the courts beginning to sketch the principle of legitimate expectation, permitting a fair hearing where an expectation of a hearing or a benefit had been disappointed.[14]

It should be said that through each of these phases, as I have called them, there were of course cases which went in a contrary direction. Even in the 1970s the courts bowed to the executive when national security was invoked to nullify the need for a fair hearing (*Hosenball*),[15] and the courts would not go so far as to review a prerogative power, such as the power of the Attorney General to refuse to act in relator proceedings (in the *Gouriet*[16] case).

Stage Four begins in the late 1970s and takes us to the present day. It is a phase of rapid increase in applications for judicial review and the beginning of a more coherent, and less pragmatic approach to the subject. In 1978 a unified application for judicial review was[17] introduced which widened standing to sue and simplified the procedures for review. Applications for judicial review have, since then, increased dramatically (although again, to put that in perspective, it should be remembered that over half the applicants for judicial review are refused leave to apply, and less than a third of those granted leave are ultimately successful in obtaining the remedy they seek).[18]

---

[14] Starting with the reference to the legitimate expectation by Lord Denning in *Schmidt* v. *Secretary of State for Home Affairs* [1969] 2 Ch. 149. See also *R.* v. *Liverpool Corporation ex p. Liverpool Taxi Operators' Association* [1972] 2 QB 299.

[15] *R.* v. *Secretary of State for Home Affairs, ex p. Hosenball* [1977] 1 WLR 766.

[16] *Gouriet* v. *Union of Post Office Workers* [1978] AC 435.

[17] Rules of The Supreme Court (Amendment No. 3) 1977, SI No. 1955 (L.30). See also Judicature (Northern Ireland) Act 1978, ss. 18–25, and see Supreme Court Act 1981, s. 31.

[18] There was a growth from 558 applications for judicial review in 1981 to 3,604 in 1995. See *Judicial Statistics for England and Wales* 1995, Cm 3290, June 1996. See M. Sunkin, L. Bridges and G. Mészáros, *Judicial Review in Perspective: An*

During the 1980s and 1990s some major breaches of executive immunity have taken place. In the *GCHQ* case in 1984[19] the House of Lords held that the prerogative power, if justiciable, was open to challenge in the courts. That case also endorsed the notion of legitimate expectation giving rise to a fair hearing and held that the mere assertion by the executive of national security was not an automatic bar to review; some evidence of danger to national security had to be provided. In 1989, prompted by the European Court of Justice, the Lords for the first time issued an injunction against the Crown, initially where Community law was directly effective,[20] but later when only domestic law was in issue.[21] In *Re M*, the House of Lords assumed the jurisdiction to make a finding of contempt against a minister of the Crown who disobeyed an undertaking given in the course of judicial review proceedings.[22] A duty to provide reasons for decisions, while not yet general, is being progressively imposed.[23] Meanwhile, the cases in which ministers, particularly the Home Secretary of late, have fallen foul of the courts are too numerous to summarize. So much so that the past two years have witnessed the outbreak of what has been described as a 'turf war' between the executive and the judiciary.[24] Events over the past few months have been unprecedented, with senior judicial figures openly justifying rigorous judicial review of official action, sometimes in the political forum offered to Law Lords by the House of Lords,[25] and in a spate of speeches and articles in learned journals.[26] Ministers and even shadow ministers have

Investigation of Trends in the Use and Operation of the Judicial Review Procedure in England and Wales (London, 1993); B. Hadfield and E. Weaver, 'Trends in Judicial Review in Northern Ireland' [1994] PL 12.

[19] *Council for Civil Service Unions v. Minister for the Civil Service* [1985] AC 374.

[20] *R. v. Secretary of State for Transport, ex p. Factortame (No. 2)* [1989] 1 AC 603.

[21] *R. v. Secretary of State for Employment, ex p. Equal Opportunities Commission* [1995] 1 AC 1.

[22] *M. v. Home Office; sub nom. Re M* [1994] 1 AC 377.

[23] *R. v. Secretary of State for the Home Department, ex p. Doody* [1994] 3 WLR 154.

[24] The words are those of *The Economist*, Dec. 1995.

[25] On 5 June 1996 a debate on the subject of judicial review was initiated by Lord Irvine of Lairg, then Shadow Lord Chancellor, in the House of Lords.

[26] e.g. Sir John Laws, 'Is the High Court the Guardian of Fundamental Constitutional Rights?' [1993] *PL* 58 and 'Law and Democracy' [1995] *PL* 72; Sir

vigorously opposed what they see as undue political interference by judges.[27] The press has openly sided with one or other of the protagonists.[28]

This brief narrative raises fundamental questions about the judicial role. Why did the judges become so deferential during Phase Two? And what led them to be more assertive in Phase Three? In any of these phases, was the approach to their own role proper? In progressively reducing the former zone of immunity surrounding the executive, were the judges seeking improperly to expand their own power? Were they in fact indulging in politics, inappropriate to their function?

Before answering these questions we have to establish the proper role of the judge in public law. Let me here put forward two models which we might agree are not appropriate, not suitable to the role of a judge in a democracy. The first is the judge as policy-maker. The second is the judge as bureaucrat.

The judge as policy-maker makes a decision which is based upon his own evaluation of its social or economic advantage. The decision openly engages in a calculation of the public good.[29] We instinctively feel that this role is not appropriate to a judge because in a democracy policy-making is the province of the legislature (or legislature as delegated to the executive or other authorities). So we reject this role for the judge as *constitutionally* inappropriate to the judicial function.

A distinction should be made between those decisions that are constitutionally outside the role of the judge and those decisions to which the process of adjudication is not *institutionally* suited. Judicial review in this country has always rested on the assumption that judges are limited in their capacity, irrespective of their constitutional role, to pronounce on the merits of a decision on

Stephen Sedley, 'Human Rights: A Twenty First Century Agenda' [1995] *PL* 386 and 'The Sound of Silence: Constitutional Law Without a Constitution' (1994) 110 *LQR* 270; Lord Browne-Wilkinson, 'The Infiltration of a Bill of Rights' [1992] *PL* 397; Lord Woolf, 'Droit Public—English Style' [1995] *PL* 57; Lord Ackner, 'Does Judicial Independence Really Matter in an Advanced Democracy?' NLJ (1996).

[27] e.g. Lord Irvine QC, 'Judges and Decision-Makers: The Theory and Practice of *Wednesbury* Review' [1996] *PL* 59.

[28] See A. Le Sueur, 'The Judicial Review Debate', *Government and Opposition*, Winter 1996, 8.

[29] See Ronald Dworkin's distinction between 'principle' and 'policy' in *Taking Rights Seriously* (London, 1977), 82–7.

judicial review. This is because the administrator is assumed to possess the relevant expertise which the courts lack, and because the procedures of judicial review lack the capacity to deliver the relevant arguments. In addition, the issue itself may not be justiciable, because the decision lacks the possibility of objective determination, or because it contains interacting points of influence with other decisions that the judge is not able to take.

Many decisions from which a judge should be disqualified because of the lack of *constitutional* competence will also involve *institutional* incompetence. The adjudicative process has limited capacity to assess whether site A, B, or C is the most suitable for a new London airport or to assess the economic arguments in favour of or against shutting a series of coal pits or setting levels of taxation. This institutional bar coincides with a constitutional one. These decisions belong in the legislative sphere.

On the other hand, there are cases where there is concurrent constitutional competence, but a question about which branch of government is institutionally more suited to deciding the matter. Judges have recently denied themselves the opportunity of pronouncing upon questions such as whether a local authority's expenditure was 'excessive',[30] or the question of a university's rating for the quality of its research,[31] or whether a hospital ought to provide an expensive treatment with low risk of long term success to a suffering child.[32]

The live issue of sentencing of criminal offenders is a case in point. It is surely within the legislative competence to lay down some rules in respect of minimum or maximum sentences, taking into account prison resources, the safety of the public, the sense of public outrage, and other factors legitimate for a legislature to entertain. Decisions on sentencing also properly lie in the constitutional realm of the judiciary, who are able, in the light of the facts revealed in the specific trial of an individual offender, to determine with relative precision the extent to which a punishment may be tailored to fit both the offender and the crime. Both the judiciary

---

[30] *R. v. Secretary of State for the Environment, ex p. Hammersmith & Fulham LBC* [1991] AC 521, *per* Lord Bridge at 596–7.

[31] *R. v. Higher Education Funding Council, ex p. Institute of Dental Surgery* [1994] 1 WLR 242 (the issue here was whether reasons ought to be provided for the decision, but 'justiciability' was at the core of the judgment).

[32] *R. v. Cambridge Health Authority, ex p. B* [1995] 2 All ER 129.

and the legislature thus share a legitimate constitutional role in respect of sentencing functions. The current debate is in large measure about the division of institutional competence; the question of which of the two institutions is better able to decide on different aspects of sentencing and which should be left to the other.

A second model is the judge as bureaucrat. The role of the bureaucrat is to implement state policy, ensuring compliance with the commands of the organs of state power and ensuring that these commands are not unduly obstructed or distorted. Despotic regimes are marked by the existence of seemingly independent judges who are, in practice, rarely critical of the exercise of public power. Lord Ackner has recently reminded us of the telephone judges in the former Soviet Union who, after hearing a case, would telephone the Kremlin to receive their instructions on the result.[33]

The notion of judge as Aparachic is not attractive here, nor applied, but a weaker form of the notion of bureaucrat judge is often expressed. Former Chief Justice Lord Parker once argued that the courts have 'a positive responsibility to be the handmaidens of the administration rather than its governor' and 'have a duty to facilitate the objects of administrative action as approved and authorised by parliament'.[34] And there is a strongly-held view among commentators in this country that the role of the judge is to 'sustain the legitimacy of public power' or 'enforce the will of Parliament'.[35] This role is opposed to the role of the judge as protector of individual rights against illegitimate incursions of state power.

This notion of bureaucrat-judge in its weaker meaning has a certain logic on its side. Since the supremacy of Parliament is our prime constitutional principle, then the role of courts is to ensure that those charged with the exercise of official power, power conferred by Parliament, is exercised in accordance with Parliament's will. Judges then become instruments to ensure that legislative designs are fulfilled; enforcement officers on behalf of the sovereign Parliament.

---

[33] N. 26 above.

[34] Quoted in D. G. T. Williams, 'The Donoughmore Report in Retrospect' [1982] *Pub. Admin.* 273 at 291.

[35] See e.g. John Griffith, *Judicial Politics Since 1920* (London, 1993).

This conception of the judicial role is further supported by the doctrine that the basis of all judicial review is *ultra vires*. If jurisdictional error or patent error of law is the only trigger for judicial review, then indeed the judge's sole function is to ensure that the decision maker acts within his *vires* or jurisdiction, within the four corners of his powers as determined by Parliament.

But to justify judicial review in this way ignores the fact that by no means all of judicial review involves the interpretation of statutory power (although a great deal does). When the statute is silent, or when prerogative power, these days, or contractual power is in issue, the judges pronounce upon the procedural or substantive fairness of a decision. Even where the decision is within the four corners of the statutory power, judges intervene when that power was unreasonably exercised or abused. Judicial intervention in these cases is, therefore, justified not by notions of *vires* or jurisdiction, but by independent principles of common law,[36] or, better still, constitutional principle—by which we mean standards expected in a functioning democracy. The application of these principles requires the judge to perform a role that is wider than that of Parliament's servant.

Our judge should therefore be neither policy-maker—in the sense of acting outside his constitutional or institutional competence. Nor should he be a bureaucrat, in its strong or weak sense. What about the judge as politician?

There are two senses in which a judge may be said to be political (and I use that term as distinct from judge as policy-maker, as I have just outlined it). In its first sense, the political judge will bias his decisions towards his own political preferences and inclinations. Thus the conservative judge will be predisposed towards conservative values and interests and against socialist interests.

Professor Griffith, in a book that has circulated very widely,[37] claims that judges in general in this country, by virtue of their training and class background, are inherently biased in favour of conservative interests. He also claims that that bias is translated

---

[36] See Dawn Oliver, 'Is the *ultra vires* rule the basis for judicial review?' [1987] *PL* 543; Sir John Laws, 'Illegality: The Problem of Jurisdiction' in M. Supperstone and J. Gouldie (eds.) *Judicial Review* (London, 1994), chap. 4. But see Sir William Wade and C. F. Forsythe, *Administrative Law*, 7th edn. (Oxford, 1994) 340 ff.

[37] J. A. G. Griffith, *The Politics of the Judiciary*, (4th edn., London, 1991).

into their decisions. Many of Griffith's examples of the bias of the conservative judge are taken from judicial decisions against the interests of organized labour, in favour of property rights or against labour party governments or local authorities.

It is of course impossible entirely to eliminate personal bias and political predilection, but there are ways to reduce the likelihood of bias, for example through the selection of judges from a broad range of backgrounds and interests. Another way is for judges to isolate themselves from policy-making, by allowing the necessary space to make policy to other bodies which are properly empowered and properly equipped for the task of policy-making.

A perennial issue over the years has been the extent to which local authorities are empowered by Parliament to engage in frankly politically-motivated decisions: to raise the wages of women employers to parity with those of men;[38] to grant concessionary railfares to the elderly,[39] to lower London transport fares by significant amounts;[40] to boycott the products of firms trading with South Africa in the days of apartheid;[41] or to ban stag hunting in the Quantock hills.[42] By intervening in these decisions judges are easy prey to allegations that they are acting politically. But in most, if not all, of these cases, it was by no means an open and shut question whether the local authority had been conferred power sufficiently wide to permit its social programme or the expression of moral outrage and, if so, whether the authority had otherwise acted improperly.

There can be no doubt that any judge who persistently confuses law with his or her personal values invites attack upon judicial independence.[43] But it must be noted that the 1990s have been marked by a series of decisions overturning Conservative ministers, so Griffith's allegations of bias are not easy now to sustain, if they ever were.

---

[38] *Roberts* v. *Hopwood* [1925] AC 578.
[39] *Prescott* v. *Birmingham Corporation* [1955] Ch. 210.
[40] *London Borough of Bromley* v. *Greater London Council* [1983] 1 AC 768.
[41] *R.* v. *Lewisham LBC, ex p. Shell UK Ltd* [1988] 1 All ER 938.
[42] *R.* v. *Somerset County Council, ex p. Fewings* [1995] 1 WLR 1037.
[43] Archibald Cox, 'The Independence of the Judiciary: History and Purposes', *U. of Dayton L Rev*. 196, 566, and cited in Lord Lester of Herne Hill QC's Suffian Lecture in Malaysia, Jan. 1997, 'Human Rights and the Rule of Law: Memories and Reflections'.

There is, however, a second way in which judges may be said to act politically: when they engage in techniques to ensure the public acceptance of their own decisions. Here we observe judges as political actors not in the sense of biasing their decisions in favour of their political predispositions or their socio-economic preferences, but of acting so as to maximize the legitimacy of their decisions. Judges here are in the political arena in the sense of winning and maintaining support for their constitutional role. There is nothing improper about that.

Judges have proved astute politicians in that sense over the years, employing a variety of presentational techniques: They may decide a case on the narrowest ground, a technique designed to avoid controversy, while not compromising the result.[44]

Judges sometimes claim that judicial review involves only procedure or at most the way decisions are reached, but never touches on matters of substance; a dubious statement, but one that reassures the public that judges are not trespassing on the legislative terrain.[45]

Recently the courts have even put out press releases to try and persuade us that their decisions were in no way meant as usurpations of the minister's authority, and that the decisions were by no means meant personally.[46]

Examining Phase Two of judicial review, the war years up to the 1960s, it seems clear that judges were acting as bureaucrats. There was little reason in logic or principle why the former broad duty to decide anything fairly was narrowed where a privilege rather than a right was in issue, and where the body was acting administratively rather than judicially. Those distinctions were manufactured and spurious. Judicial review by no means came to a complete standstill in those years, but by and large, when discretion was conferred upon a public official, the courts were over-anxious to ensure that the free exercise of that discretion not be obstructed, and they were

---

[44] As in *Ex p. Shell UK Ltd.*, n. 41, above and *Wheeler* v. *Leicester City Council* [1985] 1 AC 1054 (HL)—compare the more expansive approach of Browne-Wilkinson LJ in the CA, *ibid*. at 1064–5.

[45] e.g. in *R.* v. *Chief Constable of North Wales, ex p. Evans* [1982] 1 WLR 1155, *per* Lord Brightman; *R.* v. *Secretary of State for Home Affairs, ex p. Brind* [1991] AC 696, *per* Lords Ackner and Lowry.

[46] As was done in the recent judgment of the CA, *R.* v. *Secretary of State for the Home Department, ex p. Fayed* [1997] 1 All ER 228.

little interested in seeking any broader principles guiding the
limitation of official power.

What caused the judiciary to become deferential to official
power, to devise technical barriers to judicial intervention? The
answers normally provided to this question are these: the world
wars and the growth of the welfare state. Parliament, from 1914
on, conferred sweeping powers on ministers so that they could act
flexibly and swiftly in the interest of national security. At about the
same time we witness the rise of the welfare state. At the beginning
of the century the state was barely noticeable outside the odd
policeman and post office.[47] From the second decade the scope of
the state, as provider, regulator, as well as protector grows
exponentially. Discretion is required for its new and complex tasks.
Nevertheless, the discouragement to judicial activism was not often
explicitly contained in the governing statutes. It was largely of the
judges' own doing.

Looking back now at the writings on the constitution during that
period one is struck by the unanimity that the role of the courts
should not be too prominent. Professor Jennings took issue with
Dicey's notion of the Rule of Law,[48] which for Dicey principally
meant that law should be certain·and predictable. Discretionary
power was for Dicey inherently unpredictable and therefore offends
the rule of law. For Jennings the rule of law could impede the
necessary introduction or the implementation of discretionary
powers, and thus obstruct a great deal of the new activity carried
out by the state. Aneurin Bevan, health minister in the 1945
Labour government, established a system of tribunals in his newly
created national health service so as to insulate decisions from the
danger of what he called 'judicial sabotage of socialist legislation'.[49] Attention was drawn to the perils of an overweening
executive. Lord Hewart, the Lord Chancellor, had warned of the
new despotism in a book of that title.[50] William Robson, in his
book *Justice and Administrative Law*,[51] identified what he called

---

[47] As pointed out by A. J. P. Taylor in *English History, 1914–1945* (London,
1965), 1.
[48] Sir W. Ivor Jennings, *The Law and the Constitution* (London, 1933), 309–11.
[49] HC Rep., 23 July 1946, col. 1983.
[50] Published in 1929, but mainly directed towards the dangers of delegated
legislation, then considered by the Donoughmore Committee in 1932.
[51] First published in 1928.

the 'hegemony of the executive' (a phase which has a surprisingly modern—or post modern—ring to it) and favoured new measures to control the executive, but preferably through tribunals outside the judicial realm.

Judges during this period were content to accept all this advice to act as loyal civil servants. What was the cause of the almost abrupt switch to a more activist, less bureaucratic attitude of the judiciary in the 1960s? Why at that time, under what authority, did this change of course occur? The usual explanation is that a combination of events brought this about.

Most accounts focus on influence of two judges, Lords Reid and Denning.[52] Lord Reid was the presiding judge at the time in the House of Lords, and all the path-breaking cases I earlier mentioned bear his leading judgment. Lord Denning, then Master of the Rolls, was involved in all but one of those cases (*Ridge* v. *Baldwin*[53]) and in all those cases had been the sole dissenter in the Court of Appeal. Lord Denning had already set out his approach in his Hamlyn lectures in 1949, entitled *Freedom Under the Law*. These lectures contain the germ of a number of the later 'grounds' of review and additional search for new principles, some of them explicitly taken from French administrative law, to control discretionary powers. In 1953, in his book *The Changing Law*, Denning begins with an account of the social revolution in this century which he said was accompanied by a constitutional revolution. 'In legal theory', he wrote, 'Parliament is still sovereign, and we still claim to be under the rule of law: but anxiety is raised in many quarters by the growing powers of the executive.'[54] Throughout that book he staked a role for law and judges (sometimes called 'upright' or 'independent' judges) as arbiters of the constitution and protectors of freedom against the abuse of power. Well before *Ridge* v. *Baldwin*, Lord Denning had been paving the way for a broader duty to provide natural justice in his decisions about the powers of domestic tribunals and in some of the judgments bearing his hand in the Privy Council.[55]

Other explanations for the abrupt change in judicial attitudes stress the influence of the Franks Committee on Administrative

---

[52] See the account by Griffith in *Judicial Politics Since 1920*, n. 35 above.
[53] N. 10 above. [54] At 1.
[55] E.g. *Kanda* v.*Government of Malaya* [1962] AC 322.

Tribunals and Enquiries,[56] which came to the conclusion that these techniques of decision-making should be set in the sphere of justice rather than administration. The Franks report led to the judicialization of a number of tribunals and inquiries, so the path to more participative adminstration had been officially accepted, at least in respect of fair hearings in quasi-judicial settings.

A psycho-social explanation for the change is also sometimes offered.[57] The habit of deference in the people had been broken, whether through the experience of observing the incompetent behaviour of the officer classes during the First World War, or refusing to accept the patronage of the civil service in the allocation of welfare benefits to the deserving poor, or through a new questioning of the professional arrogance of the planners as they ordered closely knit communities to make way for motorways and modern monoliths.

Then there were the influences from abroad. Citizen participation and welfare rights were cries that carried across the Atlantic at a time of American ascendancy. The echo of the songs of the freedom marchers in Mississippi was joined by different voices demanding different rights of different kinds in different countries.

In 1951 Britain acceded to the European Convention on Human Rights. We were the first signatory. The Convention has never been incorporated into our domestic law, but in 1966 the right of direct petition to the Court of Human Rights at Strasbourg was permitted to British citizens. At least in international law, the primacy of rights over convenience was now recognized.[58] In the mid 1970s, European Community law incorporated into its jurisprudence the jurisprudence of the European Convention—so the Convention had to be applied in all directly effective EC law.[59]

And the textbooks were available. In 1959 Professor de Smith set out the principles of judicial review in a massive thesis, citing 1,800 cases, thus proving even to the positivist that a subject existed to be applied.[60] Professor Wade's book followed, and endorsed the

---

[56] Cmnd. 218 (1957).

[57] See e.g. Professor Griffith's account in 'The Political Constitution' (1979) 42 *MLR* 1.

[58] Note also the laws prohibiting race and sex discrimination enacted from 1964, which established positive statutory rights to equality in those areas.

[59] *Nold* v. *Commission*, Case 4/73 [1974] ECR 491.

[60] S. A. de Smith, *Judicial Review of Administrative Action* (London, 1959), now in its 5th edn. as de Smith, Woolf, and Jowell.

enterprise.[61] Some law departments in the United Kingdom began to teach administrative law to the students, although even in the late 1970s Lord Scarman was urging that the subject be compulsory and that it be systematically taught everywhere, as it was not then being done.

All these factors may well have played their parts in the restraint of the state by judges from the mid-1960s. We must still ask, however, whether it is *proper* for the judiciary to respond to social trends or attitudes in this way. Were not the judges, in discarding their old deferential ways, themselves acting out of political motivation, perhaps even relishing the fact that ministers of a labour government were the principal objects of their reproach during those heady days?

The relationship between public attitudes and legal principle in public law needs more careful consideration than the historians have yet provided. If the public bray for blood should the judges satisfy them any more then if they rage for rights?

It is surprising that our legal historians of this century ignore, in their accounts of the development of public law, one of the two factors that, according to Sir Isaiah Berlin, have shaped human history in this century. Berlin writes in an essay in 'The Crooked Timber of Humanity':

There are, in my view, two factors that, above all others, have shaped human history in this century. One is the development of the natural sciences and technology, certainly the great success story of our time—to this great and mounting attention has been paid from all quarters. The other, without doubt, consists in the great ideological storms that have altered the lives of virtually all mankind: the Russian Revolution and its aftermath—totalitarian tyrannies of both right and left and the explosions of nationalism, racism, and, in places, of religious bigotry, which, interestingly enough, not one among the most perceptive social thinkers of the nineteenth century had ever predicted.

When our descendants, in two or three centuries time (if mankind survives until then), come to look at our age, it is these two phenomena that will, I think, be held to be the outstanding characteristics of our century, the most demanding of explanation and analysis.

---

[61] H. W. R. Wade, *Administrative Law* (Oxford, 1969), now in its 7th edn. as Wade and Forsythe.

The ideological storms of this century passed by these islands, to their eternal credit. But the fallout has been significant. Germany in the 1930s demonstrated how possible it was that a democratically elected regime could, in the name of the popular will, transform itself into totalitarian tyranny. The Soviet Empire graphically displayed the results of the ruthless pursuit of popular and even noble ends if those ends were pursued without regard to the means necessary to achieve them. Democracy could never again be confused with majority rule, or the fulfilment of the majority will. Rights against the state should not in future be conferred merely by gift of the state. These rights, to life itself, and to expression, among others, are inherent in the respect that democracy must accord to every citizen in equal measure. The great symbol of that respect is the right to a vote which carries, for each voter, equal weight. But the respect extends beyond that into the way government treats with each individual, even between elections, and irrespective of the will of the electorate or the word of Parliament.[62] Democracy could no longer be confused with majority rule, or even with the sovereignty of Parliament. A true democracy contains at its centre principles recognizing that certain rights should be permanently protected even from the will of a temporal majority.

None of this was spelled out at the time. In 1974 Lord Justice Scarman, in his Hamlyn Lectures, argued for an entrenched bill of rights by means of incorporation of the European Convention into domestic law.[63] That apart, the approach via judicial review was essentially empirical; applying justice in the individual case, but without rooting the decisions in any constitutional soil or referring explicitly to any expected principles in a democracy.

The *GCHQ* case, in 1984,[64] in my view opened the door to a more coherent approach, especially in the speech of Lord Diplock. *GCHQ* was one of the last cases in which Lord Diplock sat before he died. He was ailing at the time. In his last few years he had confessed to being a convert to the merits of judicial review.[65] (Lord Diplock had been in the majority in the Court of Appeal in

---

[62] 'Equal concern and respect' is a phrase employed by Ronald Dworkin who has played an important role in conceptualizing the notion of limited government (as well as the proper role of the judiciary in a democracy). See especially his *Law's Empire* (London, 1986) and *Freedom's Law* (New York, 1996).

[63] *English Law—The New Dimension* (London, 1974), 14.

[64] N. 19 above.   [65] *O'Reilly* v. *Mackman* [1983] 2 AC 277.

virtually all the cases I mentioned earlier in which Lord Denning had dissented in the 1960s.) When he reached the House of Lords Lord Diplock had quietly been fashioning, with Lord Wilberforce, a notion of public law being conceptually distinct from private law.[66] In *GCHQ* he had the opportunity to apply that distinction in a way which positively aided the appellants. They would have no rights under private law, but public law required a focus on the way the state should act towards an individual, and, in this case, a legitimate expectation gave rise to a public law duty to provide a fair hearing (or would have, had national security not interceded).

But perhaps the most significant advance was made in a passage in Lord Diplock's speech in *GCHQ*, hardly necessary for the judgment itself, but which attained immediate impact. It was the passage in which he enunciated what he called the 'grounds' of judicial review.[67] These were: illegality, procedural impropriety, and irrationality. These grounds were seized upon by practitioners as categories within which to frame applications for judicial review. Their acceptance played more of a part than mere convenience; they finally released judicial review from its dependence upon the technicality of jurisdictional error as the only permissible ground of review, apart from patent error of law. The narrow and elusive nature of jurisdictional error was never satisfactory or indeed entirely comprehensible. From then on it was unlawful administration that was subject to judicial review (under the newly defined grounds), not jurisdictionally wrong administration.

Of even greater significance was the fact that Lord Diplock separated the ground of illegality (under which a body contravenes or exceeds the terms of the power authorizing the decision) from procedural impropriety (bias or failure to provide a hearing) and irrationality (which I shall come to in a moment). By so doing, he exploded the fiction that all judicial review is concerned with the interpretation of Parliament's will. Much of it is so concerned, and that question is considered under the ground of legality. But a decision may faithfully pursue the purpose of a statute and still fail the tests of procedural impropriety or irrationality. These two grounds therefore invite justification on the ground of constitutional principle outside parliamentary supremacy.

---

[66] e.g. in *Gouriet* v. *Union of Post Office Workers* [1978] AC 435.
[67] [1985] AC 374, at 410–11.

Procedural propriety provides this obviously. It rests upon the requirement in a democracy that, where possible, individuals should participate in decisions that affect them. But what of rationality, or 'unreasonableness', as it is still sometimes called?

Lord Greene's formulation of an unreasonable decision in the *Wednesbury* case in 1947[68] as one which is not just unreasonable but 'so unreasonable that no reasonable authority could so decide', as awkward as it was, sought, quite properly, to enjoin the judge from interfering with a decision on the ground of policy, or lightly challenging its merits. *Wednesbury* thus seeks to confine judges to their appropriate constitutional role and to restrict them to the area of their own institutional competence. It has also proved a deft tool of judicial politics. The mere incantation of its tautological formula tends to mesmerize the listener into accepting that judges do not interfere with the merits of decisions. The truth is that the *Wednesbury* formulation does permit judges so to interfere, but only where the decision is manifestly unreasonable, in extreme cases, where the decision is, to use current terminology, 'perverse' or 'absurd'.[69]

There is of course something deeply unsatisfactory about the logic of this approach. If *Wednesbury* seeks to proclaim a principle limiting the judge's constitutional and institutional competence, what justifies the relaxation of that principle in extreme or manifest cases? How robust can be a principle which is programmed to collapse under pressure? Or only to be triggered *in extremis*? In the absence of a more precise delineation of *when* a case is manifest or extreme, of the situations in which intervention is sanctioned, *Wednesbury* is hardly useful as a guide to the public and decision-maker. It is also an unreliable predictor of judicial behaviour.

In the *GCHQ* case Lord Diplock appeared to understand the fragile logic of *Wednesbury*, and recast its definition. He defined irrationality as 'a decision which is so outrageous in its defiance of logic or accepted moral standards that no person who had applied his mind to the question to be decided could have arrived at it'.[70]

Although by no means abandoning the notion of judicial reserve

---

[68] *Associated Provincial Picture Houses Ltd.* v. *Wednesbury Corporation* [1948] 1 KB 223.

[69] See *R.* v. *Secretary of State for the Environment, ex p. Notts. CC* [1986] A.C. 240, *per* Lord Scarman at 247–8.   [70] [1985] AC 374, at 410.

(Lord Diplock's irrational decision still had to be 'outrageous') the altered formulation was important for its more specific reference to the logic and ratiocination of a decision. Most significantly, moral standards are recognized as a feature of the exercise of state power, thus inviting the judicial elaboration of the moral duties of the state, and moral rights against the state.

What in practice lies under the cover of unreasonableness? First are decisions that are strictly irrational, in the sense of lacking logic or intelligible justification.[71] Here we have the arbitrary decision, one failing to rest on any evidential basis or justified by incomprehensible reasons. The intensity of review in these cases is not evidently low, but by definition perhaps these decisions are absurd or perverse.

But there are other unreasonable decisions where the margin of appreciation is not adjusted in favour of the decision maker; where scarcely any regard is paid to the *Wednesbury* reserve. One such example is the recent acceptance of a legitimate expectation as grounding a substantive right not to have that expectation disappointed. Thus the Inland Revenue may not resile without notice from an authorized and unqualified representation made to a taxpayer as to how he may organize his affairs.[72] Another example is the increasing acceptance of the notion of unequal treatment as grounding a claim of unreasonableness. Immigration regulations have been struck down as 'manifestly unjust and unreasonable' because they had the effect of discriminating against immigrants from less affluent countries.[73]

Both these examples rest on specific principles. The legitimate expectation rests on the principle of legal certainty, which underlines the Rule of Law. The second example rests on the principle of equality, which requires not only consistent treatment of like cases (again an element of the rule of law) but also, as in the immigration regulations case, substantive equality, namely, that similar situations ought not to be treated differently unless properly

---

[71] See de Smith, Woolf and Jowell, *Judicial Review of Administrative Action* (London, 1995), paras. 13–019–024.

[72] *R. v. Inland Revenue Commission, ex p. Matrix-Securities Ltd.* [1994] 1 WLR 334; *R. v. Inland Revenue Commission, ex p. Unilever plc* [1996] STC 681, [1996] COD 421.

[73] *R. v. Immigration Appeal Tribunal, ex p. Manshoora Begum* [1986] IAR 385.

justified (this second sense of equality is wider than that en-
compassed under the rule of law).[74]

In European Community law, legal certainty and equality are
proclaimed as 'general principles of law', assumed to be common to
all countries of the European Union, inherent in their democratic
structures.[75]

There are, however, categories of decision where the courts do
require something 'overwhelming' or 'outrageous' before being
willing to intervene. First are cases where the decision maker placed
excessive weight on one particular consideration, even though it
was lawful to take that consideration into account. The balance of
relevant considerations should in principle be primarily a matter for
the decision-maker. But the judges have intervened in cases such as
where the Home Secretary, in a decision not to release a prisoner,
took into account the prisoner's misdemeanour while on temporary
release some years back.[76] The weight accorded to the relatively
minor   misdemeanour   rendered   the   decision   unreasonable.
European law—both that of the Court of Justice and Court of
Human Rights—would here invoke the principle of proportionality, the third general principle of EC law, to justify intervention.[77]

A second situation where proportionality would be applicable
under European law is the case where the impact of the decision on
the applicant was oppressive, because it caused unnecessary
hardship or onerous infringements of his interests or rights.
Decisions of this kind include onerous conditions attached to
planning permissions.[78] The principle of proportionality would
contend that the means in these cases were excessive and
unnecessary to achieve the legitimate end. A less restrictive
alternative should have been sought.

In the *GCHQ* case[79] Lord Diplock tantalizingly suggested that
proportionality could possibly become a fourth ground of judicial

---

[74] For an elaboration of this distinction see J. Jowell, 'Is Equality a Constitutional
Principle?' (1994) 47 *CLP* 1.

[75] See D. Wyatt and A. Dashwood, *European Community Law* (London, 1993),
95–8.

[76] *R.* v. *Secretary of State for the Home Department, ex p. Handscomb* (1988) 68
Cr.App.R. 59; *Ex p. Walsh* [1992] COD 240.

[77] See J. Schwartze, *European Administrative Law* (London, 1992) chap. 5.

[78] *R.* v. *Hillingdon LBC, ex p. Royco Homes Ltd.* [1974] QB 720.

[79] N. 70 above.

review in England. It has not yet been authoritatively accepted or rejected, although sometimes applied. Lord Lowry in the *Brind* case strongly urged that proportionality is foreign to our judicial review because it does not contain the *Wednesbury* reserve and permits review on the merits of the case.[80] In practice, however, the margin of appreciation under proportionality in European Community law is elastic. When interpretation of a fundamental provision of the Treaty of Rome is in issue, then proportionality is strictly construed. The function of review in such a case is equivalent to the English court's function under the ground of illegality, where the margin of appreciation to the decision maker need not be extended. In respect of the exercise of discretion in the making of policy choices in a complex area of regulation, however, where decisions are made in respect of the common agricultural policy, the European Court is essentially deferential towards the administration, and will intervene only where the measures are 'manifestly inappropriate'.[81]

Proportionality is perhaps, therefore, *unreasonableness* under a different name, but it is a more pointed principle than unreasonableness, a specific aspect of unreasonableness, and one that is better able to focus on a particular quality of desirable decision-making, namely, that less restrictive alternatives should be considered, as should the relation between legitimate ends and appropriate means. It is, after all, one of the hallmarks of tyranny that means may be sacrificed to ends. And a hallmark of liberty that fidelity to the ends of public policy should not inevitably justify the means of attaining it.

Perhaps the most striking current development on the ground of unreasonableness is in respect of cases where fundamental human rights have been in issue. Over the past decade the courts have explicitly recognized, in the absence of inconsistent legislation, rights such as freedom of speech.[82] In judicial review, they have lowered the *Wednesbury* threshold in cases involving asylum

---

[80] R. v. *Secretary of State for Home Affairs, ex p. Brind* [1991] AC 696 at 766–7.
[81] This point is clearly brought out in G. de Burca, 'The principle of proportionality and its application in EC law' (1993) 13 *Yearbook of European Law* 105. For a recent illustration see *Germany* v. *Council (Bananas)*, Case C–280/93, 5 Oct. 1994.
[82] e.g. *Derbyshire County Council* v. *Times Newspapers Ltd.* [1993] AC 534.

seekers, where their right to life was in issue, to impose 'anxious' or 'heightened' scrutiny of the decision of the Home Secretary.[83] In the *Brind* case, the House of Lords refused to strike down the Home Secretary's ban on the broadcasting of the direct spoken words of various proscribed organizations in Northern Ireland. The conferment of broad discretionary power by Parliament to the Home Secretary was held not to be ambiguous, which did not permit the matter to be decided under the standards of the European Convention as a treaty obligation. The ban was held not unreasonable, but the majority of their Lordships held that, in assessing whether the decision was unreasonable, the more substantial the interference with human rights, the more the court will require by way of justification before it is satisfied that the decision is unreasonable.[84] This approach has been continued, and was applied by the Court of Appeal in a recent case where the Minister of Defence's ban on homosexuals in the armed forces was in issue.[85]

One of the clearest expressions of this trend was provided in 1992 in the case of *Leech (No. 2)*. The Prison Rules permitted interference with a prisoner's correspondence with his legal advisor. The Court of Appeal held the Rules invalid. Steyn LJ, as he then was, held that the Rules interfered with the prisoner's 'constitutional right' of access to justice. Using the language of proportionality, he also held that there was no 'self evident and pressing need' for the exercise of that power.[86] That important decision has already been followed in a number of cases.[87]

The *Leech* case, and others that are now flowing from the courts, show that the disaggregation of unreasonableness is gathering speed. In place of *Wednesbury*'s obscurity, a set of clearer principles are being articulated: principles of rationality, certainty, equality, perhaps proportionality, along with explicit recognition of human rights.

[83] e.g. *Bugdaycay* v. *Secretary of State for Home Department* [1987] AC 514, 531, *per* Lord Bridge, 537–8, *per* Lord Templeman.

[84] [1991] AC 696, *per* Lords Bridge, Roskill, and Templeman.

[85] *R.* v. *Ministry of Defence, ex p. Smith* [1996] QB 517.

[86] *R.* v. *Secretary of State for the Home Department, ex p. Leech (No. 2)* [1994] QB 198.

[87] e.g. *R.* v. *Secretary of State for The Home Department, ex p. Simms and O'Brien, The Times*, 17 Jan. 1997.

These principles themselves require interpretation, but they are more specific by far, and more predictable, than the *Wednesbury* test. Decisions based on them also stand out as being different in kind, not merely in category, from policy decisions, or decisions on the merits of a case. It cannot be disputed that judges are expected, and equipped and required to elucidate and apply those principles which are necessary to support a constitutional democracy.

Finally, it must be briefly asked, looking to the future, how the incorporation of the convention into our domestic law might affect the business of judicial review and, the quality of our democracy.

The argument against incorporation rests largely on the fear that it will involve a reallocation of power from the elected legislature towards an unelected judiciary. This spectre of a future government by unelected judges is both exaggerated and flawed. It is exaggerated by ignoring the trends in judicial review I have mentioned, and the fact that English judges have even now to apply the Convention when they apply directly effective European Community law, which incorporates the jurisprudence of the Convention. It is flawed as it places far too much emphasis on judicial decision-making and far too little on the moral consequences of constitutional principle. Judicial review, even in a country with a written constitution and a bill of rights is, as Professor de Smith pointed out, peripheral and sporadic.[88] Judicial intervention will of course be made from time to time, but only to test the margins of a provision, to elaborate upon an ambiguity, to define the limits of an exception. A bill of rights makes its impact on behaviour and indeed on attitudes irrespective of judicial intervention. It endorses and declares as operative a set of principles inherent in a democracy. These principles, as Dicey recognized, possess their own gravitational force, settling on the minds and the actions of officials in all governmental institutions. The Bill of Rights will be taught in the schools, and be instructed to the police. Much, though perhaps not all, of the principles that now guide our constitutional behaviour will be explicitly and officially endorsed, and thus be more apparent and accessible. Better predictions of acceptable official behaviour will be able to be made, and more precise prohibitions to be warned against.

[88] In the words of de Smith, *Judicial Review of Administrative Action* (1959–95 edns.), 1.

The unpredictable 'ideological storms' which swirled around us with such ferocity during this century seem, at its close, to have abated. In the century's last decade, one of the most formidable casualties of those storms, the Soviet Union, quietly folded its banner of absolutist government and withered away, although not to an end that Marx had predicted for the final stage of socialism. Insofar as ideologies vie with each other now, they quibble rather than quarrel over the finer tunings of the limits of a free economic market. Accord over the limits of government is perhaps less apparent. Countries now seeking a choice between unrestrained majoritarianism and limited government would be risking too much if they left the resolution of that dilemma to an unwritten constitution. They could, however, do worse than consult both the practice of our polity and the judgments of our courts which have together carved, from crooked timber, a model of democracy which portrays the necessary power of the state—yet demarcates its necessary limits.

THE CRITICAL CONDITION
OF CRIMINAL LAW

Ian Dennis

Introduction

Criticism of the state of criminal law in England is hardly a new phenomenon. It has been a feature of the legal landscape since at least the first half of the nineteenth century, when the Criminal Law Commissioners issued their series of eight reports recommending substantial reforms to the content of the law and codification of its form.[1] In 1874, some twenty years after the collapse of the first attempt at codification, Sir Alexander Cockburn, the Lord Chief Justice of the day, uttered a sentiment with a familiar modern ring. It was, he said, a matter for regret that the criminal 'law of England should be suffered to remain in its present state of confusion, arising from it being partly unwritten and partly in statutes so imperfectly drawn as to be almost worse than unwritten law'.[2] A glance at the extensive modern literature on criminal law shows that criticism has continued to develop in quantity and intensity for more than a century. This criticism takes many forms[3] and has

---

[1] *First Report, Parl. Pap.* (1834) XXXVI 105; *Second Report, Parl. Pap.* (1836) XXXVI 183; *Third Report, Parl. Pap.* (1837) XXX 1; *Fourth Report, Parl. Pap.* (1839) XIX 235; *Fifth Report, Parl. Pap.* (1840) XX 1; *Sixth Report, Parl. Pap.* (1841) X 1; *Seventh Report, Parl. Pap.* (1843) XIX 1 183; *Eighth Report, Parl. Pap.* (1845) XIV 161. For an illuminating discussion see R. Cross, 'The Reports of the Criminal Law Commissioners (1833–1849) and the Abortive Bills of 1853' in (P. Glazebrook (ed.), *Reshaping the Criminal Law* (London, 1978).
[2] See the App. to the *Select Committee Report on the Homicide Law Amendment Bill, Parl. Pap.* (1874) ix, cited in P. Glazebrook, 'Still No Code! English Criminal Law 1894–1994', in (M. Dockray (ed), *City University Centenary Lectures in Law* (London, 1996). 1, 6.
[3] Ranging from the detailed points of doctrine and interpretation to be found in practitioners' texts such as *Archbold* (for a strong example see the critique of the decision of the CA in *Gomez* [1991] 3 All ER 394 in the 44th ed. (London, 1992), para. 21/45 ff.) to the comprehensive attacks by scholars in the critical legal studies

many different targets; common to much, although not all, of it is what William Twining has described in another context as optimistic rationalism.[4] As one might expect, optimistic critics frequently disagree over how the law should be interpreted or reformed, but they generally accept the underlying premise that correct interpretation and rational improvement of the law are both possible and desirable. Some of the more trenchant rationalists have been fierce in their condemnation of the modern law. For example, Peter Glazebrook has commented tersely in a recent retrospect that the condition of the criminal law is now decidedly worse than it was at the time of Cockburn's comment in 1874.[5]

It is this critical comment which provides an appropriate starting-point for my article. In line with the aspirations of the current series I propose to offer some reflections on aspects of the development of the criminal law in the twentieth century, and in the concluding part of the article to speculate somewhat briefly on the prospects for the future. It seems to me that Glazebrook's comment, taken in the context of what we might call a critical mass of scholarship, provokes the following questions. In what kinds of ways, and to what extent, can English criminal law be said to be in a seriously defective state? If it is in such a state, and I shall be expressing the view that its condition is critical, how and why has this happened? What is the ætiology of the present state of the law? Finally, depending on the answers we give to these latter questions, what, if anything, should be done? In attempting to answer the last question I shall join ranks with the optimistic rationalists. I believe that we can and should do better, although I also think that the task of rescuing the criminal law from its present plight is becoming increasingly difficult.

My study will focus on that part of the criminal law which forms the bulk of virtually all degree courses on criminal law and which accounts for much of the work of the criminal justice system in practice. I refer to the general principles of criminal liability together with specific offences of violence, stealing, and vandalism.

---

tradition: see, e.g., M. Kelman, 'Interpretive Construction in the Substantive Criminal Law' (1981) 33 *Stanford LR* 591; A. Norrie, *Crime Reason and History* (London, 1993).

[4] *Rethinking Evidence* (Oxford, 1990), chap. 3, esp. at 75.

[5] N. 2 above, 8.

These offences are central to the criminal law. They protect the fundamental interests that all people have in the security of their persons and property.[6] In so far as the content of any of the criminal law is uncontroversial, there is virtually universal acceptance of the necessity for these offences.[7] This is not to say, of course, that there may not be important differences over their proper scope and limits. Instances of these offences are regularly reported as news stories in the media, and in that sense they are the most public and visible part of the criminal law. In practice offences of violence, theft, and criminal damage between them account for 96 per cent of recorded offences.[8] The general part of criminal law, which includes the general principles of culpability, is relevant not just to these offences but to all offences investigated and prosecuted. Leaving aside problems with other areas of the criminal law, of which there are many, it is this mainstream, everyday, criminal law that I wish to suggest is now in a critical condition.

Critique

(I) STANDARDS OF ASSESSMENT

Any such critique presupposes standards against which the law is to be measured. I claim no great originality for the standards I wish to employ. If we subscribe to certain fundamental moral and political values embodied in the liberal democratic ideal,[9] then I think we are entitled to demand that our criminal law should respect and express those values. In particular this means that the criminal law should give effect to three basic principles. These are the principles of legality, fairness, and coherence. All three might be described, in

---

[6] P. Stein and J. Shand, *Legal Values in Western Society* (Edinburgh, 1974), 31, cited by Lord Edmund-Davies in *DPP* v. *Majewski* [1976] 2 All ER 142, 168.

[7] N. MacCormick, *Legal Right and Social Democracy* (Oxford, 1982), 28.

[8] *Criminal Statistics* (London, 1995). I include in theft related offences such as burglary and handling stolen goods.

[9] These are the values of respect for the rights of individuals, particularly rights to various kinds of individual freedoms, respect for the rule of law and respect for fair procedures. It is beyond the scope of this essay to mount a detailed defence of the priority given to these values, but in making claims for them as fundamental I am drawing on classic liberal writing over the last thirty years, including H. L. A. Hart, *Punishment and Responsibility* (Oxford, 1968); R. M. Dworkin, *Taking Rights Seriously* (London, 1977); J. Raz, *The Morality of Freedom* (Oxford, 1986).

Gallie's terminology, as essentially contestable concepts,[10] but I suggest that in this context we can assign meanings to each which will command a reasonable degree of support. With Ashworth,[11] I take the principle of legality to embody 'Rule of Law' arguments: that penal law should not be retrospective and that it should give fair warning to citizens of the conduct which the state prohibits. As regards fairness, I agree with Simester and Smith that it is essential that rules of criminal liability express morally relevant differences between cases, and that in other respects like cases are treated alike.[12] We might also add here Thomas' point that the form of the criminal law should be suited to the functions of the criminal justice process.[13] In this way the chances of controlling over-extensive discretion and achieving accurate and consistent outcomes of criminal process are maximized.[14] For the purposes of this article I will put to one side all the numerous issues concerned with the fairness of the process itself. They are the subject for another occasion. Finally, coherence requires the law to be based on reasonably clear and consistent principles which can provide both rational justification for decisions falling within the scope of existing rules and also guidance for decisions in situations of uncertainty. Issues of theory and structure of the law would be subsumed under this heading.[15]

Certain intermediate instrumental standards help to serve these fundamental principles. They were set out in the the Law Commission's 1989 *Report on the Draft Criminal Code*,[16] and it is

[10] W. Gallie, 'Essentially Contested Concepts' (1955–6) *Proceedings of the Aristotelian Society* 167.

[11] A. J. Ashworth, *Principles of Criminal Law* 2nd edn. (Oxford, 1995), 67 ff. . The principle of non-retroactivity is set out in Art 7.1 of the European Convention on Human Rights.

[12] A. P. Simester and A. T. H. Smith, 'Criminalisation and the Role of Theory' in A. P. Simester and A. T. H. Smith, (eds.), *Harm and Culpability* (Oxford, 1996) 1.

[13] D. A. Thomas, 'Form and Function in Criminal Law' in *Reshaping the Criminal Law*, n. 1 above, 21.

[14] See further D. J. Galligan, 'Regulating Pre-Trial Decisions' in I. H. Dennis (ed.) *Criminal Law and Justice* (London, 1987), 177; N. Lacey, 'Discretion and Due Process at the Post-Conviction Stage', *ibid.* 221.

[15] See, for a penetrating discussion, N. Lacey, 'Contingency, Coherence and Conceptualism: Reflections on the Encounter between "Critique" and "the Philosophy of the Criminal Law" ' in A. Duff (ed.), *Philosophy of the Criminal Law* (Cambridge, 1997).

[16] *A Criminal Code for England and Wales* (Law Com. No. 177, London, 1989), Vol. 1, paras. 2.1–2.11.

useful to remind ourselves of their concerns. The Law Commission *Report* proposed standards for the criminal law of accessibility, comprehensibility, consistency, and certainty. Accessibility—the standard that the law should be reasonably easy to find—and comprehensibility—the standard that the law should be reasonably easy to understand—are essential for several reasons. One is instrumental efficiency: law which is hard to find and/or which is expressed in archaic or obscure terms is likely to produce not just expensive and time-consuming legal argument as to what the law is, but also an increased risk of the court misunderstanding the law. This risk is magnified by the extensive use of lay decision-makers in the criminal courts and by the numbers of part-time judges used in the Crown Court, many of whom may have had little previous experience of criminal work.[17] Secondly, errors in finding and stating the law may produce unfairness in outcomes. Dispositive justice fails, for example, if defendants are wrongly convicted on a misdirection which even their own lawyers fail to spot. Conversely, an error corrected on appeal may result in the quashing of a conviction of a person against whom there is a substantial case on the merits. An order for a retrial, available since 1988, lessens the possibility of a failure to do justice in such cases, but the order is discretionary. Thirdly, it seems self-evident that law which is inaccessible or incomprehensible may be inadequate for the purpose of giving citizens fair warning of the reach of the criminal law. It is perhaps worth emphasizing that these values I have referred to of legality, fairness, and coherence cut across traditional crime-control and due-process debates. The competing priorities of social protection and individual liberty may equally be jeopardized by law which is defective in these respects.

Lack of certainty in the criminal law also threatens these values. Uncertainty produces inefficiency in the form of unnecessary legal argument about issues which could be settled in any competent criminal code. It may lead to unfairness in the form of discouraging prosecution of culpable defendants because of difficulty in assessing the realistic prospect of conviction. Alternatively, where charges are brought, uncertainty may lead to wide and strained interpretations of the law in ways not envisaged by the legislature. At this point

---

[17] *Ibid.*, para. 2.5; Law Commission, *Offences Against the Person and General Principles* (Law Com. No. 218, London, 1993), para. 4.4.

considerations of fairness merge into those of legality. Uncertainty presents an obvious threat to the principle of legality, a risk which is magnified by the common law technique of retrospective declaration of the law.[18]

Lack of consistency is in some ways the most serious problem. Inconsistency may take many forms. It may be conceptual, terminological, doctrinal, theoretical. It betrays confusions and contradictions within the law itself, as Norrie has recently demonstrated in a sustained critique.[19] One result of inconsistency is inefficiency because doubt is raised about the correctness of existing law and about the ways in which the law should be developed. Inconsistency is a major threat to fairness because it may produce disparity in the treatment of defendants, a disparity which cannot be coherently rationalized.

(ii) The Law of Violence

I now turn to assess what I have described as mainstream criminal law against these criteria. It is not possible to attempt a complete analysis, but it is easy to demonstrate that the present law falls seriously short of the standards in several respects. It is convenient to begin with the law relating to violence. This law is still to be found partly in the common law offences of murder, manslaughter, and assault, and partly in the numerous offences contained in the Offences Against the Person Act 1861. Despite John Gardner's attempt to defend the 1861 Act[20] most commentators are agreed that the Act is long overdue for the scrapheap. In *Mandair*[21] Lord Mustill described it as an unsatisfactory statute which requires 'replacement by legislation which is soundly based in logic and expressed in language which everyone can understand'.[22] The Birmingham circuit judges were even less kind when they referred

---

[18] *Shaw* v. *DPP* [1962] AC 220 remains the classic example of a modern decision which flouted the principle of legality. It is strongly arguable that the decision of the HL in *R* [1992] 1 AC 599 to abolish the common law doctrine of immunity for marital rape did so also, although the European Court of Human Rights managed to hold that there was no violation of Art. 7 of the European Convention (*CR* v. *United Kingdom* [1996] 1 FLR 434). One wonders whether the Court would have reached this conclusion so easily if the policy arguments for abolition had not been so widely accepted.   [19] N. 3 above.
[20] 'Rationality and the Rule of Law in Offences Against The Person' [1994] *CLJ* 502.   [21] [1995] 1 AC 208.   [22] *Ibid.* 221.

to it as containing a 'great deal of arcane rubbish',[23] and a former Chairman of the Law Commission has called its operation 'a disgrace'.[24] The main charges against the Act are that its key provisions, and we can leave aside curiosities such as the offences of obstructing clergymen and assaulting magistrates trying to preserve wrecks, use archaic and misleading terminology, fail to distinguish adequately between serious and minor injury, have an incoherent penalty structure, and do substantive injustice by punishing defendants for doing harm that they neither intended nor foresaw. These criticisms were developed at length in the Law Commission report on *Offences Against the Person and General Principles*.[25] It is worth remembering that the 1861 Act was itself a consolidation which arose, like the other consolidations of 1861, out of the wreckage of the first failed attempt at codification in 1853. Greaves, the draftsman, admitted that he had made no attempt to introduce consistency as to substance or form.[26] It is extraordinary that this dustbin of an Act is still in everyday use 136 years later. Judges and juries are still having to wrestle with the meaning of the old term 'maliciously', a word whose ordinary meaning bears no relation whatsoever to its technical meaning in law. There are at least six reported decisions where appellate courts have had to correct errors by trial judges about this meaning.[27] Because of the failure to reform the law of non-fatal offences appeal courts are now having to decide whether the offence of 'assault occasioning actual bodily harm', an offence designed for street brawls, can be interpreted to include telephone calls which cause psychiatric illness. In the recent case of *Ireland*[28] the Court of Appeal has held that it can, and a more extreme example of strained interpretation would be hard to find.

The situation is no better when we turn to the common law of

---

[23] Law Com. No. 218 (London, 1993), para. 3.4, fn. 18.

[24] Brooke J, 'Call for New Law on Assault', *Guardian*, 17 Nov. 1993.

[25] Law Com. No. 218 (London, 1993).

[26] See J. C. Smith in [1991] Crim. LR 43, summarizing Greaves' own explanation of his consolidation enterprise in C. S. Greaves, *The Criminal Law Consolidation and Amendment Acts of the 24 and 25 Vict.* (2nd edn., London, 1862), xxvi.

[27] *Mowatt* [1968] 1 QB 421; *W v. Dolbey* (1983) 88 Cr.App.R 1; *Grimshaw* [1984] Crim. LR 108; *Rainbird* [1989] Crim. LR 505; *Savage* [1991] 2 All ER 220; *Parmenter* [1991] 2 All ER 225. The interpretation of the term 'malicious' in s. 20 of the 1861 Act adopted in these cases was confirmed by the HL in *Savage* [1992] 1 AC 699.   [28] [1997] 1 All ER 112.

homicide. In *Scarlett*[29] Beldam LJ referred to the 'antiquated relic of involuntary manslaughter based on the commission of an unlawful act' and described the law as being in urgent need of reform.[30] His remarks were echoed by the Law Commission which commented in a Consultation Paper that the doctrine of constructive manslaughter was unattractive in principle and an inappropriate feature of modern criminal law.[31] This is a good example of an offence which is both uncertain and inconsistent. It is inconsistent because the form of constructive liability it embodies ought to have been abolished in 1957 when Parliament got rid of its counterpart in the law of murder, the doctrine of constructive malice. It is uncertain because we do not know for sure whether the unlawful and dangerous act doctrine requires the act to be targeted at a potential victim.[32] In addition, now that the House of Lords in *Adomako*[33] has revived the concept of gross negligence for breach of duty cases, we do not know whether recklessness now has any role to play in manslaughter and, if so, what type of recklessness is involved. [34]

The offence of murder, like that of manslaughter, has never been defined by statute. This is a fact which foreign lawyers, particularly European lawyers, frequently find astounding. However, the elements of murder have been considered by the House of Lords on no fewer than five occasions since 1961. The first of the Lords' decisions[35] was reversed by statute six years later,[36] following intense criticism. The second decision[37] was reversed ten years later by the fourth.[38] Part of the fourth decision was almost immediately rewritten by the fifth,[39] and the fifth decision had subsequently to

---

[29] [1993] 4 All ER 629.

[30] *Ibid.* 631. For an equally critical comment on manslaughter by gross negligence see *Prentice* [1993] 4 All ER 935 (Lord Taylor CJ).

[31] Law Com. CP No. 135 (London, 1994), paras. 2.52–2.54.

[32] Compare *Dalby* [1982] 1 All ER 916 with *Goodfellow* (1986) 83 Cr.App.R 23 and *Ball* [1989] Crim. LR 730.   [33] [1995] 1 AC 171.

[34] J. C. Smith and B. Hogan, *Criminal Law* (8th edn., London, 1996), 385 takes the view that the 'objective' recklessness species of manslaughter adopted in *Seymour* [1983] 2 AC 493 has been wholly replaced by the gross negligence test, but it is not clear that this is so for any case not involving a pre-existing duty of care. Alternatively it may be that the fault element in such cases is 'subjective' recklessness requiring foresight of harm. Cf. *Pike* [1961] Crim. LR 114.

[35] The notorious case of *DPP* v. *Smith* [1961] AC 290.

[36] Criminal Justice Act 1967, s. 8; *Frankland and Moore* v. *R.* [1987] AC 576.

[37] *Hyam* v. *DPP* [1975] AC 55.   [38] *Moloney* [1985] AC 905.

be reinterpreted by the Court of Appeal to make it more intelligible to trial judges.[40] Only the third decision[41] has survived unscathed, and that one confirmed a rule which both the Criminal Law Revision Committee[42] and the Nathan Committee[43] have said should be abolished. This line of cases represents a 20 per cent success rate on clarifying and settling the law. This, if I may say so, is well below the pass mark, and in this college would not even qualify for a resit! We have now arrived at the position where the mental element required for murder is an intention to kill or cause serious injury, but the meaning of 'intention' in this context is a matter of considerable obscurity. I will return to this point shortly.

(III) THE LAW OF THEFT

Turning to the law of stealing, we find different, but equally severe, problems. The law of stealing was reformed in 1968, and again in 1978, when features of the original reform proved to be a 'judicial nightmare'.[44] The principal change effected by the Theft Act 1968 was to abandon the ancient common law conception of larceny as a trespass against another's possession of property and to replace it with a conception of theft as an offence against ownership. This conception was founded on the notion of the prohibited act being a conversion of the property, a notion which the Criminal Law Revision Committee sought to encapsulate in the term 'appropriation'.[45] In *Gomez*[46] the House of Lords resolved two earlier inconsistent decisions of its own[47] by holding that a person who obtains another's property by deception also appropriates and therefore steals it. This has the effect of turning almost all fraudsters into thieves, even where they obtain a voidable title to

---

[39] *Hancock* [1986] AC 455.

[40] *Nedrick* [1986] 3 All ER 1.

[41] *Cunningham* [1982] AC 566.

[42] 14th Report, Offences Against the Person (London, 1980), para. 21.

[43] *Report of the Select Committee on Murder and Life Imprisonment* (London, 1989), para. 68.

[44] *Per* Edmund Davies LJ in *Royle* [1971] 3 All ER 1359, 1363, commenting on s. 16 of the Theft Act 1968.

[45] 8th Report, *Theft and Related Offences* (London, 1966), paras. 32–5.

[46] [1993] AC 442.

[47] *Lawrence* v. *Metropolitan Police Commissioner* [1972] AC 626; *Morris* [1984] AC 320.

the property, and was not a result intended by the CLRC.[48] By itself
this might not matter so much. The law reports are full of cases
where judicial interpretation of statutes has not corresponded to
the intentions of the framers of the legislation, although the use of
offence-widening techniques in the criminal law may threaten
values of fairness and legality, as I have indicated. However, in the
case of theft we now have an offence whose *actus reus* consists of
doing anything at all to the property of another, even with their
consent.[49] Countless everyday transactions, ranging from borrowing a library book to shopping in a supermarket, constitute the act
required for an offence punishable with seven years' imprisonment.
The consequence of emptying the prohibited act of any significant
content is that the whole weight of the offence now falls on the
requirement of dishonesty. The offence has thus changed its
juridical form. It has shifted from what Fletcher has called the
pattern of manifest criminality,[50] whereby the offence is founded
on some objectively wrongful act, to the pattern of subjective
criminality, whereby the offence is essentially founded on the
defendant's culpable state of mind. It is now the presence or
absence of dishonesty which essentially determines whether any
dealing with another's property amounts to theft. The meaning of
dishonesty is therefore critical because it is this meaning which
provides the principal criterion of liability. Astonishingly, dishonesty turns out to have very little meaning in law. Section 2 of the
Theft Act 1968 sets out three specific examples of conduct which is
not dishonest, but says nothing about the general run of cases. The
Court of Appeal has held that dishonesty is generally to be left as a
question of fact for juries and magistrates to determine the current
standards of ordinary decent people and the defendant's awareness
of those standards.[51] This is a very problematic strategy.[52] There is

---

[48] 8th Report, n. 44 above, para. 38: 'Obtaining by false pretences is ordinarily
thought of as different from theft, because in the former the owner in fact consents
to part with his ownership. . . . To create a new offence of theft to include conduct
which ordinary people would find it difficult to regard as theft would be a mistake'.
In other words, the CLRC thought there was a morally relevant difference between
the two types of invasion of interests in property, a difference which *Gomez* ignores.

[49] Smith and Hogan, n. 34 above, 519.

[50] G. Fletcher, *Rethinking Criminal Law* (Boston, Mass., 1978), 115–22.

[51] *Feely* [1973] QB 530; *Ghosh* [1982] QB 1053.

[52] E. Griew, 'Dishonesty: The Objections to Feely and Ghosh' [1985] Crim. LR
341; A. T. H. Smith, *Property Offences* (London, 1994), paras. 7–55 ff.

first of all the obvious point that in an increasingly pluralistic and fragmented society universal 'current standards' may not exist, and in any event different tribunals are likely to have different perceptions of what they are. A more fundamental point is this. In an offence structure where dishonesty had an essentially exculpatory function, that is where the absence of dishonesty was in effect an excuse for an act that was *prima facie* wrongful, it might be defensible to allow lay tribunals to say that the act was not blameworthy by contemporary standards. An open-ended context-sensitive excuse may be the appropriate way to resolve conflicting norms and expectations in a modern society where people deal with each other's property in a wide variety of socio-economic situations. However, where the offence structure is such that dishonesty does all the work and has an essentially inculpatory function then it is wrong in principle that the concept should be so indeterminate.[53] There are clear threats here to principles of fairness and legality which we should not tolerate. It is worth emphasizing that the structural shift took place in the absence of any generally agreed structure for offences in English law or for the respective functions of act and fault elements in offence definitions.

(IV) GENERAL PRINCIPLES OF CRIMINAL LIABILITY

I turn next to the general principles of criminal liability. In modern law the key concepts of criminal fault, or *mens rea*, are intention and recklessness. Very broadly speaking a person is not liable for an act causing harm unless he or she intended to cause the harm or was reckless whether the act caused the harm. What meaning does the law assign to these terms? In the case of intention the courts curiously refuse to say. According to the authority beginning with the decision of the House of Lords in *Moloney*,[54] intention can generally be left to the jury as an ordinary word of the English language. This can only mean that juries are expected to apply a

---

[53] A point strongly supported by E. Griew, *The Theft Acts* (7th edn. London, 1995), para. 2–123. As an example of the far-reaching implications of criminalization by reference to jury standards consider *Greenstein* [1976] 1 All ER 1 (share-stagging operations).

[54] [1985] AC 905. See also *Hancock* [1986] AC 455; *Nedrick [1986] 3 All ER 1*; *Walker* (1990) 90 Cr.App.R 226.

conception of intention as the defendant's aim or purpose, since this is the ordinary meaning of the word, and we have the extra-curial authority of Lord Goff for saying so.[55] Few would argue with the principle that a decision deliberately to cause harm is blameworthy in the absence of a recognized justification or excuse. The difficulty arises with cases of what Bentham called 'oblique intention',[56] where the issue is whether the defendant intended certain harms which occurred as side-effects of acts done for other purposes. The authorities say that in these cases judges should give juries further help, but the help takes the form of a mystifying direction. Juries should be told what intention is not, namely that it is not the same as desire or motive, which are themselves somewhat ambiguous concepts. Then, after learning that a person may intend something he does not desire, juries are told that they may infer intention from the defendant's foresight that the harm was virtually certain to occur. This is a question of fact to be determined on a consideration of all the evidence, but the cases do not explain what it is that is being inferred. It is apparently a matter for them how they interpret this direction. This leads Smith and Hogan to make the following comment:

Faced with such a direction, the jury can do no more than decide to call the defendant's awareness of virtual certainty 'intention' if they think that, in all the circumstances of the case, he ought to be convicted of the offence charged; and not to call it intention if they think he ought to be acquitted.[57]

There is a fundamental structural point involved here which the cases have notably failed to deal with. Treating this form of intention as a question of fact rather than legal stipulation allows for consideration of the defendant's own explanation of what he was about, as Lord Bridge explicitly recognized in *Moloney*.[58] Such an explanation may be contextual in the sense that the defendant will point to circumstances which he claims justify or excuse his performance of a deliberate act in the knowledge that it was

---

[55] 'The Mental Element in Murder' (1988) 104 *LQR* 30, 42–3.
[56] *Introduction to the Principles of Morals and Legislation* (ed. Harrison, Oxford, 1948), 202.
[57] N. 34 above, 58.
[58] [1985] AC 905, 929.

virtually certain to produce harmful side-effects.[59] The jury will thus be asked to exercise their communal judgment on whether, given the explanation, the defendant should be convicted of the relevant offence of 'intent'. This assigns a large role to community values in the assessment of the legitimacy of justifications and excuses. It presupposes a moral judgment as part of the *mens rea* of the offence. This was a proposition, incidentally, which the House of Lords was at pains to deny in the different context of involuntary intoxication. In *Kingston*[60] Lord Mustill drew a clear distinction between the mental and the moral aspects of a crime.[61] Now, it might be thought that there is a parallel between intention and dishonesty, whose excusatory role in theft may be defensible, as I have just indicated. However, the parallel is dangerously misleading. The problem with allowing matters of justification and excuse to bear generally on the issue of intention is that any overt restrictions of policy or principle on their scope as defences may simply be bypassed. The point may be tested by an example based on the notorious case of *Steane*,[62] the authority cited by Lord Bridge in *Moloney*.[63] Steane was effectively allowed to plead an intention to avoid threats to send his family to a concentration camp in answer to a charge of intending to assist the enemy by making propaganda broadcasts. This was so even though he presumably knew that assistance would be the inevitable result of making the broadcasts. But what if he was a compulsive smoker and his intention had been to avoid threats to withdraw his supply of cigarettes?[64] Are we prepared to allow the limitation of the

---

[59] Cf. *Gillick* v. *West Norfolk and Wisbech Area Health Authority* [1986] AC 112 (doctor giving contraceptive advice to a girl under 16 lacks the intention required for aiding and abetting unlawful sexual intercourse if he or she acts for the purpose of preventing unwanted pregnancy or the transmission of disease, despite foreseeing that the advice is virtually certain to facilitate intercourse). The case has generated a substantial literature. For a recent review of the issues see A. J. Ashworth, 'Criminal Liability in a Medical Context: The Treatment of Good Intentions' in *Harm and Culpability*, n. 12, above 173.   [60] [1994] 3 All ER 353.

[61] At 360–1. The relationship between *mens rea*, blameworthiness, and defences is a complex and difficult subject which it is beyond the scope of this essay to investigate in full. My point for present purposes is that English law has no agreed structure or theory for deciding such issues when they arise, witness the very different approaches in *Kingston* of Lord Taylor CJ in the CA and Lord Mustill in the HL.   [62] [1947] KB 997.   [63] [1985] AC 905, 929.

[64] Cf. Glanville Williams, *Criminal Law The General Part* (2nd edn.) (London, 1961), 41.

defence of duress to threats to cause death or serious injury to be
outflanked by permitting lesser threats to affect the issue of
intention? Major structural and policy questions are thus concealed
by the judicial preference for leaving the meaning of intention at
large. The problem is unlikely to arise in the same form in the case
of dishonesty, where the defendant cannot substitute his own value
systems for the external standard provided he is aware of what that
standard is.

With recklessness the judicial approach is very different. The
meaning of recklessness is not a question of fact. Recklessness is a
technical term and has a specific legal meaning. Or, to be precise, it
has three legal meanings. Its meaning differs according to the
offence involved. In the law of violence the inquiry is into the
defendant's cognition: so-called *Cunningham*[65] recklessness
requires him actually to have foreseen a risk of causing injury when
he acted. In the law of sexual offences, which many would regard as
a subset of offences of violence,[66] the law mixes cognitive and
attitudinal questions by asking whether the defendant 'couldn't
care less' whether the victim consented while allowing for a positive
belief in consent to negative recklessness.[67] In the law of vandalism
recklessness retains the extended meaning assigned to it by Lord
Diplock in the notorious case of *Caldwell*.[68] This equates a
culpable lack of awareness of risk with conscious risk-taking, thus
giving the concept a considerably wider ambit than it has in
offences against the person. This leads to the result noted by Smith
and Hogan that it is easier to convict the person who discharges
what he believes to be an unloaded shotgun into someone's face of
damaging the victim's spectacles than of injuring the victim's
eye.[69] The result is curious because we would regard the latter harm
as more serious and therefore more deserving of protection by the
criminal law. The incoherence of the law is compounded by the fact
that the maximum penalty for inflicting grievous bodily harm
under the 1861 Act is exactly half that for causing criminal damage.

These radically different approaches to the twin pillars of *mens*

---

[65] [1957] 2 QB 396.

[66] See J. Temkin, *Rape and the Legal Process* (London, 1987), 93–5; N. Lacey,
C. Wells, and D. Meure, *Reconstructing Criminal Law* (London, 1990), 321 ff.

[67] *DPP* v. *Morgan* [1976] AC 182; *Kimber* [1983] 1 WLR 1118; *Satnam and
Kewal* (1983) 78 Cr.App. R 149.   [68] [1982] AC 341.

[69] N. 34 above, 71.

rea are impossible to rationalize. No coherent theory of culpability can account for the state of a law which delegates to the jury the meaning of intention as an open-ended question of fact while assigning stipulative legal definitions to recklessness. Other inconsistencies and contradictions abound throughout the general part of criminal law. One further example comes from legislation rather than case law. The Criminal Damage Act 1971 provides a lawful excuse for damaging another's property if the actor believes that it is necessary to do so immediately to protect his own property and he believes that the means of protection are reasonable. The test for this excuse is wholly subjective. The defendant's belief in the necessity for immediate protection and the reasonableness of the damage are determinative. On the other hand, although the law permits the use of force in self-defence or the prevention of crime, the force used must be no more than is reasonable in the circumstances. This is an objective test. Despite some recent doubts,[70] it seems to be clear that the defendant's belief that the amount of force used was reasonable is only evidence and is not determinative of the issue.[71] Consequently we have doctrinal inconsistency capable of producing absurd results. Suppose that the defendant is attacked by her neighbour's dog. It is arguable whether she may kill the dog to protect her legs (was this necessary and reasonable in fact?), but she can certainly kill the dog to protect her trousers if she believes this is a reasonable thing to do in the circumstances.[72] Presumably the more expensive the trousers the more reasonable the belief.

To complete this selective critique, I will make one more point about the law of criminal damage. Lord Diplock's test of recklessness states that a defendant is reckless if he gives no thought to a risk of causing damage which would be obvious to the reasonable person. In a number of cases the defendant has argued that the test should be modified to take account of the defendant's incapacity to give thought to the risk. Thus it has been suggested that minors should not be judged by the standards of knowledge

---

[70] *Scarlett* [1993] 4 All ER 629.

[71] So held by the CA in *Owino* [1996] 2 Cr.App.R 128, and assumed by the HL in *Clegg* [1995] 1 All ER 334.

[72] This vivid example was given by Professor J. C. Smith in 'Codifying the Criminal Law' [1984] *Statute Law Review* 17.

and foresight that the law expects of adults. This has been rejected by the Court of Appeal on more than one occasion,[73] despite the fact that a similar argument succeeded in the House of Lords in relation to the objective test for provocation.[74] The Court of Appeal expressed sympathy for the point but held that a conceptual analysis of the Diplock test precluded the suggested modification. Again this demonstrates an inconsistency, this time founded on theoretical incoherence. In so far as English law embodies any kind of theory of excuses it gives some effect to Hart's principle that a person should not be blamed and punished unless he or she had the capacity and a fair opportunity to adjust their behaviour to the law.[75] The principle finds its main application in the law of mental disorder, but it can be argued to underpin the approach taken to the capacity issue in provocation. It could and should have been applied to mitigate the severity of the *Caldwell* test.

Inquest

(1) HISTORICAL: THE PIECEMEAL AND UNSYSTEMATIC DEVELOPMENT OF THE LAW

This critique, and it could be expanded to include many other examples,[76] provides strong support for the claim that English criminal law falls seriously short of the standards set out above. I turn now to inquire how and why the law has got into this critical condition. What are the reasons for its failure to meet the standards of legality, fairness, and coherence?

It is plain that there is no single explanation for the current state of affairs. We are dealing with a historical process shaped by many different forces. Institutions, individuals, and the wider political and intellectual climate have all played important roles. This is not the occasion to attempt a full systematic account of the criminal law in the twentieth century, but I think it is possible to isolate a number of major factors and recurring themes which help to account for the way in which the law has developed.

I will take first the role of the legislature. Government inertia is

---

[73] *Elliott* v. C (1983) 77 Cr.App.R 103; *Stephen Malcolm R* (1984) 79 Cr.App.R 334; *Coles* [1994] Crim. LR 820.
[74] *DPP* v. *Camplin* [1978] AC 705.   [75] N. 9 above, 181.
[76] Norrie, n. 3 above.

the principal reason that we are still living with the Offences Against the Person Act 1861. The government has been told repeatedly in the last twenty years that the Act must be replaced,[77] but nothing has been done. Blame for this inaction can be laid squarely at the door of the Home Office and successive Home Secretaries. The Home Office is notoriously a reactive rather than proactive institution, and its reactions are largely determined by political forces and the size of its postbag. Sir Henry Brooke, the former Chairman of the Law Commission, recently indicated that the Home Office gave him to understand when he took office that law reform was not something which excited politicians or the general public.[78] This brings to mind Sir Henry Maine's complaint in a letter written to the Permanent Under-Secretary at the India Office in 1868: 'As to the Penal Code, nobody cares about the Criminal Law—except theorists and habitual criminals.'[79] In this respect at least nothing has changed. The theorists have no more clout now than they did 130 years ago.

Of course this is not to say that there has been no legislative activity in the criminal law. Many statutes have increased the range of criminalization, either as part of a broader scheme of regulation or in response to specific moral panics. Substantial reforming statutes have also been passed in recent years, but this is mostly because of their connection with the achievement of some overt political goal. The Criminal Attempts Act 1981, which was the vehicle for the repeal of the unpopular and discriminatory offence of 'sus', is a good example.[80] Other more limited measures have sometimes succeeded as Private Member's Bills. The main examples of major statutes in modern times enacted specifically in the cause of law reform are the Theft Act 1968 and the Criminal Damage Act 1971. These were the work of the Criminal Law Revision Committee[81] and the Law Commission[82] respectively. They were

---

[77] Criminal Law Revision Committee, *14th Report* (London, 1980); Law Commission, *Draft Criminal Code* (Law Com. No. 177, London, 1989); Law Commission, *Offences Against the Person and General Principles* (Law Com. No. 218, London, 1993).

[78] 'The Law Commission and Criminal Law Reform' [1995] *Crim. LR* 911, 917.

[79] Cited in Glazebrook, n. 2 above, 26.

[80] E. Griew, *Current Law Statutes Annotated* (London, 1981), 47/8–9.

[81] 8th Report, *Theft and Related Offences* (London, 1966).

[82] *Report on Offences of Damage To Property* (Law Com. No. 29, London, 1970).

passed during a period of a few years when, unusually, the political climate favoured law reform. That period lasted a decade or so from the early 1960s to the mid-1970s and included other reforming landmarks such as the abolition of capital punishment[83] and the reform of the law on abortion.[84] The window of opportunity for criminal law reform began to close again in the 1970s and has largely remained shut since then.

Most of the legislation in criminal law has related to specific offences. General principles of criminal liability are largely still the work of the judges, and it is to those principles that I now return. Immediately a very striking feature presents itself, and it is this feature which provides a further significant part of the explanation for the current state of criminal law. The notion that there are *general* principles of criminal liability took a long time to establish. Its origins go back at least to the work of the Criminal Law Commissioners,[85] but its developed form is largely an invention of the second half of the twentieth century. In fact it is fair to say that most of the judicial development of the general principles really only began in the 1960s. Two simple comparisons provide revealing insights into the nature and the scale of this development. The first is a comparison of the organization of the Law Commission's draft Criminal Code of 1989 and the Draft Code which was appended to the Report of the Royal Commissioners who reported in 1879.[86] The latter code was based on the code originally drafted by Stephen,[87] inspired by his experience as a colonial draftsman in India, which had been referred to a small but high-powered Royal Commission in 1878. The Law Commission's code opens with Part I, headed 'General Principles'. This contains fifty-two clauses covering preliminary matters, issues of prosecution and punishment such as double jeopardy and alternative verdicts, proof, external elements, fault, parties, incapacity, defences, and preliminary offences. These topics more or less correspond to the organization of the subject in Smith and Hogan's standard text on criminal law.[88] By contrast the 1879 code had a

---

[83] Murder (Abolition of Death Penalty) Act 1965.

[84] Abortion Act 1967.

[85] N. 1 above, particularly the Fourth and Seventh Reports.

[86] *Report of the Royal Commission on the Law Relating to Indictable Offences* (1879) C. 2345.

[87] See S. Kadish, 'Codifiers of the Criminal Law' (1978) 78 *Col.LR* 1098, 1121–1130.   [88] N. 34 above.

Part I containing just six preliminary provisions. Parties and preliminary offences were dealt with in Parts IV and XXXVI respectively. There was also a Part III on defences, headed 'Justification and Excuse for Acts Which Would Otherwise be Offences'. Most of this was taken up by elaborate rules on the use of force for various public and private purposes, rules now largely replaced by the single provision in section 3 of the Criminal Law Act 1967.

My second comparison is based on Smith and Hogan. The first edition appeared in 1965. It contained 160 pages on general principles and 109 pages on offences of violence (that is, homicides and non-fatal offences of wounding, causing grievous or actual bodily harm, and assault). Much of the material on general principles consisted of systematic analysis of old authorities. The eighth edition, published in 1996, contains exactly the same number of pages on offences of violence, but the section on general principles has more than doubled to 334 pages. This reflects the dramatic growth in the area of the general part in the last thirty years. The great bulk of the growth is the product of the work of the higher courts. It would be an exaggeration to say that the House of Lords and the Criminal Division of the Court of Appeal have virtually created the general part in this short time. However, it is not that much of an exaggeration. Almost all the topics that conventionally make up the general part have been fashioned or re-fashioned by the courts during this period. It is significant that this sustained judicial creativity has taken place contemporaneously with the Law Commission's attempt to codify the law. I will return to this point.

These comparisons are intriguing and require further explana-tion. At the risk of over-simplifying complex processes I will venture the following observations. The organization of the 1879 code reflected a prevailing nineteenth-century conception of criminal law. According to this conception criminal law consisted largely of a collection of specific offences, each free-standing with its own separate elements which required separate interpretation.[89]

---

[89] Lacey, n. 15 above, has described Stephen's conception of criminal law as 'rooted in the old view that an act presumptively discloses the subject's will and hence that the basis for judgments of criminal culpability lies primarily in the quality of *conduct*'. Part of the explanation for the old view is the difficulty, if not the

The task of interpretation was subject only to some limited and miscellaneous common law rules, such as those relating to parties, which applied generally to supplement or modify narrow offence definitions. There was, I suggest, no developed conception of a general part of criminal liability consisting of broad principles of responsibility applicable across the whole range of specific offences. The effective absence of a general part mirrored the absence of a developed and articulated theory of criminal culpability. This is well exemplified by a brief consideration of the old maxim of the common law, *actus non facit reum nisi mens sit rea*. Everyone knows that this maxim required a wrongful act to be accompanied by a guilty mind, but nineteenth-century judges had no agreed conception of a guilty mind. There was no general theory of *mens rea* which could be applied consistently across offences.[90] In *Prince*[91] the judges of the Court for Crown Cases Reserved offered four different analyses of the *mens rea* of the offence of abduction. In *Tolson*[92] Stephen J, the same Stephen responsible for drafting the code of 1879, explicitly denied even the possibility of generalizing the content of a formal requirement of mens rea. After pointing out that the mental elements for different crimes differ in their terminology, he said:

It appears confusing to call so many dissimilar states of mind by one name. The principle involved appears to me, when fully considered, to amount to no more than this. The full definition of every crime contains expressly or by implication a proposition as to a state of mind. Therefore, if the mental element of any conduct alleged to be a crime is proved to have been absent in any given case, the crime as defined is not committed.[93]

The concept of a general part of criminal liability embracing detailed principles of culpability is largely a twentieth-century invention. Its recognition and development owes much to the work of a distinguished line of academic writers, whose members include

impossibility, of gaining access to the best evidence of the accused's state of mind by direct questioning of the accused. The accused was not a generally competent witness before 1898, and pre-trial questioning of suspects by the police became common practice only in this century.

[90] Cf. J. Horder, 'Two Histories and Four Hidden Principles of Mens Rea' (1997) 113 *LQR* 95.

[91] (1875) LR 2 CCR 154.

[92] (1889) 23 QBD 168.

[93] At 185.

Kenny,[94] Turner,[95] Glanville Williams,[96] and J. C. Smith.[97] Pre-eminent amongst these is Glanville Williams, whose massive treatise, *Criminal Law The General Part*, first appeared in 1953 and went into its second and final edition in 1961. This work is undoubtedly one of the most important law texts of this century. Its influence has been, and continues to be, remarkable. It has informed the work of virtually all writers on criminal law subsequently. It had a direct and profound input into the work of the Criminal Law Revision Committee, which Williams was instrumental in establishing,[98] and of the Law Commission which appointed Williams to its Working Group in 1968. The analysis and the arguments in the treatise have frequently been cited to the courts, both in their original version and through their use in Smith and Hogan's textbook. Williams offered a lucid and persuasive synthesis capable of providing a framework for judicial develop-ment of the law, and this synthesis appeared at the optimum time for a spurt of growth in the criminal law.

In retrospect it is striking, but not surprising, how little development there was in criminal law for the first sixty years of this century. The procedural requirement of the Attorney-General's fiat to take a case to the House of Lords resulted in their hearing very few criminal appeals. Their decisions were for the most part undistinguished, and several have been subsequently reversed or overtaken by later developments. The one great exception is the landmark case of *Woolmington* v. *DPP*[99] establishing the modern rule on the burden of proof in criminal cases. The Court of Criminal Appeal was notoriously under-powered[100] and appeared to have little taste for the kind of legal arguments used before its

---

[94] C. S. Kenny, *Outlines of Criminal Law* (Cambridge). Kenny produced the first edition of his textbook in 1902 and twelve further editions to 1929.

[95] J. W. C. Turner edited the last three editions of Kenny, and also *Russell on Crime* (12th edn.) (London, 1964). See also his essay, 'The Mental Element in Crimes at Common Law', in L. Radzinowicz and J. W. C. Turner (eds.), *The Modern Approach to Criminal Law* (London, 1945) 195.

[96] N. 64 above; *Textbook of Criminal Law* (2nd edn.) (London, 1983).

[97] Smith and Hogan, n. 34 above.

[98] See the Foreword by Lord Edmund-Davies to *Reshaping the Criminal Law*, n. 1 above.

[99] [1935] AC 462.

[100] *Jackson's Machinery of Justice* (ed. J. R. Spencer, Cambridge, 1989), 201.

civil counterpart.[101] Finally, it was difficult to obtain legal aid to take a criminal case on appeal. In consequence of these factors nineteenth-century conceptions and practice of the criminal law tended to linger on largely unchecked by review and revision in the higher courts.

It was not until the 1960s that this picture of judicial inactivity began to change radically. In 1960 the need for the Attorney-General's fiat to take a case to the House of Lords was abolished and replaced by the present requirements of certification and leave.[102] This easing of a significant restriction opened up the possibility of taking to the Lords any case involving a point of law of general public importance. This necessarily included almost any issue of general principle in the criminal law. In 1966 the Court of Appeal, Criminal Division, replaced the Court of Criminal Appeal.[103] The new court brought with it increased status, improved judge-power, and a different mindset that has made it more receptive to arguments on points of law. With the expansion in 1967 of criminal legal aid to fund appeals[104] the stage was set for a dramatic expansion of judicial activism in the criminal law.

These institutional changes took effect at a time when the socio-political climate was attuned to development and reform of the law. In 1959 the Home Office established the Criminal Law Revision Committee as a standing advisory body of experts. That committee produced eighteen reports in the years up to 1986, fourteen of them by 1980. 1965 saw the foundation of the Law Commission following Gerald Gardiner's initiative as Lord Chancellor. In its *Second Programme of Law Reform*, published in 1968, the Law Commission set out as one of its objectives codification of the criminal law. This followed a commitment to codification made by the government of the day,[105] a commitment which has never been formally withdrawn. The objective of codification has formed the background to a great deal of the Commission's work in criminal

---

[101] For a restrained critique see D. Seaborne Davies, 'The Court of Criminal Appeal: The First Forty Years' (1951) 1 *JSPTL (NS)* 425, 436–40.

[102] Administration of Justice Act 1960 s 1.

[103] Criminal Appeal Act 1966.

[104] Criminal Justice Act 1967.

[105] In a speech by the then Home Secretary, Mr Roy Jenkins. The text is set out in *Codification of the Criminal Law A Report to the Law Commission* (Law Com. No. 143, London, 1985), 3.

law for almost thirty years. Finally, there appeared in the 1960s a series of highly influential texts developing the theory of the criminal law, particularly liberal theory, to a much more sophisticated and far-reaching level than it had previously attained. I have already mentioned the second edition of *The General Part* and the first edition of Smith and Hogan. To these one should add Hart's *Law Liberty and Morality*[106] and *Punishment and Responsibility*,[107] Packer's *The Limits of the Criminal Sanction*,[108] and the American Law Institute's Model Penal Code.[109]

It was the combination and interaction of these various factors that produced an explosion in the content and the literature of the criminal law. In many respects the subject has been transformed over the last three decades, and the explosion is still continuing. As one might expect, these developments reflect a wide variety of inputs. Disagreement has been frequent. The views of individual judges, for example, have played crucial roles in the decision of key issues of policy and principle. The availability of duress as a defence to murder has depended on the composition of the court determining the question.[110] Lord Diplock, who had an expansive and coherent conception of criminal fault,[111] failed to persuade his colleagues to agree with him on the definition of intention but succeeded in obtaining support for his extended meaning of recklessness. These instances demonstrate two deeper underlying truths. The development of the criminal law, particularly the general part, has been an essentially piecemeal and unsystematic development, heavily dependent on the accidents of litigation and, in the case of legislation, shifting political concerns. Above all it has not proceeded according to any generally agreed theory or structure

---

[106] (Oxford, 1963).   [107] (Oxford, 1968).
[108] (Stanford, 1968).   [109] (Philadelphia, Pa., 1962).
[110] Three of the four cases to reach the HL or the PC on duress as a defence to murder or attempted murder have been decided by bare majorities and have produced some of the most dramatic justifying rhetoric in the criminal law: see *DPP for Northern Ireland* v. *Lynch* [1975] AC 653; *Abbott* v. *R.* [1977] AC 755; *Howe* [1987] AC 417; *Gotts* [1992] 2 AC 412.
[111] See his judgments in *Sweet* v. *Parsley* [1970] AC 132 (negligence and mistake); *Hyam* v. *DPP* [1975] AC 55 and *Lemon* [1979] AC 617 (intention); *Sheppard* [1981] AC 394 (wilfulness); *Caldwell* [1982] AC 341; and *Lawrence* [1982] AC 510 (recklessness).

of criminal liability.[112] The absence of a code to provide a structure and a coherent set of principles of liability has left a vacuum at the heart of the criminal law which has been filled by a variety of preferences and approaches. We have witnessed a prolonged power struggle between courts, individual judges, the legislature, law reform agencies, and academics to supply these missing elements which would enable the law to develop with some degree of orderliness and consistency. The result of the struggle is the seriously defective state of the law which I have identified.

The real loser in this struggle is, I regret to say, the Law Commission. Throughout this explosive period of development the Law Commission has been engaged on a project which aspired to supply exactly what has been missing. Codification offered the prospect of defined concepts, a coherent structure of liability, the removal of inconsistency and uncertainty; all this set out in an accessible statute drafted in comprehensible language. But codification has not happened and, frankly, shows no sign of ever happening. Why is this? What has gone wrong? In the next section of the paper I attempt to explain why I think the project has failed, but before developing these reasons in more detail I need to give some consideration to the theory of criminal liability which has underpinned the Commission's code. As we shall see, it is the challenges to this theory which have partly helped to undermine the case for the code.

(II) THEORETICAL: ORTHODOX SUBJECTIVISM AND THE CHALLENGES TO IT

This theory is what Duff[113] has called orthodox subjectivism. Subjectivism has dominated the approach of the Law Commission to both the codification project and specific issues of criminal law reform. The Criminal Law Revision Committee also accepted this approach, most notably in its 1980 report on offences against the

---

[112] This is a matter of which the higher judiciary is increasingly conscious. In recent years reference in HL judgments to academic literature has become more common, and in *Luc Thiet Thuan* v. *R.* [1996] 2 All ER 1033, where the PC had to decide a difficult issue on the objective test on provocation, Lord Goff noted with apparent regret that their Lordships had not been supplied with any theoretical analysis of provocation.

[113] R. A. Duff, *Intention, Agency and Criminal Liability* (Oxford, 1990).

person. It was the prevailing orthodoxy amongst many criminal law scholars throughout most of the recent period of development, but it has come under increasing challenge in recent years from a number of different directions. The collapse of the project to provide the criminal law with a structure and principles grounded in subjectivist theory is bound to accentuate this theoretical power struggle. In order to appreciate the nature of this struggle, and to understand its implications, we need to begin with the principal characteristics of subjectivist theory. Inevitably, in the account that follows, I shall have to simplify some complex arguments and gloss over some important differences. Not all subjectivist theorists subscribe to the same tenets, but most would assent, more or less, to most of these propositions.

Orthodox subjectivism is founded on the political values of individualism, liberty, and self-determination. Maximum freedom from state interference and coercion is desirable to enable individuals to choose their life plans and to pursue their own conceptions of the good.[114] The law thus addresses the individual, in Kantian terms, as a subject with an entitlement to respect and concern.[115] Coherently with this political position the law accepts the philosophical postulate that individuals have free will and are able to make rational self-interested choices of action in the world.[116] The criminal law therefore accords individuals the status of autonomous moral agents who, because they have axiomatic freedom of choice, can fairly be held accountable and punishable for the rational choices of wrongdoing that they make.[117] As a general principle subjectivism then stipulates that informed voluntary choices of action are both necessary and sufficient to justify blame and punishment. The necessity for an informed choice means that a defendant must act intentionally, knowingly, or with advertent recklessness with respect to bringing about the relevant

---

[114] J. Feinberg, *Harm To Others—The Moral Limits of the Criminal Law* (Oxford, 1984), 206–14. Inspiration for this position is usually traced to J. S. Mill, *On Liberty* (1859).

[115] R. M. Dworkin, *Taking Rights Seriously* (London, 1977); D. Richards, 'Rights, Utility and Crime' (1981) 3 *Crime and Justice: An Annual Review* 274.

[116] A. Kenny, *Freewill and Responsibility* (Oxford, 1978).

[117] H. L. A. Hart, *Punishment and Responsibility* (Oxford, 1968), chap. 1; A. J. Ashworth, 'Belief, Intent and Criminal Liability' in *Oxford Essays in Jurisprudence* (3rd series, ed. J. Eekelaar and J. Bell, Oxford, 1987), 1.

harm.[118] The requirement is also interpreted as meaning that the defendant's liability falls to be assessed on the facts as he or she believed them to be.[119] A voluntary choice for this purpose is one that the defendant had the capacity and the freedom to make. According to Hart, it is, or should be, a feature of this theory that a person may not be blamed and punished unless he or she had the capacity and a fair opportunity to act otherwise.[120] Such an informed voluntary act is sufficient in the sense that much of the defendant's life and personality is excluded from the determination of liability. Character, lifestyle, upbringing, education, environment, and motive are not taken into account at the stage of conviction or acquittal. They are relevant only to the question of disposal on conviction.

Three implications of the theory need to be highlighted. First, it tends to adopt narrow conceptions of 'harm' for the purpose of criminalization decisions. The orientation to the protection of individual freedom generally leads to a preference for individual over collective welfare, so that it is only the more obvious setbacks to individual interests that count uncontroversially as harms.[121] Secondly, a strict subjective test of responsibility tends to the minimum criminalization of individuals, particularly when it is combined with the presumption of innocence. Many would regard this as a strength of the theory, on the basis that the criminal law is a blunt, expensive, and sometimes discriminatory, instrument of social control. They would agree with Bentham that it should be used sparingly and only when nothing else will do.[122] Thirdly, the focus of the forensic enquiry is narrow. The court examines the act done, the state of mind with which it was done, and the presence or absence of any operative justification or excuse at the time. The defendant thus answers for conduct in a small time-frame of his or her life, but answers only to that extent.

---

[118] Glanville Williams, n. 64 above, 31; Smith and Hogan, n. 34 above (8th edn.), 73. This is a key issue for some subjectivists. Others may disagree. Hart, e.g., was prepared to allow liability for negligence provided it took account of the defendant's capacity to foresee risks.

[119] Ashworth, n. 11 above, n. 117.

[120] N. 107 above, 181.

[121] See generally Feinberg, n. 114 above, and his further three volumes in the same series: *Offense To Others* (Oxford, 1985); *Harm To Self* (Oxford, 1986); *Harmless Wrongdoing* (Oxford, 1988).

[122] N. 56 above, chap XIII.

Orthodox subjectivism has enjoyed a considerable measure of success. It was adopted, as I have said, by both the major law reform agencies. It formed the basis of several important pieces of legislation,[123] and it has scored some notable successes in the courts. Decisions such as *Morgan*,[124] *Camplin*,[125] *Beckford*,[126] and others give clear effect to subjectivist principles. However, the theory has by no means had things all its own way, and it now faces a number of challenges. As regards the courts, orthodox subjectivism suffered major defeats in *Majewski*,[127] *Caldwell*,[128] and *Howe*.[129] The subjectivist principle of full correspondence of *actus reus* and *mens rea* has rarely succeeded in the law of violence, where offences of homicide and non-fatal injury alike are almost entirely based to varying degrees on constructive liability.[130]

This form of liability has its defenders. Some argue that it is not unfair to hold defendants liable for a greater degree of harm where they intended or foresaw a lesser degree.[131] Other writers have espoused objective forms of liability based on negligence. They argue against the necessity for a fully informed rational choice of action on the basis that criminal responsibility should extend to include at least some cases of inadvertence. On this view a person who has the capacity to foresee risks, but who negligently either assumes there are none or fails to consider the matter at all, is arguably as culpable as the person who knowingly takes a risk. A sophisticated version of this argument is put by Antony Duff in terms that responsibility should be founded on a person's attitude to risk.[132] Failure to consider risk may be symptomatic of an attitude of what Duff calls 'practical indifference' to legal norms. Such an attitude to the causing of harm is not as blameworthy as a deliberate decision to do harm, but it may betray a similar contempt for the values protected by the criminal law sufficient to

---

[123] Criminal Damage Act 1971; Criminal Law Act 1977, Part I; Forgery and Counterfeiting Act 1981; Criminal Attempts Act 1981.

[124] [1976] AC 182. [125] [1978] AC 705.

[126] [1988] AC 130. [127] [1977] AC 443.

[128] [1982] AC 341. [129] [1987] AC 417.

[130] *Newbury* [1977] AC 500; *Savage* [1992] 1 AC 699.

[131] See, e.g., J. Gardner, 'Rationality and the Rule of Law in Offences Against The Person' [1994] *CLJ* 502; J. Horder, 'A Critique of the Correspondence Principle in Criminal Law' [1995] Crim. LR 759.

[132] R. A. Duff, *Intention, Agency and Criminal Liability* (Oxford, 1990), chap. 7.

justify punishment. Another kind of attack on the necessity for informed rationality at the time of the act argues that it may give a misleading and unduly favourable picture of the defendant's culpability. This approach seeks to enlarge the 'time-frame' for assessing culpability, and has various doctrinal manifestations. These range from the notion of a 'continuing' act,[133] or of an act followed by an omission,[134] where *mens rea* is not present at the outset but supervenes later, to the concept of the 'one transaction' for a series of discrete acts,[135] to the case of voluntary intoxication where recklessness in becoming intoxicated is illogically equated with the recklessness required for harm-doing.[136]

Challenges from an opposed standpoint maintain that informed rationality at the time of the act should not be sufficient. The claim here is that this makes for too narrow a test of responsibility. It is said that the test takes inadequate account of the social, economic, and political environment in which the defendant committed the relevant act.[137] We should aim instead for a more context-sensitive account of the defendant's conduct. This kind of argument may well be allied to an attack on the supposed objectivity and rationality of the law. Thus some feminist critics have argued that the law of defences shows systematic gender bias in its deployment of concepts derived from the psychology of male responses to aggression and stress.[138] The law fails, it is said, to take account of women's experience and behaviour when confronted with threatening situations and abusive relationships. Arguments of this type have already had a widening effect on the law of provocation[139] and may yet achieve some softening of the immediacy requirement in the law of self-defence. Norrie, in his sustained critique of the criminal law, has pointed to the law's attempted exclusion of motive from issues of *mens rea* and defences, and has criticized the criminal law for its depiction of defendants as juridical abstract individuals divorced from their socio-political environment.

---

[133] *Fagan v. Metropolitan Police Commissioner* [1969] 1 QB 439.
[134] *Miller* [1983] 2 AC 161.
[135] *Thabo Meli v. R.* [1954] 1 WLR 228; *Church* [1966] 1 QB 59; *Le Brun* [1991] 4 All ER 673.   [136] *Majewski* [1977] AC 443.
[137] Norrie, n. 3 above.
[138] K. O'Donovan, 'Defences for Battered Women Who Kill' (1991) 18 *Jo. of Law and Society* 219; A. McColgan, 'In Defence of Battered Women Who Kill' (1993) 13 *OJLS* 508.
[139] *Ahluwalia* [1992] 4 All ER 889; *Thornton (No. 2)* [1996] 2 Cr.App.R 108.

This is the most far-reaching of the various challenges to what I would call orthodox subjectivism. At one level it reflects a scepticism about the allocation we make of information about the defendant and the circumstances of the offence between the liability decision and the sentencing decision. What is the justification for recognizing only a few, tightly limited, excuses as relevant to liability, but a much broader range of contextual matters as capable of mitigating the defendant's culpability? Inevitably such a question leads to a further inquiry into the adequacy of our theory of excuses and doubt as to how the limits of responsibility are to be defined. At this point it becomes clear that such challenges may not just carry subjectivism to its logical limits by eliminating objective constraints on the scope of defences. Lurking in the background of strong versions of these approaches may be a philosophical antipathy to the concept of free will itself and a preference for some form of determinism.[140] Ultimately we may reach a rejection of the entire conceptual structure of blame, conviction, stigma, and punishment. The best-known exponent of an alternative vision of what Hart called a regime of 'social hygiene'[141] is still Lady Wootton, whose ideas first circulated almost forty years ago.[142] That vision has never taken a firm hold, possibly because of its paternalistic, even totalitarian, resonance, but it serves as a valuable reminder of the problem of indeterminacy when the limits of orthodox subjectivism are expanded beyond a narrow context for the defendant's act.

The Future of Codification

In the final part of this article I offer some speculations about the future of codification of the criminal law. It seems to me that it is still the case that only codification can rescue English criminal law from its current critical condition. The litigation process is too haphazard and unsystematic to permit the courts to do it, and in any event there are constitutional limits on their ability to rewrite

---

[140] One can detect such an antipathy in Norrie's work, but his recent article, 'The Limits of Justice: Finding Fault in the Criminal Law' (1996) 59 *MLR* 450, adopts a more ambivalent stance towards liberal theories of responsibility.

[141] N. 107 above, 193, 207.

[142] *Crime and the Criminal Law* (2nd edn.) (London, 1981).

or update unsatisfactory legislation. New piecemeal legislation may make some improvements, but there is a substantial risk that without the foundation of an agreed structure and principles for criminal liability it will end up being part of the problem. But how is codification to be achieved, given the lack of progress on the Law Commission's project?

Before dealing with the political dimensions of this issue I want to draw attention to a recurring problem with the Law Commission's codification strategy.[143] This is a problem which has been exacerbated by the speed and the nature of the growth in the general part in the last thirty years. The problem is that the Commission's strategy has not been consistent. It has gone through three distinct phases, each of which has unfortunately, and possibly unavoidably, generated different obstacles to the achievement of the codification goal.

The first phase was the period between 1968, when the codification project was announced, and 1980, when the Commission effectively admitted that it did not have the resources to do the job as it originally planned. The strategy at this time[144] was the incremental approach, representing an Anglicized version of the method adopted by the American Law Institute in drafting the Model Penal Code. It involved the Commission, and at this stage the Criminal Law Revision Committee, producing legislative proposals in succession for all the major topics in criminal law. The proposals would contain any necessary reforms, arrived at by the usual process of working paper, consultation, and final report. It was envisaged that Parliament would pass a series of Bills enacting the proposals, and at the end of the process there would be one large consolidation Bill which would effectively create the criminal code. On any view this was an ambitious strategy, and with hindsight it looks clearly to have been an over-optimistic strategy for both the Commission, a new body with limited resources and many other reform projects, and the CLRC, a part-time body

---

[143] I wish to emphasize that in what follows I am speaking only on behalf of myself and not for the code team which assisted the Law Commission in the preparation of the Draft Code. I hope it is not necessary to add that my comments are of course not made in any spirit of hostility to the Commission.

[144] See Sir Derek Hodgson, 'Law Com. No. 76–A Case Study in Criminal Law Reform' in *Reshaping the Criminal Law*, n. 1 above, 240, 245–8.

dominated by judges and practitioners. Perhaps even more un-realistically the strategy presupposed unlimited access to Parliamentary willingness and time to support the project. By the mid-1970s it was clear that the strategy was not going to work, and by 1980 it had undoubtedly run into the sands. At this point the Commission switched track. It accepted a proposal from the Criminal Law Committee of the Society of Public Teachers of Law that a team drawn from its members should assist the Commission in the production of a draft code. The team, of which I was privileged to be part, envisaged a code containing a reasonably complete statement of general principles plus, initially, represent-ative specific offences illustrating the operation of the general part. The team's report,[145] setting out this proposal with a draft Bill, was favourably received on consultation.[146]

Following the consultation, the Commission decided to expand the team's approach by including substantially more offences so as to provide a practically complete code which would cover more than 90 per cent of the day-to-day work of the criminal courts. This can, I think, be fairly described as the 'big bang' approach. Instead of codification by degrees and over many years we would have one big Bill to do the whole job immediately. However, it was sought to allay fears of the possible effects of the change with the reassurance that the draft code was essentially a restatement of the present law, together with certain reform proposals made by official bodies who had found the present law to be defective. It was here that the trouble started. The restatement principle had been the foundation on which the original SPTL proposal to the Commission had been constructed. It made coherent sense in 1980, which was probably the high water-mark of the acceptance of orthodox subjectivism by the courts and the legislature. At that stage it certainly looked feasible to construct a code based on subjectivist principles and to claim fairly that it represented the fundamental principles of English law. By 1989 this claim was more controversial. The courts had moved off in different directions in a number of areas: intention, recklessness, duress, parties, and so on. Criticism of orthodox subjectivism was beginning to make itself felt on several

---

[145] Law Com. No. 143 (London, 1985).
[146] Law Com. No. 177 (London, 1989), para. 1.15.

fronts,[147] and by the time the draft code was published in 1989 there was some feeling in the Commission itself that two crucial areas of the code needed a structural rethink.[148] Consequently the draft code faced two major barriers as soon as it was published. Much criminal law reform is inherently controversial. The amount of reform in the draft had grown, and there was now more than enough potential for controversy to alarm politicians, civil servants, and practitioners in equal measure. Restatement, on the other hand, is not politically problematic to the same extent, but it has led to trouble from a different direction. Informed critics have argued either that the code does not restate the law accurately[149] or that it has merely succeeded in replicating the existing confusions, contradictions, and unsound policy embodied in the law.[150] It became clear at a seminar early in 1990 that it would be extremely difficult to take forward the draft code as a whole;[151] in consequence the Commission switched track yet again.

The third approach has abandoned the big bang technique in favour of a curious mix of pragmatism, radicalism on a few discrete topics, and codification by stealth. Thus, in the space of just five years the Commission has produced the following: a radical working paper on parties,[152] of which nothing has been heard since 1993; a radical working paper on intoxication,[153] which was followed not long afterwards by a return to orthodoxy accompanied

---

[147] Contemporary writings include J. McEwan and St J. Robilliard, 'Recklessness: the House of Lords and the Criminal Law' (1981) 1 *LS* 267; C. Wells, 'Swatting the Subjectivist Bug' [1982] Crim. LR 209; J. E. Stannard, 'Subjectivism, Objectivism and the Draft Criminal Code' (1985) 101 *LQR* 540; R. A. Duff, 'Codifying Criminal Fault: Conceptual Problems and Presuppositions' in *Criminal Law and Justice*, n. 14 above, 93; N. Lacey, *State Punishment* (London, 1988), chap. 3.

[148] The areas were complicity (see Law Com. CP 131, *Assisting and Encouraging Crime* (London, 1993)) and intoxication (see Law Com. CP 127, *Intoxication and Criminal Liability* (London, 1993)).

[149] See, e.g., G. de Burca and S. Gardner, 'The Codification of the Criminal Law' (1990) 10 *OJLS* 559; Glanville Williams, '*Finis* for *Novus Actus*' [1989] *CLJ* 391.

[150] Norrie, n. 3 above; P. R. Glazebrook, 'Structuring the Criminal Code: Functional Approaches to Complicity, Incomplete Offences and General Defences' in *Harm and Culpability*, n. 12 above, 195.

[151] A brief account of the seminar is given in [1990] Crim. LR 141.

[152] *Assisting and Encouraging Crime*, Law Com. CP 131 (London, 1993).

[153] *Intoxication and Criminal Liability*, Law Com. CP 127 (London, 1993).

by an appallingly and unnecessarily complex draft Bill;[154] a much-delayed report on conspiracy to defraud, which postpones final decisions yet again to the outcome of a review of dishonesty;[155] two working papers in succession on consent;[156] a good report on involuntary manslaughter,[157] which contains a valuable and innovative proposal on the vexed subject of corporate manslaughter; and, most importantly, crucial proposals for replacing the Offences Against the Person Act in a draft Bill which smuggles in selected parts of the general part of the 1989 code.[158] In the light of these varied and somewhat inconsistent developments it is not easy to make sense of the Commission's current vision of the future of English criminal law. Is there now a clear sense of the structure, principles, and style of the criminal code? Assuming that the Commission retains its thirty-year commitment to codification, does it have any real reason to think that its current strategy is going to produce the result which the earlier strategies have failed to achieve?

It is of course true that the Commission has been a victim, both of the speed of change in the last thirty years and of the disappearance of political interest in codification long before any draft was ready. Codification has not been on any political agenda since the late 1960s. It is not identified with the crime control concerns which have dominated Conservative approaches to criminal justice in recent years, nor is it directly linked with other parties' proposals for human rights legislation. In my view it will be essential to re-establish codification as a political priority before there is any realistic prospect that it can be achieved. I stress this point for two related reasons. One is that the case for the code as a piece of desirable law reform has failed. As long as we can continue to muddle on, and in one sense we clearly can, arguments that the criminal law is in a serious mess will not make much headway. The

---

[154] *Legislating the Criminal Code: Intoxication and Criminal Liability*, Law Com. No 229 (London, 1995).

[155] *Criminal Law: Conspiracy to Defraud*, Law Com. No 228 (London, 1994).

[156] *Consent and Offences Against the Person*, Law Com. CP No 134 (London, 1994); *Consent in the Criminal Law*, Law Com. CP No 139 (London, 1995).

[157] *Legislating the Criminal Code: Involuntary Manslaughter*, Law Com. No 237 (London, 1996).

[158] *Offences Against the Person and General Principles*, Law Com. No 218 (London, 1993).

political climate does not favour large-scale law reform for its own sake, and there is an insufficient constituency pressing for change. The other reason is the hazards of the legislative process. In his recent article Sir Henry Brooke has revealed that this is a major stumbling-block to Law Commission proposals for criminal law reform.[159] It appears that cross-party support will not be forthcoming in the absence of a blessing from a House of Commons Committee. However, it is difficult to see how any such committee could be precluded from considering afresh all the numerous issues of principle and policy raised by a criminal code. The delay in such a procedure would be infinite, and the inevitable compromises and restructuring would undermine some of the principal objectives of codification. I very much doubt whether a criminal code Bill can be handled in a similar way to the procedure recently adopted for the Law Commission's Bills to reform the civil law: such a code Bill would have to be taken forward as a Government's programme measure. Its size and importance would mean that it would inevitably be the centrepiece of the Parliamentary session; it might even have to be dealt with over the course of two sessions.

If this perception is right, the political dimensions of codification need to be reconsidered. There will have to be something additional to the pressing need to improve the criminal law to make the difficulty of enactment of the code worthwhile. At the present time I can see only two possibilities. One has some degree of realism, the other is little more than a fantasy. To deal briefly with the fantasy, a speculative possibility is that codification may become part of the European agenda. If a federal Europe containing the United Kingdom represents the political future in the twenty-first century, and it is of course a huge if, then sooner or later demands are likely to arise for harmonization of penal law in the European Union. Harmonization would be a logical consequence of political union, and its arrival would be hastened by increasing European co-operation in law enforcement, particularly against organized and transnational crime.[160] At this point the United Kingdom would

---

[159] 'The Law Commission and Criminal Law Reform' [1995] Crim. LR 911, 918–19.

[160] Some discussion of the possibility of harmonization has already taken place, but the prevailing tone is one of scepticism: see C. Harding and B. Swart, 'Intergovernmental Co-operation in the Field of Criminal Law' in P. Fennell, C. Harding, N. Jorg, and B. Swart (eds.), *Criminal Justice in Europe* (Oxford, 1995) 87, 104–5.

find itself at a distinct disadvantage. It is inconceivable that harmonization would not take the form of a pan-European criminal code, and it is easy to predict that the leading candidates for the basic draft would be the modern codes of France and Germany, revised in 1994 and 1975 respectively. Our obscure and muddled English law would be marginal in this particular codification exercise. This is not to say that we would necessarily find the content of a Franco-German code distasteful. In many respects the similarities of substantive Continental criminal law with English law are greater than the differences, certainly greater than Continental similarities with English criminal procedure. It would nonetheless be a humiliating experience to have a European-inspired code imposed in this country after decades of failure to enact an indigenous code.

The alternative scenario also has a constitutional dimension, but it is a more realistic one in the short to medium term. It can be developed through a parallel with one other modern piece of legislation in the criminal justice area. The Police and Criminal Evidence Act 1984 was a major programme measure which codified and reformed much of the law relating to the enforcement of the criminal law, notably the law of police powers. It has become increasingly clear that this Act represented a new constitutional settlement between citizens and state in relation to law enforcement. Certainly, this is how it has been judicially interpreted in connection with such issues as the unlawful denial of access of suspects to legal advice and breach by the police of the requirements for recording interviews with suspects. Decisions of the courts in the law of criminal evidence have demonstrated clear concern to uphold the integrity of the settlement and its introduction of what have been described as fundamental rights.[161] A criminal code has an equally significant constitutional dimension. It is in a sense the most direct expression of the relationship between a state and its citizens, containing as it does a set of official notices of the conduct which the state prohibits its citizens from engaging in.

---

[161] *Samuel* [1988] QB 615; *Keenan* (1990) 90 Cr.App.R 1; *Canale* (1990) 91 Cr.App.R 1; *Walsh* (1990) 91 Cr.App.R 161. I have discussed the underlying theory of these decisions in I. Dennis, 'Instrumental Protection, Human Right or Functional Necessity? Reassessing the Privilege Against Self-Incrimination' [1995] *CLJ* 342, 351–3.

It is the logical counterpart of PACE, and the analogy with PACE provides a strong argument for saying that we should seek Parliamentary approval, not just to rescue criminal law from its present critical condition, but to re-establish its constitutional legitimacy after so many years of piecemeal incoherent development.

This argument would be strengthened further if we are to have a Bill of Rights based on the European Convention of Human Rights. The commitment of the Convention to standards of legality and fairness would underpin the case for the code which is ultimately founded on the securing of those values. A criminal code would be a logical follow-up to a Bill of Rights because it would complete the constitutional re-ordering that a Bill of Rights would represent. Persuading politicians of the case for enacting this form of concrete expression of the values of human rights law now represents the best prospect for codification in the short to medium term.

This route to codification will require both a change of attitude on the part of those in government and a solution to a long-running territorial battle. It has always been anomalous that responsibility for criminal policy rests with the Home Office whereas most of the initiatives for criminal law reform emanate from the Law Commission, which is attached to the Lord Chancellor's Department. The former has always had an effective power of veto over the latter, at least as far as major criminal law measures are concerned. This is not the place to revive the tired debate about a Ministry of Justice for England and Wales, although we might reasonably expect such a Ministry to take control of all work on criminal law reform, including any project for codification. My proposal is more modest. It is that after thirty years it is time for the Law Commission and for others to take stock of the progress of the code project. If no-one really believes in it any more then we should ask whether it is worth continuing to devote resources to something that is never going to happen. If, on the other hand, there really is a political wish to take it forward, then it seems to me that a round-table conference is needed at which all parties can try to agree at least on the type of code that they want and, equally importantly, on how it is to be drafted and taken through the political process. It is clear that the 1989 draft code will need some fairly substantial revision in the light of both recent developments and the criticism it has received. We may even have reached the stage where what is needed is a new

...uropean Union has moved with extreme caution about urging ...rmonization in this area of law.

Thus the topic for this article. Can criminal law and justice be ...obalized? Or is this already happening? And how are trans-...ational crime and the fear of such crime pushing developments in ...riminal justice? These are rather large questions and I cannot offer ...nything more than an introduction to some of the issues which ...ey raise, around which there is a rapidly growing, though as yet ...nsynthesized, literature. I shall begin by evoking the fears which ...ocus either on the spread or the response to transnational crime as ...xamples of the type of problems associated with the globalization ...f crime. I shall then say something about the meaning of ...obalization and the various ways this phenomenon relates to ...riminal justice more generally. Finally I shall consider more ...arefully the claim that organized crime is globalizing, drawing also ...n my empirical research into organized frauds against the ...ubsidies programmes of the European Union started many years ...go when I still worked in University College.[1] I should say that it is ...ot my intention in this article to debunk concern over the spread ...f organized crime as no more than a new 'moral panic'. If only it ...ere that simple! Descriptions of the growth of this type of crime ...an be exaggerated, as can descriptions of the threat posed by the ...rganization of police efforts to deal with it.[2] But calling for ...aution is unlikely by itself to have much influence over rapidly ...volving events. What needs to be carefully questioned is the single-...mindedness of policy-making which claims to rely on an allegedly ...rrefutable logic: since crime now knows no frontiers, it follows ...hat systems of criminal justice can no longer afford to be based on ...he nation state but must do their best to form a common front.

---

[1] See N. Passas and D. Nelken, 'The Legal Response to Agricultural Fraud in the European Community: A Comparative Study' (1991) 6 *Corruption and Reform* 237, and 'The Thin Line Between Legitimate and Criminal Enterprises: Subsidy Frauds in the European Community' (with N. Passas) in (1993) 20 *Crime, Law and Social Change* 223.

[2] See K. G. Robertson, 'Practical Police Cooperation in Europe: the Intelligence Dimension' in M. Anderson and M. den Boer (eds.), *Policing across National Boundaries* (London, 1 994), 106 at 117 ('the conspiracy theorists of European policing are wrong when they see a vast surveillance State, for the reality is that a true intelligence system is not an easy monster to produce but is one of the rarest of creatures').

model penal code which needs to be drafted as a whole and put out to consultation as a whole.

The kind of conference I am advocating would require the presence and input of politicians, civil servants, especially the Home Office, the Law Commission, the judiciary, practitioners, and academics. It would be an ambitious undertaking and it might fail to reach sufficient agreement to justify further work. But, given the urgency and the constitutional importance of the project, it is surely worth making the effort. If we do not make the effort, there is no alternative to the traditional English remedy of muddling through. However, in the case of the criminal law this is not the remedy, but the disease. I hope that the law is not going to require intensive care in the next century, but I fear this will be the case unless we have the vision and the energy to undertake necessary surgery now.

THE GLOBALIZATI
CRIME AND CRIM
JUSTICE
Prospects and Proble

David Nelken

Earlier this year the following letter from a M
postgraduate student in Iraq, arrived for me at Un

Dear Mr Nelken
I am Ali from Mosul. I am studying for a Mast
Criminal Law. My thesis is about Nolle Pro
discontinuance of military criminal proceedings by
Defence under military criminal law. I wish for you
send me modern reports and research about it as so

Unfortunately, Ali was asking the wrong person if h
an expert in military criminal law. But his letter re
law is both the most local and the most universal o
cultural phenomena. Ali's letter might be though n
carries the assumption of law as somehow being so
culture that it becomes feasible to turn to a very diffe
the potential source of useful ideas about how militar
could be developed in Iraq. But we should not be so
law's reach. Just such a spreading of legal ideas has o
past (I live in Bologna not far from the tombs of
whose rediscovery of Roman law helped shape t
Europe), and something similar is happening today
ence of a new *lex mercatoria* for international busines
or in the attempt to extend human rights law. The
that some forms of law do seem to travel better
Criminal law for example is usually seen as v
quintessential part of national sovereignty, and not fo

Instead, I shall try to show why the relationship between globalization, crime, and criminal justice is a lot more complex than this thought captures.

Two Opposite Fears

It is possible to detect two types of anxiety in current writing about the globalization of crime. The first of these stems from the argument that globalization is a process out of control, or even beyond control, which is creating enormous opportunities for business and organized crime which locally based criminal justice systems are struggling to keep up with and perhaps are always destined to be behind. The old-new category of 'transnational crime' is taken to embrace a wide variety of threatening behaviours including terrorism, espionage including industrial espionage, drugs and arms trafficking, the international wholesaling of pornography and prostitution, smuggling and trade in people and body parts, counterfeiting, crimes related to computer technology, international fraud and other financial crimes, tax evasion, theft of art, antiques, and other precious items, crimes against the environment, trade in endangered species, and internationally co-ordinated racial violence. What is more, much of this transnational crime is assumed (rightly) to be organized by foreign criminal enterprises such as the Sicilian Mafia, the Colombian drug cartels, the Yakuza in Japan, the Chinese and Taiwanese Triads, or sophisticated fraudster networks in Nigeria. Increasingly, attention is also being paid to the challenge represented by the Mafias of Russia and other countries in Eastern Europe who are seen as amongst the main beneficiaries of the break-up of the former Soviet Union, the run down of the Red Army, the privatization programmes or foreign investments and aid payments, and so on.

As is confirmed by the recent redeployment in Britain of the secret services to carry out intelligence against them, organized criminals have slipped easily into the slot of public enemy number one which was previously reserved for the anti-democratic menace of communism. And this is even more true of the United States. As Louise Shelley, an influential American expert on organized crime, argues, the world is now facing a new non-state based form of authoritarianism which subjects people to coercion, corrupts law, privatizes weak states for its own goals, and threatens those journalists—and criminologists—who try to expose it.[3] Her conclusion (these arguments always arrive at the same one) is that 'the legal institutions of the world are still bound to the nation state but the forces of coercion are transnational; existing state based legal systems therefore cannot protect citizens from the new authoritarian threat provided by transnational organised crime'.[4] According to this view the globalization of crime thrives on the inability of the criminal law to globalize. And the European Union is the best illustration of this. As another American writer put it:

crooks were the last item on the European Community's agenda in 1990. Engrossed in plans to make money, economic leaders had given scarcely a thought to the opportunity for criminals to do likewise—no common police academy or training existed, each country had its own laws on extradition, rights of asylum, hot pursuit, exchange of police and intelligence information, undercover agents, controlled drug deliveries, jail terms for drug traffickers, money laundering or phone taps.[5]

But there also mirror image fears. The claim here is that police forces are in fact using these fears about transnational crime to forge alliances which are not democratically accountable. America has long been in the lead here in exporting abroad its war against drugs and terrorism, but in Europe this is also well illustrated by the inter-state TREVI or EUROPOL policing agreements; the European Commission itself only has observer status, the European Parliament still less say. Criminal justice is thus globalizing along with everything else (and in the same way) and efforts at transnational police action represent a real danger to democratic structures which themselves presuppose the national state. As one author claims 'it is by looking at the enforcement practices of the transnational law enforcement enterprise that we can best come to understand the political form of the emergent transnational world system'[6] or, as

---

[3] L. Shelley, 'Transnational Organized Crime: The New Authoritarianism', paper presented at the Law and Society Conference, Glasgow, 13 July 1996.

[4] *Ibid.*, 3.

[5] C. Sterling, *Thieves' World: The Threat of the New Global Network of Organised Crime* (New York, 1994), 40.

[6] L. W. E. Sheptycki, 'Law Enforcement, Justice and Democracy in the Transnational Arena: Reflections on the War on Drugs' (1996) 24 *International Journal of Sociology of Law* 61, 64. See also L. W. E. Sheptycki, 'Transnational Policing and the Makings of a Postmodern State' (1993) 33 *British Journal of Criminology* 613; E. Nadelman, *Cops across Borders* (London, 1993); M. Anderson and M. den Boer

Rosa Luxembourg is alleged to have said, 'the police are the one true International'. What is more, powers and techniques which are demanded or taken in order to deal with the threat of menacing forms of organized crime often end up being used against more low level or local forms of criminality. Insofar as borders are defended the focus is often on keeping out those immigrants who in the present economic climate are once again assumed to be surplus to requirements;[7] thus illegal immigration is now included alongside drugs and terrorism as one of the three major threats against which what is increasingly being called *Fortress Europe* needs to be defended. For these commentators on transnational policing the solution is often worse than the problem—not only because it is symmetrically authoritarian—but also because there is ample evidence that unaccountable policing can itself involve illegality or engage in crime in its own account.

So far the differences between systems and the obstacles to international collaboration are as significant as the moves to common forms of policing and punishment. But even if progress to a unified order of international criminal law is so slow, or perhaps just because it is so slow, we should also note that measures taken to deal with transnational criminality by *individual* nation-states already have serious implications for civil liberties. If INTERPOL is said to have files on 130,000 people of whom 80,000 are drug offenders; researchers quote the police in Britain alone as claiming to have records on the 60 per cent of Colombians living in London who, they say, are involved in the drug trade (as many as 42,000 out of a total of 70,000).[8] An intelligence agent was recently quoted in the *Sunday Times* as saying, 'We are one of the very few countries in the world to have legislation that allows us to work very aggressively overseas . . . We take the view that stealing money from a crook is a good thing and if it's from an account in a foreign country who cares? We are hardly likely to be sued, and anyway

---

(eds.) n. 2 above; M. Anderson et al. *Policing the European Union* (Oxford, 1995); C. Fijnaut and G. Marx, *Undercover: Police Surveillance in Comparative Perspective* (The Hague, 1995).

[7] The current politics of exclusion of immigrants to the European Community is the subject of large literature which I cannot summarize here, but there is still much to be studied about the relationship between this pattern of exclusion and internal forms of exclusionary social control.

[8] Sheptycki, 'Law Enforcement . . . .' n. 6 above.

there are no fingerprints to lead back to us'[9] (according to the report these remarks allegedly met with the approval of a leading London legal academic). The 1992 decision of the American Supreme Court in the *Alvarez Machain* case seemed to authorize state kidnapping of a drug dealer from Mexico. In the same year in the decision in R. v. *Governor of Pentonville Prison, ex p. Chinoy*[10] the English courts refused to took at illegalities which had allegedly occurred in the gathering of evidence in France. In sum, whatever globalization may or may not be doing to crime, talk about globalization is increasingly serving as a means by which national criminal justice systems seek to augment their resources and (re)legitimate themselves.

How far can discussions about globalization help us to place these fears about organized crime and transnational enforcement in some wider context so as to give us a better grasp of what is happening? Certainly there have been other periods, such as the early years of this century, which witnessed widespread levels of concern about international drug traffic—though it is worth remembering that Britain, and even more Holland, were then counted amongst the countries accused of profiting from the trade. This and other campaigns against foreign threats were accompanied by a level of xenophobia and fear of immigration even more severe than that being witnessed today. What difference does globalization make? Certainly it would be important if we could show that organized criminals engaged in transnational crimes were simply responding to the pressures and opportunities which were re-shaping legal and illegal enterprise alike. For if we were to treat globalization as the real villain of the piece, we could hardly assume that transnational policing could provide the answer. It could certainly do little to offset the many other effects of globalization on levels of crime in different countries and cities. Rather than setting the secret services on the trails of the Mr Bigs of organized crime, the challenge we would face would be better analysed as having to do with the political choice whether to regulate or deregulate globalization processes more generally (together with the problem of whether and how such regulation could be made effective).

[9] *Sunday Times*, 17 Nov. 1996.   [10] [1992] 1 All ER 317.

Understanding Globalization

But what exactly is meant by globalization? Is it just the latest jargon phrase wheeled out so as to describe a series of otherwise unrelated matters or is it the magical key to making the connections which otherwise are so hard to find when living through a period of rapid change? The term is now being used in a variety of academic disciplines. I have the space here to say only a little about some of the definitions, aspects, and theories of globalization which I have gleaned from the literatures of sociology and management science. Because it is rare to find much specific reference to crime and criminal justice in these discussions our task will be to tease out the implications of globalization for our subject (as well as to consider how developments in crime and criminal justice and criminology may themselves affect globalization).

In a recent social science text with this title, Malcolm Walters[11] defines globalization as 'a social process in which the constraints of geography on social and cultural arrangements recede and in which people become increasingly aware that they are receding'. Thus globalization has both objective and subjective elements. However, though Walters tends to see these as going together it will sometimes be useful for our purposes to distinguish them. Starting from a concern with criminal justice we might want to ask—does globalization really destroy the local basis for allocating blame? In particular could it be one of the functions of criminal justice, for better or worse, to reflect or attempt to recreate a sense of group solidarity which does not coincide at all with changing economic constraints?

Anthony Giddens similarly defines globalization as 'the intensification of social relations which link distant localities in such a way that local happenings are shaped by events occurring miles away and vice versa'.[12] What this means for our argument is that what happens in a local neighbourhood of a city, including of course its levels of crime, is increasingly likely to be influenced by factors such as world money and commodity markets which operate at an indefinite distance from the neighbourhood itself. For

---

[11] M. Walters, *Globalisation* (London, 1995), 3.
[12] A. Giddens, *Consequences of Modernity* (Oxford, 1990), 64, and cf. A. Giddens *Modernity and Self Identity* (Oxford, 1991).

Giddens globalization should be treated as part of the process of modernization (not postmodernization), a secular trend through which time and space come to be separated from a person's location or the cycles of the seasons. It represents a further stage in the lifting out of social relations from local contexts of interaction and their restructuring across time and space through symbolic tokens such as money, media and expert systems. Those who live in modern times trust their societies and lives to be guided by such impersonal flows of expertise so that to know what to do it is necessary to have resort to a constantly changing forms of knowledge. (In the jargon without which sociology would become too user-friendly this is known as 'time-space distanciation', 'disemebedding', and 'reflexivity'). Each of these changes in the relationship of the individual to her social world has potential implications for crime and its control. A recent attempt to draw conclusions for criminology[13] suggests that Giddens has described a world of relativized and individualistic choices which helps weaken social controls and makes it more difficult to define and reinforce outer boundaries of cultural and legal systems. What replaces these boundaries is our drawing on expert systems so as to create bubbles of security in defined areas of housing and shopping malls which have to be fortified against the risks posed by those members of the population who have been displaced from the economy by processes of global change.

Globalization has manifold economic, political, and cultural aspects and there is predictable disagreement about which of these is driving the others.[14] As compared to what are described as more culturalist approaches other authors lay more stress on economic factors. Wallerstein argues that the world capitalist system has always been integrated not by nation-states but by global commercial and manufacturing relationships which determine which countries belong to the core, semi-periphery, or periphery of this system.[15] In these terms, changes in the dependent nation-state

---

[13] A. Bottoms and P. Wiles, 'Crime and insecurity in the City' in C. Finjaut, J. Goetals, T. Peters, and L. Walgrave (eds.), *Changes in Society, Crime and Criminal Justice in Europe*, Vol. I (The Hague, 1996).

[14] See M. Featherstone (ed.), *Global Culture* (London, 1990).

[15] I. Wallerstein, *The Capitalist World-Economy* (Cambridge, 1979): for another attempt to situate globalization in historical perspective see also R. Robertson, *Globalisation, Social Theory and Global Culture* (London, 1992).

system, world military order, and the international division of labour and trading relationships can all be expected to have consequences for the type and levels of crime. Another leading writer stresses the importance of transnational global companies, the transnational capitalist class, and the cultural ideology of consumerism and focuses in particular on what he calls the 'key transnational practices' which characterize globalization.[16] These practices, which originate with non-state actors and cross state borders, involve among others major capitalist institutions, globalizing bureaucrats, executives of transnational companies, and professional and consumerist elites in the first and third worlds. From a criminological perspective it would certainly be relevant to examine how the spread of consumerist ideology increases expectations without necessarily providing the income to satisfy them.

A similar stress on political economy, though without the Marxist flavour, is found in the management science literature.[17] It argues that the increasing integration of the world economy is an objective trend which can be measured by descriptive indicators such as price and interest rates convergence. Economic actors are increasingly having to take greater account of the way their actions in one nation state influence their actions in another. The State loses influence because political action is increasingly dominated by world financial and real goods markets and governments encounter particular difficulties in pursuing policies of regulation which are out of line with other countries. New forms of interdependence also pose governments with other problems such as how to tax information flows (though no doubt they will find out how to do so one day). In part as a reaction to these difficulties there is an increasing number of regional groupings, not only the EU or NAFTA, but also the IMF, which has grown in membership from forty-four to 178 countries. This literature is specially useful when we come to consider the globalization of organized crime as an aspect of how and why legitimate businesses are integrating world wide.

Where is globalization leading? What would a fully globalized

---

[16] L. Sklair, *The Sociology of the Global System* (Hemel Hempstead, 1991).

[17] See the entries on globalization in M. Warner (ed.), *International Encyclopedia of Business and Management* (London, 1996).

society look like? Walters[18] tells us it would exhibit a high level of differentiation and multicentricity and there would be no tight set of cultural preferences and prescriptions. Insofar as culture is unified it will be extremely abstract, expressing tolerance for diversity and individual choice. Importantly for the future of criminal justice, we are told that territoriality will disappear as an organizing principle for social and cultural life. But looking that far ahead is not all that convincing. We would do better to concentrate on trying to clarify our ideas about what is happening now to crime and criminal justice as it is shaped by or tries to resist these trends.

Globalization and Crime

In trying to apply theories of globalization it is all too easy to go from the sublime to the meticulous. On the one hand we have sweeping futuristic visions; on the other all too concrete descriptions of what is happening on the ground in police co-operation or the emergence of new forms of transnational crime, with only an impoverished account of how this relates to wider social changes. We lack a middle-range theory which makes developments in crime and criminal justice central to its concerns. But is it even plausible to expect to find one theory which would successfully explain all types of crime linked to globalization—from genocide to insider trading to computer 'hacking'—and which could also succinctly explain the common denominator of globalizing moral panics from pædophilia to political corruption (though current developments in Belgium suggest that there can be surprising and disturbing links between such apparently unrelated crimes)? What we can do is at least try to provide a framework which could help us to sort out the various relationships between globalization and developments in crime and criminal justice.

Which should be the axis of such a framework? One important distinction to bear in mind is that between increasing homogenization and increasing interdependence (of other kinds). On the one hand there is the phenomenon of the 'global village' (which we can call *homogenization*), in which up to 800 million of the world's population can be found watching an American superbowl game on television whilst eating pizza and drinking coca cola—or the

---

[18] N. 11 above.

scene in Nani Moretti's film *Dear Diary* where an Italian devotee of soap opera desperately shouts at some American tourists visiting the Etna volcano to find out what has happened in the latest instalments of his favourite soap which had been broadcast in the USA, but not yet in Italy. The spread of American films, television series, and novels which feature (particular) images of crime and criminal justice illustrates this sort of globalization. On the other hand there is the *interdependence* vividly illustrated by the Chernobyl nuclear disaster or the way a military coup in Nigeria affects the price of oil in Rotterdam and brings about a collapse of prices on the Tokyo Stock exchange. In the sphere of crime we could consider the part played by organized crime pyramid frauds in the recent collapse of order in Albania, or the multiple consequences of reckless or fraudulent speculation by merchant banks or other players on the commodities markets.

Globalization may further either or both of these processes. What is important is to see that interdependence does not necessarily presume or produce homogeneity.[19] As sociologists of modernity from Durkheim to Luhmann have emphasized, it thrives on difference and differentiation. But there is also a further distinction which needs to be made which is obscured in many discussions of globalization which describe growing interdependence. It is often unclear whether such interdependence is something planned as a *strategy* of integration (for example under the impetus of multinationals such as McDonalds), or whether it is rather (by definition) a process which is beyond control, as in the way money flows to where it can obtain the best return. Of course both of these processes may sometimes be relevant for different purposes, but all this needs careful sorting out. To allow this we need a framework which helps us to see how globalizing processes may involve homogenization and integration in varying degrees.

One final note of caution. We must not assume that developments in crime and criminal justice are merely a *consequence* of globalization; they may also, as already noted, be one of the causes

---

[19] See S. Yearley, *Sociology, Environmentalism, and Globalization* (London, 1996), 23: 'A global world is not a uniform world. But it is one in which key processes—manufacture, food production, cultural transmission—are increasingly being organized at a transnational level.'

of whether or not people feel part of a global order. Notoriously, criminal law functions by creating boundaries between insiders and outsiders; by responding to real or constructed threats it helps define enemies or create scapegoats.[20] Whilst this will often, and perhaps typically, tighten the definition of who can count as an insider, attempts to extend the reach of the law, as for example through the creation of the International War Crimes tribunals, or in legislation aimed at dealing with 'sex tourists' who victimize children abroad, may also broaden this definition of who counts as an offender or a victim. In addition, discourse about crime, like that about victims, is itself one of most universalizing of current ideologies—after the alleged death of merely political ideologies. As its influence spreads, criminology, like other types of expertise, can also be seen as a bearer of globalization, though it puts one in mind of Beck's remark that expertise secures its survival as much through its failure as its success.[21]

Globalization may even *constitute* and not simply cause or facilitate crime. Typically this will be when it increases the levels of criminalization of certain types of behaviour which not long before had been considered as acceptable, or at least containable, within acceptable limits, especially as long as they were confined to local insiders. One interpretation of the move to legislate against a crime which is aptly named 'insider trading', which accompanied the so-called 'big bang' liberalization of the London stock exchange, is in terms of the need to ensure predictability and trust in the globalized City of London once it was opened up to outsiders. As Clarke puts it, 'it would have perplexed leading members of these institutions up to the end of the 1950s to be told they were doing anything reprehensible in acting on such information. It was precisely because of access to such information that one was part of the city, and one was part of the city in the clear expectation of making a considerable amount of money'.[22] Similarly, it is not easy to decide how much the campaigns against political corruption of the 1990s merely reflect an increase in such misbehaviour in the 1980s or also the effects of globalization in making such conduct ' more 'costly'

---

[20] Cf. J. O'Neill, 'Aids as a Globalizing Panic', in n. 13 above, 329–42.
[21] U. Beck, *The Risk Society: Towards a New Modernity* (London, 1992).
[22] M. Clarke, *Business Crime: Its Nature and Control* (Oxford, 1990), 162.

or increasing the centrality of penal law as a political resource.[23]

Table 1: Crime, Criminal Justice and Two Aspects of Globalizing
Processes of Interdependence

1. High homogenization, Low integration

Global spread of criminal techniques e.g. car ramming and strategies of
control e.g. technological methods of surveillance;

Developments and fashions in criminal justice e.g. the decline of
rehabilitation, fixed sentencing, community policing, local crime prevention, 'victim's rights', mediation, (the 'reintegrative shaming' approach in
criminology).

Global spread of images of crime ('Miami Vice') and criminal justice
('Perry Mason'). Influence of (American) criminology and the Anglo-
American concept of 'criminal justice'.

2. High integration, High homogenization

Greater flows of illegal trade e.g. of pornography, drugs, etc., as well as
more opportunities for financial crime, as part of increased legal trading;

New criminal laws to fight counterfeiting, to protect new information
property rights, regulate financial markets, computer 'hacking', the use of
the INTERNET etc.

Development of international criminal law, creation of war crimes
tribunals, international and regional policing agreements e.g. *Schengen*

3. Low integration, Low homogenization

Local differences in types and levels of crime in countries, cities (and parts
of cities) in the core, semi periphery, and periphery of the 'world system'
which result from market- and technology-driven changes in the flows of
trade, information, and people.

Other effects of the 'hollowing out' of the State and of 'localization' as a
reaction to (or aspect of) globalization.

---

[23] See e.g. D. della Porta and Y. Meny (eds.) *Corruzione e Democrazia: Sette
paesi a confronto* (Naples, 1995); D. Nelken and M. Levi, 'Introduction' in M. Levi
and D. Nelken (eds.), *The Politics of Corruption and the Corruption of Politics*
(Oxford, 1996); and A. Garapon and D. Salas (eds.), *La République Pénalisée*
(Paris, 1996).

4. High integration, Low homogenization

Pax Mafioso—strategic agreements between organized crime groups exploiting national differences in law and sentencing. The export of hot money, arms, dangerous waste, unsafe products and working practices by state/organized/business criminals. Competition for 'hot money' and money laundering, growth of tax havens.

Pax Americana—American foreign crime policy in Latin America and elsewhere. Fortress Europe: *TREVI, EUROPOL*; IMF and world bank pressures on developing countries.

Table 1 sets out the four cells of the framework which I have been outlining, with some illustrative examples (many more could of course be added) showing how increasing global interdependence may influence or be influenced by crime and criminal justice. It allows us to draw a number of lessons for the currently popular claim that the crucial threat which globalization represents is the way it facilitates the integration of organized crime (to which the only answer is a similar response by the international forces of order).

In the first place, and most importantly, it suggests the complexity of teasing out the connections between crime and globalization. While some forms of crime result from processes of integration, others belong more to homogenizing processes and some aspects of globalization cannot be fitted into either of these categories. Criminal justice or other agencies need to be aware of this variety; even more, their responses are themselves part of the phenomenon that needs to be understood.

More specifically, the table shows us why an exclusive focus on the threat of transnational criminals fails to capture many of the other ways globalization may affect opportunities for crime. As cell 3 suggests, many of the problems caused by globalization have nothing to do with deliberate integration by organized criminals but result from the differential effects of globalization on different countries, cities, or parts of cities which governments cannot or will not attempt to control. From a criminological point of view the drive to economic integration can, and often will, lead to social and anomic disintegration. It will therefore be of small help to integrate at the level of criminal justice responses whilst leaving the underlying causes untouched. The disintegrative effects of economic integration may even be exacerbated by some of the homogenizing globalizing processes which affect criminal justice (as can be seen in cell 1). It is enough to think of the way the rehabilitative approach to punishment fell widely out of favour just at the same time as the welfare state faced fiscal pressures because of changes in global competitiveness and oil prices.

We also need to question the assumption that there is an inverse relationship between the problem posed by organized crime and success in achieving agreement on the harmonization of national systems of criminal law and enforcement. The table reminds us that some homogenization of criminal justice (the increasing adoption of the accusatorial model for example) is already taking place as a result of globalization, despite the alleged dependence of criminal law on the nation state and local culture. But a comparison of cells 2 and 4 should again remind us of the limits of law as a response, whether uniform or not. It is true that organized crime is able to organize strategically to exploit differences in the economic and legal order—just as these differences are exploited and reinforced also by *legitimate* business in its 'forum shopping' for favourable legal systems and the way it puts pressure on weak states to soften regulatory regimes. But organized and economic crime has also benefited from the opportunities opened up by increasing *homogenization* of the world economic and legal order (including the enormous increase in the issue of bonds consequent on the internationalization of the banking system). Greater harmonization of legal procedures and penalties (even apart from the conceptual difficulties this raises) will do little as such to change the balance of incentives which lead to the world wide distribution of crime even if it may help in the processing of the few who are apprehended. And, in practice, integration of enforcement efforts usually tends to involve subordination rather than homogenization, as in the way the United States attempts to enforce its priorities in South America.

The dialectic between crime and control will not be understood as long as we stick to the idea that the forces of order are waging a losing war against an insidious foreign enemy. Increasing certain sorts of control efforts may even act as an incentive to criminal action, as in the case of drugs and other illegal products and activities in which organized crime specializes. Insofar as crime and control can, for some purposes, be separated this will depend on our ability to distinguish the dynamics of criminal behaviour and of changes in criminal justice which are highlighted in each of the four cells. How far do crime and control evolve by following the same or different logics? What are the organizational and inter-organizational challenges which each face? How far is it true that organized crime strategies reflect a strictly economic logic whereas the growth of international policing responds to more political considerations at both national and international levels? And what are the implications of any such differences?

Trend, Tactic, or Trope?

Before concluding this brief, and necessarily oversimplified, over-view of the relationship between globalization and criminal justice there is one further reflection which can be drawn from the social science literature. This warns us to be wary of taking globalization to be something inevitable. There is certainly some evidence to justify talking about globalization as a current trend, just as it made sense—a generation ago—to talk about the economic and cultural 'convergence' between nations that would inevitably eventually be produced through their common reliance on modern technology. But, as that counter-example shows, historical inevitability is not so easily discerned (the move towards market systems in the former communist states may be more attributable to their failure to keep up in the technological battle). Presupposing the inevitability of globalization is itself a loaded description of current developments. Insofar as globalization is to be defined not simply or always as a process out of control, but also as a strategy or tactic which is followed by determinate economic and political actors, there will almost always be some room for alternative strategies and resistance.

The progress of globalization is thus not determined simply by the extension of new technologies in communication and transport-ation but is also the result of social and political action, including decisions (and non-decisions) by governments about regulating and deregulating the national and international economy. Talking about globalization as if it were inevitable is itself often a tactic for gaining resources, for favouring one or other policy choice—or what is often the same thing, making an alliance with one or other national or international actor or set of actors. It is precisely *not* the case that 'Global economic interaction poses an identical legal and law enforcement dilemma for industrialized and newly industrializing nations—opening their borders, economy, and society to the free exchange of people, capital, and goods, without sacrificing domestic order and protection of the international interests of their citizens'.[24] Even allegedly global environmental problems do not have the same costs for all, just as some countries or groups pay a higher price for trying to deal with them.[25] In particular there are likely to be systematic differences in judgments of globalization from the perspective of members of countries in the semi-periphery or periphery of the capitalist world system—as they experience its effects as packaged by the IMF and the world bank in its curious mixture of economic liberalism and human rights.

This point is often lost sight of because of the way talk about globalization has become a trope or metaphor which carries arguments over all or any obstacle. Take, for our own topic, the following quotation from the same article published in an allegedly radical criminological journal. 'Economic and social change', we are told, 'is apparent across the face of a transformed globe, reshaped by technological winds blowing across the global landscape as forcefully and as steadily as the Trade winds carried explorers and colonists to reshape the New World. Virtually every institution within industrialized and newly industrializing economies is undergoing rapid evolution to keep pace with the speed of technologically induced social and political change save *one*, law and law enforcement'.[26] With this type of metaphoric reasoning it is no surprise to find that our author later assumes, rather than demonstrates, the happy arrival of global consensus when he asserts blandly that organized crime (his concern is the Chinese and Taiwanese variety) 'imperils the attainment of international objectives like political harmony and economic advancement through free trade'.[27]

Less scholarly (even less scholarly!), though more widely read

---

[24] W. H. Myers III, 'The Emerging Threat of Transnational Organised Crime from the East' (1996) 24 *Crime, Law and Social Change*, 181, at 182. Myers himself immediately acknowledges that 'the economic burdens and social effects of maintaining this tension fall unequally upon industrialized and newly industrializing nations' but (illogically) insists nonetheless that 'all nations have an equal share in the consequences of failing to act'.   [25] See Yearley, n. 19, above.

[26] W. H. Myers III, n. 24 above, 182.   [27] *Ibid.*, 213.

accounts of organized crime—which one suspects may influence or echo even more closely some levels of official thinking—make regular resort to questionable metaphors rather than sober evidence. Crime, we are told, 'skids out of control around the globe'.[28] In particular the European Union 'faces an uncontrollable invasion of migrants from every direction'[29] and, in 1992, 'every kind of criminal was riding in on this human tide' so that 'Western Europe lay like a vast open city under murderous criminal bombardment'.[30] Even what purports to be evidence in such accounts is far from meeting minimum requirements, as in the claim that 'crime is the fastest growing industry in Britain' or the fatuous assertion that Holland, 'an island of civility on a turbulent continent', 'has more crimes per capita than . . . the United States'.[31] Nobody had told our author (an American living in Europe)—assuming she was in good faith—that it is the high level of bicycle theft in that country which so biases its crime statistics.

The Strategy and Culture of Organized Criminals

The exaggerations of those trying to grab our attention with metaphors should not be taken as an excuse to conclude that there is nothing to be worried about regarding organized crime or that globalization is irrelevant to its strategies. But if we are to take seriously both the fears mentioned at the outset of this article what can be done about the real threat of organized crime other than entrust the police and the intelligence services with ever-increasing (and uncontrollable) powers?

The first step must be to understand more about the changing strategies of organized criminals.[32] The management science

---

[28] N. 5 above, 38.   [29] *Ibid.*, 39.   [30] *Ibid.*, 41.
[31] *Ibid.*, 38.

[32] There is no space here to expound on the many differences between organized crime groups. But it is at least worth noting that describing organized crime as a new authoritarian menace to the democratic state fails to bring out the contrast between organized crime groups, or strategies, which aspire to military control over a territory (offering or exacting protection) and those, on the other hand, which thrive on the collusion of complicit weak States which allow them to accumulate wealth (e.g. through international frauds or drug smuggling) without drawing attention to their criminal activities.

literature, for example, explains the advantages of global integration for business multinationals in terms which can apply equally well to organized crime. Thus we read of alliances, protection from competition, economies of scale, the securing of stable supplies and markets, assistance in diversification and bringing products to market, the possibilities of taking advantage of expertise and local knowledge, the reduction of risks, the financing of large-scale projects, and the acquisition of technology.[33] The opportunities which globalization has opened up for organized crime also reflect the extent to which such crime enterprises have integrated not only with other organized crime groups but also with legitimate and semi-legitimate international business. For example only 5 per cent of the more than 175 billion dollars a day of international transactions is connected to flows of world trade directly.[34] The remainder is made up of capital on the look out for short-term liquid or semi-liquid speculative investments. This total has grown enormously as a result of the internationalization of banks and holding companies since the 1960s, the elimination of restrictions and controls on foreign investments and currency swaps, and the impact of electronic technology on the individual national capital markets. As important as the globalization of markets or the technological marvels of electronic money transfer is the development of privileged territories where transactions of huge dimensions can take place without any form of regulation and control—the tax havens and Eurodollar markets at the intersections of main routes of legal and illegal trade. In order to recycle their illegal profits organized criminals have thus increasingly established relationships with the institutions and locations harbouring homeless capital and bought themselves into systems of offshore banks and holding companies.

But the dirty money derived from illegal activity is only a minor part of all the 'hot money' ready to move from one end of the globe to the other at the smallest change in interest rates, legal

---

[33] See M. Warner, n. 17 above.

[34] P. Arlacchi, 'Corruption, Organized Crime and Money Laundering World Wide' in M. Punch et al., *Coping with Corruption in a Borderless World* (The Hague, 1993), 89. The best discussion of these matters is still R. T. Naylor, *Hot Money and the Politics of Debt* (New York, 1987).

regulations, economic policies, or political regimes. There are two other main sources of hot money apart from that produced from illegal transactions. A second source is the profit produced in the underground or informal economy which runs at 10–15 per cent of gross product in developed countries. This money, made by those otherwise law-abiding, cannot be declared because it is the result of transactions organized to avoid paying tax. It needs to flow out of the country until it can reappear safely. A third source of hot money is so-called 'flight capital' leaving indebted countries in the third world. In the period 1973–81, for example, multinational bank managers came to depend on the volume, not the quality of, loans extended without deposits. Highly-placed members of foreign governments spent the loans on public works, armaments, and luxurious consumer goods but a large part returned to Western countries in the form of illegally exported capital often deposited with the very banks that gave the credits in the first place. The short-sighted complicity of the largest banks in the world revealed itself as short-sighted when countries began defaulting. But when the banks curbed the credit flow to the developing world from 1981 the problem grew worse as frightened members of the middle classes began expatriating their savings; something like 200 billion dollars was allegedly transferred between 1976 and 1985 to the USA and the tax havens of Europe, Asia, and the Caribbean, leaving their own countries without foreign exchange reserves.

In some parts of the world the destinies of legal and illegal commerce now (again?) seem to be fatally intertwined. One chapter of a recent biography of Pablo Escobar (the former Colombian drug baron) begins:

Every morning, on the fifth floor of the north Bogota headquarters of one of Colombia's biggest financial and industrial conglomerates there arrives a fax from its main office in the United States. The fax gives the daily US dollar price of cocaine on the streets of New York. Immediately the information is keyed into a computer performance chart. Two parallel lines run across the middle of the graph. When the price spikes through the upper line, it indicates a supply blockage. The scarcity of cocaine in New York means a scarcity of US dollars in Colombia. The company's domestic sales are damaged. When the price bursts through the lower line it heralds the presence of a major new cocaine supplier and a spate of killings and informant related seizures until the supply drops back to normal levels. In the meantime with US dollars flooding to Colombia, it is a good moment to buy them cheaply. According to a technician who worked for the conglomerate, the chart was installed in 1986.[35]

Earnings from the illegal drug trade in Colombia are said to be the same as that from legal exports and to have helped to save the economy from debt-related torment, hyper-inflation, and economic stagnation which affected so many other countries in South America in the 1980s.[36]

Even in the most developed Western countries there is a blurring of legal and illegal commerce, as in the arms trade,[37] and this is as often sustained as attacked by the police and intelligence services. A good example is provided by the collapse of the Bank of Credit and Commerce International.[38] The BCCI grew to be the World's seventh largest private bank with assets of $23 billion and operations in seventy-two countries. The criminal enterprises it helped fund included smuggling, drug trafficking, money launder-ing, illegal arms trade, transfer of nuclear technology, public corruption and capital flight, illegal ownership of US banks, financing of terrorism, frauds against depositors, and the methods adopted ranged from false accounting to the use of violence. The bank's main beneficiaries were 3,000 powerful customers who included the Colombian drug lords, ruthless dictators such as Duvalier, Somoza, Saddam Hussein, Marcos, and Noriega. But the uses made of the bank by the CIA and other Western secret services also played an important part in postponing its hour of reckoning. As Passas argues:

in order to better understand and fight organized international crime groups, one has to explore their links with legitimate organizations and (Western and other) government policies that provide crime facilitative conditions and/or create demands such as those fulfilled by BCCI. BCCI reflects and is deeply rooted in the world's structural problems and conflicts.[39]

There are ever more reports of research findings which illustrate the increasing overlap between organized crime, corporate crime,

---

[35] S. Strong, *Whitewash*, (London, 1996).
[36] *Ibid.*
[37] R. T. Naylor, 'Loose Cannons: Covert Commerce and Underground Finance in the Modern Arms Market' (1995) 22 *Crime, Law and Social Change* 1.
[38] N. Passas, 'BCCI?' (1996) 23 *Crime, Law and Social Change* 293–300, at 308.
[39] *Ibid.*, 245.

and ordinary business.[40] But whilst it is essential to explore the full extent of symbiosis between legitimate business and organized crime I am uneasy about the temptation in some parts simply to *equate* business and organized crime or to treat organized crime as no more than a special form of capitalist enterprise.[41] It seems to me that, for all the similarities in strategy, there are also significant differences in culture, differences which could perhaps be exploited in seeking to contain the threat posed by this form of criminality. Interviews carried out under my guidance with members of organized crime groups in Italy who are involved in defrauding the European Union, for example, show that there is an uneasy relationship between the locally based organized criminals and the more cosmopolitan legal and accounting experts on whom they have increasingly to rely.[42] There also persisting, if subtle, differences in philosophy between organized criminals and businessmen (notwithstanding the now widely-accepted accounts of the affinity between the approach of the New Mafia and that of business entrepreneurs).[43] The following extract from a longer interview with two members of the Mafia responsible for organizing European Union fraud in Sicily reveals, amongst other things, a fatalistic zero-sum approach to life which is, in some ways, far from the capitalistic ethic.

The interview was carried out at the height of the judges' attack on corruption in Italy. Asked whether the judges' campaign was bad for business the senior of the two men replied:

all the screaming and excitement can never go on for very long—still less can it cause any permanent damage except to those who allow themselves to be frightened. You stop your activities for a moment and wait while the crows scream and get all excited. Then everything returns as it was before.

---

[40] See e.g. N. Passas and D. Nelken, 'The Thin Line . . .', n. 1 above; P. Van Kuyne 'Implications of Cross-border Crime Risks in an Open Europe' (1993) 20 *Crime, Law and Social Change* 99; and P. Van Duyne and A. A. Block, 'Organized Cross-Atlantic Crime: Racketeering in Fuels' (1995) 22 *Crime, Law and Social Change* 127.

[41] D. Gambetta, *The Sicilian Mafia: The Business of Private Protection* (Oxford, 1993); V. Ruggiero, *Organised Crime and Corporate Crime in Europe* (Aldershot, 1996); cf. D. Nelken, 'White-Collar Crime', in M. Maguire, R. Morgan, and R. Reiner (eds.), *Oxford Handbook of Criminology* (2nd edn.) (Oxford, (forthcoming).

[42] The following extracts are taken from D. Nelken, 'Inflated Claims: Organised Crime and European Union Fraud' in A. Febbrajo, D. Nelken, and V. Olgiati (eds.), *European Yearbook of Sociology of Law* (forthcoming).

[43] P. Arlacchi, *Mafia Business* (Oxford, 1995).

No-one (Nothing) can fundamentally upset [the order of] the forest: trees may dry up and die but other ones just the same will take their place, animals die, but others are born. Things can change their position and form but always remain essentially the same.[44]

Q But the world, the larger society in which we live, isn't actually a forest, and man is not only an animal . . .

A1 Man can be any of the things you want but in the end he remains nothing other than an animal. He can wear any type of clothes imaginable, and non-imaginable, but under these clothes the only concrete, real and true thing is his body which needs to eat, drink, piss, fuck, kill, defend itself, work, steal, win, dominate, and command.

Q . . . And, above all, love.

A1 Why, do you think that he who kills is unable also to love? It all depends what values we associate or give to love and what rules or concepts we relate it to. Love comes in infinite forms and substance!

A2 These ways of talking don't do any one any good. Everyone has their own way of thinking about this subject. Everyone loves and behaves according to his own lights. In the end it is always the strongest who triumphs.

Q It depends what you mean by 'the strongest'. . . . In any case Don . . ., (as you conceded) when the crows shout and get excited you do need to stay a little quieter and therefore you will be suffering losses. How do you make up for or at least limit these losses?

A1 You always want to understand, to discover. Don't let your brain overwork or your stomach will complain of hunger.

Q There are those who are satisfied by meat and others who are only sated by thoughts and discoveries. You can give me to eat the food that is best suited to my digestion . . .

A1 You really are the son of . . . a really good woman! . . .[45] Well, we always get to know much in advance if the crows are about to start their screeching. We have men who are predisposed for this role, planted in the appropriate positions. We invest major capital expenditures so as to maintain these special observers who are above suspicion. We always know to stop in time, before the rumpus starts. And so we are able to freeze every activity in time, and destroy any path that might lead to us. In those cases where it is necessary we also set in motion manoeuvres or entire apparatuses aimed at throwing the investigators off the scent.

---

[44] This is the well known thesis of *Il Gattopardo*.
[45] A way of saying 'you son of a whore'.

A2 Sometimes one is also obliged to throw someone or something to the crows so as to quieten them down.

A1 But nothing is decided on the spur of the moment. The less hasty decisions are taken the more one can be certain that the world will carry on going as it always has.

Q Doesn't the very use of the word 'truffa' (fraud/ swindle) bother you?

A1 And why on earth should it? It is a 'truffa'. But watch out, my boy, not everything that you think of as wrong really is so. It all depends, as I said before, on which rules you follow. For you the EEC is a legal and good system, for me it is itself nothing other than a 'truffa'. A real fraud just because it is so accepted and well defended . . . but come and visit me one day and we will speak at greater length about this. Real honesty is so rare as to be almost Utopian. On this earth perhaps only one man has ever succeeded in being really honest—and we put him on the cross. Meanwhile we all go to Mass and listen to the words of men who swindle and mislead us . . . Have you ever asked yourself why we and the Church keep going trying always not to step on each others toes. This is because at bottom we are both systems which, with different rules and rites, seek similar or even identical goals. But let's not speak any more about this now, otherwise you would be capable of wearying me with questions until tomorrow morning.
. . .

Q You pursue power and wealth, but it seems to me that you never get the chance to relax and enjoy its fruits because you are always obliged (to fight to) hold on to it and to defend yourselves from everyone and everything. You have to watch out both for institutionalised legality and your own many internal enemies. So doesn't it all seem without any sense?

A1 But this is just what life is! All systems are forced to fight to survive and to defend themselves continuously. Man's only choice is whether to be essentially the hunter or the prey. All this is natural. And perhaps we (Cosa Nostra) are the most quintessentially natural of all systems . . .

A2 It is not easy to change a system. And it would in any case be useless and unproductive to try because no system could ever be really and deeply different from what came before. Revolutions only change the form of things but the substance always remains the same. So it is better to continue with what there has always been. Why waste energy uselessly?

Interviews with members of the Camorra-based organized crime groups in the Campagna region of Italy also provide equivocal evidence of the effects of globalization on the culture of organized criminals. Here is a member of the New Camorra confirming the changes brought about over the past few years.

A1 ... The old Camorra had difficulty in getting beyond regional boundaries, and rarely went beyond national frontiers. Its links were with local politicians, together with a very few national politicians and Euro parliamentarians. It preferred to concern itself with matters that happened in its own backyard, in the political locality: contraband, prostitution, (protection) rackets, extortion, the 'pizzo',[46] illegal gaming, illegal football pools, betting as well as other similar 'businesses' and enterprises of various kinds. The New Camorra, on the other hand, has preferred to modernise itself, to turn itself into a full scale industry, and to organise at national and (even) international level. As a result its 'connections' have grown considerably both in number and sophistication. Our mode of operating nowadays is surgical, almost scientific.

On the other hand, listen to these comments by an accountant compromised into working for the Camorra—the only hopeful signs in his generally bleak picture of the dominance of this crime group in his part of Italy.

A ... The children of those entrepreneurs who rely on this fraudulent way of running their business are beginning to rebel against their parents. These young people all come from studying at the University where they have had the chance to acquire an approach to business which is ethically correct, and relies on management skills. They have been made aware of the [rules of the] market, of market equilibrium at both national and international level. Furthermore, all of them, even if some more than others, having had experience of industries in the North (of Italy), have had the chance to come across their way of doing things and so come to understand that the way things are done where they grew up is completely mistaken. They feel humiliated both personally and in their role as businessmen. That is the reason therefore why, when they take over the reins of their father's business, they rebel against the compromises with organized crime to which their fathers have sunk. But this rebellion is enclosed for the time being within the walls of the home. Word of it never comes out. It is within the family that the young are fighting to change things, even at the price of being killed. I myself have many times been a witness to bitter family arguments in the homes of my industrialist friends. And I have seen the force, the courage and the determination of these young people. They choose to fight these battles out in the privacy of the home so as not to undermine the image of a united family in the eyes of acquaintances and the larger community.

---

[46] The 'pizzo' is the widespread practice of demanding a rake-off or 'cut' from all business activities in areas under control and/or subject to the threats or blandishments of organized crime.

It is thus worth remembering that globalization may help undermine the opportunities for some crimes as well as increase them. European Union fraud, like many other of the activities of organized crime in fact thrives on protective legislation rather than on globalized market freedom—in this case the common agricultural policy which is explicitly designed to keep out competition from food producing nations outside the European Union.

Think Global, Act Local?

I have no pretensions in this article to offer any worked out solutions to the new challenges of transnational crime. My task has been the more modest one of trying to clarify what is at stake and warn against over-simple remedies. Relying on increased police enforcement is likely to be illusory,[47] though there is much more to be done in seeking to reconcile the values of accountability and effectiveness in reshaping the role of the police at national and international level. But if we are not just to leave the battle against organized crime to the police there may be a need for more, rather than less, local action. The slogan of 'thinking globally and acting locally' adopted by the green movement has had deserved success in raising ecological consciousness about the wider implications of local action for the fate of common resources. There may be a need for similar consciousness-raising in order to see the links between organized crime and the financial and other choices made by businesses, banks and ordinary consumers of illicit services.[48] What could also repay further investigation is the extent to which organized criminals are really orientated to *local* cultural values; we could even say that organized crime 'thinks locally even as it acts globally'.

And what about the attempt to think globally in the letter sent by Ali from Masul? In my reply, I supplied him with information

---

[47] See G. Farrell, K. Manshur, and M. Tullis, 'Cocaine and Heroin in Europe 1983–93: A Cross-national Comparison of Trafficking and Prices' (1996) 36 *British Journal of Criminology* 255 who argue, at 279, 'the implications of this analysis for increasing the effectiveness of European law enforcement are not encouraging. The balance of evidence suggests increasing enforcement will impact only marginally upon prices due to rapidly diminishing marginal returns'.

[48] See M. Levi, 'Pecunia Non Olet: Cleansing the Money-Launderers from the Temple' (1996) 16 *Crime, Law and Social Change* 217, who notes the difficult practical and policy issues involved.

about two more appropriate experts to help him with his research. The handbook of the Society of Public Teachers of Law provided me with the name of a scholar in Liverpool who specializes in military law. But I also sent Ali the name of a law professor at Tel Aviv active in defending soldiers in military trials who refuse to obey orders they regard as illegitimate. The chances that a law student in Iraq dare write to a law professor in Israel are admittedly low, but then that too tells us something about how far the trend to globalization still has to go.

THE STIRRING OF CORPORATE SOCIAL CONSCIENCE
From 'Cakes and Ale' to Community Programmes

Ben Pettet

I. Profit Maximization and Community Programmes

Almost exactly 100 years ago, company lawyers all over Britain were digesting the latest of a series of House of Lords cases which were establishing fundamental doctrines of company law.[1] This one was to become the most famous of them all, and the reference to the case is etched on the hearts of all who have come subsequently to the subject; [1897] Appeal Cases 22.[2] The lawyers and the corporate world were no doubt pleased with what they read. The case made it clear beyond further doubt that a company was a separate person in law from the shareholders and that the shareholders of a limited company did indeed have limited liability.

On the centennial anniversary of this event and on the fiftieth anniversary of the publication of the first volume of *Current Legal Problems* it is a great privilege to write this article, to take stock of the past, and to peer into the future.

Also a century ago, although considerably less exactly, another landmark case was decided, *Hutton* v. *West Cork Railway Company*.[3] The Cork and Bandon Railway Company was buying

---

[1] Others were *Ashbury Railway Carriage and Iron Company* v. *Riche* (1875) LR 7 HL 653 (*ultra vires*); *Trevor* v. *Whitworth* (1887) 12 App. Cas. 409 (company may not purchase its own shares); *Ooregum Gold Mining Company of India* v. *Roper* [1892] AC 125 (unlawful to issue shares at a discount).
[2] Judgment had been given on 16 Nov. 1896.
[3] (1883) 23 Ch. D. 654.

the business of the West Cork Railway Company for £141,934. The West Cork Railway Company was in the process of being wound up when a general meeting endorsed a proposal of the directors to apply £1,050 in compensating the managing director and other paid officers of the company for the loss of their employment, not because of any legal claim for salary that they then had, but as a gratuity.[4] Some of the debenture-holders had voting rights similar to shareholders. Hutton was one of these and he had dissented from the resolution of the meeting. He brought an action to restrain the company from applying the money in the manner proposed. He was successful. The Court of Appeal held (by majority) that the payments would be *ultra vires* the company. They approved an earlier case[5] which had held that the directors could not be restrained from paying a gratuity to their servants. The directors of a trading company had the power to do it because it was done with a view to getting better work from their servants in the future. But that did not apply here:

The company was gone as a company carrying on business for the purpose of making a profit, and the sums paid, therefore, to its officials and managing directors, could not be looked upon as an inducement to them to exert themselves in future, or as an act reasonably done for the purpose of getting the greatest profit from the business of the company, but must be looked upon as a gratuity ... without any prospect of its in any way reasonably conducing to the benefit of the company.[6]

Bowen LJ put it in more colourful language:

Take this sort of instance. A railway company or the directors ... might send down all the porters at a railway station to have tea in the country at the expense of the company. Why should they not? It is for the directors to judge, provided it is a matter which is reasonably incidental to the carrying on of the business of the company, and a company which always treated its employe[e]s with Draconian severity, and never allowed them a single inch more than the strict letter of the bond, would soon find itself deserted—at all events, unless labour was very much more easy to obtain in the market than it often is. The law does not say that there are to be no cakes and ale,

---

[4] Also to apply about £1,500 in remuneration for the past services of the directors, who had never received any remuneration.
[5] *Hampson v. Price's Patent Candle Company* (1876) 24 WR 754, and also a similar case, *Taunton v. Royal Insurance Company* (1864) 2 H & M 135.
[6] Cotton LJ at 665–6.

but there are to be no cakes and ale except such as are required for the benefit of the company.[7]

Unlike the *Salomon* case, 'company' here of course effectively means 'shareholders'.[8] *Hutton* enshrines the profit-driven mechanism of our capitalist system—it is unlawful to give the workers anything unless it is good for the shareholders, meaning, unless it increases efficiency and therefore increases profits. *Hutton* cements the shareholders' legal rights to the efficient use of resources at the disposal of the board of directors. It also contains a frank but probably unguarded warning for labour—if labour becomes easy to obtain in the market, it can expect to be treated 'with Draconian severity'—almost a judicial piece of advice for labour to combine.

Whilst the *Salomon* case stands more or less unchallenged[9] the same cannot be said of *Hutton*. The idea that the cakes exist only for the shareholders has been subjected to continual assault both by political events this century and in the writings of political philosophers and modern legal theorists. To some of that we will return later.[10]

The subsequent career of the *ultra vires* doctrine is a story that has been told many times. This century, particularly the last half of it has witnessed a change of approach. A change by the courts and the legislature. A shift from a didactic rule making stance of *Ashbury Railway Carriage and Iron Co. Ltd. v. Riche*[11] to an approach facilitative of the wishes of the business community. It had really started only five years afterwards in *Attorney General* v.

---

[7] *Ibid.*, 672–3.

[8] The word 'company' in this kind of context is usually construed to mean something like 'present and future members'; see Megarry J in *Gaiman* v. *Association for Mental Health* [1971] Ch. 317, 330, where, in construing the phrase 'in the interests of the company', he said 'I would accept the interests of both present and future members of the company as a whole, as being a helpful expression of a human equivalent.'

[9] The *Salomon* principle has however been subjected to some legislative incursions: see 298–299 below. It is also true that there has been considerable academic interest in the concept of an unlimited liability regime for companies, but it cannot be said that the topic has attracted a great deal of interest from the public at large or the legislatures; see e.g. H. Hansmann and R. Kraakman 'Towards Unlimited Shareholder Liability for Corporate Torts' (1991) 100 *Yale LJ* 1879. For further references and analysis see my own article on this subject 'Limited Liability—A Principle for the 21st Century?' (1995) 48 *Current Legal Problems* 125.

[10] See 303–312 below.   [11] (1875) LR 7 HL 653.

Great Eastern Railway,[12] where the House of Lords held that the doctrine should be 'maintained' but 'reasonably and not unreasonably . . . applied' so that 'whatever may be fairly be regarded as incidental to' the objects ought not to be *ultra vires*.[13] The ameliorating process continued in 1918, with the House of Lords decision in *Cotman* v. *Brougham*[14] the effect of which was to permit (once more)[15] the use of long objects clauses to evade at least some of the ramifications of the doctrine. The *Bell Houses* case[16] in 1966 gave the directors some discretion (albeit limited) to extend the objects of the company,[17] and in 1982 most important of all in the context of corporate giving, *Re Horsley & Weight*[18] established that:

> The objects of a company do not need to be commercial; they can be charitable or philanthropic; indeed they can be whatever the original incorporators wish, provided they are legal. Nor is there any reason why a company should not part with its funds gratuitously or for non-commercial reasons if to do so is within its declared objects.[19]

Largely seen as an out-of-date nuisance, especially by our new European partners, the *ultra vires* doctrine was partially and not very successfully abolished, in 1972,[20] as part of an attempt to implement the first Harmonization Directive,[21] and more successfully in 1989, although still with somewhat mysterious effects.[22]

---

[12] (1880) 5 App. Cas. 473.   [13] *Ibid*. 478, *per* Lord Selbourne LC.
[14] [1918] AC 514.
[15] *Re German Date Coffee Company* (1882) 20 Ch. D 169 had diminished the effectiveness of long clauses by the adoption of a 'main objects rule' of construction which identified one of the clauses as a main object and the others as merely ancillary to it. *Cotman* v. *Brougham* held that that construction would be excluded (at least as far as the *ultra vires* doctrine was concerned) by the adoption of a clause which made it clear that the sub-clauses in the objects clause were to be construed as separate and independent objects.
[16] *Bell Houses* v. *City Wall Properties* [1966] 2 QB 656; and see Lord Wedderburn, 'The Death of Ultra Vires' (1966) 29 *MLR* 673.
[17] See also *Newstead* v. *Frost* [1980] 1 All ER 363 and B. Pettet, 'Unlimited Objects Clauses?' (1981) 97 *LQR* 15.
[18] [1982] 3 All ER 1045.   [19] *Ibid*. 1052, *per* Buckley LJ.
[20] S. 9(1) of the European Communities Act 1972. Later (in 1986) there followed the 'DTI Consultative Document: Reform of the Ultra Vires Rule' by Professor Dan Prentice. Unfortunately his approach was not fully adopted in the later legislation.
[21] Art. 9(1) (68/151/EEC) [1968] OJ L65/8.
[22] Companies Act 1989, ss. 108–112; and see J. Poole, 'Abolition of the Ultra Vires Doctrine and Agency Problems' (1991) 12 *Co. Law* 43.

Nevertheless, subject to modifications, the doctrine continues to govern relationships between the company and its shareholders.[23]

Hutton itself was not spared legislative reform. It had been followed in the *Daily News* case in 1962[24] but this was then overturned in the Companies Act 1980[25] so that in circumstances of cessation of business a company can make provision for employees, even though it is not in the best interests of the company.[26] But this is only in circumstances of cessation; while the company trades, the profit-maximization theory of *Hutton* still applies.[27]

As a result of some of these diminutions in *ultra vires*, and particularly *Re Horsley & Weight*, modern-day corporate giving, to employees or wider community, has a firmer foundation in law than in the past, although some of it has no doubt always proceeded on the basis of the shareholders, and sometimes possibly the courts, turning a blind eye to it. Even Bowen LJ in *Hutton* was prepared to concede that the directors might 'when a meritorious servant is leaving their service, present him with a £5 note'.[28] And obviously within the constraints of the profit-maximization doctrine itself, corporate giving can often be legally justified as improving employer and employee relations,[29] and even giving to the wider community, justified, as advertising, as building a corporate image of power, an image of benevolence and an image of concern for the environment.

Relations with employees can only have been improved by Levi

---

[23] Companies Act 1985, s. 35(2), (3).

[24] *Parke* v. *Daily News* [1962] Ch. 927 trenchantly criticized by Lord Wedderburn in 'Ultra Vires and Redundancy' (1962) *CLJ* 141.

[25] Companies Act 1980, s. 74; now in s. 719 of the Companies Act 1985.

[26] *Ibid.*, s. 719(2).

[27] It is noticeable that s. 309, which requires the directors to have regard to the interests of the company's employees, does not have any provision in it corresponding to s. 719(2) although it is perhaps arguable that even as it stands, s. 309 might make a board's occasional departure from profit maximization more difficult to attack in some circumstances.

[28] (1883) 23 Ch. D 654, at 673, although he was careful to confine even this to what was necessary in the reasonable management of the company. The finding of a benefit to the company in *Evans* v. *Brunner Mond* [1921] 1 Ch. 359 is possibly an example of judicial blind eye.

[29] As suggested in *Hutton* '[T]hat sort of liberal dealing with servants eases the friction between masters and servants, and is, in the end, a benefit to the company': (1883) 23 Ch. D 654, at 673, *per* Bowen LJ.

Strauss's recent proposal for a £500 million cash bonus amounting to an extra year's pay for each member of its global workforce.[30]

There is obviously much scope for ingenuity in modern day versions of 'cakes and ale'. Another recent example:

> Chase Manhattan has rewarded employees with free relaxation therapy
> ... While white-shirted, red-braced figures wave their telephones in the
> anxiety-laden atmosphere of the dealing room, others are relaxing with a
> half-hour session of aromatherapy, holistic massage or acupuncture ...
> senior management were the last ones to come along.[31]

From the beginning of the 1980s Britain has seen a significant increase in corporate giving to the wider community. Dr Saleem Sheikh in his valuable research into corporate social responsibility[32] cites statistics showing a substantial rise during the 1980s.[33] The glossy annual reports of many of our larger companies show how much importance is attached to these philanthropic activities. In its role as a model company the London Stock Exchange has, for some years,[34] in its annual reports contained a whole page devoted to what it calls the 'Community Programme' starting with a statement of policy:

[30] *Financial Times*, 13 June 1996.
[31] The *Financial Times*, on 5 Feb. 1997 carried an item by Richard Donkin under the heading 'Staff Benefits—There's the Rub'.
[32] S. Sheikh, *Corporate Social Responsibilities: Law and Practice* (London, 1996).
[33] *Ibid.* 45 and n. 22: 'in 1980 the estimated donations made by the top *200* British companies amounted to £25.4m but by 1988 this had risen to £170m'. In this field generally, there are considerable difficulties in compiling accurate statistics, particularly over a long period of time. It is also hard to make comparisons over long periods, as the methods of compiling the statistics change, and thus it is difficult to get a precise picture of very long-term trends. However, statistics during the 1990s taken from *The Major Companies Guide 1997–1998* (Directory of Social Change), 9, show increases in corporate giving, funded by increases in profits (although the percentage of pre-tax profit being given has fallen). Thus Top *400* Corporate Donors:

> 1990–91: Charity Donations 133m (%ptp 0.25%) and Community Contributions 225m (0.42%)
> 1995–96: Charity Donations 182m (0.21%) and Community Contributions 252m (0.29%)

[34] e.g. 1993, 1994, 1995. The 1996 Report disappointingly gives a lower profile to the Community Programme, although the amount of donation is not reduced. However the LSE has been going through an unhappy patch of late, and has perhaps felt the need to project an image of a company looking inward at its own difficulties, and solving them. Early 1996 saw a fundamental strategy review aiming to cut costs and create a 'leaner stock exchange': *Financial Times*, 1 July 1996.

Last year the focus continued to be on charitable donations and support for communities within the Inner London Area . . . The Exchange endeavours to build on existing relationships with target charities . . . Donations . . . have been made to organisations within the following categories: the arts, community services, education, enterprise, medical and environment. Donations over the year[35] totalled £117,000[36] including over £5,000 to match donations raised by staff . . . Exchange charity events over the year have included two successful quiz nights involving over 200 staff which raised £3,300.

Guinness plc, one of our largest companies by market capitalization, has a three-page spread[37] devoted to what it calls 'Community', its policy statement:

Responsible corporate citizenship is central to Guinness's activities around the world. Whether in the promotion of responsible drinking—Guinness published its own employee guide to sensible drinking in five languages in 1995—or in environmental performance, with clear targets set for energy usage and waste, the Company continues to develop an active programme in line with best practice worldwide.

Its worldwide contributions for charitable purposes totalled £6.3 million.

According to the 1996 report of another large company:

Cable and Wireless takes very seriously its responsibility to the communities in which it operates. Through donations and sponsorships—which in 1995/96 totalled £6.9 million—it contributes to a wide range of local and international causes. In all its activities, it aims to build mutually beneficial partnerships with those in whom it is investing. It also aims to encourage its own employees to be personally involved.

Many companies, as is well known, give contributions to political parties, historically mainly the Conservative Party. Tate & Lyle have a refreshingly different approach; their Annual Report for 1996 disclosing gifts of £15,000 to the Conservatives, £7,500 to Labour, and £2,500 to the Liberal Democrats. This was on the basis that the board believed that political parties should be state funded and not have to rely on their historical sources for income.[38]

---

[35] This is taken from the 1995 Report.
[36] Not much compared with the two examples which follow, but of course, the Stock Exchange is a much smaller company.
[37] Report and Accounts 1995, 18–20.
[38] Annual Report 1996, 34.

Not all companies have yet reached such heights of altruism, but after all, its slogan on the cover of that Report is '[Tate & Lyle] A world leader in sweeteners and starches'. Corporate donations to political parties raise legal and ethical issues of public law which cannot be explored here, but they are currently getting a good deal more public attention than in the past.[39]

II. The Greening of Company Law

1. CORPORATE SOCIAL CONSCIENCE

The concept of the caring company is not new.[40] There can be no doubt that much of corporate giving is done for reasons of indirect benefit eventually leading to profit, and to project what are currently regarded as the politically and culturally correct images of big business. This kind of social activism also raises difficult theoretical problems, some of which will be considered later. Nevertheless, as we try to take stock of the position at the turn of the century, it does seem that there is a new spirit abroad. Whether it is the earnest staff at their quiz nights at the Stock Exchange, or the journalists writing in our daily newspapers, or the politicians giving their speeches (in Singapore or elsewhere), there is currently unprecedented national interest in the company becoming something more than it has been in the past.

In my view, the conscience of a corporation resides in the moral values of all those who are connected with it, whether by managing it, working for it, electing the managers, or otherwise; the values being those that they hold in relation to their respective roles in it and in relation to its role in society. With regard to the company's social responsibility, that conscience is stirring.[41]

---

[39] See e.g. the two-page analysis of Conservative Party funding in *Financial Times*, 19 Dec. 1994. The banning of foreign funding of political parties is also being mooted: *Financial Times*, 13 Jan. 1997. See also K. D. Ewing, 'Company Political Donations and the Ultra Vires Rule' (1984) 47 *MLR* 57; K. D. Ewing, *The Funding of Political Parties in Britain* (Cambridge, 1987).

[40] See the account of the historical background in Sheikh, n. 32 above, 1–14, 37–43.

[41] This is a simple notion which serves only for the broad purposes of this article. There have been many views about the nature of the corporate conscience: e.g. A. A. Berle in *The Twentieth Century Capitalist Revolution* (London, 1955) saw it as

About a quarter of a century ago a Law Professor at Yale wrote of his country as being:

[O]ne vast, terrifying anti-community. The great organisations to which most people give their working day, and the apartments and suburbs to which they return at night, are equally places of loneliness and alienation. . . .[42]

. . .[W]e may be in the grip, not of capitalist exploiters, but of mindless, impersonal forces that pursue their own non-human logic.[43]

Charles Reich saw a need to develop a new consciousness, a new culture through which to change society, not by tearing down the institutions of the 'Corporate State', but by changing them from within through fundamental changes of attitude. He saw a new consciousness developing in his country, 'like flowers pushing up through the concrete pavement',[44] a 'greening' of America.

It is arguable that the story of company law in England this century, but mainly the second half of it, has been the beginning of a 'greening', in the sense, at last, of a greater infusion into the law of concepts of respect, of fair play, of an awareness of the need to serve the business community, and, slowly, an awareness of the need to serve the wider community. We have already seen the development of the *ultra vires* law along these lines; what of the rest of it?

---

something which must be 'built into institutions so that it can be invoked as a right by the individuals and interests subject to the corporate power': *ibid.* 89–90 and that it was a limitation on economic power '. . . intangible . . . but wholly real. It may be called limitation by "public consensus". This is the existence of a set of ideas, widely held by the community, and often by the organisation itself and the men who direct it, that certain uses of power are "wrong" that is, contrary to the established interest and value system of the community': *Power Without Property* (New York, 1959), 90. See also G. Teubner's summary of academic views about the nature of the legal person that stress its 'dynamic social reality' in his 'Enterprise Corporatism: New Industrial Policy and the Essence of the Legal Person', 36 *American Journal of Comparative Law* 130–55 (1988) reprinted in Wheeler, *Reader on the Law of the Business Enterprise* (Oxford, 1994), 53–4. Teubner's challenging analysis is that 'the social substratum of the legal person is neither an assemblage of people nor a pool of resources nor a mere organisational structure. Nor is it adequately characterised as an action system or as a formal organisation. The substratum is conceived properly as a "collectivity" or "corporate actor", i.e. the self-description of a (usually formally) organized social action system that brings about a cyclical linkage of self-referentially constituted system identity and system elements': *ibid* 58.

[42] C. Reich, *The Greening of America* (New York, 1970), 5.
[43] *Ibid.*, 8.   [44] *Ibid.*, 290–1.

2. A DEVELOPING SOCIETY AND NEW LEGAL RESPONSES

In 1898 Albert Venn Dicey delivered his 'Lectures on the Relation
Between Law and Public Opinion in England during the Nineteenth
Century'.[45] Dicey spoke of the 'close and immediate connection . . .
which . . . exists between public opinion and legislation'[46] and that:

> In England . . . the beliefs or sentiments which, during the nineteenth
> century, have governed the development of the law have . . . been public
> opinion, for they have been the wishes and ideas as to legislation held by
> the people of England, or, to speak with more precision, by the majority of
> those citizens who have at a given moment taken an effective part in public
> life.[47]

and for Dicey, here, legislation included case law, being the laws
'indirectly but not less truly enacted by the courts'.[48] So he was
really looking at the effects that different currents of informed
opinion were having on the legal structure, looking at what were
the movements and trends which have shaped law reform. Professor
Jim Gower, when giving his lecture at the London School of
Economics in their half-way-through-the-century series of lectures,
also modelled on Dicey's book, described his own task as being to
review the changes which had come about in the last five decades,
and to attempt to assess 'how far these changes were in response to
public or business opinion and how far they reflect particular
policies or theories'.[49]

This century the pace of world change has been unprecedented.
In England the semi-feudal Edwardian Empire has given way to a
democratic multicultural welfare state. The expectation of democracy, the reception of Continental and American ideas of
psychoanalysis, and increases in material living standards have
brought into existence an increasingly literate, assertive, and
sophisticated populace. People, even the less well-off, have a greater
sense of their own social legitimacy than ever before, and they
expect more from their public figures, politicians, and each other.
Political satire is not a new phenomenon in this country, but

---

[45] 2nd edn. (London, 1914). Originally published in 1905.
[46] *Ibid.*, 7.   [47] *Ibid.*, 9–10.   [48] *Ibid.*, 17.
[49] Ginsberg, *Law and Opinion in England In The Twentieth Century* (London,
1959), 144.

nevertheless these changes in attitude, together with the growth of media and information technology, have ensured that modern-day public figures and those in authority are subjected to scrutiny and criticism as never before. The economy has changed and our companies have grown hugely, in number, size, and economic power.[50] One would expect that our laws, and in our case, our company law, would have changed to reflect all this. As we shall see, although there have been many different strands of thought inputting to the reform of company law, the one that most frequently recurs is the demand for fair treatment, for an escape from Reich's 'impersonal . . . non-human logic'.

At about the time the first volume of *Current Legal Problems* was published, someone called Greenhalgh was wrestling with some of the 'non-human logic' of company law. And in Lord Greene's words, he deserved 'some measure of sympathy because, with great determination, he has fought for what he conceives to be his rights, and it has landed him in a series of unsuccessful actions'.[51] It had all started because the company was in financial difficulties and Greenhalgh put a small fortune into it to put it back on its feet. In return, arrangements were put in hand to give him voting control of the company.[52] Almost immediately the others set in chain a series of technical manœuvres aimed at wresting this control from him. Starting in 1941 he waged a ten-year battle against them. It ultimately involved him bringing seven actions, taking five of them to the Court of Appeal. Let us consider this one,[53] about half-way through: by this stage, there were two types of shares in the company, two-shilling shares and ten-shilling shares. Greenhalgh held most of the two-shilling ones. The other faction had enough votes to pass an ordinary (51 per cent), resolution but they probably wanted[54] to be able to pass a special

---

[50] See L. C. B. Gower's review of 'Business Developments' in Ginsberg n. 49 above, 144–5, where he shows that at the turn of the century there were only 29,000 companies, with a paid up capital of £1,600m. The present position is of around 1m companies (public and private), with a UK market capitalization in excess of £1 trillion (i.e. £1,000 billion); *Financial Times*, 14 Jan. 1997.

[51] *Greenhalgh* v. *Aderne Cinemas Ltd.* [1946] 1 All ER 512, 513.

[52] See [1945] 2 All ER 719, 720–2, *per* Vaisey J.

[53] Actually the fourth action; *Greenhalgh* v. *Aderne Cinemas Ltd.* [1946] 1 All ER 512 (CA).

[54] Presumably; in view of what subsequently happened in *Greenhalgh* v. *Aderne Cinemas Ltd.* [1950] 2 All ER 1120.

(75 per cent) resolution, so that they would be in a position to alter the articles of association and further whittle away his position.[55]

Did company law contain a process of alchemy which would enable them unilaterally to alter the balance of power in this way? Yes it did. The prevailing Companies Act[56] contained a power, as it still does, exercisable by ordinary resolution whereby shares of say, £1 nominal value, could be subdivided into multiple shares of a smaller amount; there is a sound technical reason for having such a facility.[57] But it was not relevant here. Here that facility was misused to destroy the constitutional protection which the scheme of the Companies Act was supposed to give to Greenhalgh. The other faction passed an ordinary resolution subdividing each of their ten-shilling shares into five shares, of two shillings each. That gave them five times as many votes as they had had a few minutes earlier![58] And so now they could pass the special resolution and alter the articles. Greenhalgh, ever trustful, thought that law which had failed him on several occasions in the past would at least give him a remedy here. And Greenhalgh had a strong case, for the ability of even a three-quarters majority to alter the articles of association is trumped by a yet further constitutional protection, a further checks and balance mechanism given by the company law system, for class rights[59] cannot be varied without the consent of

---

[55] Lord Greene spoke of his shareholding as 'his safeguard against the passing of special resolutions or extraordinary resolutions which might be contrary to his wishes': [1946] 1 All ER 512, 514. They did eventually pass a special resolution, to satisfactory effect: see *Greenhalgh* v. *Aderne Cinemas Ltd.* [1950] 2 All ER 1120.

[56] 1929; the provision was s. 50 (combined with art. 37 of the prevailing Table A); now s. 121(2)(d) of the 1985 Act and art. 32 of the 1985 Table A.

[57] Growth in the real or market value of shares results in a share price which is higher than the nominal value of the shares as originally issued. A share price of over about £2 can 'make the shares harder to trade and artificially depresses the price. . . . When a company feels its share price is "heavy" . . . it can split its shares into shares with a smaller par value.' See G. Holmes and A. Sugden, *Interpreting Company Reports and Accounts* (3rd edn.) (Cambridge, 1987), 15.

[58] 'It was that remaining measure of control (see n. 52 above) which was attacked and sought to be destroyed by the next manœuvre, which was the passing of the resolution now in question under which the issued 10s shares were split, with the consequence that the holders of each of those shares had acquired five times as many votes as they originally had': [1946] 1 All ER 512, 514.

[59] The CA assumed, without holding, that the two-shilling shares were a separate class: *ibid.*, 515. Vaisey J at first instance ([1945] 2 All ER 719) adopted a similar approach, although he seemed a little more persuaded, referring to *Re United Provident Assurance Co. Ltd.* [1910] 2 Ch. 477 which had, surely, settled the point.

the class,[60] and where the sole member of the class is against the proposal what we are really looking at is a power of veto.[61] But here even, there was a surprise in store for Greenhalgh. Had his rights been varied? No, said the Court of Appeal, they were just the same; the enjoyment of them had been affected, but not the rights themselves; so he lost. It seems wrong, and even Lord Greene was constrained to admit: 'Instead of Greenhalgh finding himself in a position of control, he finds himself in a position where the control has gone, and to that extent the rights of the . . . 2 s[hilling] shareholders are affected, as a matter of business.'[62] But, so he held, 'As a matter of law . . . they remain as they always were—a right to have one vote per share.'[63]

This is surely wrong. Voting rights are only a relative concept; no one votes on their own, if they are the only voter in the constituency. The concept only has human meaning when a person is set against others who vote, and then you add them up and see who wins. If the votes of one side are quintupled, that must vary the rights of the other side. The court conceded that as a matter of business this *was* true, but as a matter of law it was untrue. The reasoning is technical, legalistic, and the factual result, both in the instant case and in the saga generally, was profoundly unfair; Greenhalgh did indeed deserve sympathy. The full story can be found in the fourth edition of Professor Gower's *Principles of Modern Company Law*,[64] told there as an illustration of the vulnerability of a minority shareholder.

Greenhalgh represents an ultra-formalistic approach to company law; an approach which interprets and makes law by looking only to the letter of the law and not its real effects on people, and which rewards and encourages a culture of cynical ingenuity. One more example, chosen as much for its subsequent history as for its illustration of lawful chicanery, is *Re Windward Islands*,[65] although this differs from the previous example in that the judge's hands here were largely tied by the rules of statutory interpretation

---

[60] The current provision is s. 125 of the Companies Act 1985; in Greenhalgh's case it was a provision in the articles of association.

[61] See e.g. *Cumbrian Ltd.* v. *Cumberland & Westmoreland Newspapers Ltd.* [1987] Ch. 1. [62] [1946] 1 All ER 512, 518.

[63] *Ibid.*, 518. As Lord Greene had earlier observed 'these things are of a technical nature;': *ibid.*, 516. [64] At 624–7

[65] (1988) 4 BCC 158.

and the failure to get a good result comes about through the inactivity of the legislature. The Companies Act 1948 contained an important minority shareholders power in section 132[66] whereby members holding 10 per cent or more of the voting shares could require the directors of the company to requisition a meeting. The obvious purpose of it was to enable a minority to get a forum within the company to discuss and resolve matters of dispute. The relevant mechanics of the section provided that: '[t]he directors of a company . . . shall . . . on the requisition of members . . . forthwith proceed duly to convene . . . [a meeting].' On 13 April 1982 the minority deposited a requisition with the company with the aim of having a meeting to remove two of the directors, and sixteen days later the directors sent out a notice convening the meeting. It was going to be held in August, at lunchtime, on Sunday 22nd. Nourse J carried out an impeccable clinical analysis of the statutory provisions and correctly held that this was lawful. The distinction between *convening* a meeting and *holding* one was there in the statutory provisions.[67] It was an old dodge and, as the learned judge pointed out, had been criticized twenty years earlier by the Jenkins Committee,[68] but their recommendations had not been implemented. It was, as he said, '[a]n oddity, in regard to a section whose evident purpose was to protect minorities'.[69] Taken as a whole, the response of the legal system, the legislative part of it, here, was inadequate.

The subsequent history of the *Windward Islands* problem is instructive. In 1948 the legislature had put a new provision into the Companies Act[70] designed chiefly to provide a remedy for minority shareholders in small partnership-style companies where the breakdown of relationships between them had made the carrying on of the company no longer feasible. The remedy was to be an alternative to winding up on the just and equitable ground and the courts were given unlimited discretion as to the remedies which

---

[66] Now s. 368 of the Companies Act 1985.

[67] See s. 132(3) which had in its last clause the distinction between 'convened' and 'held': 'If the directors do not within twenty-one days from the date of the deposit of the requisition proceed duly to convene a meeting, the requisitionists . . . may themselves convene a meeting, but any meeting so convened shall not be held after the expiration of three months from the said date.'

[68] (London, 1962) Cmnd. 1749, para. 458.

[69] (1988) 4 BCC 158 at 161.   [70] S. 210.

could be granted. The judges had shown no great enthusiasm for this new discretion and in the thirty-two years until its repeal there were only three successful reported cases.[71] The new jurisdiction was largely defined out of existence once the judiciary had decided that a shareholder director who was excluded from management and remuneration was oppressed in his capacity as a director, and not, as the statute required, in his capacity as a member.[72] Following recommendations by the Jenkins Committee in 1962,[73] although somewhat tardily, Parliament tried again in 1980 with a new section (now section 459), giving a remedy to a shareholder who had suffered 'unfair prejudice'.[74] Despite a shaky start[75] a new spirit was abroad in the Chancery Division, and the judges gave remedies where none had existed before, the floodgates of litigation had opened, and the new cases streamed into the equally new specialist law reports.[76] The shareholder director who suffered a lockout could now get an order that the majority must buy his shares at a fair value.[77] Eventually we came to see attempts to restrict the jurisdiction[78] revealing differences in judicial policy which continue to the present day.[79] The approach of the Court of Appeal in *Re Saul Harrison*[80] was an attempt to reduce the number of petitions by requiring that we must look mainly to existing cases to know whether something is unfairly prejudicial.[81] Shortly

---

[71] *SCWS v. Meyer* [1959] AC 324; *Re Harmer* [1959] 1 WLR 62; *Re Stewarts* [1985] BCLC 4.   [72] *Re Lundie Bros.* [1965] 1 WLR 1051.

[73] *Report of the Company Law Committee* (London, 1962), Cmnd. 1749, para. 212.

[74] As subsequently amended s. 459 now provides that a member may petition for an order 'on the ground that the company's affairs are being or have been conducted in a manner which is unfairly prejudicial to the interests of its members generally or of some part of its members (including at least himself) or that any actual or proposed act or omission of the company . . . is or would be so prejudicial'.

[75] e.g. the decision in *Re A Company* [1983] Ch. 178.

[76] Butterworths Company Law Cases (BCLC) and CCH's British Company Cases (BCC). Also Palmer's Company Cases (PCC), a series which was subsequently discontinued.

[77] e.g. *Re a Company* 00477/86 (1986) 2 BCC 99171.

[78] *Re a Company* 004377/86 (1986) 2 BCC 99520 and *Re a Company* 006834/88 (1986) 2 BCC 99520.

[79] *Re Abbey Leisure* [1990] BBC 60 (CA), and *Re a Company* 00330/91, ex p. *Holden* [1991] BCC 241 were examples of attacks on the restrictive approach which has recently returned in *Re a Company* 00836/95 [1996] BCC 432.

[80] [1994] BCC 475.   [81] *Ibid.*, 488.

afterwards, the Chancery Division hastened to diminish the restrictive effect of *Saul Harrison*, giving back to the section its original power: 'the words of the section are wide and general and, save where the circumstances are governed by the judgments in *Re Saul Harrison*, the categories of unfair prejudice are not closed'; the words of Arden J. in *Re BSB Holdings (No 2)*.[82]

The full extent of the astonishing power of section 459 can be appreciated when we consider what happened to the *Windward Islands* problem. In *McGuinness, Petitioners*[83] some of the shareholders deposited their requisition with the company on 4 November 1987 and 'forthwith' on 23 November their Glasgow-based company convened the meeting, to be held, in London, the following June. The Court of Session affirmed the analysis of Nourse J in *Windward Islands*, but held that the shareholders were entitled to expect that the meeting would be held within a reasonable period and that in the circumstances this was unfairly prejudicial to their interests. Thus, when applied head on against a statutory anomaly section 459 can simply reverse the result. In the next Companies Act the legislature amended the statute,[84] and so by 1990 the difficulty had ceased to exist.

The *Greenhalgh* example cannot be disposed of quite so neatly although it is extremely unlikely that it represents the law today. Even before the appearance of the unfair prejudice remedy, Foster J in *Clemens v. Clemens*[85] was prepared to recognize the element of negative control possessed by a 45 per cent shareholder (in that she could block a special resolution), and an issue of shares to people who would vote with the 55 per cent holder was set aside.[86] With the advent of the unfair prejudice remedy came a series of cases[87]

---

[82] [1996] 1 BCLC 155, 243.   [83] (1988) 4 BCC 161.

[84] Companies Act 1989, Sched. 19, para. 9. It added what is now s. 368(8) which provides: '[t]he directors are deemed not to have duly convened a meeting if they convene a meeting for a date more than 28 days after the date of the notice convening the meeting.'   [85] [1976] 2 All ER 268.

[86] A similar result was reached in *Pennell* v. *Venida*, noted by S. J. Burridge, 'Wrongful Rights Issues' (1981) 44 *MLR* 40.

[87] *Re Cumana Ltd.* [1986] BCLC 430; *Re DR Chemicals Ltd.* (1989) 5 BCC 39; *Re Kenyon Swansea Ltd.* (1987) 3 BCC 259; *Re A Company 007623/84* (1986) 2 BCC 99191; *Re A Company 002612/84* (1984) 1 BCC 92262; *Re A Company 005134/86* [1989] BCLC 383. Also, obviously, s. 89 of the 1985 Act (introduced in 1980) will sometimes be relevant in these kinds of cases; see e.g. the discussion in *Re DR Chemicals* (above) at 51.

putting paid to attempts to water down control and voting rights; in my view it is inconceivable that the trick played on Greenhalgh would survive a section 459 petition at the present day.[88]

3. Wider Case and Statute Law Responses

In these examples we have been seeing technical lawyers' law being turned inside out by fairness-based responses from the legal system. And to a large extent, that is the history of the development of company law this century and most intensely in recent years. Nevertheless this approach has not visited all areas; for instance in the doctrine of separate corporate personality, virtually no judicial[89] progress has been made in the 100 years since the *Salomon* case; the Court of Appeal in *Adams* v. *Cape*[90] has recently made it clear that it is not permissible to pierce the corporate veil just because the interests of justice might be thought to require it and has reduced most of the decisions when the corporate veil has been pierced or circumvented to the status of aberrations or rare examples of narrow exceptions.[91] Many other areas have fared differently. The courts steadily developed the idea that shareholders owe a kind of quasi-fiduciary duty in certain circumstances, as an exception to the normal rule that their shares are property rights and they can vote how they please, selfishly in their own interests, and that the majority vote will rule, a doctrine entrenched, again in that last quadrant of the nineteenth century in *North West Transportation* v. *Beatty*.[92] However, starting already in 1874, it

---

[88] The CA decisions in *White* v. *Bristol Aeroplane Co.* [1953] Ch. 65 and *Re John Smith's Tadcaster Brewery* [1953] Ch. 308 (capitalization issue of bonus ordinary shares is not a variation of rights of preference shares), although having some similarities with Greenhalgh, are also distinguishable in some respects, e.g. they lack the improper motive present in Greenhalgh, the long course of unfairly prejudicial conduct, and, further, the liability to watering by bonus issue could be seen as part of the generally understood commercial relationship between preference and ordinary shares. In my view it is not altogether clear that these cases would not be followed at the present day. On the problems in this area generally, see further B. Reynolds, 'Shareholders' Class Rights: A New Approach' [1996] *JBL* 554.

[89] Legislation has removed some of the unfair aspects of the corporate entity doctrine; see nn. 114 and 123.   [90] [1990] Ch. 433.

[91] Recently followed in *Re Polly Peck International plc* [1996] BCC 486 and applied in *Re H* [1996] 2 All ER 391. The first instance decision of *Creasey* v. *Breachwood Motors* [1992] BCC 638 is difficult to reconcile with *Adams* v. *Cape*.

[92] (1887) 12 App. Cas. 589.

was being held that there were certain things which it was unacceptable for the majority to do to the minority, for this would be a fraud on the minority; the cases *Menier* v. *Hooper's Telegraph Works*,[93] followed by *Cook* v. *Deeks* in 1916.[94] The idea was put more helpfully and perhaps in more juristic form many years later, by Megarry J in *Estmanco* v. *GLC*,[95] when he spoke of conduct 'stultifying the purpose for which the company was formed'.[96] Fundamental alterations of the constitution also attracted attention, in the year 1900, with *Allen* v. *Gold Reefs of West Africa*[97] holding that where the articles were being altered the shareholders needed to vote *bona fide* for the benefit of the company. Later it was held that shareholders in a class meeting owed a duty to vote *bona fide* for the benefit of the class[98] and, as described already, a shareholder's existing negative control would sometimes be protected.[99] In the development of directors' duties the story is rather different, starting early on with fierce concepts of probity borrowed from trusts law and the eighteenth-century case of *Keech* v. *Sandford*[100] the judges of the Chancery Division had no difficulty in fixing the directors with duties of utmost good faith.[101] As this century has developed, more attention has had to been given to that other aspect of the director's function, namely his role as a man of business who must take risks with the shareholders' (company's) funds in order to make money. Here the earlier subjective duties of care and skill[102] have been replaced by objective duties of reasonableness, reflecting the transition of the judicial concept of the role of directors as a part-time gentlemanly activity[103] to one which carries objective responsibilities.[104] The courts have recently had to grapple with the potential unfairness produced by the

---

[93] (1874) LR 9 Ch. App. 350.   [94] [1916] 1 AC 554 (PC).
[95] [1982] 1 All ER 437.   [96] *Ibid.*, 448.
[97] [1900] 1 Ch. 656.
[98] *Re Holders' Investment Trust Ltd.* [1971] 1 WLR 583.
[99] See e.g. *Clemens* v. *Clemens*, n. 86 above.
[100] (1726) Sel. Cas. Ch. 61.
[101] An approach confirmed by the HL in *Regal (Hastings) Ltd.* v. *Gulliver* [1942] 1 All ER 378.
[102] See e.g. *Re City Equitable Co.* [1925] Ch. 407; *Dorchester Finance Co. Ltd.* v. *Stebbing* [1989] BCLC 498, 501–2.
[103] E.g. *Marquis of Bute's Case* [1892] 2 Ch. 100.
[104] *Norman* v. *Theodore Goddard* [1992] BCC 14; *Re D'Jan Ltd.* [1993] BCC 646.

trust duty in the context of business, for that principle, fanatically applied in *Regal* v. *Gulliver*, produced an unfair claw-back of part of the purchase price which the buyer of the company had agreed to. More recently *IEF* v. *Umunna*[105] shows us that in some contexts fairness will require that a rigid application of the duty be set aside when measured against the director's own expectations of entrepreneurial reward and his own lifetime stock-in-trade of know-how. There are other examples of fairness-based responses: the development of the doctrine of identification opened the way for companies to be convicted of a much wider range of crimes and strengthened the regulatory regime surrounding the business activities of some companies;[106] the inclusion of the creditors within the meaning of 'company' in some circumstances.[107]

The story of legislative change is of even more significance. To a large extent the increase in the number of companies, and perhaps the growth of our economy, is traceable to a legislative policy, of facilitating the perceived needs of the business community, starting with the Board of Trade's original decision to permit the creation of companies by registration, which found expression in the Joint Stock Companies Act of 1844. The price for this indulgence was, and has remained, the policy of regulation, of policing, which until relatively recently mainly found expression in the doctrine of disclosure.[108] Disclosure is a handy compromise between contractual sanctity of bargain and the need to have a legislative policy which asserts at least some standard of fair dealing, the aim of regulation being, as Professor Jim Gower has put it, 'to protect reasonable people from being made fools of'.[109] Hence we have disclosure of accounts to the shareholders, and to the public by virtue of the registration requirement.[110] Disclosure of accounts is not a

---

[105] [1986] BCLC 460.

[106] *DPP* v. *Kent and Sussex Contractors Ltd.* [1944] KB 146.

[107] *Winkworth* v. *Baron* [1987] BCLC 193; *West Mercia Safetywear Ltd.* v. *Dodd* (1988) 4 BCC 30.

[108] The disclosure doctrine has increasingly been supplemented by the creation of a tougher regulatory regime surrounding companies. In particular, recent years have seen the web of financial services regulation spawned by the Financial Services Act 1986 and a growing emphasis on detecting and prosecuting City fraud, as evidenced by the high-profile formation of the Serious Fraud Office by the Criminal Justice Act 1987.

[109] See L. C. B. Gower, *Review of Investor Protection—Report: Part I* (London, 1984), para. 1.16.

[110] See generally Companies Act 1985, Part VII.

policy which has had a steady history; for instance the 1844 Act contained a requirement that companies publish (by registration) an annual balance sheet.[111] But then this requirement was dropped by the 1856 Act[112] and publication reinstated only in 1907, on the recommendation of Lord Loreburn's Committee. This century has seen substantial increases in the levels of disclosure required although, again, at times the legislature has blown hot and cold[113] but it still remains a major plank in the maintenance of a 'level playing field'. Disclosure of accounts is of course, only one area of a much wider disclosure doctrine.

If we look at few examples from the other main legislative developments this century we see here too facilitation and fairness; we see that facilitation of business needs and the enforcement of some level of fairness in the business world are the recurring themes in the development of our company law.

In 1929 fraudulent trading was introduced[114] to curb abuses of the limited liability principle; also in that year were the first provisions against a company giving financial assistance for the purchase of its shares to curb the abuse of companies being purchased using their own assets.[115] The 1948 Act contained new provisions designed to overturn the decision in *Drown* v. *Gaumont Picture Corporation*[116] requiring that share premiums be treated as undistributable reserves and so not available for dividends. The Acts of 1967, 1976, and 1980 among other things strengthened the provisions designed to ensure fair dealing by directors. During the 1980s there were many developments designed to facilitate the laissez-faire business culture of those days, so that we had exemptions from share premium account to facilitate takeovers,[117] and exemptions from the financial assistance rules were introduced for private companies to help along the new corporate finance

---

[111] 7 & 8 Vict. c. 110 (1844), s. 43.

[112] Joint Stock Companies Act 1856.

[113] For example the 1981 Companies Act implementing the EC 4th Directive, provided exemptions for certain small and medium-sized companies; *ibid.*, ss. 1, 5–8, sched. 1.

[114] Companies Act 1929, s. 275; see now Insolvency Act 1986, s. 213 and Companies Act 1985, s. 458.

[115] Companies Act 1929, s. 45; see now Companies Act 1985, ss. 151–158.

[116] [1937] Ch. 402.

[117] Companies Act 1981, ss. 36–41; now Companies Act 1985, ss. 131–134.

techniques of venture capitalists.[118] Similar reasons prompted allowing the purchase of shares out of capital[119] by private companies and the new facility of redeemable equity shares.[120] The year 1985 saw the greatest overhaul of insolvency legislation[121] for over a century (work largely completed in 1989),[122] introducing new procedures such as administration orders designed to facilitate the rescue of companies before the onset of irremediable insolvency. Abuses of limited liability were further curbed by the introduction of wrongful trading, and there were laws to curb recurrent scandals such as the 'phoenix phenomenon' under which an insolvent company could sell its business to a new company bearing the same name, and thus rise from the ashes, so to speak, freed from its debts and with the same characters in charge.[123] Disqualification of directors was toughened up in 1985, since when thousands have been disqualified.[124] The major corporate scandals of the 1980s showed that grave breaches of criminal law are a not uncommon feature of corporate life. Here too the system responded with the setting up of the Serious Fraud Office,[125] which, having lost some high-profile cases, has an unfortunate public image, but in the hit and miss area of complex frauds actually has a tolerably decent conviction rate of 63 per cent.[126] And in terms of enforcing fairness, how can one not mention the 1986 revolution in the regulation of financial services, the creation of the SIB and the 'alphabet soup' of practitioner-based SROs—enforcing 'Honesty,

---

[118] Companies Act 1981, ss. 43–44; now Companies Act 1985, ss. 155–158.

[119] To the extent of the permissible capital payment; see Companies Act 1981, ss. 46–62; now Companies Act 1985, ss. 162–181.

[120] Companies Act 1981, ss. 45; now Companies Act 1985, ss. 159–160.

[121] Insolvency Act 1985, largely consolidated (with parts of the Companies Act 1985) into the Insolvency Act 1986.

[122] Companies Act 1989, Part II, contained provisions regulating the appointment of auditors and regulating the profession of insolvency practitioner.

[123] Insolvency Act 1986, ss. 88–27, 214–215, and 216–217.

[124] First introduced in the Companies Act 1948, s. 188, the provisions were gradually extended by the Insolvency Act 1976, the Companies Act 1981, and the Insolvency Act 1985. Many hundreds a year are disqualified, e.g. 355 in 1994, 633 in 1995 (Insolvency Service Statistics).

[125] See n. 108 above.

[126] The total number of prosecutions brought being 153 (statistics supplied by telephone conversation with an official of the Office on 19 Feb. 1997). The CPS annual conviction rate in the Crown Courts is 90.4% (year ending March 1996; statistics supplied by telephone conversation with an official of the Service on 19 Feb. 1997).

Solvency, Competence', the three basic requirements for conduct of
investment business in the United Kingdom?[127] In its early days the
system was said to be self-regulatory, but that was early on seen to
be a myth.[128] Those who break the rules face heavy fines, as
stockbrokers Greig Middleton recently found out with their
£200,000 fine from the SFA.[129] Those who have insisted on
carrying on as if the system does not exist are likely to be even more
firmly dealt with, as the Court of Appeal case *Fallon* v. *SIB*,[130]
shows, where the defendant persisted in carrying on investment
business without the authorization required by the Financial
Services Act and was eventually committed to prison for nine
months.

4. ENERGY IN LAW REFORM

Where has the policy-making energy for all these reforms come
from?[131] The historical role of the DTI[132] here has already been
alluded to, and it is a role that shows no real sign of diminishing, as
witnessed by the 1992 announcements of the wide-ranging
Company Law Review which has given birth to a veritable stream
of carefully written consultation documents, followed in some cases
by speedy legislation.[133] Since 1992 the Treasury also has had a
role in the field of investor protection. The European Commission,
too, has made its input. The policy of harmonization of the
company laws of the Member States has been effected through a
series of complex directives[134] which have been painstakingly

---

[127] Financial Services Act 1986, Sched. 2, para. 1, requires that members of SROs
must be 'fit and proper' which has been interpreted to mean 'Honesty, Solvency and
Competence': see *Re Noble Warren Investments Ltd.* [1989] JBL 421.

[128] L. C. B. Gower's view, even in 1988, was that the Government's description
of it in their White Paper as 'self-regulation within a statutory framework' was more
accurately expressed as 'statutory regulation monitored by self-regulatory organisations recognised by, and under the surveillance of, a self-standing Commission': see
' "Big Bang" and City Regulation' (1988) 51 *MLR* 1, 11.

[129] *Financial Times*, 19 Apr. 1995. The contractual basis of the levying of fines by
SROs is unlikely to diminish their impact.   [130] (1994) LEXIS.

[131] What follows is not an exhaustive list; merely the main sources of input.

[132] The Board of Trade until 1970.

[133] E.g. in Feb. 1995 the DTI Consultative Document, 'Resolutions of Private
Companies', preceded the Deregulation (Resolutions of Private Companies) Order
1996 (SI 1996 No 1471) amending the Companies Act 1985, ss. 381A–C.

[134] And occasionally through an EC Reg.: e.g. the EEC Merger Reg. 4064/89,
[1989] OJ L395/1.

implemented by the DTI since 1972. By and large these have made very many technical changes to our laws, but not really to much of their basic policy and direction. As Lord Templeman put it in his 'Forty Years On' lecture in 1990, '[i]n most cases Community Law has not gone further or faster than Parliament would wish in relation to its domestic legislation.'[135] Most of those that would make major changes, such as the draft Fifth Directive, have been blocked by the United Kingdom.[136] Also inputting over the years have been the various company law committees, some of which have already been mentioned,[137] and individual academics or practitioners commissioned to produce reports on various areas of problem; Professor Jim Gower on *Share Purchases by Companies*,[138] and of course the regulation of *Financial Services*,[139] Professor Dan Prentice on *Ultra Vires*,[140] Sir Kenneth Cork on *Insolvency Law*.[141] Others have conducted their own campaigns from the sidelines; Professor Len Sealy led a crusade[142] against unnecessary burdens on small businesses during the 1980s; the ideas caught on, and by the close of the decade we had seen the introduction of the elective regime, new rules on written resolutions,[143] and, indeed, not pertaining to company law, a general Deregulation Statute.[144] Others, such as Judith Freedman, have studied the mechanisms of law reform themselves[145] and their criticisms may be paying off; is it any coincidence that we are currently awaiting actual draft legislation on financial assistance,

---

[135] Lord Templeman, 'Company Law Lecture—Forty Years On' (1990) 11 *Co. Law* 10, 13.

[136] Also the draft 13th Dir. which would make a major changes to UK takeover regulation by putting it on a legal basis. The UK government's fear is that this will lead to American-style litigation in takeover battles.

[137] The main ones this century being: Loreburn 1906, Wrenbury 1918, Greene 1926, Cohen 1945, Jenkins 1962.

[138] *The Purchase by a Company of its own Shares* (London, 1979), Cmnd. 7944.

[139] *Review of Investor Protection—A Discussion Document* (London, 1982); *Review of Investor Protection—Part 1* (London, 1984), Cmnd. 9125 and *Part 2* (London, 1985).   [140] See n. 20, above.

[141] *Report of the Review Committee on Insolvency Law and Practice* (London, 1982), Cmnd. 8558.

[142] See e.g. L. Sealy 'A Company Law for Tomorrow's World' (1981) 2 *Co. Law* 195; L. Sealy, *Company Law and Commercial Reality* (2nd edn.) (London, 1984).

[143] Companies Act 1989, ss. 113–117.

[144] Deregulation and Contracting Out Act 1994.

[145] See J. Freedman, 'Reforming Company Law' in F. Patfield (ed.) *Perspectives on Company Law: 1* (Deventer, 1995).

the process having already had the benefit of a detailed consultation exercise?[146] Last but by no means least, we have the input of the Law Commission which, since 1992, has been taking a special interest in company law. Their thoughtful consultation document on shareholder remedies[147] will no doubt bear legislative fruit in due course, and their report recommending a new crime of corporate killing may, when implemented, have an important input to make in the process of stirring corporate social conscience[148] and altering corporate behaviour.

5. The Role of Self regulation

Company law also has a self-regulatory element which should not be forgotten, and indeed in recent years has achieved a high profile nationally. Introduced in 1959 the self-regulatory City Code on Takeovers and Mergers, administered by the Panel since 1968, has in the eyes of most commentators been a highly successful venture; and today in the supportive environment in which it operates its non-legal status seems hardly to matter; in the words of a former secretary of the Panel, '[t]he code is non-statutory, but voluntary it is not.'[149] As is often the case with areas that are primarily self-regulatory, there is a skein of legal rules haphazardly interwoven with the self-regulatory area, and in particular here there has since 1948[150] been legislation regulating the monopoly aspects of takeovers.

In the early 1990s the nation's despairing accountants[151] and City constituencies set up the Cadbury Committee which produced

---

[146] 'DTI Company Law Review: Proposals for Reform of Sections 151–158 of the Companies Act 1985' (1993). There have been various subsequent DTI releases.

[147] Consultation Paper No. 142.

[148] *Legislating the Criminal Code: Involuntary Manslaughter*, Law Com. No. 237. Also of note in the company law field is *Fiduciary Duties and Regulatory Rules*, Law Com. Consultation Paper No. 124.

[149] Richard Godden (1990). Also part of the self-regulatory structure are the Substantial Acquisitions Rules (SARs), formerly promulgated on the authority of the Council for the Securities Industry (CSI), now on the authority of the Panel.

[150] Monopolies and Restrictive Practices (Inquiry and Control) Act 1948. The area is now covered by the Fair Trading Act 1973 and by Arts. 85 and 86 of the Treaty of Rome and EEC Council Reg. 4064/89 [1989] OJ L395/1.

[151] For a comment on their unfortunate position see my article 'Limited Liability—A Principle for the 21st Century?' (1995) 48 *Current Legal Problems* 125, 140–1.

the now world-famous *Report on the Financial Aspects of Corporate Governance*. The Greenbury Committee followed, after the press publicity given to the high levels of directors' remuneration, particularly in recently privatized industries, had fuelled the existing doubts about the governance structures in private-sector plcs. It is clear that despite initial doubts the self-regulatory non-legal nature of it is not rendering it valueless and the corporate governance movement seems to have engendered a wide degree of enthusiasm. Currently awaited is the report of the Hampel Committee which is conducting 'a fundamental review of all aspects of corporate governance in the UK'.[152]

6. THE PATH TO A STAKEHOLDER COMPANY LAW

To some extent, the above developments have been the product of, and are evidence of, a 'greening' of company law—fairness, facilitation, respect, care, and productive energy in law reform. But there is one area, above all, where fresh growth is evident. I have already previewed the idea of corporate social responsibility in brief glimpses of the development mainly of one narrow area of this: corporate donations; from the begrudged 'cakes and ale' to the multi-million pound community programmes of our larger plcs. To 'corporate responsibility' we must now return. The jurisprudence which this has given rise to is colossal.

In the USA, in 1932, Berle and Means[153] had shown that in many of the largest corporations, there was a separation of ownership and control; disparate shareholdings, each with a small stake in the company, were not able effectively to control management, who were thus largely at liberty to pursue their own goals of high salaries, job security, and personal prestige. The truly great power which the managers possess can then be said to lack legitimacy, for in democracies power is only legitimate if it is subjected to effective controls.[154] The early 1930s also saw the famous Berle and Dodd

---

[152] *Financial Times*, 8 Dec. 1995.

[153] A. A. Berle and G. Means, *The Modern Corporation and Private Property* (revised edn.) (New York, 1968). First published in 1932.

[154] *Ibid.*, esp. 219–43, 293–313. It may need to comply with other norms also. For a modern analysis see M. Stokes 'Company Law and Legal Theory' in W. Twining (ed.), *Legal Theory and Common Law* (Oxford, 1986), 155 reprinted in S. Wheeler (ed.), *A Reader on the Law of the Business Enterprise* (Oxford, 1994), 80.

debate on the question 'For whom are corporate managers trustees?'[155] Did the directors hold their powers in trust for the entire community or solely for the shareholders? Now broadened into the arguments about creating a stakeholder society and communitarian philosophy, the debate continues to the present day.[156] To some extent it has already left its recent mark on company law legislation;[157] the majority of states[158] now have a constituency provision in their corporation statutes, although it is probable that the motives for putting them there are sadly compromised.[159] For example, the Illinois Business Corporation Act[160] provides:

In discharging [their] duties . . . the . . . directors . . . may, in considering the best long term and short term interests of the corporation, consider the effects of any action . . . upon employees, suppliers and customers of the corporation . . ., communities in which offices or other establishments of the corporation . . . are located, and all other pertinent factors.

In England the corporate social responsibility question, although largely in the form of the related industrial democracy debate, had acquired a high public profile by the late 1970s, when the majority

---

[155] A. A. Berle, 'Corporate Powers as Powers in Trust' (1931) 44 *Harvard L Rev.* 1049 and E. M. Dodd, 'For Whom are Corporate Managers Trustees?' (1932) 45 *Harvard L Rev.* 1145. For a detailed analysis of the debate and the later literature see: Sheikh, n. 32 above, 153–7 and Sommer, n. 156 below, 36 ff.

[156] On communitarianism the main source is A. Etzioni, *The Spirit of Community—Rights, Responsibilities and the Communitarian Agenda* (New York, 1993). Recent journal sources on corporate responsibility are: A. Sommer, 'Whom Should the Corporation Serve? The Berle-Dodd Debate Revisited Sixty Years Later' (1991) 16 *Delaware Journal of Corporate Law* 33; A. Fejfar, 'Corporate Voluntarism: Panacea or Plague? A Question of Horizon' (1992) 17 *Delaware Journal of Corporate Law* 859; M. De Bow and D. R. Lee, 'Shareholders, Nonshareholders and Corporate Law: Communitarianism and Resource Allocation' (1993) 18 *Delaware Journal of Corporate Law* 393. There are also distinguished collections in [1993] *Washington and Lee Law Review* 1373–1723 and in (1993) 43 *University of Toronto LJ* 297–796. For earlier material see the extensive bibliography in J. Parkinson, *Corporate Power and Responsibility: Issues in the Theory of Company Law* (Oxford, 1993).

[157] In this regard, I am grateful for discussions I have had with Professor Ron Jensen, my colleague on the London Programme of Pace University.

[158] Hamilton, *Cases and Materials on Corporations* (St Paul, Minn., 1995), 597 refers to there being 28 in 1992.

[159] It would help directors to resist takeover offers by giving them a vague and wider ground on which to recommend rejection: *ibid.*, 598.

[160] At 5/8.85, *ibid.* 597.

report of the Bullock Committee recommended having worker representation on company boards.[161] In 1980 Parliament enacted that boards of directors must have regard to the interests of their employees as well as their members.[162] In broadening the constituency in this way company law had taken a great leap, even though the technicalities ensured that it would be virtually impossible for employees to get any legal remedies.[163] During the 1980s, numerous academics emphasized the challenges posed for company law by industrial democracy.[164] In his influential article, 'The Legal Development of Corporate Responsibility—For Whom will Corporate Managers be Trustees?',[165] Lord Wedderburn wrote:

No solution for managerial authority can be found ... without some renegotiation of the legitimacy on which corporate government rests; and

---

[161] *Report of the Committee of Inquiry on Industrial Democracy* (London, 1977), Cmnd. 6706.

[162] Companies Act 1980, s. 46; now Companies Act 1985, s. 309.

[163] See my analysis in 'Duties in Respect of Employees under the Companies Act 1980' (1981) 34 *Current Legal Problems* 199, 200–4. Conservative government policy remained one of promoting employee involvement voluntarily; a further nudge towards this was contained in the Employment Act 1982, s. 1, which amended the legislation relating to the contents of the directors' report so that it requires that where a company employs more than 250 persons then among the matters to be included in the report is 'a statement describing the action that has been taken during the financial year to introduce, maintain or develop arrangements aimed at—a) providing employees systematically with information on matters of concern to them as employees, b) consulting employees or their representatives on a regular basis so that the views of employees can be taken into account in making decisions which are likely to affect their interests, c) encouraging the involvement of employees in the company's performance through an employee share scheme or by some other means, d) achieving a common awareness on the part of all employees of the financial and economic factors effecting the performance of the company', now in Companies Act 1985, sched. 7, Part V.

[164] Lord Wedderburn, 'The Legal Development of Corporate Responsibility: For Whom Will Corporate Managers be Trustees?' in K. Hopt and Teubner (eds.), *Corporate Governance and Directors' Liability: Legal, Economic and Sociological Analyses of Corporate Social Responsibility* (Berlin, 1985); Lord Wedderburn, 'The Social Responsibility of Companies' (1985) 15 *Melbourne University Law Review* 1; Lord Wedderburn, 'Trust, Corporation and the Worker ' (1985) 23 *Osgoode Hall LJ* 203; G. Teubner, 'Corporate Fiduciary Duties and their Beneficiaries: A Functional Approach to the Legal Institutionalisation of Corporate Responsibility' in Hopt and Teubner (eds.), *op. cit.* above; L. Sealy, 'Directors' Wider Responsibilities—Problems Conceptual, Practical and Procedural' (1987) 13 *Mon LR* 164; P. G. Xuereb, 'The Juridification of Industrial Relations Through Company Law Reform' (1988) 51 *MLR* 156; Lord Wedderburn, 'Companies and Employees: Common Law or Social Dimension?' (1993) 109 *LQR* 220.

[165] N. 164, above.

that cannot be accomplished without the acceptance of the workers as an integral constituent—albeit a conflictual constituent—in the business corporation. Where the corporate group is transnational, that constituency too is multinational.[166]

and then:

The need is for mechanisms, both internal to and external to the enterprise, through which wider social responsibility can emerge, procedures which will inevitably modify the objective of maximising profit without attempting to replace it at a stroke by some other substantive formula.[167]

This decade, scholarly and political interest has expanded; interest both in industrial democracy and in the development of wider social responsibilities. The term 'corporate governance' is now being used to describe the whole question of for whose benefit the company is run and through what structures (and not merely addressing the problem of making existing structures work effectively); as it was put recently, 'Corporate Governance is thus the system whereby managers are ultimately held accountable to all stakeholders for their stewardship.'[168] Published in 1993, Parkinson's *Corporate Power and Responsibility: Issues in the Theory of Company Law* contains a painstaking analysis of most of the issues raised by the (predominantly American) literature.[169] Sheikh's interesting work has already been mentioned.[170] Stakeholder books have appeared: Will Hutton's influential work *The State We're In*[171] argued that the financial system needs to be 'comprehensively republicanised'[172] and a few weeks ago Plender's *A Stake in the Future—The Stakeholding Solution*[173] was published, taking a milder line than Hutton, and setting out the theoretical basis of the doctrine as he saw it. The stakeholder concept has been taken up by the Labour Party, launched by Tony Blair's speech in Singapore[174] last year although it is possible that it has been backpedalled somewhat, to a call for cultural changes in companies.[175] The TUC has stated its position in an intensely

---

[166] At 43.   [167] *Ibid.* 44.
[168] IPPR Report, *Promoting Prosperity: A Business Agenda for Britain* (London, 1997), 103.   [169] See n. 156 above.   [170] N. 32 above.
[171] London, 1995.   [172] See n. 194 below.   [173] London, 1997.
[174] *Financial Times*, 9 Jan. 1996. Labour Party thinking in this area is set out in *Vision for Growth: A New Industrial Strategy for Britain* (London, 1996).
[175] See *Financial Times*, 26 June 1996 and Plender, n. 173 above, 15–16.

carefully argued document, *Your Stake at Work: TUC Proposals for a Stakeholding Economy.*[176] And perhaps[177] less closely linked to the Labour Party, we have the recent Report of the Commission on Public Policy and British Business called *Promoting Prosperity— A Business Agenda for Britain.*[178] There has also been the report of the *Tomorrow's Company* inquiry from the Royal Society of Arts.[179] In addition, there have been numerous 'stakeholding' articles.[180] The genuine public interest in the stakeholder debate in Britain represents a natural desire to search for social consensus, for community, and, it has to be said, for the left of centre to fill the ideological void created by the current unpopularity of Marxist/ Socialist ideology. Thus it is political and highly contentious; its opponents write of 'Snares of stakeholding' 'Silly slogans of stakeholders,'[181] and there is the CBI document, *Boards without Tiers.*[182]

In the 1990s the movement towards industrial democracy has speeded up. It is well known that in the face of opposition from the United Kingdom little satisfactory progress has been made with the draft EC Fifth Directive, the earliest draft of which would have required larger companies to have a two-tier board structure, consisting of a top-tier supervisory board and an executive, management board, and some form of worker representation.[183] Work on the earlier Vredeling Directive[184] and on the European Company Statute has a similar history.[185]

---

[176] London, 1996.

[177] A political furore resulted from the accusation by the then Deputy Prime Minister, Michael Heseltine, that some of the leading businessmen involved in the report had allowed themselves to be used by the Labour Party; see *Financial Times*, 22 and 23 Jan. 1997.   [178] See n. 168 above.

[179] Royal Society for the Encouragement of Arts, Manufactures and Commerce, 1995.

[180] e.g. J. Kay and A. Silberstone, 'Corporate Governance', *National Institute of Economic and Social Research Review*, August 1995, 84; Alcock, 'The Case Against the Concept of Stakeholders' (1996) 17 *Co. Law* 177; P. Ireland, 'Corporate Governance, Stakeholding, and the Company: Towards a Less Degenerate Capitalism' (1996) 23 *Journal of Law and Society* 287.

[181] Samuel Brittan, *Financial Times* 1 Feb. 1996 and 7 Jan. 1995.

[182] London, 1996.

[183] The full story of the subsequent drafts is analysed in detail in J. J. Du Plessis and J. Dine, 'The Fate of the Draft Fifth Directive on Company Law: Accommodation Instead of Harmonisation' [1997] *JBL* 23.   [184] [1983] OJ C217.

[185] For detail of the proposals see J. Dine, 'The European Company Statute' (1990) 11 *Co. Law* 208; A. Burnside, 'The European Company Re-proposed' (1991) 12 *Co. Law* 216.

However, the 1992 Maastricht Treaty on European Union and its annexed Protocol and Agreement on Social Policy authorized the Member States, although excluding the United Kingdom, to adopt directives for the information and consultation of employees, and so, despite earlier UK opposition, the European Works Council Directive[186] was adopted in 1994. It covers about 1,500 or so European companies (namely those employing over 1,000 workers with more than 150 in at least two Member States[187]) and requires them to establish company-wide information and consultation committees for their employees. Described by Padraig Flynn, the EU Social Affairs Commissioner, as 'one of the most important legislative steps ever taken by the EU in the field of Social policy',[188] the directive is a catalyst for a major change in corporate culture. Currently, about 100 UK-based companies may be covered by the Directive by virtue of their undertakings in other Member States, and about half of these[189] have already set up councils which have voluntarily included their UK employees. About 200 companies based elsewhere have set up councils which include UK employees employed by their UK subsidiaries. According to Padraig Flynn, the UK experience can be summed up as 'de jure it is out, de facto it is in'.[190]

Whether through clenched teeth or not, the attitude of some of the companies doing this seems to have been very positive. British Steel, for instance, when setting up its arrangements 'said it wanted to "build on its strong tradition of consultation" with all its workers and create a flexible works council that suited its business circumstances'.[191] The unions are not always happy with the

---

[186] Council Dir. 94/45/EEC on the establishment of a European Works Council or other procedure in Community-scale undertakings or Community-scale groups of undertakings for the purposes of informing and consulting employees [1994] OJ L254/64. It came into force on 22 Sept. 1996. See C. McGlynn, 'European Works Councils: Towards Industrial Democracy?' (1995) 24 *Industrial LJ* 78. There have been important developments in relation to related dirs. (Collective Redundancies Dir., Acquired Rights Dir., Health and Safety Framework Dir.); see M. Hall, 'Beyond Recognition? Employee Representation and EU Law' (1996) 25 *Industrial LJ* 15; and see generally B. Bercusson, 'The Dynamic of European Labour Law after Maastricht' (1994) 23 *Industrial LJ* 1.   [187] Art. 2.

[188] *Financial Times*, 18 Sept. 1996.

[189] Statistic supplied in a telephone conversation with an official of the TUC Works Councils Monitoring Unit on 17 Feb. 1997. The figure may be as high as 57.

[190] *Financial Times*, 12 July 1995.

[191] *Financial Times*, 1 Aug. 1996.

arrangements, but in this case the general secretary of the ISTC, the main steel union, said he was '[a]bsolutely delighted . . . The new body is of the highest standard and best practice among European Works Councils'. The British Steel proposal was for 'a 29-strong works council with 16 representatives from its UK plants, three from Sweden, two from Germany and one each from Holland, France, Finland, Denmark, Ireland, Belgium, Norway and Italy. It intends to include six full-time national trade union officials with five of them from the UK and the others in rotation from recognised unions in other European countries involved . . . [it] will meet twice a year but extra sessions may be held in emergencies. . . . The council's agenda will include broad strategy, manpower and employment, business reorganisation and areas such as health and safety and the environment where these issues have a transnational impact.'[192]

Before we can consider any future developments, we need to ask further what really is stakeholding, and what are its implications for company law? The word 'stakeholders' originates in the USA and Paddy Ireland tells us that it developed as a deliberate play on the American word for 'shareholders', namely 'stockholders'.[193] Perhaps also it had a deep historical appeal to the American psyche, carrying the connotation of the hardworking and deserving settler 'staking a claim' by ringfencing a plot of land and thus acquiring it; it denotes a moral claim for participation and for rights not yet recognized by the law. Stakeholder theorists argue that the concept is needed to make society better, not by removing capitalism, but by making it, in Hutton's words, less 'degenerate'.[194] In the process, not only do people have a greater sense of worth and well-being, but the economy becomes more efficient and grows faster. As Plender put it, '[a] stakeholder economy is one which derives

[192] *Ibid*: ' "Under no circumstances" will the council become involved in or discuss "any issues relating to collective bargaining or negotiations within the group undertakings" said the company.'

[193] See P. Ireland, n. 180 above, 295 and n. 47.

[194] 'Thus the great challenge for the twentieth century, after the experience of both state socialism and of unfettered free markets, is to create a new financial architecture in which private decisions produce a less degenerate capitalism. The triple requirement is to broaden the stake-holding in companies and institutions, so creating a greater bias to long term commitment from owners; to extend the supply of cheap, longterm debt; and to decentralise decision-making. The financial system, in short, needs to be comprehensively republicanised': n. 171 above, 298.

competitive strength from a cohesive national culture, in which the exercise of property rights is conditioned by shared values and cooperative behaviour'[195] and (later) 'the stakeholding solution offers a means of legitimizing the tempestuous mechanics of capitalism and of preserving human and social capital in the interests of competitive advantage'.[196] Some of the efficiency is said by economists to come from lower transaction costs: fewer monitors are needed in the workplace, commercial contracting is simpler and cheaper because of a higher level of trust and shared values between the parties, less state legislation and costly regulation is needed.[197] Stakeholder theory emphasizes the importance of inclusion, the role of intermediate institutions, companies, unions, churches, clubs, campaigning groups.[198]

The agenda produced by stakeholder theory for the reform of company law is difficult to pin down, but at present it involves participation of employees and other constituencies in corporate decision-making structures, varying the scope of directors' duties, either by including the wider constituencies as the subjects of the duty or redefining the company so as to include them. There are many other suggestions; the TUC document[199] contains proposals, ranging from rights to training, to requirements for companies to produce a social audit.[200]

Most stakeholder proposals involve a greater or lesser degree of what may broadly be called 'corporate voluntarism'[201] or 'profit-sacrificing social responsibility;[202] that is, some level of departure from the principle of running the company for the sole benefit of the shareholders. Over the years corporate voluntarism has been subjected to a great deal of theoretical analysis and criticism. The

---

[195] Plender, n. 173 above, 23.   [196] *Ibid.*, 256.

[197] Plender, n. 173 above, 24. 'The historic success of stakeholder economies such as Germany, Switzerland or Japan is partly explained by their lower transaction costs, both inside and outside the firm.'

[198] *Ibid.*, 256: 'For the left, it provides a sophisticated alternative to the notion of equality, although one which is not necessarily at odds with that slogan since it is rooted in the idea of fairness.'

[199] See n. 176 above.

[200] In fact in view of the TUC's enthusiasm for their interpretation of stakeholder ideals it is difficult to see whether the industrial democracy debate survives as a separate issue.

[201] e.g. as in A. Fejfar, 'Corporate Voluntarism: Panacea or Plague? A Question of Horizon' (1992) 17 *Delaware Journal of Corporate Law* 859.

[202] J. Parkinson, n. 156 above, 304.

debate revolves around three main criticisms, although these are overlapping and linked and there are many other angles.[203]

It is argued, first, that the pursuit of corporate goals other than profit is inefficient, and so in the long run we would all be worse off for it; a viewpoint usually identified with Milton Friedman, who said that 'A corporate executive's responsibility is to make as much money for the stockholders as possible'.[204] Further it is said that the company and its shares are private accumulations of capital, and any goal other than profit for shareholders is an infringement of private property, a naked redistribution of wealth, sometimes called the shareholders' money argument. Thirdly and alternatively, boards of directors are the wrong people to be making decisions about the distribution of wealth; they are not elected by or accountable to the populace, and it extends their already overlarge powers; it is a state function and they should defer to the state, which can make appropriate redistributions through the taxation system. This is sometimes called the deference argument.

Various replies can be mounted. The efficiency argument can be met head on by pointing to the counter-efficiencies produced by the reduction of social friction which stakeholder policies would produce. Germany and Japan have forms of worker involvement in larger companies and have clearly been doing better than many of us in recent decades. In his recent book, *Competitive Advantage Through People*,[205] Jeffrey Pfeffer, Professor of Organizational Behaviour at Stanford Graduate School of Business used the example of the five top-performing US companies between 1972 and 1992. Stocks which produced average returns of 18360 per cent during the period, 'exceptional economic returns in highly competitive almost mundane industries'.[206] The factor they had in common was 'how they manage their workforce'. Employment security, high wages, and greater employee share ownership can all

---

[203] For a more detailed analysis see *ibid*. 304–346.

[204] Interview with Playboy Magazine, Feb. 1973 at 59, reprinted in Hamilton, n. 158 above, 589. See further M. Friedman, *Capitalism and Freedom* (Chicago, Ill., 1962); according to Sheikh's analysis (n. 32, above) he later modified his views: *ibid*., 24–27.   [205] Boston, Mass., 1994.

[206] *Ibid*., 5. Top performing in terms of the percentage returns on their shares. They were South West Airlines, Uhl-Mart, Tyson Foods, Circuit City, and Plenum Publishing. The figure of 18360% is my calculation of the average growth from the statistics Pfeffer gives on 4.

produce efficiencies and so enhance competitiveness.[207] The shareholder's money argument is diminished by the legitimacy problem created by the immense power that companies in fact exercise over the lives of individuals and in the lack of sufficient controls on that power, especially since shareholders usually do not even bother to exercise what minimal controls there are.[208] The deference argument is in my view probably the most challenging, but its strength can be diminished by the argument that the general cultural improvement in society resulting from stakeholder policies diminishes the need for strict adherence to democratic theory.[209] Also, since currently about 70 per cent of shares are owned by institutions[210] then one can point to the spread of ownership as already creating a kind of democracy in ownership which makes it less compelling to defer to formal democratic structures. As the TUC document proclaims 'We're the shareholders now';[211] not as a slogan celebrating a recent triumphant seizure of property, but as a simple but significant statistical fact.

III. Looking Ahead

Looking ahead, what does the future hold for company law? Legislative reform in many areas will continue; we have not yet reached Utopia. In the very long term a slow but radical restructuring along stakeholder lines is highly likely.[212] English society is slowly

---

[207] *Ibid.*, 4. See also the recent study showing similar results by Bilmes, Wetzker, and Xhonneux, *Financial Times*, 10 Feb. 1997, 'in one of the first studies of its kind, our analysis of more than 100 German companies reveals a strong link between investing in employees and stock market performance'.

[208] See e.g., n. 176 above, 14: 'Less than 15% of the votes of pensions funds are cast at AGMs and witness Cadbury's efforts to coax the institutional shareholders into activity: *Report of the Committee on the Financial Aspects of Corporate Governance* (London, 1992), para. 6.11.

[209] e.g. Plender, n. 175 above, 256: 'By emphasizing the role of intermediate institutions . . . the stakeholding concept consciously downgrades the role of the state'.

[210] 69.9% in 1992; see *Stock Exchange Fact Book* (London, 1994).

[211] N. 176 above, para. 1.43.

[212] Berle and Means were probably not far wrong when in 1932 they wrote prophetically: '[a]s an economic organism grows in strength and its power is concentrated in a few hands . . . the demand for responsible power becomes increasingly direct. . . . How will this demand be made effective? To answer this question would be to forsee the history of the next century': Berle and Means, *The Modern Corporation and Private Property* (New York, 1932), 310.

becoming more and more egalitarian; expectations rise continually. But within the current political spectrum a full-blown stakeholding economy, as envisaged by the TUC and by Hutton, is a radical package and it is debatable whether the political will to do it all soon exists within any of the major parties. Hutton himself is fairly pessimistic about this.[213] What is more likely is a gradual implementation of a succession of amendments to company law, broadly in the direction of stakeholder ideas. In the immediate future some thought could usefully be given to extending section 309 of the Companies Act 1985 so that it requires that directors should have regard to the interests, not just of the employees, but also the company's suppliers, customers, and the community in which the company is located. As it stands at the moment, it looks a little odd and almost old-fashioned; if the constituencies are to be extended beyond shareholders at all, then why just to the employees? The suggestion can no doubt be deprecated as minimalism, and as channelling stakeholding into a dead end. It is true that what is needed in the long run are structural mechanisms which ensure that constituencies other than shareholders are involved in the management and decision-making processes. But stakeholder theory will only really work if people generally are enthusiastic about it,[214] and people need time to adjust to ideas. According to the Engineering Employers Federation many companies, when they learned of the impact of the European Works Councils Directive, were put into 'a state of deep shock'.[215] This is not conducive to a new spirit of co-operative enterprise. It would be a pity if nothing at all were done for the next half century, merely because the claims for law reform had been pitched too far above the political consensus. Corporate social conscience is stirring, but stirring (in the transitive sense) also is necessary. If the *Conservative* government of 1980 could introduce section 309, then there must surely currently, and in the near future, be a comfortable consensus for extending it. Indeed a

---

[213] N. 171 above. [214] e.g. *ibid.*, 320 ff.

[215] 'Mr Reid [European Affairs Co-ordinator of the Engineering Employers Federation] said that the federation's roadshow had put many companies into a state of "deep shock" when they heard about the impact of the directive': *Financial Times*, 6 Feb. 1996, the point being that if a Labour government is elected it will sign the Protocol.

recent MORI Poll[216] suggests that 87 per cent of people in Britain now believe that large companies have a responsibility to the community.

What will company law look like in 1,000 years time? We are after all, at the end of the millennium as well as at the end of the century. The most fundamental changes to our company law will be brought about if the free market economies of the Western World have been abandoned in favour of some kind of command economy and the eventual demise of the market economy is a distinct possibility. It is true that there has been a slump in world demand for command economy ideology and a boom in free market ideology. But with computers anything is possible; computer technology in some of our supermarkets monitors every purchase that is made and sets up the necessary replacement orders. Similarly a command economy run by a computer instantaneously matching the supply of scarce resources to demand throughout the whole system might be many times as efficient as our present markets, which depend on buying and selling decisions made on the basis of imperfect knowledge of the economy. Countries that did not have it would be in the Stone Age. If so, the world's democracies will eventually find that they need to go down that road; and company law will be there as well.

---

[216] Poll conducted for the organization Business in the Community 1996, cited in M. Suzman, 'A Fine Act to Follow' in [1995] *Business in the Community Annual Report* 4. See also Plender *op. cit.* 9.

FAMILY VALUES AND FAMILY JUSTICE

Michael Freeman

Introduction: 'Family Law' in 1900

Family law has come a long way in the twentieth century. When the century opened there was divorce for adultery only—aggravated adultery where wives were the petitioners.[1] A wife who committed adultery forfeited her right to maintenance and to property, even property she had brought into the marriage. Domestic violence had been discovered[2] and largely forgotten: it was assumed the separation order invented in 1878 had solved the problem.[3] A recent reform was the introduction of separation of property in 1882,[4] fought for by middle-class women[5] and of no relevance to most. Married women still lacked full contractual capacity, a

---

[1] Matrimonial Causes Act 1857. This Act changed process and procedure: it did not change the substantive law of divorce. And see Colin S. Gibson, *Dissolving Wedlock* (London, 1994), chap. 4.

[2] See A. James Hammerton, *Cruelty and Companionship: Conflict In Nineteenth Century Married Life* (London, 1992); Carol Bauer and Lawrence Ritt, ' "A Husband is a beating Animal": Frances Power Cobbe Confronts the Wife-abuse Problem in Victorian England' and 'Wife-abuse, Late-Victorian English Feminists, and the Legacy of Frances Power Cobbe' (1983) 6 *Int. J. Women's Studies* 99, 195 (on Frances Power Cobbe and her legacy). On the US see Reva B. Siegel, ' "The Rule of Love": Wife beating as Prerogative and Privacy' (1996) 105 *Yale LJ* 2117, and Linda Gordon, *Heroes of Their Own Lives: The Politics and History of Family Violence* (New York, 1988).

[3] Matrimonial Causes Act 1878 (the 'future safety' of the wife had to be 'in peril'): this proviso was removed in 1895 by the Summary Jurisdiction (Married Women) Act 1895.

[4] Married Women's Property Act 1882, on which see Lee Holcombe, *Wives and Property: Reform of the Married Women's Property Law In Nineteenth-Century England* (Toronto, 1983).

[5] See Dorothy M. Stetson, *A Women's Issue: The Politics of Family Law Reform in England* (Westport, Conn., 1982).

disability that was to survive for more than a third of this century.[6] Not surprisingly the ability of a married woman to pledge her husband's credit for necessary goods and services assumed an importance that seems barely credible today.[7]

The law of marriage was firmly in place: reforms in 1753[8] and 1836[9] had opened the institution to public scrutiny and provided for a centralized system of state regulation.[10] Lord Penzance's definition[11] of 'Christian' marriage as a 'voluntary union for life of one man and one woman to the exclusion of all others' was unchallenged and, it seemed, unassailable. Polygamous marriage was not only denied matrimonial remedies and relief but was judged not to be marriage at all.[12] Of transsexualism[13] we knew nothing: the gay[14] were more likely to find their way into Reading gaol than its register office.[15] Quasi-marital relationships were denied legal status: a case[16] in the early years of this century stigmatized the contract involved as akin to one for prostitution.

Beyond the law of wardship[17]—and this then existed more to

---

[6] It was removed by the Law Reform (Married Women and Tortfeasors) Act 1935, s. 1.

[7] Though the common law presumption has not been formally abolished. The agency of necessity has: see Matrimonial Proceedings and Property Act 1970, s. 40.

[8] Marriage Act 1753 (Lord Hardwicke's Act). Elite public opinion began to favour reform in the 1730s, but Bill after Bill failed: opposition was greatest in the House of Commons.

[9] Marriage Act 1836. The Births and Deaths Registration Act was passed the same year. See further Diana Leonard, 'The Regulation of Marriage: Repressive Benevolence' in G. Littlejohn *et al.*, *Power and the State* (London, 1978). See also the thesis of Jacques Donzelot, *The Policing of Families* (New York, 1979).

[10] For the situation before see Lawrence Stone, *Uncertain Unions: Marriage in England 1660–1753* (Oxford, 1992).

[11] *Hyde* v. *Hyde and Woodmansee* (1866) LR 1 P & D 130. But John Cairncross notes that many prominent thinkers including Milton and perhaps Newton thought polygamy consistent with Christianity: *After Polygamy Was Made A Sin* (London, 1974).

[12] *Re Bethell* (1888) 38 Ch.D 220.

[13] *Corbett* v. *Corbett (orse Ashley)* [1971] P 83 was English law's first confrontation with the phenomenon.

[14] But for evidence of same-sex unions in pre-modern Europe see John Boswell, *The Marriage of Likeness* (New York, 1994).

[15] On the Oscar Wilde trial see Richard Ellmann, *Oscar Wilde* (London, 1987), chap. XVII.

[16] *Upfill* v. *Wright* [1911] 1 KB 506.

[17] On which see John Seymour, 'Parens Patriae and Wardship Powers: Their Nature and Origins' (1994) 14 *OJLS* 159.

protect property than the welfare of children[18]—there was little child law. The child's welfare only became a relevant consideration in custody disputes in 1886: it was not until 1925 that the child's welfare became the 'first and paramount consideration', and this only because of feminist pressure for mothers to have equality with fathers.[19] There was a rudimentary law of child protection in existence[20]—it had taken three generations since a similar law to protect domestic animals[21]—but no understanding of child abuse.[22] As for sexual abuse, incest was not even a crime[23]—for this we had to wait until 1908.[24] There was no law of adoption,[25] no child welfare system,[26] no legitimation by subsequent marriage.[27] The law placed full responsibility on the mother rather than the father for bringing about the undesirable situation of illegitimacy. Laws relating to illegitimacy were emblematic of the negative and

[18] Despite comments such as Lord Cottenham's in *Re Spence* (1847) 2 Ph. 247, 251, and Kay LJ's in *R v. Gyngall* [1893] 2 QB 232, 248. And see N. V. Lowe and R. A. H. White, *Wards of Court* (2nd edn.) (London, 1986), 4, and the Latey Report on the *Age of Majority* (Cmnd. 3342) (London, 1967), para. 193.

[19] See respectively Guardianship of Infants Act 1886 and Guardianship of Infants Act 1925.

[20] The Prevention of Cruelty to Children Act 1889. See for the origins of this C. K. Behlmer, *Child Abuse And Moral Reform in England 1870–1908* (Stanford, Cal., 1982). But Linda Pollock in *Forgotten Children: Parent–Child Relations from 1500 to 1900* (Cambridge, 1983) shows there was public concern about cruelty to children well before the 1889 Act (385 cases in *The Times* between 1785 and 1860 and only 7% resulted in acquittals).

[21] This had been passed in 1823. The sponsor of the 1889 Bill was 'anxious' that children should be given 'almost the same protection' (HC Debs., vol. 337, col. 229).

[22] For this we had to wait until the 1960s: see M. D. A. Freeman, *Violence In The Home* (Farnborough, 1979), chap. 2.

[23] It had been an ecclesiastical offence (except between 1650 and 1660) though ecclesiastical authority was in decline long before 1908 (and see Lord Penzance's remarks in *Phillimore* v. *Machon* (1876) 1 PD 481).

[24] Punishment of Incest Act 1908. On the origins of the 1908 Act see V. Bailey and S. Blackburn, 'The Punishment of Incest Act 1908: A Study in Law Creation' (1979) *Crim. LR* 708. Prosecutions for incest in church courts seem to have been rare in early modern England. See Martin Ingram, *Church Courts, Sex and Marriage in England 1570–1640* (Cambridge, 1987), 245–9.

[25] For this we had to wait until 1926: see Adoption of Children Act 1926.

[26] This developed after the Second World War: important triggering events were a scandal (the O'Neill death), a famous letter to *The Times* (by Lady Allen of Hartwood on 5 July 1944), and the Curtis Report (*Care of Children*, Cmd. 6922, London, 1946). See further Jean Packman, *The Child's Generation* (Oxford and London, 1975).

[27] Introduced by the Legitimacy Act 1926. It had been rejected by the Barons at the Council of Merton in 1236.

punitive approach to family regulation. The law showed no compassion towards the child, who could not even inherit from a mother who died intestate until 1926.[28]

Family Law: An Academic Discipline

As the century opened there was no academic discipline of family law. For this we had to wait until after the Second World War. The London School of Economics was the first institution to teach family law—the law of domestic relations as they called it. The initiative came from the distinguished comparativist, Otto Kahn-Freund, whose tradition was very different from that just described.[29] UCL did not teach family law until the 1950s: it too called it 'the law of domestic relations'.[30] The subject lacked an academic text until 1957.[31]

Family Law: A Discrete Entity

As an academic discipline, family law developed much as other law subjects. The early textbooks, particularly *Bromley*, were firmly rooted within a positivistic and legalistic framework. Family 'law' was a discrete entity, not part of a social continuum.[32] Viewing the discipline in this way had a number of consequences.

The law was seen apart from the values it embodied and helped to structure and restructure—and it is by no means a one-way process. Thus, to take an example, the relationship between law and patriarchy,[33] so essential to an understanding of family law, was not understood. Consider the resurrection of the 'one-third rule' in *Wachtel* v. *Wachtel*:[34] Lord Denning MR justified this on

---

[28] The ecclesiastical courts, however, gave a right of support: see R. H. Helmholz, 'Support Orders, Church Courts and the Rule of Filius Nullius' (1977) 63 *Virginia LRev.* 431.

[29] In a public lecture, he recalled the scepticism with which the innovation was greeted, particularly amongst practitioners for whom divorce was synonymous with family law.

[30] And see Roscoe Pound, *Jurisprudence* (St. Paul, Minn., 1959), vol. III, 68.

[31] When P. M. Bromley's *Family Law* (London, 1957) was published. The main practitioner text (first published in 1910) was called simply *Divorce* until its 16th edn. in 1991.

[32] And see Judith Shklar, *Legalism* (Cambridge, Mass., 1964).

[33] On this see Michael D. A. Freeman, 'Legal Ideologies, Patriarchal Precedents, and Domestic Violence' in Michael D. A. Freeman (ed.), *State, Law and Family: Critical Perspectives* (London, 1984), 51.   [34] [1973] Fam. 72.

the ground that on divorce the ex-husband would have greater expenditure than his former wife. He would 'have to go out to work all day and must get some woman to look after the house', whereas the ex-wife 'will not . . . have so much expense . . . she will do most of the housework herself'.[35] Compare his reasoning in *Button* v. *Button*[36] with that in *Cooke* v. *Head*.[37] Ignore the values involved and the cases may readily be distinguished. Ms Cooke was what we would now call a cohabitant. But look at the values. In *Button* the argument was that 'a wife does not get a share in the house simply because she cleans the walls or works in the garden or helps her husband with the painting and decorating'.[38] In *Cooke* v. *Head*, by contrast, where the female cohabitant did 'quite an unusual amount of work for a woman',[39] using a sledgehammer to demolish old buildings, working a cement mixer, and doing other 'male' activities (in effect demonstrating she was a crafts*man*), her work was richly rewarded. The message is clear: what women normally do, or are expected to do, has no economic value, but 'real' work must be compensated.

Family Law's Image of the Family

A second consequence of the way family law as a discipline developed was that what emerged as family law, in the eyes of most family lawyers, academics, and practitioners, was a narrow and distorted image both of the subject of the discipline (the family) and of the processes which regulate the family.

First, let me explain this in relation to 'the family'. Family law is about husbands and wives (or those who live in relationships 'like' husbands and wives) and the children they produce. Of course, in part this is true, but I would suggest only in part. Why is it that we take it for granted that the family revolves around a sexual tie? Why is the 'sexual family' invested by our culture and society with exclusive legitimacy? Why is it, and here I quote Martha Fineman,[40]

---

[35] *Ibid.* 94.
[36] [1968] 1 All ER 1064.   [37] [1972] 2 All ER 38.
[38] N. 36 above, 1067.   [39] N. 37 above, 40.
[40] *The Neutered Mother, The Sexual Family and Other Twentieth Century Tragedies* (New York, 1995). Though I agree with this analysis, I do not accept Fineman's maternalist vision of the way in which the family should be conceived and structured. There is an excellent review article by M. M. Slaughter (1995) 95 *Columbia LR* 2156.

the 'foundational institution'? The sexual tie may not be a marital bond, it may even exist between members of the same sex, but it remains at the core of our understanding of intimacy and family connection.

In these terms single mothers are deviant: we never talk of married mothers because mothers are assumed to be married or in equivalent relationships.

We define children, even today, in terms of the relationship between their parents. Although the terms 'legitimate' and 'illegitimate' no longer exist in English law[41] and the legislation eschews terms like 'marital' and 'non-marital' (contrary to Law Commission advice[42] which favoured such epithets), the relationship between the child and his/her father still depends on the father's relationship with the mother.[43]

Step-children are only children of the family when 'treated'[44] as such by both their parent and the person to whom their parent is now married, and anything less than marriage will not do. This, it may be thought, is odd: are the 'couple' and their children not a family?

Relationships between parents and adult children, even adult dependent children, for example the many 'twenty somethings' who, in the absence of employment or marriage, have returned home fit ill within conventional concepts of the family. This is well illustrated by the discomfort the law feels when confronted by a family provision application by an adult child. Take the case of *Re Jennings (Deceased)*.[45] Jennings separated from his wife in 1945 and died in 1990. After the separation the only thing he did for his son, who was less than two at the time, was to send him ten shillings in a birthday card on his second birthday. The son from

---

[41] Family Law Reform Act 1987, s. 1.

[42] See Law Commission, *Illegitimacy* (Law Com. No. 118) (London, 1982), para. 4.

[43] Unmarried fathers do not automatically have parental responsibility: see Children Act 1989, s. 2(2)(b). They can acquire it (see s. 4), but very few do (see I. Butler *et al.*, 'The Children Act 1989 and the Unmarried Father' (1993) 5 *JCL* 157).

[44] See Matrimonial Causes Act 1973, s. 52(1). A child born to the wife after a marriage has been dissolved is not a child of the family: *Fisher* v. *Fisher* [1989] 1 FLR 423. There are similar, but not identical, provisions in the Inheritance (Provision for Family and Dependants) Act 1975 and the Marriage (Prohibited Degrees of Relationship) Act 1986 (and see the facts of *Smith* v. *Clerical Medical and General Life Assurance Society* [1993] 1 FLR 47).

[45] [1994] 1 FLR 536.

modest beginnings had done quite well. Now 50, he was comfortably off. Nevertheless, he wanted to claim financial provision from his father's estate. Did Jennings have 'any obligations and responsibilities'[46] towards his son? Wall J thought he did: the phrase was 'not limited to obligations existing solely at the date of death, but is wide enough to include obligations and responsibilities arising in infancy which were not discharged'.[47] The Court of Appeal did not agree: the reference in the Act to obligations and responsibilities which the deceased 'had' could not mean 'had at any time in the past'. Nourse LJ reasoned, '[a]n Act intended to facilitate the making of reasonable financial provision cannot have been intended to revive defunct obligations and responsibilities as a basis for making it',[48] and in answer to an alternative submission that a failure to meet legal obligations imposed a continuing moral obligation, the judge said the 'only factor on which the [son] can rely is the relationship between the deceased and himself as father and son, and this was not the intention of Parliament'.[49] Henry LJ, supporting this conclusion, said that 'it is not the purpose of the 1975 Act to punish or redress past bad or unfeeling parental behaviour when that behaviour does not still impinge on the applicant's present financial situation'.[50] The issue is rendered more complex because, despite twentieth-century reforms,[51] English law, unlike its civilian counterparts, still recognizes freedom of testation, and family provision is but an exception grafted on to this. Nevertheless a conclusion such as that reached in *Re Jennings (Deceased)* sits uncomfortably with the emphasis we would now wish to place on parental responsibility.

Family Law and Social Control

If the image of the family was narrow, so too was our understanding of the state's involvement with it. As with other areas of law we saw

---

[46] See Inheritance (Provision for Family and Dependants) Act 1975, s. 3(1)(d). An excellent discussion is Kate Green, 'The Englishwoman's Castle—Inheritance and Private Property Today' (1988) 51 *MLR* 187.

[47] N. 45 above, 542.   [48] *Ibid.* 543.   [49] *Idem.*

[50] *Ibid.* 548. And see S. M. Cretney, 'Reforms of Intestacy: The Best We Can Do?' (1995) 111 *LQR* 77, 96–7.

[51] Beginning in 1938 with the Inheritance (Family Provision) Act. This Act was the initiative of Eleanor Rathbone. Lord Astor had six times failed to get his bill passed. And see *Re Coventry (Deceased)* [1980] Ch. 461, 474.

the law's involvement—thus also the state's—only at the point of breakdown.[52] It is true that the law refrains from intervention in ongoing relationships, though this can be over-emphasized.[53] This relative abstinence is said to reflect the values we place on autonomy, integrity, and privacy.[54] But, in seeing the law as occupying a central hegemonic position, we overlook the ways in which the family is controlled other than by legal rules and principles. Order is not just constructed by law.

We have begun to notice this now with the transfer of child maintenance to a regulatory body (The Child Support Agency)[55] and with the shift in the Family Law Act of 1996 away from law and lawyers and the new emphasis on process and on alternative methods of family dispute resolution, in particular mediation. But, if we had not totally immersed ourselves in the law reports, we would have seen the subtle and less than subtle ways in which family interactions were socially controlled. The boundaries between what is intimate and what is public have become blurred.[56] Marriage has become 'medicalized',[57] subjected to expert knowledge, guidance, and intervention. This has grown out of the interventionist strategies which developed in the nineteenth century to modernize the 'backward' parts of society, the lower social orders.

There are two discourses on marriage. One emphasizes social control, the other autonomy. The social control discourse is dominated by a view of marriage as an institution involving constraints, clear and prescribed social roles, and penalties for those who break the conventions and norms governing marital relations. The autonomy discourse emphasizes choice and depicts

---

[52] See Otto Kahn-Freund, Editorial Introduction to John Eekelaar, *Family Security and Family Breakdown* (Harmondsworth, 1971), 7.

[53] e.g. see John Eekelaar, *Family Security and Family Breakdown* (Harmondsworth, 1971), 76 (see also his *Family Law and Social Policy* (London, 1978)). But see M. D. A. Freeman, 'Towards A Critical Theory of Family Law' (1985) 35 *CLP* 153.

[54] But see Carole Pateman, *The Disorder of Women* (Cambridge, 1989), chap. 6 on the public/private dichotomy and Freeman, n. 53, 166.

[55] See Child Support Act 1991 and Mavis Maclean, 'Child Support In The U.K.: Making The Move From Courts To Agency' (1994) 31 *Houston LR* 515.

[56] See Richard Sennett, *The Fall of Public Man* (Cambridge, 1974).

[57] See David Morgan, *The Family, Politics and Social Theory* (London, 1985). See also Christopher Lasch, *Haven In A Heartless World* (New York, 1977), referring to the 'new religion of health'.

the social actor as a rational person empowered to shape family life in accordance with his or her life projects. These discourses express 'ideal-types'; they are ends of a continuum, and marriage and those who work with marriage—institutions ranging from the courts to mediators and counsellors—operate in the space between these polar positions.

If we narrow our focus, as the discipline of family law has tended to do, to family legislation and to what the courts are doing, it is easy to conclude that the autonomy discourse is in the ascendancy. The removal of the matrimonial offence,[58] a relaxed attitude to whom one may marry[59] and now where,[60] greater tolerance of polygamy,[61] even now of polygamous ceremonies by those domiciled in this country,[62] more recognition of quasi-marital relationships,[63] can be seen as freedom-enhancing, humanistic measures giving people greater space to do their own thing. But, even looking just at legal developments, the picture is blurred. Freedom extends only so far: we cannot change our sex[64] (the law is firmly rooted in biological determinism); we cannot marry persons of the same sex as ourselves:[65] countries which allow registered partnerships

---

[58] By the Family Law Act 1996. See, generally, Ingleby, 'Matrimonial Breakdown and the Legal Process: The Limitations of No-Fault Divorce' (1989) 11 *Law and Policy* 1. On the US see Herbert Jacob, *Silent Revolution* (Chicago, Ill., 1988).

[59] See Marriage (Prohibited Degrees of Relationship) Act 1986. Australia has gone further, removing all restrictions based on affinity (see H. A. Finlay, 'Farewell To Affinity and the Calculus of Kinship' (1976) 5 *Univ. of Tas. LR* 16).

[60] Marriage Act 1994 (civil marriage may take place in 'approved premises' such as stately homes and hotels but not 'behind the bushes', *per* Gyles Brandreth MP, HC Debs., vol. 250, col. 1330).

[61] Matrimonial relief has been available since 1972 (see now Matrimonial Causes Act 1973, s. 47). On succession are *Chaudhry* v. *Chaudhry* [1976] Fam. 148.

[62] See Private International Law (Miscellaneous Provisions) Act 1995, ss. 5 and 6.

[63] See generally Michael D. A. Freeman and Christina M. Lyon, *Cohabitation Without Marriage* (Aldershot, 1983). The Scottish Law Commission has recommended that a former cohabitant should be able to apply to a court within a year of the end of cohabitation for financial provision (*Report on Family Law*, Scot. Law Com. No. 135 (1992)). There are precedents in New South Wales (De Facto Relationship Act 1984, s. 27) and Ontario (Family Law Act 1986, s. 26).

[64] A person's sex is fixed at birth: *Corbett* v. *Corbett* (*orse Ashley*) [1971] P 83. The accepted view is that *Corbett* still represents English law (see *R.* v. *Tan* [1981] QB 1053; *Rees* v. *United Kingdom* [1987] 2 FLR 111).

[65] See Matrimonial Causes Act 1973, s. 11(c): parties must be respectively male and female. In the US see the Defense of Marriage Act, Pub. L. No. 104–199, § 3(a), 110 Stat. 2419 (1996).

usually draw the line at same-sex marriages,[66] and a legitimate interpretation of the growth of cohabitation law would see it not so much as an enhancement of autonomy to shape relationships as the thrusting, Malvolio-like, of marriage on those who would wish to escape from it.[67]

If we broaden our focus, we witness not so much a withdrawal of social control but what Stanley Cohen has called its 'dispersal'.[68] An effect of the 'triumph of the therapeutic' has been to 'increase rather than decrease the *amount* of intervention . . . and, probably, to increase rather than decrease the total *number* who get into the system in the first place'.[69] Cohen was writing of the criminal justice system, but the parallels with family regulation are too close to ignore. A generation ago we were flushed with enthusiasm for a Family Court,[70] described as a ' "caring court" with social and welfare services integrated within it as part of a total team operation'.[71] At least then these services were projected as part of a court. Now it is accepted that the focus—and with it the values— should be a clinic.[72] We are told that mediation will not be compulsory, though in practice it will become so, particularly for those who will also require state-subsidized legal services, in effect

---

[66] See Danish Registered Partnership Act, No. 372 (1989), Norwegian Act on Registered Partnerships for Homosexual Couples, No. 40 (1993), Swedish Law Regarding Registered Partnerships (1994). See also the Hawaii case of *Baehr* v. *Lewin*, 852 P 2d 44, *clarified* 852 P 2d 74 (1993). See also William Eskridge, *The Case for Same-Sex Marriage* (New York, 1996) and David J. Chambers, 'What If?' (1996) 95 *Michigan LRev.* 447).

[67] See Freeman and Lyon, n. 63 above, 183 (see also Freeman and Lyon (1980) 130 *NLJ* 228). A formidable defence of this is Ruth Deech, 'The Case Against Legal Recognition of Cohabitation' in J. Eekelaar and S. Katz (eds.), *Marriage and Cohabitation in Contemporary Societies* (Toronto, 1980), 300.

[68] 'The Punitive City: Notes on The Dispersal of Social Control' (1979) 3 *Contemporary Crises* 339.

[69] *Ibid.* 347. See also S. Cohen, 'Prisons and The Future of Control Systems' in M. Fitzgerald *et al.* (eds.), *Welfare In Action* (London, 1977), 217.

[70] I questioned this in 'Questioning the Delegalization Movement in Family Law: Do We Really Want A Family Court?' in J. M. Eekelaar and S. N. Katz (eds.), *The Resolution of Family Conflict* (Toronto, 1984), 7.

[71] *Per* A. H. Manchester, 'Reform and The Family Court' (1975) 125 *NLJ* 984. The model then was the Finer report, *One-Parent Families*, Cmnd. 5629 (London, 1974), part IV, ss. 13 and 14. It is now accepted that the jurisdictional reforms of the Children Act 1989 are as much as we are likely to get.

[72] And see John Eekelaar, 'Family Justice: Ideal on Illusion?' (1995) 48 *CLP* 190, 193.

the poor (and particularly women) whose personal lives have long been more intensively policed than the rest of the population.

Family Law's Neglect of Family Issues

A third consequence of the way family law developed has been its continuing neglect of areas of life and social regulation, without an understanding of which it is not really possible to grasp what are generally agreed to be its central features. This is less so now of housing law or homelessness legislation or social security law than it was, but it remains the case with what is euphemistically called 'community care'.[73] Perhaps because family law has revolved around a sexual tie, it has been easy to overlook the elderly. In an ageing world, should not family law embrace family relationships with, and responsibilities towards, the elderly?[74] When, for example, will elder abuse (once distastefully called 'granny-bashing') be taken seriously?[75] When will family law acknowledge that this social problem comes within its horizons? The legislation is ahead of the textbook writers on this: elderly relatives come within a category of 'associated persons' and thus may use the domestic violence remedies in the new Family Law Act 1996[76] and, presumably, others may invoke remedies on their behalf.[77] The plight of elderly victims barely featured in the Law Commission Report from which this legislation derives, or in debates, discussions, or commentaries on the new legislation (including mine).[78] But that should not really surprise us: we have not as yet grappled with the problem.

Of greater significance is family law's neglect of community care.

---

[73] See National Health Service and Community Care Act 1990. Richard Titmuss referred to its 'comforting appellation' in *Commitment To Welfare* (London, 1968), 104.

[74] See John Eekelaar and David Pearl, *An Aging World-Dilemmas and Challenges for Law and Social Policy* (Oxford, 1989).

[75] See P. Decalmer and F. Glendenning, *The Mistreatment of Elderly People* (2nd edn.) (London, 1997), and B. Penhale, 'The Abuse of Elderly People: Considerations For Practice' (1993) 23 *British Journal of Social Work* 95, where similarities and differences with child abuse are discussed. On the gendered nature of elder abuse see Simon Biggs, 'A Family Concern' (1996) 47 *Critical Social Policy* 63.

[76] See s. 63(3)(c) and (d).   [77] Family Law Act 1996, s. 60.

[78] It is mentioned in the Law Commission report. See *Domestic Violence and The Occupation of The Family Home* (London, 1992), para. 3.8.

Community care could not be more inappropriately labelled. It is care by the family, which means disproportionately care by women.[79] It raises important questions which family law has barely begun to address. If the state is imposing responsibility for caring for the elderly on to daughters and daughters-in-law, is it also giving them any status? It has taken us long enough to move from parental rights to parental responsibility.[80] Ought we to consider the rights and responsibilities involved in this caring relationship? It is perhaps a relationship best understood by reference to, or at least by analogy with, the trust relationship. This may fit better here than it does with the parent–child relationship, which some have wished to characterize in terms of a trust model.[81] The implications of extending a woman's homecaring role, particularly if she has to give up work (again), similarly needs exposing. In terms of property interests and financial provision, should any significance be attached to whose parent (his or hers) she is looking after? (It is to be assumed that it is a contribution towards the welfare of the family,[82] but this is to give 'family' a broader meaning than it usually has). More broadly, the issue of community care raises all sorts of issues about state regulation and social control, as social workers become increasingly involved with 'normal' as opposed to deviant families, traditionally their clientèle. Could they yet become embroiled in the lives of 'normal' families outside this context? Is the final triumph of a therapeutic state in sight?

---

[79] See J. Finch and D. Groves, 'Community Care and the Family: A Case For Equal Opportunities?' (1980) 9 *Journal of Social Policy* 487; C. Ungerson, *Policy is Personal: Sex, Gender and Informal Care* (London, 1987); J. Lewis and B. Meredith, *Daughters Who Care* (London, 1988).

[80] Parental responsibility was only encoded into English law in 1989 with the Children Act 1989, ss. 2 and 3. It did, of course, take much longer to recognize the authority of the mother: this was encoded in the Guardianship Act 1973, after attempts to achieve this in 1925 failed (on this see S. M. Cretney, 'What Will The Women Want Next?' (1996) 112 *LQR* 110, and J. Brophy, 'Parental Rights and Children's Welfare' (1982) 10 *Int. J of Soc. L* 149).

[81] See C. Beck *et al.*, 'The Rights of Children: A Trust Model' (1978) 46 *Fordham L Rev.* 669 and the criticisms of Chris Barton and Gillian Douglas, *Law and Parenthood* (London, 1995), 22–8. See also John Eekelaar, 'Are Parents Morally Obliged To Care For Their Children?' (1991) 11 *OJLS* 51.

[82] Matrimonial Causes Act 1973, s. 25(2)(f). And see Julia Twigg, 'Carers, Families, Relatives: Socio-Legal Conceptions of Care-giving Relationships' (1994) *JSWFL* 279.

Family Law and Opinion

In Dicey's view law was based on opinion.[83] In *Law and Public Opinion in England during the Nineteenth Century* he quotes David Hume to the effect that 'the governors have nothing to support them but opinion' of the governed.[84] He also believed, somewhat paradoxically, that legislation could 'foster or create law-making opinion'.[85] He saw the law then both as secondary, taking its moral legitimacy from society, and as a primary force with potential for social engineering. Later writers[86] have shown that law is better able to effect social change in so-called 'instrumental', or morally neutral, areas of life than with so-called 'expressive' activities, of which family living is the quintessential example. Dicey recognized this: 'changes in the law which affect family life always offend the natural conservatism of ordinary citizens'.[87] But he also recognized—and was right to do so—the complex inter-relationship of law and opinion in the process of family law reform.

He uses two examples, the divorce reform of 1857[88] and the married women's property legislation of 1870–93.[89] Of the first divorce legislation he says, 'on the face of it [it] did no more than increase the facilities for obtaining divorce'. However:

in reality [it] gave national sanction to the contractual view of marriage, and propagated the belief that the marriage contract, like every other agreement, ought to be capable of dissolution when it fails to attain its end. This Act and the feelings it fostered are closely related to the Married Women's Property Acts 1870–1893.

Nor, Dicey adds:

can any one doubt that these enactments have in their turn given strength to the belief that women ought, in the eye of the law, to stand substantially

---

[83] *Law and Public Opinion in England During The Nineteenth Century* (2nd edn.) (London, 1914, originally published in 1905), 1.

[84] *Ibid.* 2 (see also 14).   [85] *Ibid.* 41.

[86] e.g. Y. Dror, 'Law and Social Change' (1959) 33 *Tulane LR* 787; G. J. Massell, 'Law as An Instrument of Revolutionary Change In a Traditional Milieu' (1968) 2 *Law and Society Review* 179.   [87] N. 83 above, 385.

[88] Matrimonial Causes Act 1857.

[89] One of the earliest statements of the need for reform is Eliza Lynn's essay 'One Of Our Legal Fictions', 9 *Household Words* 260 (Apr. 1854). In 1854 also Barbara Leigh Smith published 'A Brief Summary of The Law Concerning Women' (London, 1854).

on an equality with men, and have encouraged legislation tending to produce such equality. In this matter laws have deeply affected not only the legislative but also the social opinion of the country as to the position of women.[90]

And he concludes, 'law and opinion are here so intermixed that it is difficult to say whether opinion has done most to produce legislation or laws to create a state of legislative opinion'.[91] It is striking that Dicey should have seen the 1857 reform as a 'triumph of individual liberalism'[92] for it was legislation which upheld the interests of the community and of Christian morality. It was, further, censorious and discriminatory. It is, we would think, to the reform of 1969[93] that we should look to find the beginnings of a divorce law which embodies individualistic rather than collectivist ideology. And the dichotomy ill-suits the latest divorce legislation[94] which straddles the two.

Of married women's property legislation Dicey writes at length. Consistent with his thesis that law-forming opinion emerges from the ideas of great thinkers,[95] he attaches considerable importance to John Stuart Mill whose 'authority among the educated youth of England was greater than may appear credible to the present generation'.[96] Dicey is amazed at the speed with which married women's property rights developed in English law. His explanation was that rather than try to work any 'sudden revolution' in the law, Parliament had been content to engage in 'judicial legislation', that is, 'the reproduction in statutory shape of rules originally established by the courts'.[97] Although 'the simpler mode of proceeding was to enact . . . that a married woman should, as regards her property

---

[90] N. 83 above, 43–4.   [91] *Ibid.* 44.

[92] *Ibid.* 347. But in the 'Introduction To The Second Edition' Dicey uses divorce reform as an example of the contrast between the 'individualistic, or democratic, and the socialistic view of life' (see lxxix). In Dicey's terms Lord Mackay would be 'socialistic'!

[93] The Divorce Reform Act 1969 (if only in the provision allowing divorce on the fact of five years' separation: s.2(i)(e)).

[94] The Family Law Act 1996. The new law is individualistic in that ultimately s/he who wants a divorce will almost invariably get one irrespective of the wishes of the other: the hurdles erected in the way of this goal, together with much of the language of the law, particularly that embodied in its principles, suggest valorization of the community over the individual.

[95] N. 83 above, 21–6.

[96] *Ibid.* 386 (see also 22, where Mill's *On Liberty* is quoted to the effect that 'wise' 'noble' things come from 'individuals').   [97] *Ibid.* 362.

and rights or liabilities connected with property, stand on the same footing as an unmarried woman',[98] Parliament instead made the property of a married woman 'her "separate property" in the technical sense which that term had acquired in the Courts of Equity'.[99] At long last the procedures that were 'framed for the daughters of the rich, have been extended to the daughters of the poor'.[100] This analysis is interesting but, like many accounts by lawyers, when they venture into the field of the sociology of law creation, far from accurate. It is an explanation of legal development but it is separated off from the political context and hence its political meaning. What is missing is an understanding of the existence of an alternative vision of what the law governing married women's property should be. And this was found in the feminists who campaigned for the original legislation in 1868: Lydia Becker, Ursula and Jacob Bright, Elizabeth Wolstenholme Elmy (all of whom were ignored by Dicey[101]), and John Stuart Mill.[102] The principle of the original bill was that with respect to her property a married woman should be able to act as a feme sole. The feminist reformers sought legal equality between husband and wife: they got an extension to all women of the protection and special status that the few wives with 'separate property' had long enjoyed.

These examples draw attention not only to the complexity of the inter-relationship between law and opinion, and do so from a historical distance, but they also raise many questions about law creation: about how a seemingly objective condition becomes a social problem when it was not one previously,[103] about moral entrepreneurship[104] and definition, about the impact of different interest groups and different ideologies,[105] about the relationship of courts and legislatures.

---

[98] *Ibid.* 387.   [99] *Ibid.* 387–8.   [100] *Ibid.* 395.

[101] But see Mary Lyndon Shanley, *Feminism, Marriage and the Law In Victorian England* (Princeton, NJ, 1989). On these feminist thinkers see Barbara Caine, *Victorian Feminists* (New York, 1992).

[102] Dicey lauds Mill, attributing the earliest married women's property legislation in 1870 to his 'influence' (n. 83 above, 386). Dicey underestimates the importance of the 1870 Act: he overlooks the fact that for the bulk of women 'earnings' were more significant than 'property'.

[103] See Willard Waller, 'Social Problems and the Mores' (1936) 1 *American Sociological Review* 922.

[104] On which see Howard S. Becker, *Outsiders* (New York, 1963), 147.

[105] See William J. Chambliss and Marjorie S. Katz, *Making Law* (Bloomington Ind., 1993).

As a generalization it would be true to say that in the area of family regulation it is social forces which have shaped and altered law, rather than the reverse. But this does not tell us much. Certainly, this was the case with the first adoption legislation in 1926, with attempts at informal adoptions long antedating long-delayed legislation.[106] But this is less so in other areas concerned with the status of children, in particular in relation to children born outside marriage where even a proposal to allow for legitimation by subsequent marriage met resistance as late as 1920.[107] The growth of a law of cohabitation since the 1970s is clearly a response to the upsurge in alternative living arrangements and the perceived need to do justice between such partners:[108] the contrast between what the Court of Appeal was saying in 1959[109] and in the cluster of cases in the early 1970s beginning with *Cooke* v. *Head* could not be stronger. But the treatment of cohabitation as if it were marriage is not applied consistently through National Insurance, the tax system, or the maintenance regime.[110]

The courts are even prepared to accept that words can change their meaning in accordance with common and accepted parlance. Thus, in 1975 the Court of Appeal had no difficulty in construing 'member' of the tenant's family to include a woman who had lived with the deceased tenant for twenty-one years, though Parliament in passing the original legislation would not have had such a person within its contemplation.[111] What society understood as 'family', not what the legislature meant by 'family' more than fifty years earlier, was the determining consideration.[112] When, in the late 1940s, the House of Lords decided that a marriage could be consummated despite the use of a condom, and despite the Book of

---

[106] Though the acceptance by the state of adoption is both co-optation and regulation.

[107] The first Bill sponsored by the National Council for the Unmarried Mother And Her Child (founded in 1918) was introduced by Neville Chamberlain in 1920 and would have allowed for legitimation, as well as increasing the maximum affiliation payment and providing officers to collect such payments (see Jenny Teichman, *Illegitimacy* (Oxford, 1982), 162–4).

[108] It is largely judge-made law. See further Freeman and Lyon, n. 63 above.

[109] In *Diwell* v. *Farnes* [1959] 2 All ER 379.

[110] Or in family law generally: see e.g. *Burns* v. *Burns* [1984] Ch. 317.

[111] See *Dyson Holidays* v. *Fox* [1976] QB 503.

[112] Increase of Rent and Mortgage Interest (Restrictions) Act 1920, s. 12(1)(g).

Common Prayer's admonition about marriage being about pro-creation of children, it did much the same thing, putting a concept into the context of common practice.[113] The courts in both these cases were, it may be thought, right. But was the Court of Appeal also right to conclude that a woman who lived in council accommodation with another woman, a secured tenant, and who shared a 'committed, monogamous, homosexual relationship' with her was not a 'member of the tenant's family'?[114] Their decision accorded with common usage (and prejudice): was this an occasion on which the courts should have taken a lead? Is it within the judicial province even to contemplate doing so?[115]

To attribute a change and development in family law to social forces does not advance our understanding by much and is, above all, simplistic. There can be few areas of life upon which there is less consensus. As a result family law reform is commonly controversial and contested. The major divorce reforms this century (in 1923, 1937, 1969, and 1996) have all encountered opposition. The reforms of 1937—though not the three-year bar on divorce—had been recommended by a Royal Commission as long ago as 1912.[116] At least the reforms of 1969 and 1996 were immune from organized clerical opposition (indeed, the Church acted as a catalyst for reform in 1969).[117] The passage of the latest Act was so stormy that a government eager not to lose its 'pro-family' divorce measure was forced into concessions on a variety of matters including pension-splitting.[118]

---

[113] In *Baxter* v. *Baxter* [1948] AC 274.

[114] See *Harrogate BC* v. *Simpson* [1986] 2 FLR 91.

[115] The House of Lords in *R* v. *R* [1992] 1 AC 599 thought it could remove the very long-standing marital rape immunity, and rejected what had existed for more than 300 years because of social change ('marriage is in modern times . . . a partnership of equals').

[116] Royal Commission On Divorce and Matrimonial Causes (Cd. 6478) (the Gorell report) (London, 1912).

[117] See Archbishop of Canterbury Group, *Putting Asunder: A Divorce Law For Contemporary Society* (London, 1966): this was a major source of the Divorce Reform Act 1969. Contemporaneously, the Archbishop of Canterbury told the House of Lords that the matrimonial offence existed for historical reasons and not 'for any reasons of Divine necessity' (HL Debs., vol. 278, col. 271).

[118] On pension splitting see s. 16, the result of a government defeat in the House of Lords (see HL Debs., vol. 569, cols. 1610–35). In the House of Commons it was made 'crystal clear' that the Family Law Bill would not pass without this provision being added.

Change in law is a complex subject. Changes can be subtle and not so subtle. These can be changes in function without change in form with tenacity of conceptual thinking cloaking the uses to which those concepts are put.[119] Major changes can result from seemingly minor alterations in process: the introduction of the 'special procedure' in 1973 may have had greater impact on the reform of divorce than the Divorce Reform Act in 1969, but it was not even debated in Parliament and attracted little interest and less controversy.[120] The growth of legal aid and its subsequent near-withdrawal may have had greater effects on divorce than any alterations in grounds or judicial interpretations.[121]

It is common to talk about law and social change in terms of lag. Dicey was one of the first to attempt to explain why the law was often in arrears of social change, and critics are apt to seize upon the perceived gap between law and society and attribute this to the law's 'natural' conservatism. The American sociologist Ogburn built a theory around 'lag', what he called 'cultural lag'.[122] He tried to show how legal culture could hang over after material conditions had changed: one example he gave was the doctrine of common employment and industrial world in which it developed.[123] But resistance to change can only be characterized as 'lag' where there is one 'true' definition of a problem and one, and only one, 'true' solution.[124] The legal process is part of the total culture and in the normal case can only, and will, respond to demands levelled at it.

There are areas concerned with family regulation where it is difficult to believe that there is more than one 'true' solution. The 1923 divorce reform, giving wives the same rights as husbands, is such an example—at least from our perspective, though it was not so perceived then.[125] The removal of a wife's domicile of

---

[119] See Karl Renner, *The Institutions of Private Law and Their Social Functions* (London, 1949).

[120] See P. T. O'Neill, 'Divorce: A Judicial or An Administrative Process?' (1974) 4 *Family Law* 71.

[121] See C. Gibson, 'The Effect of Legal Aid on Divorce In England and Wales' (1971) 1 *Family Law* 90, 122.

[122] See W. G. Ogburn, *Social Change With Respect To Culture and Original Nature* (New York, 1950).   [123] *Ibid.* 236.

[124] Lawrence Friedman and Jack Ladinsky, 'Social Change and The Law of Industrial Accidents' (1967) 67 *Columbia LR* 50.

[125] It was the fourth attempt at reform since the ending of the War. It gained support from the fact that married women had recently been granted the vote: see Lawrence Stone, *Road To Divorce: England 1530–1987* (Oxford, 1990), 394–6.

dependency[126] (Lord Denning called it the 'last barbarous relic of a wife' servitude'[127]) is another. The final extirpation, by judicial[128] and legislative reform,[129] of the marital rape immunity is perhaps a third example, but then we are reminded that the Criminal Law Revision Committee, as recently as 1984, recommended by a majority to retain the immunity in all cases except where the parties were living apart.[130]

These cases—and of course there are others—are the exception. Today, as before, across a range of family issues there is little or no consensus. The new divorce law remains controversial (should the period for reflection and consideration be longer where there are children of the family under sixteen?[131] Should there be no circumstances in which the basic waiting period can be reduced?[132] Why a waiting period at all when reflection and consideration have already taken place? Why, some will still say, is adultery not a ground for divorce?). Financial provision remains controversial (for example, many would think its assessment ought to take greater account of matrimonial misconduct.)[133] The rights of first and reconstituted families remains contentious: the controversies ignited by the Child Support Act in 1991 have not died away despite reforms.[134] The attitude the law should adopt towards those who live together outside marriage continues to excite passions, as witnessed by the angry, at times irrational, response to the domestic

---

[126] By the Domicile and Matrimonial Proceedings Act 1973.

[127] In *Gray* v. *Formosa* [1963] P 259, 267.

[128] See n. 115. This withstood challenge in the European Court of Human Rights: see *CR* v. *United Kingdom* [1996] 1 FLR 434.

[129] In the Criminal Justice and Public Order Act 1994, s. 142.

[130] *Sexual Offences* (Cmnd. 9213) (London, 1984).

[131] The Law Commission rejected the idea that the period should be longer if there were children (see *The Ground for Divorce*, Law Com. No. 192, para. 28). Cf. s. 7(11), (13), but note s. 7(12)(b).

[132] It cannot be reduced in any circumstances: the government adamantly resisted amendments to allow for abridgement (see HL Debs., vol. 568, col. 961; vol. 570, col. 18).

[133] This may be taken into account if in the opinion of the court it would be 'inequitable to disregard it' (Matrimonial Causes Act 1973, s. 25(2)(g), as amended by the Family Law Act 1996, Sched. 8, para. 8(3)(b)). It is now emphasized that conduct may be taken into account whatever its nature, though in most cases where it has been taken into account it has been extreme (e.g. *Evans* v. *Evans* [1989] 1 FLR 351; *H* v. *H* [1994] 2 FLR 801; *A* v. *A* [1995] 1 FLR 345: cf. *F* v. *F* [1996] 1 FLR 863).

[134] See M. Horton, 'Improving Child Support—A Missed Opportunity' (1995) 7 *CFLQ* 26.

violence bill in 1995,[135] and the eccentric provision in the Family Law Act 1996 stating as a normative proposition the 'fact' that couples who live together outside marriage have not shown the 'commitment' that is involved in marriage.[136]

On child law issues, similarly, the consensus, where it exists, is thin. There is agreement that child abuse is a 'bad thing', but not upon what constitutes child abuse.[137] There is a 'spectrum of abuse' and an 'index of harm'; that much is acknowledged.[138] But there is a belief among some, not only the leading thinkers Goldstein, Freud and Solnit, that sexual abuse and psychological and emotional abuse are too vague and value-laden to warrant state intrusion.[139] There is even less consensus on corporal chastisement by parents, though a number of countries have followed Sweden's lead and outlawed the practice.[140] It might have been thought that legislation to ban corporal punishment in state schools[141] would have had the effect of fostering or creating law-making opinion as regards the hitting of children by parents, but it has not done so. On adoption too there are big differences, so much so that the then government abandoned its plans to implement adoption reform in the 1996–7 session fearing it would provoke dissent on race and sexual orientation issues.[142] The issue of 'open' adoption also divides, including in constituencies within the child welfare movement.[143]

[135] See Teresa Gorman, 'No Backbenchers in the Bedroom', *Independent*, 7 Nov. 1995.   [136] See Family Law Act 1996, s. 41(2).

[137] *Working Together* (London, 1991) lists four categories for the register and for statistical purposes (neglect, physical injury, sexual abuse—which was not recognized officially in 1980—and emotional abuse). Domestic violence is not included (on which see Audrey Mullender and Rebecca Morley, *Children Living With Domestic Violence* (London, 1994)).

[138] *Per* Ward LJ in *Re B* [1990] 2 FLR 317.

[139] See Joseph Goldstein, Albert J. Solnit, Sonja Goldstein and Anna Freud, *The Best Interests of the Child* (New York, 1996), 112, 122. See the critique by Michael Freeman, 'The Best Interests of the Child?' (1997) 11 *Int. J. of Law, Policy and the Family* 360.

[140] Sweden was the first country to do so (in 1979): others to follow are Finland (1983), Norway (1987), Austria (1989), and Cyprus (1994).

[141] Education (No. 2) Act 1986, largely a response to *Campbell and Cosans* v. *United Kingdom* (1982) 4 EHRR 293.

[142] See *Adoption—A Service for Children* (London, 1996), containing a consultative Adoption Bill.

[143] See Murray Ryburn, *Open Adoption: Research, Theory and Practice* (Aldershot, 1994). Secrecy has a relatively short history (it dates from 1949 in England).

The development of family law does reflect the felt necessities of powerful interest groups, both their ability to construct law to further their meanings and interests and their ability to keep alternative agendas out.[144] Laws are arenas for the contestation of meaning. Those with the power to impose their meanings, and block out alternative visions/revisions, can present these meanings as more than consensual, as natural. There is no better example than the notorious section of the Local Government Act 1988 (section 28) which defined lesbian and gay relationships as 'pretended families'.[145] Such imagery is calculated to defuse conflict: who can believe in 'pretended' as opposed (presumably) to real families? Just as, in relation to the recent campaign, it would be difficult to find good reasons to object to 'family values' if one had no knowledge of the meanings packed into this symbol of political legitimation.[146]

The pivot for change may seem to be outside this structure of power. Often the *fons et origo* has been scandal, the Dennis O'Neill case leading to the Children Act in 1948,[147] the death of Maria Colwell being instrumental in helping to forge the Children Act of 1975,[148] the sex abuse explosion in Cleveland in 1987 becoming an effective source of the Children Act in 1989;[149] the birth of 'Baby Cotton' (as a result of supposedly the first commercial surrogate pregnancy) providing the spark for the Surrogacy Arrangements Act of 1985.[150] Sometimes there has been moral panic over real folk devils; at other times over fictive ones (for example, the large

---

[144] See Alison Diduck, 'The Unmodified Family: The Child Support Act and the Construction of Legal Subjects' (1995) 22 *Journal of Law and Society* 527.

[145] See Jeffrey Weeks, 'Pretended Family Relationships' in David Clark (ed.), *Marriage, Domestic Life and Social Change* (London, 1991), chap. 9.

[146] See as examples and for contrast David Willetts, *The Family* (London, n.d.); Patricia Hewitt and Penelope Leach, *Social Justice, Children and Families* (London, 1993). See also Kate Marshall, *Moral Panics and Victorian Values* (London, 1986).

[147] See the Monckton report (Cmd. 6636, London, 1945). Interesting insights may be found in Nigel Middleton, *When Family Failed* (London, 1970).

[148] On which see Nigel Parton, *The Politics of Child Abuse* (Basingstoke, 1985), chap. 4. For the growth of understanding in the US see Barbara J. Nelson, *Making An Issue of Child Abuse* (Chicago, Ill., 1984) and Lela B. Costin, Howard J. Karger and David Stoesz, *The Politics of Child Abuse in America* (New York, 1996).

[149] On which see M. D. A. Freeman, 'Cleveland, Butler-Sloss and Beyond' (1989) 42 *CLP* 85.

[150] On which see M. D. A. Freeman, After Warnock—Whither The Law' (1986) 39 *CLP* 33.

number of unmarried women queuing up for *in vitro* fertilization that led to the passing of section 13(5) of the Human Fertilisation and Embryology Act in 1990 which requires that a woman shall not be provided with treatment services unless account has been taken of the welfare of any child who may be born as a result of the treatment (including the need of that child for a father)).[151]

Sometimes, as Dicey wrote, change can be attributed to the thinking of 'some one man of originality or genius'[152] (he had in mind Adam Smith or Jeremy Bentham). In family law it is difficult to construct such a pantheon; John Stuart Mill and Harriet Taylor perhaps;[153] the women's suffrage movement;[154] the modern feminist movement;[155] Goldstein, Freud and Solnit.[156] All these persons (and movements) have influenced the development of family law, but often their ideas have been redefined to fit goals or programmes or have been used piecemeal (thus Goldstein, Freud and Solnit's 'psychological parent' found its way into the Children Act 1975 when permanency planning was on the agenda,[157] together with a 'child's sense of time',[158] though this was not understood by the legislature,[159] and the 'least detrimental alternative'[160] is encoded into the 1989 legislation, where there is less of an emphasis on psychological parenthood).[161]

---

[151] See Gillian Douglas, 'Assisted Reproduction and the Welfare of the Child' (1993) 46 *CLP* 53.

[152] N. 83 above, 22.

[153] See Barbara Caine, 'John Stuart Mill and the English Women's Movement' [1978] *Historical Studies* 52.

[154] See Sandra Holton, *Feminism and Democracy: Women's Suffrage and Reform Politics in Britain 1900–1918* (Cambridge, 1986); Jill Liddington and Jill Norris, *One Hand Tied Behind Us: The Rise of the Women's Suffrage Movement* (London, 1978).

[155] A good discussion is Dale Spender, *Women of Ideas And What Men Have Done To Them from Aphra Behn to Adrienne Rich* (London, 1983).

[156] See n. 139 above, and see on their influence Peggy C. Davis, ' "There Is a Book Out . . .": An Analysis of Judicial Absorption of Legislative Facts' (1987) 100 *Harvard LR* 1539.

[157] On which see June Thoburn, Anne Murdoch, and Alison O'Brien, *Permanence in Child Care* (Oxford, 1986).

[158] See n. 139 above, 41–5.

[159] See the time limit provisions of the Children Act 1975 (ss. 29, 56, 57) which take no account of the age of the child. The Children Act 1989 is more conscious of this: see s. 1(2) and the time-tabling provisions in ss. 11 and 32.

[160] See n. 139 above, 50–61.

[161] See Children Act 1989 s. 1(5).

The Family Today

To understand current debates about the family, the 'back to basics' campaign, the emphasis on family values, the concern with responsible reproduction and parenthood, the panic about divorce as well as about cohabitation and illegitimacy, some facts have to be established.

When this century opened there were 600 divorce petitions in its first year. The century has witnessed 'the emancipation of divorce'. As Gibson says:

Marriages in Victorian times were regulated by a morally and socially divisive system which sanctioned separation but harshly restricted divorce. Only a combination of statistical ignorance, historical incomprehension and legal disregard could set the 600 petitions of 1900 against some 189,000 petitions in 1992 as evidence of earlier family permanency.[162]

Until the First World War divorce was largely confined to the middle and upper classes: changes in aid given to poor petitioners in 1914, together with the effects of the war, produced an increase in the divorce rate after 1918.[163] Even so, the rate was under one per 1,000 of the married population until the Second World War. It was 5.9 in 1971. It is now 13.1 (a decline from a peak of 13.7 in 1992). Such a rate, if it continues at the 1987 divorce level and pattern, suggests that about 37 per cent of newly formed marriages will ultimately end in divorce.[164] Almost three million children under 16 experienced parental divorce in the twenty years between 1971 and 1990.[165] It is probable that if trends continue, one in four children will have first-hand knowledge of parental divorce before

---

[162] 'Contemporary Divorce and Changing Family Patterns' in Michael Freeman (ed.), *Divorce: Where Next?* (Aldershot, 1996), 9. A good example of moral regulation is the warning in *Fisher* v. *Fisher* (1861) 2 Sw. & Tr. 410 that a petitioning wife would receive no more maintenance that was necessary for her support, and that it should be assessed on a more moderate basis than for alimony in cases of judicial separation.

[163] See Jane Lewis, *Women In England 1870–1950* (Hemel Hempstead, 1984). In France in 1891, where the assistance to the poor to undertake litigation was more generous, there were 13 times more divorce petitions per 1,000 marriages than in England.

[164] See J. Haskey, 'Current Prospects for the Proportion of Marriages Ending In Divorce' (1989) 55 *Population Trends* 34.

[165] See Gibson, n. 162 above, 15.

they reach the school-leaving age.[166] Fewer divorcing couples have dependent children than was the case in 1970 (57 per cent in 1992, compared to 62 per cent in 1970); even so the annual number of dependent children involved in divorce has more than doubled to some 168,000 in 1992 as a consequence of the increase in the number of divorces.[167]

Only Denmark of Western European countries has a higher divorce rate than England.[168] However, the rate of increase in divorce numbers between 1970 and 1989 is more than twice as high as Denmark (1.7 as opposed to 0.8[169]), suggesting that it is likely that we will soon overtake Denmark and become Western Europe's divorce capital. The median duration of marriage at divorce is about 9½ years.[170] But, if the trend is observed, this time span is deceptively high. Kiernan and Wicks noted in 1990 that 10 per cent of couples who married in 1951 had divorced by their twenty-fifth wedding anniversary; for those marrying in 1961 10 per cent had divorced by their twelfth wedding anniversary, whilst amongst those marrying in 1971 and 1981 the analogous durations of marriage were 6 and 4.5 years.[171]

The number of persons marrying is also in decline, though England still has the second highest marriage rate (6.8 per 1,000 per year of the eligible population) of countries in Western Europe.[172] The peak year for marriage was 1971. The median age for marriage then was 24.6 for men and 22.6 for women, two years

---

[166] See A. Cherlin, *Marriage, Divorce, Remarriage* (Cambridge, Mass., 1992), 26. W. J. Goode, *World Changes In Divorce Patterns* (New Haven, Conn., 1993) believes it may be twice this proportion.

[167] N. 162 above, Table 2.2.

[168] Central Statistical Office, *Social Trends* (London, 1993). Incidence is higher in the US (see J. Goldthorpe, *Family Life In Western Societies* (Cambridge, 1987)). It was 21 per 1,000 in 1991. On Canada and Australia see Lorraine Fox Harding, *Family, State and Social Policy* (Basingstoke, 1996), 58.

[169] N. 162 above, Table 2.6.

[170] This is based on the length of time a marriage has existed as a legal entity. The evidence is that about a third of divorcing couples separate within five years of marrying. See Office of Population, Censuses and Surveys, *Marriage and Divorce* (London, 1992). See also B. Thornes and J. Collard, *Who Divorces?* (London, 1979) and Gibson, n. 1 above, 143–5.

[171] *Family Change and Future Policy* (London, 1990), 13.

[172] It is higher only in Portugal. In 1994 there was more than one divorce for every two marriages (158,200 divorces and 291,100 marriages): see *Population Trends* No. 85 (London, 1996).

less than it had been in 1951.[173] The sex ratio was more even (in the first half of this century and in the last century women outnumbered men). There was increasing economic prosperity and close to full (male) employment. Couples were thus enabled to marry and begin families earlier with the resources to do so and a reasonable prospect of a secure economic future.

Since 1971 the median age for marriage has risen: by 1991 it was well over 26 for men and well over 24 for women.[174] The fall in first marriage rates after 1970 was largely due to people under 25: the marriage rate declined steeply for men and even more dramatically for women. Teenage marriage rates also fell.[175] The trend has changed the prediction of those ever marrying/never marrying. According to the Family Policy Studies Centre, 'if present marriage rates continue, then the expected proportions of men and women married by age 50 would be around 77% for men and 78% for women, compared with 93% of women and 96% of men in 1971'.[176] The percentage of those marrying in church has also declined.[177] The increase in civil marriage is connected with the rise in the number of second and subsequent marriages,[178] and the general secularization of society. But it also masks a change in the understanding and meaning of marriage: there has been an ideological shift in which marriage is seen more as a terminable contract rather than a life-long and religiously sanctioned commitment. Marriage has become what Giddens refers to as a 'pure relationship', that is 'a social relation which is internally reverential, that is, depends fundamentally on satisfactions or rewards generic to

---

[173] See B. J. Elliot, 'Demographic Trends In Domestic Life 1945–1987' in D. Clark (ed.), *Marriage, Domestic Life and Social Change* (London, 1991).

[174] Office for Population, Censuses and Surveys, *Marriage and Divorce Statistics*, Series FM No. 19 (London, 1991).

[175] N. 173 above, 88 (in 1970 one in 10 teenage women and one in 40 teenage men were married: in 1987 it was one in 40 women, and one in 200 men).

[176] Fact Sheet: The Family Today; One Parent Families No. 3 (London, 1991), 1. But *Social Trends* No. 27 (London, 1997) projects that by 2020 the population of those over 16 who are married will fall to 49%.

[177] 51% of marriages were in register offices and 32% in Anglican churches in 1993 (see *Population Trends*, No. 80 (London, 1995). The proportion of civil marriages is likely to increase with the Marriage Act 1994.

[178] More than one-third of marriages are remarriages for one or both spouses. In the perspective of history this is not surprising, though in the 18th century, when the proportion was similar, most first marriages had ended on death (see L. Stone, *The Family, Sex and Marriage in England 1500–1800* (Harmondsworth, 1977).

that relation itself'.[179] It has freed itself from the traditional influences which used to shape it, such as tradition, religious dogma, and kin bargaining. The companionate, rather than the institutional, marriage is part of this quest for self-identity and self-fulfilment.[180] Other unions, gay ones for example, are part of this same quest, as is divorce, with the opportunity this presents to discover diverse family forms.

Companionate marriage, both as ideal and ideology, may have contributed to divorce, raising expectations, increasing anger and frustration, fuelling a cause of disappointment. Changes in attitudes towards marriage (and divorce) have had their effect also on counsellors, therapists, and others concerned with marriage guidance, so that there has been a shift from adopting a social control stance, where the emphasis was on marriage-saving, to one of social support, where the stress is on individual problem-solving.[181] And, where once marriage guidance took a distinctly moral Christian viewpoint, it is now less judgmental and more appreciative of the needs of those who seek its help.[182] Sometimes, in reading the debates on the Family Law Act 1996 one had to wonder whether our legislators were aware of this shift in role: certainly, they often acted as if the clock could be turned back. The 'right' sees divorce as a societal rather than an individual problem, as a problem of social order and welfare expenditure. There are those on the 'right' who are prepared to argue that the welfare benefits system should be used to coerce people into remaining married, even into getting married in the first place.[183]

It also deplores the rise in the number of people living together outside marriage. Cohabitation is common today as, of course, it was in the past when the line between marriage and cohabitation

---

[179] *Modernity and Self-Identity* (Cambridge, 1991), 244. See also Janet Finch and David Morgan, 'Marriage in the 1980s: A New Sense of Realism?' in n. 173, 55.
[180] See Janet Finch and Penny Summerfield, 'Social Reconstruction and the Emergence of the Companionate Marriage, 1945–1959' in n. 173, 7. See also M. Young and P. Wilmott, *The Symmetrical Family* (London, 1973).
[181] See Jane Lewis, David Clark, and David Morgan, *Whom God Hath Joined Together: The Work of Marriage Guidance* (London, 1992).
[182] The writings of Herbert Gray and Dr E. F. Griffith, discussed by Jane Lewis in n. 181, chap. 2 capture the flavour of early marriage guidance, including its association with the eugenics movement.
[183] eg. Patricia Morgan, *Farewell To The Family: Public Policy and Family Breakdown in Britain and the USA* (London, 1995).

was not clear.[184] We tend to think of marriage and cohabitation as discrete entities: our ancestors saw them, perhaps more accurately, as part of a social continuum. Cohabitation was not common in the 'permissive' 1960s. Only 2 per cent of women marrying before the age of 30 (both bride and groom being single) in the period 1965–9 had lived with their husbands before marriage. For those marrying in the period 1985–9 the proportion had risen to almost half (47 per cent).[185] Fewer than one in ten of those under 40 regard living together outside marriage as morally wrong.[186] Over a half of all men (55 per cent) and women (58 per cent) aged 25–29 report having lived in a extra-marital relationship.[187] It is estimated that in 1992 there were 1.3 million cohabiting couples.[188]

Cohabitation is no more stable than marriage, and is probably less so. Cohabitations tend to be short-lived, after which they either break up or are transformed into marriages. There is a finding[189] that divorce is more probable if the couple cohabits first: married couples who had cohabited were about 60 per cent more likely to have divorced or separated within fifteen years than those who had not cohabited. Whether such people by cohabiting indicated a weaker commitment to marriage or whether it is that cohabitation is practised more by less conventional people who are also for that reason more willing to divorce is not known. Nor, I suspect, would the disparity look as great if the years spent cohabiting were included in the calculation of the length of the marriage.

People are having children also outside both marriage and cohabitation. Although the law does not distinguish births within a

---

[184] See Phillipe Ariès, 'Marriage' (1980) 2 *London Review of Books* No. 20, 8. See also Freeman and Lyon, n. 63, chap. 1.

[185] Office of Population, Censuses and Surveys, *General Household Survey* 22 (London, 1993), 230. By 1993 it had leapt to 70% (*Population Trends* No. 80, London, 1995).

[186] Central Statistical Office, *Social Trends* (London, 1995), 75. The Protestant Reformation Society found in 1996 that 70% of members of the Church of England and 56% of active members did not believe it was 'sinful' for a man and a woman to live together without being married. Amongst those aged 25–35 the proportion disapproving was 12%. See *Independent*, 28 Aug. 1996.

[187] See British Household Panel Survey, *Changing Households: The British Household Panel Survey 1990–1992* (Colchester, 1994), 75, 78.

[188] *Social Trends*, No. 27 (London, 1997).

[189] See John Haskey, 'Premarital Cohabitation and the Probability of Subsequent Divorce: Analyses using New Data from the General Household Survey' (1992) 68 *Population Trends* 10.

stable cohabitation from those to single and unpartnered women, there are big differences. The global statistic that a third of births in this country are outside marriage[190] cloaks the distinction between children born to parents who are living together and those born to mothers without male partners. In 1990 75 per cent of out-of-wedlock births were jointly registered, and three quarters of these joint registrations were by couples at the same address.[191] Well over half of such births are thus likely to be cohabiting couples. About 4 per cent of all dependent children are reared in non-marital, cohabiting relationships.[192]

There has been a decrease in the proportion of households filling the 'traditional' family structure of a couple with dependent children: the proportion of families meeting this was 31 per cent of households in 1979 but only 25 per cent in 1991.[193] The proportion of families headed by a lone parent increased from 8 per cent in 1971, when there was sufficient concern to establish a Royal Commission under Sir Morris Finer,[194] to 21 per cent in 1992.[195] The United Kingdom has one of the highest rates of lone parenthood in Europe. A figure of 1.5 million lone parent families has been estimated for the year 2005: that could be close to a 300 per cent increase in a generation.[196] The number has gone up through divorce, but equally because of the number who do not marry. In 1989 one third of all lone parent families were headed by a never-married mother (there was 360,000 never-married mothers out of 1.2 million single-parent families in 1989, and they are

[190] The percentage is now 34%: (1996) 85 *Population Trends*. The sharpest increase occurred in the early to mid-1980s: see J. Cooper, 'Births Outside Marriage: Recent Trends and Associated Demographic and Social Changes' (1991) 63 *Population Trends* 8.

[191] See John Haskey, 'Estimated Numbers and Demographic Characterisations of One-Parent Families in Great Britain' (1991) 65 *Population Trends* 35.

[192] See John Haskey and Katherine Kiernan, 'Cohabitation In Great Britain—Characteristics and Estimated Numbers of Cohabiting Partners' (1989) 58 *Population Trends* 23.

[193] Office of Population, Censuses and Surveys, *General Household Survey* (London, 1991).

[194] *Report of Committee on One-Parent Families*, Cmnd. 5629 (London, 1974).

[195] Office of Populations, Censuses and Surveys, *General Household Survey* (London, 1994). 2.3 million children are growing up in lone-parent families.

[196] Family Policy Studies Centre, n. 176 above. It was 570,000 in 1971: see n. 194 above.

growing at a rate of about 17 per cent a year).[197] Concern, particularly on the 'right' has been voiced about this new 'underclass'.[198] The family behaviour of the poor and of marginal members of society has caused alarm throughout history.[199] In the 1980s and 1990s there has been particular moral panic about this 'fatherless' underclass. In the United States, though less so in Britain, this is tangled with issues of race.[200]

Family Values

In Britain the underclass 'debate' is associated with a series of polemical publications of the Institute of Economic Affairs.[201] A principal concern is welfare dependency. This is said to undermine the family. As Segalman and Marsland explain:

the family is the crucial—indeed indispensable—mechanism in producing autonomous, self-reliant personalities, capable of resisting the blandishments of welfare dependency. It is . . . only in the context of loving support and rational discipline which the family offers . . . that children can be reliably socialised . . . anything at all which weakens the fabric of families inevitably generates and escalates welfare dependency. . . . Social policies which . . . weaken the legitimate authority of parents in the socialisation of their children are likely to create environments in which only exceptional children are capable of growing up into genuinely mature and autonomous adults.[202]

I have quoted this at length both because it is so representative of 'underclass' literature and because it has so many questionable assumptions. I will look at just one: the underlying assumption that the two-parent model of the family is essential for the normal development of children. Without a father present, the children will

---

[197] See L. Burghes, *One-Parent Families: Policy Options for the 1990s* (York, 1993).

[198] See Charles Murray, *The Making of The British Underclass* (London, 1990); Norman Dennis and G. Erdos, *Families Without Fathers* (London, 1992).

[199] For insights see Gareth Stedman Jones, *Outcast London* (Oxford, 1971).

[200] As in Charles Murray and Richard Herrnstein, *The Bell Curve* (New York, 1994). For a critique see R. Jacoby and N. Glaubermann (eds.), *The Bell Curve Debate* (New York, 1995).

[201] e.g. n. 198 above and J. Davies, B. Berger, and A. Carlson, *The Family: Is It Just Another Lifestyle Choice?* (London, 1993).

[202] *Cradle To The Grave: Comparative Perspectives On The State of Welfare* (London, 1989), 121.

be improperly socialized. Implicit in this is the view that the mother's values and expectations will vary by type of family. But the only researchers to test this hypothesis, Acock and Demo,[203] did not so find. They found that parenting values held by mothers do not vary by family type. All family types had mothers who stressed the importance of following 'culturally valued guidelines for behavior'.[204] There was no statistically significant difference across family types for parental difficulties with children. Though 'first married'[205] mothers were twice as likely to be involved in school activities as continuously single mothers, there was little difference in maternal interaction across family types for pre-school children, or in mothers' involvement in the leisure activities of their school-age children. Single parenthood was found to be less stressful than pre-divorce parenthood. Divorced women living as single parents reported an improvement both in their parental status and in their functioning. The 'right' seems to assume that families without fathers account for a range of social problems, notably teenage sexual activity, drug use, and delinquency.[206] Acock and Demo show evidence of technically present but 'functionally absent fathers',[207] suggesting it is not in one type of family only that fathers are absent as active participants.

Acock and Demo found few statistically significant differences across family types on measures of the socio-emotional adjustment and well-being of children. When samples were controlled for social background, there were no significant differences across family types in academic performance. They conclude:

teachers, politicians and popular commentators are simply wrong if they assume that single mothers do not value their children's education, do not have high educational expectations for their children, or do not impose family rules. What is needed to support these families is not rhetoric but changes in social policy and the provision of social programs and special services to meet their needs.[208]

---

[203] *Family Diversity And Well-Being* (Thousand Oaks, Cal., 1994).
[204] *Ibid.* 219.
[205] Where both mother and father were in their first marriage and they had one or more biological children under 19 living at home (see *ibid.* 51).
[206] e.g. Gertrude Himmelfarb, *The Demoralization of Society: From Victorian Virtues To Modern Values* (London, 1995). See the critique of Linda C. McClain, ' "Irresponsible" Reproduction' (1996) 47 *Hastings LJ* 339.
[207] N. 203 above, 217.   [208] N. 203 above, 231.

What they get is rhetoric. In 1993 it was 'back to basics'.[209] The world was captured by the Bulger case, the trial of two 11-year-olds for the abduction and savage murder of a toddler.[210] The case was thought to illustrate graphically the supposed malaise in family life—neither Thompson nor Venables came from a traditional or functioning family. The case equally illustrated the absence of civic responsibility[211] as forty plus adults watched a distressed toddler dragged to his death, and none intervened. Would this have happened had James Bulger been a dog?

The 'back to basics' campaign lasted barely a year. It tripped on innumerable banana skins, as successive prominent government ministers were found not to know that the seventh commandment was central to the traditional values that they themselves were preaching. Its final demise, like his, came in February 1994 when a Tory MP was found hanging with an orange in his mouth and clad only in stockings and suspenders. The campaign itself was soon resurrected, this time using the catch phrase of 'family values'.[212] It is difficult to spell these out exactly. It is a moral campaign and it is pro-family. It is against welfare dependency.[213] It evokes an image of a past society characterized by stable monogamous marriage. It is a snapshot perhaps of the 1950s before liberalism, permissiveness, and feminism challenged and problematized conventional behaviour. It is a campaign directed particularly against men who fail to fulfil their parental obligations. In this respect it is more than a moral campaign: the Child Support Act can be understood as a dual discourse, in part injecting moral virtue but equally concerned with

---

[209] See M. D. A. Freeman, 'Back To Basics' (1995) 33 *University of Louisville Journal of Family Law* 329.

[210] See M. D. A. Freeman, 'The James Bulger Tragedy: Childish Innocence and the Construction of Guilt' in Anne McGillivray (ed.), *Governing Childhood* (Aldershot, 1997), 115. See also Blake Morrison, *As If* (London, 1997).

[211] On which see Suzanna Sherry, 'Responsible Republicanism: Educating for Citizenship' (1995) 62 *Univ. of Chicago LR* 131.

[212] A slogan rather than a concept. This is noted also by Steven H. Hobbs, 'In Search of Family Value: Constructing A Framework For Jurisprudential Discourse' (1992) 75 *Marquette LR* 529. He offers clues to an explanation of the concept.

[213] But see Nancy Fraser, *Unruly Practices: Power, Discourse and Gender in Contemporary Social Theory* (Cambridge, 1989): women dependent on state welfare as 'the negatives of possessive individuals' (152). Wider implications are traced in Jan E. Dizard and Howard Gadlin, *The Minimal Family* (Amherst, Mass., 1990).

saving public money.[214] It cannot be said to have succeeded in either its symbolic or instrumental goals. It subjected a vast population to a social security formula, many for the first time. It scrutinized their behaviour and their finances, not surprisingly provoked a backlash,[215] and led to some reforms.[216] It remains, until the Family Law Act 1996 is implemented, the most concrete example of family values in action. But its attempt to impose moral and financial order seems likely to fail.

But it is not just a campaign against errant fathers. It is directed against much in recent change: divorce 'the great destroyer'[217] (there are too many and they can be gained too easily[218]), freer sexual morality (cohabitation should be discouraged, abortion restricted[219]), single parenthood (irresponsible reproduction is particularly censored[220]). They want to restore traditional gender roles, so that women should not be in paid employment but in the home and available to care for children (as well as to undertake

---

[214] It was based on a White Paper called *Children Come First* (London, 1990), Cm 1263, soon dubbed 'Taxpayers Come First' by John Eekelaar, *Independent*, 2 Nov. 1990.

[215] Though much of the criticism was misconceived or distorted the scheme came close to provoking opposition on 'poll-tax' scale. A particular legal problem—the conflict between the clean break principle and a continuing obligation to support children—was seen in *Crozier* v. *Crozier* [1994] 1 FLR 126.

[216] See Child Support (Miscellaneous Amendments and Transitional Provisions) Regulations 1994 (SI 1994 No. 227); Child Support and Income Support (Amendment) Regulations 1995 (SI 1995 No. 1945); Child Support Act 1995 (and see Michael Freeman, 'Family Justice and Family Values In 1995' in Andrew Bainhaim (ed.), *The International Survey of Family Law* (The Hague, 1997), 142–6.

[217] Per Patricia Morgan, 'Conflict and Divorce: Like A Horse and Carriage?' in Robert Whelan (ed.), *Just A Piece of Paper? Divorce Reform and the Undermining of Marriage* (London, 1995), 31.

[218] Divorce reform was heralded by the Lord Chancellor before the Law Commission report was published in 1990. In a speech to the Family Conciliation Council (see *The Times*, 18 Oct. 1990) he called for a brake on 'easy' divorce. He talked of the need to strengthen marriage and make the divorce process more rigorous.

[219] Attacks on abortion are not necessarily motivated by pro-life considerations. They may equally be targeted at what are considered to be the dangers of giving women, reproductive freedom. See (in the US context) Walter Dellinger and Gene B. Sterling, 'Abortion and the Supreme Court: The Retreat from *Roe* v. *Wade*' (1989) 138 *Univ. of Pennsylvania LRev.* 83.

[220] A critical assessment is Nancy Dowd, 'Stigmatizing Single Parents' (1995) 18 *Harvard Women's LJ* 19. We should not ignore, she argues, 'implicit stories of race and gender that reek of oppression' (45). See also Martha L. A. Fineman, 'Masking Dependency: The Political Role of Family Rhetoric' (1995) 81 *Virginia LRev.* 2181.

'community care'). The family values movement is also associated with an anti-gay backlash and a moral panic about AIDS.[221]

In the name of family values the Family Homes and Domestic Violence Bill was killed off in the autumn of 1995.[222] The Bill, based on a Law Commission report,[223] was proceeding smoothly and uncontroversially under the 'Jellicoe' procedure when it encountered the opposition of the *Daily Mail*, in particular its columnist William Oddie. He was able to whip up a frenzy of opposition among a cabal of back-bench Conservative MPs. His initial blast, 'How MPs Fail To Spot This Blow To Marriage',[224] was followed by an attack on the Law Commission, 'Legal Commissars Subverting Family Values'.[225] Much of their fury was misplaced or very late: some of what they attacked has been law since 1976.[226] A novel provision[227] to which they took exception would have extended to cohabiting couples the summary procedure in section 17 of the Married Women's Property Act 1882, and presumably also by implication its case law.[228] Not only would this have given them a quicker, more informal remedy. It would also have been cheaper for them and for the state. How insisting that such property disputes be determined by High Court judges upholds family values is beyond my comprehension. Anyone reading a case like *H* v. *M*[229] would soon realize that the determination of such disputes cries out for a simpler process. Though most of the lost Bill was retrieved in the Family Law Act 1996, the Government was unwilling to court further disaster by attempting this reform again.

---

[221] In relation to gay parenting see Helen Reece, 'The Paramountcy Principle: Consensus or Construct?' (1996) 49 *CLP* 267. An interesting case study is Phyllis Burke, *Family Values* (New York, 1993).

[222] See Clare Dyer, 'Homes and Guardians', *Guardian*, 31 Oct. 1995.

[223] See n. 78 above.

[224] 23 Oct. 1995.

[225] 1 Nov. 1995. For rational responses see leading articles in the *Guardian*, 28 Oct. and 3 Nov. 1995: see also Paul Vallely, 'How The Right Wing Went For Lord Mackay', *Independent*, 2 Nov. 1995 and Helen Wilkinson, 'Fundamentally Wrong on Families', *Independent*, 3 Nov. 1995.

[226] See Domestic Violence and Matrimonial Proceedings Act 1976, s. 1(2).

[227] See Family Homes and Domestic Violence Bill 1995, cl. 26 (in the Bill as amended on Report).

[228] Notably *Pettitt* v. *Pettitt* [1970] AC 777.

[229] [1992] 1 FLR 229. See, in support, Waite J's remarks at 242.

Family Justice

The 'right' (or much of it) is also opposed to modern trends in divorce law. It would not see a link between a moral campaign on family values and the family justice embodied in the latest divorce reform (the Family Law Act 1996). The personal opinions of the Lord Chancellor, so clearly articulated in an unprecedented credo placed in the foreword in *Looking To The Future*,[230] are only partly reflected in the practical blueprint of the legislation. But he does not subscribe, nor does the Act give effect, to the view of marriage and divorce such as is found in 'family values' documents.

For them the new Act is the final nail in the coffin of marriage. It turns marriage into a 'provisional agreement, terminable at whim'.[231] It 'abolishes marriage'.[232] The end of fault, so one of them argues:[233]

will virtually kill marriage off as a concept with any legal meaning. Fault describes what happens when someone is held responsible for their bad behaviour. Abolishing fault abolishes the concept of personal responsibility. It effectively declares that the breakdown of the marriage is no-one's responsibility. Marital breakdown becomes instead something that just happens to unfortunate individuals, like meningitis or an earthquake.

She further argues that:

civil marriage does not set out the obligations of one spouse to another. They are inferred instead from the legal remedies in divorce. Duties such as staying together, being faithful to each other or treating each other reasonably exist only by virtue of the fault that accrues to desertion, adultery or unreasonable behaviour. Remove these defaults, and marriage becomes a vapid concept.[234]

This is a shallow, simplistic, and pathological view of law. Of course the law appears more visible when it is broken, just as the laws of grammar do. But sanctions do not create obligations: sanctions exist to support obligations.[235] Without sanctions (divorce

---

[230] *Looking To The Future: Mediation and the Ground For Divorce* (London, 1995), Cm 2799.

[231] Norman Barry, 'Justice and Liberty In Marriage and Divorce', n. 217 above, 39.

[232] *Per* Melanie Phillips, 'Death Blow To Marriage', n. 217 above, 13.

[233] *Ibid.* 14.   [234] *Idem.*

[235] See H. L. A. Hart, *The Concept of Law* (Oxford, 1961), 193.

for adultery, for example) the obligation (in this instance marital fidelity) may be weakened (that is an empirical question, thus far untested[236]), or redefined (adultery, these critics seem to forget, is currently defined very narrowly[237]). The truth is we do not know. However, it seems unlikely that spouses currently desist from fornicating outside their marriage because of the sanction attached to adultery.[238]

Despite what these right-wing critics and moralists think, the new divorce law does embody a vision of the family which is consistent with some of the ideals with which we associate family values. It is a divorce Act which is pro-marriage; it encourages counselling, mediation, reconciliation, the promotion of good continuing relationships. The Act begins by setting out general principles, the first one of which is that 'the institution of marriage is to be supported'. Section 1 also emphasizes marriage saving and the promotion of good continuing relationships between the parties and any children affected. It should be noted that the reference is to the 'institution' of marriage, not the marriage which is the subject of the proceedings. Marriage is an ideological enclosure, the prescribed relationship against which all else is measured, and in comparison to which all else is found wanting.[239] That cohabitation is different from marriage is stressed in section 41(2): when dealing with the relationship of cohabitants (before making an occuptaion order) the court is directed to have regard to the 'fact' (it is so stated) that the couple 'have not given each other the commitment involved in marriage'. The courts may find it as difficult to unravel this as they have previously found the concept of living together 'as husband and wife'.[240]

---

[236] There is, however, some evidence of an increase in spousal abuse in American states which have removed fault from their divorce laws.

[237] There must be vaginal penetration: see *Dennis* v. *Dennis and Spillett* [1955] P 153. So (in Scotland) A I D was held not to amount to adultery (*Maclennan* v. *Maclennan*, 1958 SLT 12).

[238] We cannot assume that the literature in commercial law recounting the necessity for preserving incentives for good faith behaviour in long-term commercial relationships has any force in the domestic context: see, e.g., Scott, 'Conflict and Co-operation In Long-Term Contracts' (1987) 75 *California L Rev.* 2005. But note Milton C. Regan, *Family Law And The Pursuit of Intimacy* (New York, 1993), 139.

[239] See Carol Smart, *The Ties That Bind* (London, 1984), 141–6.

[240] *McLean* v. *Nugent* (1980) 1 FLR 26; *Tuck* v. *Nicholls* [1989] 1 FLR 283; *Adeoso* v. *Adeoso* [1981] 1 All ER 107; and in, the context of marriage, *Fuller* v.

The new Act emphasizes marriage in other ways too. It slows up the process of divorce. 'Quickie' divorces, available when the adultery or behaviour facts are used, as they have been in 75 per cent of divorces, become a thing of the past.[241] It will now take a minimum of eighty weeks to end a marriage where there are children of the family under 16.[242] The Act is full of waiting periods: the one-year absolute bar on divorce is retained[243] (though the justifications posited for this are weak[244]); at least three months must elapse between attending an information meeting and making a statement of marital breakdown which commences the divorce process; a period of nine months and fourteen days (fifteen months and fourteen days where there is a child of the family under 16) is set aside for reflection on whether the marriage can be saved and to give space to effect a reconciliation, and for consideration of future arrangements.[245] The standard period for reflection and consideration can be extended:[246] it can never be reduced, not even in cases of extreme violence or moral turpitude, not even where the delay will detrimentally affect the health or welfare of children, not even when the applicant is terminally ill and will not survive long enough to get a divorce order, perhaps to remarry and legitimate children.[247] What does this moral absolutism imply? It can only be an attempt to convey that marriage is not to be relinquished lightly. So couples who have done their reflecting and considering and couples incapable of reflecting and considering on anything for fifteen minutes will still have to wait for fifteen months (if they have school-age children). Many, of course, will already be in other

---

Fuller [1973] 1 WLR 730 and *Santos* v. *Santos* [1972] Fam. 247. See also Mary Hayes, ' "Cohabitation Clauses" In Financial Provision and Property Adjustment Orders—Law, Policy and Justice' (1994) 110 *LQR* 124.

[241] See Gwynn Davis and Mervyn Murch, *Grounds For Divorce* (Oxford, 1988): see chap. 5 on the choice of 'fact'.

[242] See Family Law Act 1996, s. 7(11), (13).

[243] See Family Law Act 1996, s. 7(6).

[244] The Law Commission dodged the issue (see *The Ground For Divorce* (London, 1992), Law Com. No. 192, para. 5.82): *Looking To The Future*, n. 230 above, though it would help 'to protect couples rushing into re-marriage too soon without having had time to think why their previous marriage was so short-lived' (para. 4.42).

[245] See Family Law Act 1996, s. 8(2), 7(3), (11), (13).

[246] See Family Law Act 1996, s. 7(13) (for circumstances where it cannot be extended are s. 7(12)).

[247] Because, allegedly, to do so would be to re-introduce considerations of fault.

relationships, and many of these will have broken up before the marriage is ended. Oddly, the Act encourages extra-marital cohabitation (also perhaps abandonment and bigamy) by extending the uncoupling process.

Central to this new system of family justice is mediation.[248] The Law Commission recommended it, though it conceded that there were dangers in relying 'too heavily upon . . . mediation instead of more traditional methods of negotiation and adjudication'. It listed these as

exploitation of the weaker by the stronger . . . considerable potential for delay, which is damaging both to the children and often to the interests of one of the adults involved . . . and the temptation for the court to postpone deciding some very difficult and painful cases which ought to be decided quickly.[249]

The government's view, nevertheless, was that a 'greater use of mediation . . . will help achieve the objectives of a good divorce system'.[250] There were fears that mediation would be compulsory. It is not to be, though there is a clear 'encouragement'[251] to use family mediation.

Concern has been expressed about the move to mediation.[252] It constitutes a shift in the paradigm of dispute resolution away from law and lawyers.[253] Mediation is couched in the language of responsibilities—it is said to enable spouses to take responsibility for the breakdown of their marriage and to encourage them to look to their future responsibilities[254]—and there is no denying that these are important. But so are rights,[255] and law and lawyers, whatever the faults of the institution and its practitioners, have a reasonable record in protecting these. It is perfectly consistent with the move away from moral judgment (at least that found in the

---

[248] See Simon Roberts, 'Mediation In Family Law Disputes' (1983) 46 *MLR* 537. On the need for lawyers and mediators to offer a complementary service see Janet Walker, 'Is There A Future For Lawyers In Divorce?' (1996) 10 *Int. J of Law, Policy and the Family* 52.　　　　　　　　　　　　[249] N. 244 above, para. 5.34.
[250] N. 230 above, para. 5.21.　　　　　　　　[251] N. 230 above, para. 5.21.
[252] See John Eekelaar, n. 72 above; S. Cretney, 'Divorce Reform in England: Humbug and Hypocrisy or a Smooth Transition?' in Freeman (ed.), n. 152 above, 39. See also C. Piper in Freeman (ed.), n. 162 above, 63.
[253] See M. Freeman, n. 70 above.　　　　　[254] See n. 230, above, para. 5.21.
[255] Particularly to the weak: see Kimberlé Crenshaw, 'Race, Reform and Retrenchment: Transformation and Legitimation In Anti-Discrimination Law' (1988) 100 *Harvard L Rev.* 1331.

evaluation of conduct that the fault fact represented) that a process which looks to the future rather than judging the past should become dominant. But if rights are not publicized—and many mediators will not fully understand legal implications—and not protected, who will lose out? The fear is that most victims will be women. You cannot negotiate decisions and renegotiate relationships without access to full and competent information. Without it important legal rights may be unknowingly relinquished, entire issues may be overlooked, and time and money may be wasted mediating an agreement which subsequently has to be rewritten when legal advice is obtained. We do not know what attitude the courts will take to agreements negotiated during a mediation, particularly where there is a gross imbalance in bargaining power.[256]

There is concern also in the context of domestic violence[257]— perhaps the grossest example of where unequal power distorts bargaining relationships. It may be that cases of domestic violence will be exempted from mediation. But why just cases of violence? What of other forms of abuse? What of cases where there has been, and is likely therefore still to be, economic exploitation? Concern has been expressed also about the impact of mediation on children. As Martin Richards has noted, 'mediation is an adult business and, although adults may be bargaining in the shadow of their children's needs as they perceive them, children cannot be party to it.'[258] The government's response was that 'mediation services are very conscious of children's needs'.[259] It thought that soon mediators will be specifically trained to deal appropriately with the interests of children, even to receive guidance on when it is appropriate to involve children in mediation.[260] It is ironic that when the

---

[256] For evidence of pressures to agree to settlements see Gwynn Davis *et al.*, *Simple Quarrels* (Oxford, 1994). And see *Edgar* v. *Edgar* [1980] 3 All ER 887.

[257] See Trina Grillo, 'The Mediation Alternative: Process Dangers for Women' (1991) 100 *Yale LJ* 1545; Penelope Bryan, 'Killing Us Softly: Divorce Mediation and the Politics of Power' (1992) 40 *Buffalo L Rev.* 441; Felicity Kaganas and Christine Piper, 'Domestic Violence and Divorce Mediation' (1994) *JSWFL* 265.

[258] 'But What About The Children? Some Reflections On The Divorce White Paper', (1995) 7 *CFLQ* 223, 225.

[259] N. 230 above, para. 5.32. See also Adrian L. James, 'Social Work in Divorce: Welfare, Mediation and Justice' (1995) 9 *Int. J of Law and the Family* 256, arguing that mediation is becoming synonymous with child welfare.

[260] N. 230 above, para. 5.33.

competence of children to participate is more and more being recognized,[261] when they are granted more and more rights to independent representation in legal proceedings, that a shift away from law and lawyers should see this snatched away from them, particularly in an Act which strengthens their status.[262]

What the effects of the new Act will be on divorce remains contentious. It will lengthen the process of divorce. There will be some reconciliations. We may never learn how many, any more than we know why at present there are many more divorce petitions that decrees nisi, and why there is a significant shortfall between the number of decrees nisi and absolute.[263] Perhaps more cases will fall by the wayside than now. If so there will be a growing number of persons living in a status of limbo. Whether the number of divorces will go up depends on a number of matters. It is commonly said that with each divorce reform, divorce increases.[264] But this is not strictly so. To take only the most obvious example, it would seem that the number of divorce petitions rose substantially with the implementation of the Divorce Reform Act in 1971. But the 1960s saw an annual rise of 9.5 per cent to a peak of 70,575 petitions in 1970. If this yearly increase had continued there would have been over 200,000 petitions by 1990, when there were in fact 189,000.[265] Both Schoen and Baj[266] and Haskey[267] have followed birth cohorts, and each found that successive generations register a higher rate of divorce. The structure and processes of divorce law

---

[261] See Elizabeth S. Scott, 'Judgment and Reasoning In Adolescent Decisionmaking' (1992) 37 *Villanova L Rev.* 1607; Priscilla Alderson, *Children's Consent To Surgery* (Buckingham, 1993); *Gillick* v. *West Norfolk and Wisbech AHA* [1986] AC 112; and the Children Act 1989.

[262] See Family Law Act 1996, s. 11 (and see also s. 64). The significance of s. 11 can, however, be over-emphasized, as the Lord Chancellor did (see HL, Debs., vol. 567, col. 703) when he stressed that 'all arrangements will have to be decided before divorce', which is in this context is not true.

[263] Davis and Murch, n. 241 above, 53, point to a 'fall-off' rate of about 2% between nisi and absolute: the 'fall-off' from petition to decree nisi is even more pronounced (perhaps as high as 15%).

[264] Notably by Ruth Deech, 'Divorce Law and Empirical Studies' (1990) 106 *LQR* 229, 242.

[265] As observed by C. Gibson, n. 162 above, 32.

[266] 'Twentieth Century Cohort Marriage and Divorce in England and Wales', *Population Studies* 38, 439 (1984).

[267] 'First Marriage, Divorce and Remarriage: Birth Cohort Analyses', *Population Trends* 72, 24 (1993).

have little impact on the incidence of divorce or marital breakdown. What then does?

We live in a privatized world: Mrs Thatcher's notorious remark about there being no such thing as society, only individuals, was ideological, not sociological. But the society she helped to forge, one built on egoism and selfishness, was one in which divorce could be expected to flourish. We also live increasingly in a secularized world, less constrained by religious and traditional codes of morality. There is a backlash against this, and some attempt is being made to reinject a sense of community. It is in part upon the success of this that we wait to see whether the number of those getting divorced will increase or not.

It is short-sighted to think that our answers lie in systems of family justice. It is not to marital law that we should look to create better or happier families. It can play a role, but it is subsidiary to a basket of other policies. In the coda to this article I address a few of these.

Justice For The Family

Anyone who studies the family in Britain today cannot fail to be struck by the absence of a family policy, particularly when we examine the ways that our neighbours treat the family.[268]

The family values rhetoric, with its emphasis on moral malaise, on family disintegration, on the growth of an underclass, leads to policies placing greater emphasis on family obligations and responsibilities, to punitive welfare policies and to other forms of social control. There is a weak commitment in Britain towards creating the infrastructure on which an explicit and coherent family policy can be built. We lack strong institutional support for mothers' labour market chances. We are laggard in our provision of socialized child care facilities. Our provision of cash benefits subsidizing the costs of children is poor. We have long panicked

---

[268] In particular France: see Linda Hantrais, 'Comparing Family Policy in Britain, France and Germany' (1994) 23 *Journal of Social Policy* 135 and Jane Lewis, 'Gender and the Development of Welfare Regimes' (1992) 2 *Journal of European Social Policy* 159. Though dated, Sheila Kamerman and Alfred Kahn's *Family Policy: Government and Families in Fourteen Countries* (New York, 1978) is still an invaluable source. S. Zimmerman, *Family Policies and Family Well-Being* (Newbury Park, Cal., 1992) is also useful in relation to the US.

over lone mothers. It was their heavy dependence on the social security system that motivated the establishment of the Child Support Agency. Of course men should meet their obligation to children they have fathered. But more could be done to enable these women to work. Currently, they have a very low employment rate: compare Sweden where 87 per cent of lone mothers are in the labour force and, when not working full-time, hold jobs which provide the legal entitlement to work three quarters of the normal day, with all the occupational benefits accruing to full-time employees, while their children are small.[269] In France (as well as Belgium), 95 per cent of 3 to 5-year-olds have places in publicly funded childcare facilities: ten times as many French women work through their child bearing years as those in Britain.[270] We are the only country in Europe where lone mothers have a lower full-time employment rate than mothers in two-parent families.[271] The nursery voucher scheme showed the Conservative government may have begun to understand the problem, though it did not find the solution. And low pay remains a consistent feature of women's work. Britain is 'one of three countries in the EC which have the highest proportion of female low paid'.[272]

We need to find ways of assisting entry to the labour market for lone parents. Instead we have concentrated on ways of finding savings in the social security budget. So the Child Support Act of 1991 was introduced to substitute private transfers for public ones, not to augment family income for poor lone-parent families.

On maternity leave we now compare favourably. But until October 1994 we were the only country in the EC which insisted on a 'length of service' condition to maternity leave. We have not

---

[269] See A. Leira, 'The Woman Friendly Welfare State? The Case of Norway and Sweden' in Jane Lewis (ed.), *Women and Social Policies in Europe* (Aldershot, 1993).
[270] See A. Phillips and P. Moss, *Who Cares for Europe's Children? The Short Report of the European Childcare Network* (Brussels, 1988).
[271] See S. Dex and P. Walters, 'Women's Occupational Status in Britain, France and the USA: Explaining The Difference' (1989) 20 *Industrial Relations Journal* 203.
[272] S. Dex, S. Lissenburgh and M. Taylor, *Women and Low Pay: Identifying The Issues* (Manchester, 1994), p. vii. In 1995 women manual workers' hourly pay was 72% of men's (with non-manual workers it was 68%). Since women work a shorter week, their gross weekly earnings were lower (67%; and 65% respectively: see Central Statistical Office, *New Earnings Survey* (London, 1995), Table 20.1.

hitherto given entitlement to parental leave. The Conservative Government refused to comply with the EC Directive on this,[273] consistent with its decision (now likely to be revoked by the new Labour Government) to opt out of the Social Chapter of the Maastricht Treaty.[274] In France by comparison, parental levae from work can be taken by either men or women until a child is 3 and extend up to a period of three years. In Denmark parental leave is a statutory right (ten weeks at 90 per cent of earnings). Germany allows eighteen months' leave, but pays a low flat-rate payment for only six months. Italy pays 30 per cent of earnings for six months.

These examples could be multiplied. What they show is what family values could look like. We can deplore and despise the right's stand on 'family values' and still support family values. We need a policy which values the family, which upholds the integrity of all of its members, which enhances the opportunities of its members to fulfil their life chances, which offers support rather than discipline. If family law is to play a part in this reconstruction it will have to break beyond the conventional boundaries to examine social policies as they affect family members. It will also have to look beyond the boundaries of this country to Maastricht and beyond.

The Future

I doubt whether the future—certainly the short-term future—will see the development of any such family policy, though the new Labour Government is committed to adopting the Social Chapter of the Maastricht Treaty.[275] What it will see is both resistance to change and pressure for change. The new divorce law will be seen as meddlesome and onerous. The mediation system will not be able to cope and there will be demand for the new processes to be relaxed. In time the period for reflection and consideration will be reduced, probably to six months. Nor will the differential for those

---

[273] (1996) 96/34/EC: OJL 145, 4.

[274] See Peter Lange, 'Maastricht and the Social Procotol: Why Did They Do It?' (1993) 21 *Politics and Society* 5. But see Brian Burkitt and Mark Baimbridge, 'The Maastricht Treaty's Impact on the Welfare State' (1995) 42 *Critical Social Policy* 100.

[275] Bribes (tax allowances) to keep women (probably only married women) at home is a distinct possibility, but hardly a welcome one.

with children be sustained. The information meeting will disappear, to be replaced by a booklet or, as likely, the internet. By the time of the next divorce law, in 2020 or thereabouts, divorce is likely to be an administrative procedure, nothing more.

Cohabitation will become more and more like marriage, or marriage more and more like cohabitation. The pressure may be for the latter, but so long as the family is seen as an instrument of state policy, assimilation is likely to be in the direction of marriage. Same-sex marriages, though barely on the agenda in this country,[276] will be allowed. So, of course, will the marriage of transsexuals. These concessions to pluralism will liberalize, but will also colonize—the state gaining control of a wider range of relationships. Divorce law, in as much as such 'law' exists, will extend to these newly-recognized marriages and, by analogy, to cohabitation as well. We will continue to struggle to define cohabitation, but those relationships embraced by whatever definition is adopted will find a marriage-like regime imposed on them. This could lead to courts acquiring a discretion over money and property issues[277] when cohabitation is brought to an end. But the discretion the courts have now with marriage is likely to come under increasing scrutiny[278] and if fixed rules emerge, as I think they are likely to do, they will apply to cohabitation also.[279] This would be a case of marriage adopting the current legal practices of cohabitation, though, of course, the rules originate in marriage.[280] Though some will continue to call for the end of maintenance, it is more likely

---

[276] In contrast to Scandinavia, the Netherlands, and the United States. On the US see Mark Strasser, *Legally Wed: Same-Sex Marriages and the Constitution* (Ithaca, NY, 1997) and contrast Lynn Wardle, 'A Critical Analysis of Constitutional Claims for Same-Sex Marriage' (1996) *Brigham Young L Rev.* 1.

[277] Including pension issues: see *The Treatment of Pension Rights On Divorce* (London, 1996), Cm 3345. A comparative prospective (and warning) is David L. Baumer and J. C. Poindexter, 'Women and Divorce: The Perils of Pension Division' (1996) 57 *Ohio State LJ* 203.

[278] As in the United States: see Jane C. Murphy, 'Eroding The Myth of Discretionary Justice in Family Law: The Child Support Experiment' (1991) 70 *NCLRev.* 209 and Carl E. Schneider, 'Discretion, Rules and Law: Child Custody and the UMDA'S Best-Interest Standard' (1991) 89 *Mich. L Rev.* 2215; 'The Tension Between Rules and Discretion in Family Law' (1993) 27 *Family LQ* 229.

[279] But see Grace Blumberg, 'Cohabitation Without Marriage: A Different Perspective' (1981) 28 *UCLA L Rev.* 1125.

[280] And see S. M. Cretney and J. M. Masson, *Principles of Family Law* (6th edn.) (London, 1991), 231–4.

that the concept will extend to cohabitation: English law may yet come to know of 'palimony'.[281]

The driving force is likely to be the concept of responsibility. Now well entrenched in child law and child support law, it will make inroads into the law governing adult domestic relationships.[282] This will include relationships with the elderly. Family law will as assuredly embrace 'community care' as it now does children.

Students of the family values debates of the 1990s and the ensuing 1996 Act cannot fail to have been struck by the contrasting ideology and images of the family in the Children Act 1989.[283] They should therefore not be surprised that by 1996 the Children Act was coming under attack:[284] extravagant claims were made that its ideology, supposedly associated with increasing children's rights, was undermining the stability of the family. Attention was drawn to the spectre of children divorcing their parents[285] and taking parents to courts—and European ones to boot—for smacking them.[286] Concern about juvenile crime—the Bulger case[287] was a catalyst—was further fuelled by these tensions. The Children Act adopted parental responsibility[288] (as it did the concept of partnership[289]) as a central concept, refusing to withdraw it from those who acted irresponsibly or abusively.[290] Whether a future Children Act will be as committed to upholding responsibility as a normative goal where factually it is absent may be doubted. The pendulum may swing from partnership with parents to greater protection of children, with parental responsibility being upheld as an ideal but being scrutinized more intensively and removed more

---

[281] *Cf. Windeler* v. *Whitehall* [1990] 2 FLR 505, *per* Millet J.

[282] See Christine Piper, *The Reasonable Parent* (Hemel Hempstead, 1993).

[283] See Lorraine Fox Harding, 'The Children Act 1989 In Context: Four Perspectives In Child Care Law and Policy' [1991] *Journal of Social Welfare and Family Law* 179 and 285.

[284] See, e.g., the leading article in the *Daily Telegraph*, 13 Feb. 1997.

[285] See Michael Freeman, 'Can Children Divorce Their Parents?' in Michael Freeman (ed.), n. 162 above, 159.

[286] See the *Independent*, 9 Sept. 1996. See also the case in *The Times*, 4 Sept. 1996.

[287] See n. 210 above.

[288] Children Act 1989, ss. 2 and 3.

[289] Not in the Act but see Department of Health, *Principles and Practice In Regulations and Guidance* (London, 1990), 8.

[290] See John Eekelaar, 'Parental Responsibility: State of Nature or Nature of The State?' [1991] *Journal of Social Welfare and Family Law* 37.

readily. Adoption is likely to become more 'open'[291] but a concomitant of this may be a greater reliance upon it.

When the state of family law comes to be reviewed a generation from now the audit will look very different—so, it may be predicted, will the concerns and the agenda.

[291] See n. 143 above.

INDUSTRIAL RELATIONS —THE EMPIRE STRIKES BACK

R. W. Rideout

The Best of Worlds

When Professor Sir Otto Kahn-Freund arrived in this country before the Second World War he was justifiably impressed by labour relationships voluntarily regulated by unenforceable agreements. Until as late as 1950 the *Industrial Relations Handbook* suggested a marked degree of orderliness in the system. Courts were supposed to have learned not to interfere after the foray by the House of Lords against collective labour power at the beginning of the century and the response of a legislature painfully aware of its accountability to a relatively new working electorate.[1] It had been, and continued to be, the fixed policy of all successive governments to refrain from legislation in those areas regarded as appropriate for collective bargaining[2] and to maintain a reasonable balance between the negotiating power of organized labour and organized capital. This, rather than a legislative code of rights, was considered sufficient to maintain acceptable standards of employment.

Under this regime legendary trade union leaders constructed district, and subsequently national, bargaining on a narrow front primarily concerned with economic interest. A remarkable degree of national uniformity was established. In engineering in October 1938 the negotiated national rate for a fitter was £3.7.2½d per week. The average weekly earnings of such a worker were

---

[1] In *Taff Vale Railway Co. Ltd.* v. *ASRS* [1901] AC 426, and *Amalgamated Society of Railway Servants* v. *Osborne* [1910] AC 87. The legislative response was contained in the Trade Disputes Act 1906 and the Trade Union Act 1913.

[2] See O. Kahn-Freund, *Labour and the Law* (London, 1972) 29.

£3.13.8d[3] Lord Wedderburn, writing in 1986,[4] said that an observer at this time would have looked in vain for anything capable of being described as 'labour law' in Britain. So long as this is meant to indicate absence of a legal system it is an accurate assessment. Sir Otto Kahn-Freund pronounced it a healthy situation.

The lawyer, therefore, was not often called upon but saw a system regulated by collective agreement notionally producing individual agreement between employer and worker. The contract of employment was seen as the cornerstone of UK employment law.[5] Most legal commentators were content with that.[6] Sir Otto Kahn-Freund did not conceal the truth. '[T]he rules of employment,' he wrote, 'are thus, in the main either an emanation of the managerial power of the employer or they are a complex amalgam of legislation and of collective bargaining.'[7] Without the moderating effect of collective bargaining the contract of employment was not an agreement but an instrument of servitude, but few then chose to point out that this collective moderating effect operated on a narrow front and that the contract had been constructed by the courts to ensure an absence of job security and, largely, to advance managerial interests.

Disintegration

'Few branches of the law,' said Sir Otto, in 1959, of this system, 'have been less changed in their fundamentals since Dicey's day.'[8] But the apparent stability was, by that time, a deception which no one wished to shake. As Davies and Freedland say:[9]

[3] *Report of the Royal Commission on Trade Unions and Employers' Associations 1965–1968* (Cmnd. 3623), 14–15.

[4] Lord Wedderburn, *The Worker and the Law* (3rd edn.) (Harmondsworth, 1986), 1.

[5] O. Kahn-Freund, 'Legal Framework' in A. Flanders and H. A. Clegg (eds.), *The System of Industrial Relations in Great Britain* (Oxford, 1956), 47—and see my reply in 'The Contract of Employment' (1966) 19 *CLP* 11.

[6] From Smith, *Law of Master and Servant* (8th edn. by Knowles, Oxford, 1931) and Batt, *The Law of Master and Servant* (London, 1929) consistently to the latter textbook's 4th edn. (by Crossley Vaines, 1950).

[7] Kahn-Freund, n. 2 above, 41. By reference to legislation the author clearly meant those areas such as health and safety which were, historically, regarded as appropriate for legal regulation rather than negotiation.

[8] O. Kahn-Freund in *Law and Opinion in England in the Twentieth Century* (London, 1959), 215.

[9] P. Davies and M. Freedland, *Labour Legislation and Public Policy* (Oxford, 1993).

A direct challenge to free collective bargaining would, at one and the same time, have alienated the unions and deprived the government of the assistance that was proving essential in the fight against inflation and for greater exports. Government could not be sure that what it would have to rely upon in the absence of trade union co-operation would be more effective.

Something like a partnership between trade unions and government had been forged during the Second World War and was sustained at a high level for a decade thereafter. But the fight against inflation was primarily seen as a fight against wage increases where they outstripped the rise in productivity. Collective Bargaining in the United Kingdom was mostly concerned with wage increase and job protection by the maintenance of restrictive practices. Trade unions were to be asked to restrain wage increases and abandon restrictive practices. That challenge was to reveal a weakness in their structure of which those of their leaders who had moved into government may well have been unaware and which their successors would rather not acknowledge. By 1967 the nationally agreed rate for an engineering fitter was £11.1.8d. His average weekly wage was £21.7.9d, rising in vehicle building to £24. 8.5d. The Royal Commission was to make a virtue of the explanation for this phenomenon, then called wage drift, and so, from the point of view of industrial relations it may have been. But it revealed the power the local official, the shop-steward, had acquired, initially during the war, over actual wage levels. The Royal Commission saw the shop steward more as an oiler of the machinery than a spanner in the works; again, so he might have been. But his control of wage levels meant that the national union leadership in the private sector could not deliver to government what it asked of them. Even had the unions been in a position to impose the restraint the government was to seek their co-operation had depended on the maintenance of full employment. Government was to fail them as they failed government.

For a time the seriousness of this failure was not appreciated. Between 1951 and 1961 unemployment averaged 1.7 per cent. Productivity increased by an average of 2.2 per cent per year. Almost inevitably in such circumstances, wage inflation ran at 6 per cent. But the average price rise of 3.25 per cent which this produced was considered tolerable. Industrial relations looked to be working. The one-day national stoppage of engineering workers in 1953 was the first set-piece strike since that of textile workers in 1933.[10] Little notice was taken of the fact that in France, Germany, Italy, and Japan—our major trade rivals—productivity was rising at double the rate prevailing in the United Kingdom.

Perhaps it was purely coincidental that it was in the courts that signs of concern about the health of the system first clearly surfaced. In the next twenty years they were to mount a much more pronounced attack on the power of the unions than government, anchored to a philosophy of co-operation, dared. The decision of the House of Lords in *Rookes* v. *Barnard*[11] challenged the totality of the legal immunity of industrial action and sought, in a manner reminiscent of 1901, to forge new delictual liability. The Labour government responded, but not quite as enthusiastically as had the Liberal government in 1906. Professor Lord Wedderburn has pointed out[12] that the Trade Disputes Act 1965 offered the narrowest protection that could have been devised to avert that threat. The threat from the extension of tort liability to interference with commercial contracts, posed by the superficially sympathetic decision in *Thomson and Co. Ltd.* v. *Deakin*,[13] began to be more fully recognized at this time but no immunity was considered until the Royal Commission pointed out the need, and the proposal to grant immunity in that respect had to wait for implementation until 1976.[14] Much more significant of the developing breakdown in the old order was the enactment in 1965 of the first legislative social engineering attempted in the area normally left to collective bargaining.[15] In the Redundancy Payments Act 1965 the government appeared to have two principal objectives. It regarded worksharing as economically undesirable and it thought to remove

---

[10] J. Durcan, W. McCarthy, and G. Redman, *Strikes in Post-War Britain* (Oxford, 1983), 58. The fact that for much of that period strikes had been a criminal offence is, it is submitted, not a significant factor in the explanation. The criminal sanction proved ineffective when it was invoked; see *Report of the Royal Commission on Trade Unions* n. 3 above, para. 823.

[11] [1964] AC 1129. [12] Wedderburn, n. 4 above, 45.

[13] [1952] Ch. 646.

[14] Full immunity was proposed in 'In Place of Strife', Cmnd. 3888, para. 100 and the Bill drafted by the Labour government in 1969. The *Thomson* immunity was eventually provided by the Trade Union and Labour Relations Act 1976, s. 3(2) amending TULRA 1974, s. 13(1) and (3).

[15] The Industrial Training Act 1964 was itself an indication that more was needed than co-operation with trade unions and the Contracts of Employment Act 1963 represented a first small step towards legislative employment protection.

a demand to introduce it which was being supported by a considerable amount of industrial action.[16] It was also thought that employers were retaining reserves of under-employed workers who might usefully be shaken out into more productive activity. Fundamental as was this break with the policy on non-intervention it was not significantly opposed by trade unions. They, who had done little at that time to develop collective agreements to cope with the escalation of redundancies, rightly saw the legislation as a 'floor of rights' upon which they could build by collective bargaining. They, and the economy, were strong enough to support a spate of agreed redundancy procedures which, in extreme cases, could provide six times the amount of statutory compensation. So legislative intervention, far from being opposed, was welcomed. There had yet to be learned the lesson learned in the United States when the Taft–Hartley Act 1946 reversed many of the benefits to trade unions afforded by the Norris–La Guardia Act 1935, that protective legislative intervention can give rise to restrictive backlash. Of course, no one saw this as the first stage in a separate process of individualization of industrial relations. It was to acquire significance in that direction as the bare floor of rights began to reappear with the decline in bargaining power in the 1980s.

The Search for a System

By the mid-1960s everyone had realized that the unregulated voluntary system did not deal efficiently in economic terms with the increasing number of disputes generated by the increasingly recognized economic problems. In those days the first resort of a government which did not know the answer was to appoint a Royal Commission. The Royal Commission on Trade Unions and Employers' Associations, which sat from 1965 to 1968, took as its guiding principle that 'properly conducted collective bargaining is

---

[16] Statistics do not disclose this cause of industrial action as a major, or significantly increasing, problem. In 1960 it accounted for 228 disputes involving 60,300 workers and a loss of 272,000 working days—about 9% of the total under each of these heads. In 1962 this cause still only accounted for about 9% of totals at 302 disputes involving 383,000 workers. The loss of 745,000 working days, however, might suggest that it was becoming more difficult for employers to meet the demand. Statistical source: *British Labour Statistics: Historical Analysis* (London 1971), Table 198.

the most effective means of giving workers the right to representation in decisions affecting their working lives, a right which is, or should be, the prerogative of every worker in a democratic society'. It set out a plan to reconstruct industrial relations around plant bargaining which it declared to be the most effective form of dispute resolution. It had, in truth, little alternative. Local bargaining of one sort or another was effectively establishing the going rates in the private sector. But it adhered to the old idea of legal regulation as only legitimate to provide support for voluntary bargaining. Unwittingly, perhaps, a major step in the process of individualization was mooted, and subsequently implemented in the Commission's recommendation of a legislative floor of rights for workers headed by a remedy for unfair dismissal and, despite a spirited defence of the ability of the TUC to do the job put up by its trade union members, some legislative clarification of the rights of members in relation to their trade unions. Sir Otto Kahn-Freund considered that the law could play three different roles: (1) an 'auxiliary' function in support of collective bargaining (which role it had played at least since the end of the First World War); (2) a 'regulatory' function by way of a code of employment rights supplementing terms and conditions established by collective bargaining; and (3) a 'restrictive' function defining the limits of permissible conduct in pursuance of industrial disputes. Both major political parties were more attracted to the idea of a more complete legislative framework of labour relations. For the Labour government Mrs Castle proposed to confer rights on trade unions in return for restrictions on unofficial strikes and ballots before official strikes. But she also said, 'management these days can no longer function by arbitrary exercise of its traditional prerogative but only by winning the consent of its workpeople'.[17]

For Mr Carr and the incoming Conservative government in 1971 legislation was to be the primary instrument of reform, modernizing the industrial relations structure by the introduction of a much greater element of compulsion. Significantly, Lord Wedderburn saw the Industrial Relations Act which it passed as drafted by two independent phantoms; the civil servant intent on tidying the structure and the Conservative lawyer imbued with doctrines of individual (as distinct from collective) rights. There was no third

---

[17] Quoted by Wedderburn, n. 4 above, 50.

strand of the old corporatism under which control of labour relations had been conducted solely by trade unions and management. The Government saw the Act as the required systematic restructuring of the whole of industrial relations, apparently heedless of the fact that such a system was to be operated by parties who had never before participated in anything like a comprehensive regulated structure. Trade unions saw no good reason to co-operate in bringing about the end of voluntarism and of their inherent liberties. The Act had provided them with a ground on which to rally by requiring them to register in order to use the system they rejected. Unfortunately, it had located on this very ground a self-destruct mechanism.

Rarely in their history have trade unions revealed a totally united front, but they did so now in their refusal to register. Without significant registered unions to operate it the statutory machine, built under the supervision of Sir Geoffrey Howe and a thing of great technical beauty, remained silent and inoperative. Perplexed, its would-be operators activated the emergency procedures in response to a national rail strike and demonstrated that the emergency procedures could not handle emergencies.[18] Lord Wedderburn attributed some of the blame for the failure of the Industrial Relations Act to Sir John Donaldson's belief 'that industrial class conflicts were justiciable issues appropriate for courts of law to resolve'. He, with the aid of the Court of Appeal,[19] had already held a trade union vicariously liable for the actions of shop stewards whom it had expressly instructed not to take the action in question[20] when, faced with the same disobedience, this time to judicial injunction, he imprisoned six contumacious shop stewards. The mob had its martyrs and howled for a general strike in their support. Lord Denning averted something close to revolution but was unable to prevent the judiciary appearing impotent. The judiciary, at least, had obeyed its instructions. Not so management which, like the trade unions, showed no will to change the historical relationship between the law and industrial relations. Whilst the Secretary of State for Education brooded on the lessons to be applied when she became Prime Minister the great industrial relations revolution collapsed. Many who heaped

---

[18] See *Secretary of State for Employment* v. *ASLEF (No. 2)* [1972] ICR 19.
[19] *Heatons Transport (St Helens) Ltd.* v. *TGWU* [1972] ICR 308.
[20] *Ibid.*

derision on it then would wish now a similar opportunity to operate a system of regulated industrial relations.

A final effort was made by the Labour government of 1974 to 1979 to revive the spirit of co-operation between government and a now deeply suspicious trade union movement. Opinions of this 'social contract' have significantly varied. Professor Hepple[21] sees it as fulfilling all three of Professor Kahn-Freund's legislative functions in re-establishing 'collective laissez-faire, whilst simultaneously preserving the peculiarly British voluntarism based on workplace democracy'. He omits to point out that it spectacularly failed. Given every reason to be arrogant it is perhaps surprising that the unions ever tried to make the social contract work. They failed not through lack of will but through inability to deliver wage restraint and, failing, gave in to the demands of local bargaining unimpressed by arguments about the national economy. The unions, in their arrogance, had forgotten a critical rule of industrial relations. In the end you win or lose because you have, or have not, public opinion on your side. From 1980 to the present day the government has been able to rely on attacking the publicly perceived evil of trade union power which was established in these final years of supposed co-operation.

Judicial Unease

Some members of the judiciary had long thought the unions too powerful. Lord Wedderburn wrote, in 1980,[22] 'the eras of judicial "creativity", of new doctrines hostile to trade union interests, have been largely, though not entirely, co-terminous with the periods of British social history in which trade unions have been perceived by middle class opinion as a threat to the established order'. Had he written now he might have added, 'unless the courts perceive that the government is intent on dealing with that threat'. British judges have an instinct for detecting a viable solution. They clearly did not regard Salmond's invention of a tort of intimidation as such despite the effort in *Rookes* v. *Barnard*[23] to improve upon it. Lord Denning himself expressed doubts about its applicability.[24] But in *D. C.*

---

[21] B. Hepple, 'The Future of Labour Law' (1995) 24 *ILJ* 309.
[22] Lord Wedderburn, 'Industrial Relations and the Courts' (1980) 9 *ILJ* 65 at 78.
[23] N. 11 above.   [24] *Morgan* v. *Fry* [1968] 2 QB 710.

Thomson Ltd. v. *Deakin*[25] the tort of inducement to breach of contract had been extended to protect commercial contracts. In the 1960s, whenever it appeared possible to avoid statutory immunity those members of the Court of Appeal whom the Master of the Rolls selected to sit with him in such cases reconstructed that tort, paring away the restraining conditions placed upon it in that earlier case.[26] Lord Denning was to resume this construction when, the era of legislative reform in the 1970s having failed, it appeared that the problem remained.[27]

The need to remove the statutory impediment to the use of this greatly improved weapon appeared as great as ever in the late 1970s and the Court of Appeal set to with what looked like enthusiasm; despite the fact that Lord Scarman had declared[28] of section 13 of the 1976 Act that 'the law now is back to what Parliament had intended when it enacted the Act of 1906—but stronger and clearer than it was then'.[29] Lord Denning imported into the concept of immunity for 'furtherance' (of a trade dispute) meanings hitherto unknown to the compilers of the *Oxford English Dictionary*.[30] The House of Lords set aside every one of these restrictions on the scope of the immunity, not because a majority of its members disapproved of restriction, but because they were well aware of the threat to public confidence in the impartiality of the judiciary involved in such blatant alteration of the legislative intent. But whilst expressing this fear Lord Diplock made it clear that he

---

[25] [1952] Ch. 646.

[26] See e.g. *J. T. Stratford and Son Ltd.* v. *Lindley* [1965] AC 269; *Emerald Construction Co. Ltd.* v. *Lowthian* [1966] 1 All ER 1013; *Torquay Hotel Co. Ltd.* v. *Cousins* [1969] 2 Ch. 106.

[27] See e.g. *Meade* v. *Haringey London Borough Council* [1979] ICR 494 where he extended tort liability to inducement to breach of statutory duty, 'confident', he said, 'that the people at large would have supported such a move'. The HL certainly did so in *Merkur Island Shipping Corporation* v. *Laughton* [1983] 2 AC 570.

[28] In *NWL* v. *Woods* [1979] ICR 886.

[29] Not everyone in 1906 would have shared Lord Scarman's view. Lord Halsbury regarded the immunities as creating a privileged class, legalizing tyranny and likely to produce commercial distress (HL Debs., vol. 166, cols. 705 and 709). Dicey asked, 'Was there ever such a thing in a civilised country?' by which the caprice of a trade union could govern the employment condition of domestic servants, for example. See Wedderburn [1980] 9 ILJ at 89.

[30] See e.g. *BBC* v. *Hearn* [1977] IRLR 269; *NWL* v. *Woods* [1979] IRLR 478; *Express Newspapers Ltd.* v. *McShane* [1980] ICR 42; *Duport Steels Ltd.* v. *Sirs* [1980] 1 All ER 529.

disapproved of industrial muscle[31] and saw the current wage claims as aimed to bring down the economic system.[32] In *Duport Steels* v. *Sirs*[33] he said that the statutory immunity 'tended to stick in judicial gorges' and was 'intrinsically repugnant to anyone who has spent his life in the practice of the law or the administration of justice'.[34] If nothing else, the courts, both positively and negatively, had demonstrated the effect that could be achieved by defining and enforcing areas of illegality. By 1982 the programme of legislative reduction of the statutory immunity, no doubt prompted by these various indications of judicial support, had sufficiently progressed for Lord Diplock to leave the issue in the hands of Parliament.[35]

The Empire Strikes Back

As everybody knows, the last sixteen years have seen progressive restriction on the legal freedom to take industrial action, internal individualization of trade unions and more general pursuit of individualism in the cause of freeing the labour market, coupled with an economic situation inimical to trade union power. There is a complex interaction of these movements in which reduction of the power of organized labour to restrict the market is facilitated by market changes which that reduction, in turn, assists. Most significantly, security of employment is replaced by the attractively named 'flexibility'.[36] Professor Hepple summarizes the period in a sentence:

The auxiliary function of labour law was disestablished, the regulatory role was diminished, and the restrictive function was vastly enhanced by the strict control of trade unions, the confinement of trade union pressure to the plant or enterprise, and the imposition of draconian civil and quasi-criminal liability on unions.[37]

---

[31] *Express Newspapers* v. *McShane* [1980] ICR 35 at 56–7.

[32] *NWL* v. *Woods* [1979] ICR 867 at 878.

[33] [1980] 1 All ER 541 at 547.

[34] He was not alone in expressing such sentiments: see Wedderburn (1980) 9 *ILJ* at 91.

[35] *The Universal Sentinel* [1982] IRLR 200.

[36] See Mark Beatson, *Labour Market Flexibility*—Employment Department Research Series No 48 (1995) for a statistical survey of the advance of this concept.

[37] B. Hepple, 'The Future of Labour Law' (1995) 24 *ILJ* 310; and see Lord Wedderburn, *Employment Rights in Britain and Europe* (London, 1991), 211–24.

All these factors, and others, have complemented each other in weakening collective labour and enhancing individualism, but not strengthening the individual. That policy applies the central argument of the neo-Liberals that deregulation, rather than regulatory protection, is in the long-term interests of the worker. Pure theory is wisely presented as awaiting long-term proof. No proof, it is submitted, is yet apparent. Nevertheless successive governments have single-mindedly pursued this policy. A report of the Department of Trade and Industry has said that 'The United Kingdom government is committed to reducing regulatory and administrative burdens on business. No new laws may be introduced without ascertaining and minimising the costs to business.' If the European Union's policy makers share this view it is currently subordinated to the economic desire to maintain a level playing field of protective regulation. A desire to avoid distortion of the economic market by permitting social dumping prevails over a wish not to distort the labour market.[38] In the United Kingdom, from the outset in 1980, deregulatory individualization has intruded into all aspects of collectivism. The destruction of virtually all that characterized the industrial relations scene until 1971 could scarcely have been more effective. But far more significant for the future than that destruction has been the formulation of a new attitude of mind which sees no useful role for organized labour. Such collectivism as might survive is seen as workplace based consultation. The immunity upon which, regrettably, the right to strike relies has been eaten away to a point where most industrial action is tortious. Davies and Freedland[39] doubt whether an apparent programme of biennial statutes restricting both industrial action and freedom to organize was, at least initially, a planned 'step by step' reduction of the collective power of labour. One has to accept that had there been such a plan it would have seemed

---

[38] See P. Davies, 'The Emergence of European Labour Law', in Lord McCarthy (ed.), *Legal Intervention in Industrial Relations* (Oxford, 1992). The neo-Liberal theory does not go unchallenged although some of the contrary arguments similarly suffer from absence of proof. See S. Deakin and F. Wilkinson, 'Rights vs Efficiency? The Economic Base for Transnational Labour Standards' (1994) 23 *ILJ* 289. Hendy at 27 says that deregulation produces a 'Dutch auction in labour where worker competes with worker across the globe for the chance of a job at lower labour costs and in worse conditions'.

[39] N. 9 at 442.

quixotic to have appointed James Prior to carry it out.[40] But it is suggested that it is misleading to see the Employment Act 1980 as a mild exploration of how far it was necessary to go. In the name of democracy that Act set about individualizing trade unions, paradoxically, by a degree of regulatory bureaucracy antipathetic to any concept of voluntary association. The process was to reach its high point in abolition of the freeedom of a trade union to maintain the internal solidarity essential to its function as representative of the collective will by disciplining the individual who chooses to defy that will. Inevitably, it was to abolish the closed shop which neo-Liberals saw as a prime example both of an infringement of individual rights and a means of forcing up labour costs. Certainly government funding of an official with the duty to assist with advice and unlimited financial assistance individual members' legal actions against their unions is as startling as it is unprecedented.[41] Lord Wedderburn saw the prerogative action instigated by the Prime Minister against freedom of association among the staff of GCHQ as the turning point in rendering this concept meaningless in industrial relations.[42]

As early as 1982[43] the single most important step in strike control had been taken with the abolition of the total 1906 immunity for tort action of trade unions as such. Nothing less than judicial power to freeze trade union funds during an unlawful strike followed upon that measure. By 1989 the Committee of Experts of the International Labour Organization[44] felt it necessary to express concern 'at the volume and complexity of legislative change since 1980'. 'Whilst it is true,' it said, 'that most of the legislative

---

[40] See James Prior, *A Balance of Power* (London) 158. It was he who expressed it as a step-by-step policy and here it appears to be suggested that he meant thereby only to monitor the effect of measures and reinforce them if it appeared necessary. The evidence is that that was not the approach intended by the rest of the government, nor by Mr Prior's civil servants. James Prior was succeeded at the Department of Employment by Norman Tebbit who replaced the policy as much as was necessary to one of systematic sequential destruction of internal union authority and external union power. The disastrous root and branch approach of the Industrial Relations Act 1971 continued to be carefully avoided. Norman Tebbit wrote—*Upwardly Mobile* 234—'I rejected pressures to ban the closed shop—it simply wouldn't have worked, but I did set out to undermine it'.

[41] See now Trade Union and Labour Relations Act 1992, Chap. VIII.

[42] Lord Wedderburn (1989) 8 *ILJ* 38.

[43] Employment Act 1982, s. 15.

[44] 1989 Report III, Part 4a. Geneva, 1989, at 241.

measures were not incompatible with the requirements of ILO Conventions there is a point at which the cumulative effect constitutes an incursion upon the rights guaranteed by the Convention.' The Committee expressed its view that concern for the rights of the individual had not been matched by similar concern for the rights of trade unions. It might have asked whether such measures did more to increase the rights of the individual or to remove restrictions on the power of the employer.

In the midst of this process an opportunity was created to destroy the archetype of collective power—the National Union of Mineworkers. This was probably the primary purpose of the confrontation in 1984–5, but it also furnished an opportunity to test both the changes already made and the state of public opinion. If *GCHQ* is the watershed in the destruction of the freedom to associate in trade unions the defeat of the miners is the watershed of loss of the collective power of labour.[45] The trade union cause was lost before the battle was joined. Whatever the initial intention, attack upon the collective influence of labour was, by then, established government policy pursued with unprecedented determination. As Lord Wedderburn wrote,[46] '[w]hoever was right or wrong in the dispute, the unions lay like skittles bowled out into the corners of the industrial arena'. Nevertheless the propaganda coup for the policy was fortuitously greater than it might have been by reason of the arrogant leadership of the NUM, its failure to hold strike ballots in accordance with its own rules, and its public demonstration that, despite its reliance on promises made in 1974 for the future of coal, it did not carry important sections of its membership with it. The courts became part of the battleground and the principal instrument of publicity for the ultimate triumph of individualism.[47] On this occasion, however, although in line with well-established precedent they misapplied the *ultra vires* doctrine, they were not always unsympathetic to the cause of the miners.

The remainder of the story is well known. So far have the process and its accompanying propaganda now gone that expressions of

---

[45] There were, of course, other similarly significant steps such as the abolition of the National Dock Labour Scheme. See *Associated British Ports* v. *TGWU* [1989] IRLR 399.   [46] N. 4 above, 78.

[47] e.g., *Taylor and Foulstone* v. *NUM (Yorkshire Area)* [1984] IRLR 445; *Thomas* v. *NUM (South Wales Area)* [1985] 2 WLR 1081.

intention to pursue the attack are an essential part of the perpetual electioneering that now passes for government. Professor Hepple[48] regards even statements that the reform of labour law is now complete[49] as only indicative of the opinion that there is an end to labour law. He sees the disbandment of the Department of Employment as a delayed[50] culmination of a policy of decollectivizing, deregulating, and deinstitutionalizing labour law. The policy of revision of labour law is now driven by political, rather than economic, forces.

Judicial Regulation

As has been hinted, the process of individualization was to locate and thrive upon machinery already put in place with other purposes in mind. Most significant among that machinery are industrial tribunals. Naturally, they concentrate upon individual rights and, indeed, it was the conflict between their individualism and the collective functions conferred on the NIRC by the Industrial Relations Act 1971 which cast most strain upon that court. But much of the jurisdiction of the industrial tribunals goes further than mere individualism. It is founded on the contract of employment[51] and that is dominated by the employer. As Professor Hepple has said,[52]

. . . it is small wonder that statutory rights, such as those to protection from unfair dismissal, have been interpreted from the view of the 'reasonable employer' rather than that (adopted for example in Swedish law) of the employer's social responsibility for employees and the employee's right to remain employed. The contractual premises of British unfair dismissal law have led the courts and tribunals to judge reasonableness from the

---

[48] B. Hepple, 'The Future of Labour Law' (1995) 24 *ILJ* 303.

[49] The Rt. Hon. Michael Portillo MP when Secretary of State for Employment, *The Times* 3 July 1995. But see statements in 1996 by the Secretary of State for Trade and Industry of an intention to render strikes in the public service illegal if they appeared likely significantly to interfere with the provision of that service.

[50] See M. Freedland, 'The Role of the Department of Employment—Twenty Years of Institutional Change' in Lord McCarthy (ed.), n. 38 above, at 274–95 where it is suggested that the process of abolition had begun before the 1980s and would have been completed sooner had Mrs Thatcher remained Prime Minister.

[51] See B. Hepple, 'Restructuring Employment Rights' (1986) 15 *ILJ* 69.

[52] *Ibid.*, 82.

standpoint of the employer, rather than by balancing the interests of employer and employee.

The industrial tribunal, more than any other institution has judicialized British labour law. By founding that judicialization on a contractual model rather than an industrial relations model[53] legislation has greatly facilitated decollectivization. Not only have industrial tribunals been the principal machine in this process but their presence and popularity may well have made it acceptable. An opportunity to link individual rights enforceable in industrial tribunals with the collective procedures of industrial relations was missed in the 1970s probably because the Department of Employment failed to realize, and accordingly frustrated, the purpose behind the statutory provisions for registering collectively agreed disciplinary procedures as an alternative to resort to tribunals.[54] A belated plan to do so in 1997 is likely to be too late to achieve this purpose.[55] Paradoxically, the more beneficial the effect of legislation on individual rights the more it emphasizes individualism through the contract of employment. The largely unexpected effect of the Wages Act 1986 by which some 10,000 employees a year collect debts from employers obviously undermines the powers of collective representation of trade unions, and it is scarcely surprising, therefore, that a general contractual jurisdiction has now been conferred on industrial tribunals. Even the Labour Party plans an individual right to a minimum wage to replace the collective procedure of the abolished Wages Councils.

Not at all surprisingly the courts in this period have begun to show signs of assuming the regulatory role that Kahn-Freund saw as one of the three functions of labour law. They are always at their best when protecting the individual, and the most distinguished members of the judiciary have shown an enthusiasm for experimentation in the development of individual employment rights for which they would never have had the opportunity but for the

---

[53] See e.g. Browne-Wilkinson J in *Williams* v. *Compair Maxim Ltd.* [1982] IRLR 83. See also R. Rideout, 'Unfair Dismissal—Tribunal or Arbitration' (1986) 15 *ILJ* 84.   [54] See Rideout, n. 53 above.

[55] If alternative arbitration through ACAS were to achieve its most beneficial potential effect by increasing the incidence of reinstatement in employment it would probably drive employers, who fear that more than any other remedy, back to tribunals. If it were to succeed its relative cheapness would deprive trade unions of a valuable bargaining counter in achieving voluntary settlement.

legislative intervention between 1965 and 1978. Regrettably the judicial attitude to the auxiliary collective area seems not to have changed from that adopted in the late 1970s, but this, perhaps, is because they cannot fail to see the legislative disapproval of any sign of such change. An indication of this swimming with the tide, so startling that it surprised even the most hardened juro-sceptics, is the decision of the House of Lords in *Associated Newspapers Ltd.* v. *Wilson.*[56] Many employers have taken advantage of the cumulative weakness of trade unions to remove the machinery whereby they have traditionally exercised their influence. In this case two separate employers had offered higher rates of pay to employees who abandoned the collective bargaining structure, and one had derecognized the union for bargaining purposes. The plaintiffs claimed that by offering non-unionists higher rates of pay the employers were discriminating against other employees on the grounds of union membership. The Court of Appeal, following its own earlier decision,[57] held that there was no genuine distinction between union membership and resort to the normal services of a trade union, so that it was discriminatory on the grounds of union membership to pay less to those who sought to make use of those services. The legislature responded[58] by raising a presumption that where there was evidence that an employer intended to further a change in his relationship with his employees and to discriminate on grounds of trade union membership only the first intention constituted the purpose for which he took action unless the action was such that no reasonable employer would take for such a purpose. It will readily be appreciated that the two purposes are aspects of one purpose and that what the legislature is saying is that where an employer discriminates on grounds of union membership in order to alter the position of the union in relation to him his discriminatory motive is to be ignored. In face of this declaration of legislative intent all members of the House of Lords[59] concluded

---

[56] Coupled with *Associated British Ports* v. *Palmer* [1995] IRLR 258.
[57] *National Coal Board* v. *Ridgway* [1987] IRLR 80.
[58] Trade Union Reform and Employment Rights Act 1993, s. 13.
[59] The decision was primarily founded on the conclusion that 'act' does not include 'omission' in relation to such discriminatory conduct. Although Lords Lloyd and Slynn dissented, it does seem that this is correct on any reasonable grammatical construction of the legislation. Lord Browne-Wilkinson viewed this conclusion with

that, since in neither case were employees wishing to qualify for the higher rate required to give up union membership, but only their reliance on bargaining collectively through their union, the employer was not discriminating on grounds of union membership. To say, as did one member of the House, that there is much benefit left in trade union membership after collective bargaining is stripped from it reduces the trade union to a friendly society. If this is their only permitted function then the freedom to join trade unions is abolished. Even after all their effort it remains true to say, as did Sir Otto Kahn-Freund in 1972,[60] 'the contribution which the courts have made to the orderly development of collective labour relations has been infinitesimal'. This is just as well. The courts have conclusively demonstrated that they are unable to comprehend the purpose of industrial relations.

When we look to the regulatory function of individual employment protection, however, the courts appear in a very different light. Lord Woolf has spent much time and thought experimenting with public law remedies.[61] There is little doubt that the courts have retired to reconsider this experiment and they may not hurry to resume it in view of the acknowledgment of the existence of contractual rights for civil servants and the cautious, but un-doubted, development of an equally effective remedy in the injunction. Ever since Lord Denning opened the door to specific enforcement of the contract of employment in *Hill v. C. A. Parsons & Co. Ltd.*[62] the possibility has existed of using the injunction to enforce terms[63] and even to reinstate.[64] It is, of course, no objection to the effectiveness of such a remedy that it can favour either party to the relationship.[65] The same is true of the somewhat underrated, but very real, extension of protection afforded by the

---

regret because it left 'an undesirable lacuna in the legislation protecting employees against victimisation'. It is less clear why the majority should not have considered that payment of a lower rate was an act rather than an omission.

[60] Kahn-Freund, n. 2 above.

[61] See Lord Woolf, 'Droit Public—English Style' [1995] *Public Law* 57; 'Public Law—Private Law: Why the Divide?' [1986] *Public Law* 220; *R. v. East Berkshire Area Health Authority, ex p. Walsh* [1984] ICR 743.

[62] [1972] 1 Ch. 305.

[63] e.g. *Dietman v. London Borough of Brent* [1987] ICR 737.

[64] e.g. *Irani v. Southampton and South West Hampshire Health Authority* [1985] ICR 590.

[65] e.g. *Evening Standard v. Henderson* [1987] IRLR 64.

abolition of the perniciously wrong assumption that wrongful repudiation of the contract was an effective termination.[66] The degree of uncertainty which is produced by a contract which theoretically continues until there is evidence of acceptance of the repudiation is not, it is submitted, a good ground to doubt the theoretical correctness of this judicial reform.[67] The Court of Appeal did not present its decision in *Faccenda Chicken* v. *Fowler*[68] in any other light than as an application of existing law, but it was nothing of the sort. It swept away, and it was intended to sweep away, much of the restriction on the marketability of an employee's acquired skills which had developed within the implied term of respect for an employer's trade secrets as that had extended to respect for most forms of confidentiality. No one should, and the knowledgeable will not, deduce from this that the courts are committed to employee protection. One only has to refer to the decision in *Cresswell* v. *Board of Inland Revenue*[69] to observe that the courts are still addicted to the policy of sustaining the power of management to manage.

But elsewhere the courts have been equally inventive. The Employment Appeal Tribunal (EAT), under the presidency of Phillips J, had done no less than confer viability on anti-discrimination law.[70] Lord Browne-Wilkinson would probably hesitate to accept that he had performed almost as singular a service for the law of unfair redundancy in *Williams* v. *Compair Maxim Ltd.*[71]—and he may even be surprised to find the right of consultation, which he there sought to establish for trade unions, now applied to all redundancy dismissals. He would not be so surprised to find that it took the House of Lords, in which he had not then arrived, five years to implement his attack, in *Sillifant* v. *Powell Duffryn Timber Ltd.*,[72] on the pernicious rule in *British Labour Pump* v. *Byrne*. Unfortunately the House of Lords fatally hesitated in *Polkey* v. *A. E. Dayton Services Ltd.*[73] allowing a

---

[66] See particularly *Gunton* v. *London Borough of Richmond* [1980] ICR 755.
[67] See remarks to this effect in *Boyo* v. *London Borough of Southwark* [1995] IRLR 50.   [68] [1986] IRLR 69.   [69] [1984] IRLR 90.
[70] The individualization of the remedy for discrimination, which is inherently a collective problem, has perpetuated that trend to individualization of all labour law.
[71] [1982] IRLR 83.   [72] [1983] IRLR 91.
[73] [1988] AC 344, [1988] ICR 142.

somewhat reactionary EAT virtually to reintroduce the former rule.[74]

When we turn to the judicial influence upon the content of the contract of employment we find some willingness and ability to restrain employer initiative in the interest of the individual employee. For well over a century until 1971 the courts had been relatively inactive in this field for the simple reason that employees would very rarely have litigated the terms of their contracts except as a result of dismissal, and actions for dismissal, if they occurred at all, would have been brought in county courts. The High Court dealt only with untypical employees with long notice entitlement, and it is not surprising that the implied terms it developed reflected employee duties rather than rights. But in 1972 the new right to complain to an industrial tribunal of unfair dismissal, and, perhaps most significantly, the right to treat a repudiatory breach of contract by an employer as constituting a dismissal, produced vast numbers of reported cases exploring the opportunities for manipulating contractual terms.

The new era started unpromisingly with the decision of the Court of Appeal in *R.* v. *Secretary of State for Employment, ex parte ASLEF*[75] replacing the suggested implication of active co-operation[76] with a duty not wilfully to disrupt the undertaking (by industrial action such as a work to rule). But it was this decision that led to development of a compromise in the dual obligation of each party to maintain the trust and confidence of the other.[77] Lord Wedderburn[78] expresses despair that this should so clearly be seen to be capable of requiring co-operation from the employee, but it remains a major advance in common law recognition of employee

---

[74] *Duffy* v. *Yeomans & Partners Ltd.* [1994] IRLR 642.

[75] [1992] ICR 19.

[76] Some textbooks still contend for such a term relying on the occasional remark that an employee failing to co-operate might be in breach of her duty to maintain trust and confidence: e.g. *Woods* v. *W.M. Car Services* [1982] IRLR 413 (CA). Even Professor Hepple did so, categorically, in *Wood* v. *Freeloader Ltd.*[1977] IRLR 455.

[77] See e.g. *Isle of Wight Tourist Board* v. *Coombes* [1976] IRLR 413; *Courtaulds Northern Textiles Ltd* v. *Andrew* [1979] IRLR 84; *Wigan Borough Council* v. *Davies* [1979] IRLR 127; *Post Office* v. *Roberts* [1980] IRLR 347; *BBC* v. *Beckett* [1983] IRLR 423; *Bracebridge Engineering Ltd.* v. *Darby* [1990] IRLR 3; *Imperial Group Trusts* v. *Imperial Tobacco plc* [1991] IRLR 66; *Ticehurst* v. *British Telecommunications* [1992] IRLR 219; *Newns* v. *British Airways Corporation* [1992] IRLR 275.   [78] Wedderburn, n. 44 ab~

rights. In *Jones* v. *Associated Tunnelling*[79] Browne-Wilkinson J (as he then was) reversed the previous assumption that the employee, by continuing to work, was deemed to accept unilateral variation initiated by the employer. In that same case he took the massive step of saying that it was not necessary for the courts to rely on what they supposed the parties would have agreed before they could imply a term. This opened further a door to overtly independent judicial action which had been left ajar by Slynn J (as he then was) in *Mears* v. *Safecar Securities Ltd.*[80] Everyone has their moments of failure and it is regrettable that Browne-Wilkinson J should, in *Evans* v. *Elemeta Holdings Ltd.*,[81] have failed to secure the adoption of the concept of the reasonable employee to counterbalance that of the employer.

In *United Bank* v. *Akhtar*[82] an industrial tribunal had invoked trust and confidence to overcome blatantly unreasonable use of an express mobility clause. There is an obvious difficulty in suggesting that invocation by an employer of a contractual right destroys the employee's trust and confidence. An inspired EAT invented the ultimate, overriding implication in a term that one party should not use its contractual powers in such a way as to make performance by the other 'practically' impossible.

It will be objected that these are isolated incidents and that many more decisions suggest that the employer is, or could be, in control. *Akhtar*, for instance, would not have been so difficult if the common sense mobility term adopted by Browne-Wilkinson J in *Jones* had not been summarily rejected in favour of a blanket, and uninformative, express term in *Rank Xerox Ltd.* v. *Churchill*.[83] But if the will of even some of the leaders of the judiciary remains to protect the employee from exploitation there is a good chance of the common law assisting other protective devices. The will was certainly there in a majority of the Court of Appeal in *Johnstone* v. *Bloomsbury Health Authority*[84] although Browne-Wilkinson V-C perhaps showed employers the way to outwit his reconstruction of the contract of employment in that case. In *Aspden* v. *Webbs Poultry and Meat Group (Holdings) Ltd.*[85] Sedley J actually

[79] [1981] IRLR 477.
[80] [1982] IRLR 183.
[81] [1982] ICR 323.
[82] [1989] IRLR 507.
[83] [1988] IRLR 280.
[84] [1992] QB 333.
[85] [1996] IRLR 521.

dispensed with an express term which obviously did not represent the intention of the parties when a new contract was signed on the ground that the contract was 'internally inconsistent'.

Taking Stock

The second half of this century has seen growing attack from many quarters on collective labour organization, reaching a crescendo in the last sixteen years. That attack has been the more effective in the light of growing unemployment. Although it is true to say that a peak in 1979 of twelve million trade union members and a collective bargaining cover of 80 per cent[86] concealed alarming weakness in the union movement, reduction of this number by almost one third, to eight and a half million, and of collective bargaining cover to less than half the workforce, reveals the severity of the attack. The reality is probably worse than it looks. Just as effective as the law in imposing sanctions on industrial action is the fear among potential strikers, after two major recessions since 1979, of being made 'redundant'. In September 1996 there were two and a quarter million registered unemployed. This fell below two million in December 1996, but that drop was probably due to the administrative barriers to obtaining benefit raised by the job seekers' allowance.[87] The total itself is undoubtedly well short of the number in the labour force not in regular employment. So, even where unions are well organized, the incidence of industrial action is much diminished and their bargaining power sharply reduced. Of course, reduction in the number of strikes, which has been the primary objective of the attack, is economically beneficial. In 1979 strikes cost 1,272 days per 1,000 workers. In 1995 the corresponding figure was nineteen. Is the worker paying for increased profitability or is he or she benefiting from it?

Underlying this is a massive change in the nature of the

---

[86] 84%–86% in 1975, counting Wages Councils: Mark Beatson, *Labour Market Flexibility* (London, 1995) (see particularly 27–8 and 71–2) suggests a lower figure. Citing the WIRS survey 1990, which covers only establishments with more than 25 employees, he gives a coverage of 54%. Such establishments only account for 70% of the workforce. A majority of the remaining 30% are unlikely to be covered.

[87] It is not suggested that this figure is exceptional in Europe. The Sept. figure represented 8.85% of the workforce. In Germany unemployment accounted for 10% of the workforce, much of this in the former GDR, and in France 12%.

workforce. Uniform contracts are being replaced by individual variation. The long-term job is disappearing as an expectation and this greatly enhances the burden of insecurity the worker bears. One theory is that uncertainty is a spur to effort. This is probably the result of a simplistic deduction from the apparent effect of job security in the former Soviet Union.[88] However that may be, a study of the underlying causes of industrial unrest would reveal that insecurity was principal among them.

The nature of the workforce has already radically changed. Women comprise 48 per cent of it but only 55 per cent of those are in full-time employment. By no means all of these are second earners but where they are they will tend to accept low wages. They, and the substantial proportion of part-time and casual men, as well as the 3,206,000 self-employed, will be difficult to organize collectively.[89]

Virtually all the legislative infrastructure of collective bargaining has gone. The power to seek compulsory bargaining rights was removed, with the support of the then Chairman of ACAS, in 1980. The Central Arbitration Committee had lost most of its functions by 1982. Wages Councils were abolished in 1993 leaving the unions to wonder why they had been so critical of them. Across the public sector the general duty to maintain collective labour relations has disappeared with privatization. Only the individual-izing industrial tribunals flourish, despite the misplaced wish of one Prime Minister to abolish them.

Individualization and privatization in the interests of en-couraging the operation of market forces have fed into the system a reduction of both standards and security precisely at the time when economic markets throughout the world were creating similar insecurity. Nowhere was this more apparent than in the system of compulsory competitive tendering,[90] the effect of which has been

---

[88] This effect is due more to the lack of incentive in a system restricting the acquisition of wealth.

[89] The writer's estimate is that 31% of the workforce falls in the low organizability category.

[90] It is not the writer's purpose to depict this as anything but economically desirable, even necessary. Anyone acquainted, for example, with the costing systems of local authority direct works departments before the introduction of CCT must realize that only monopoly control of the operation saved such departments from economic destruction.

standardization downwards.[91] For some years this provided a frightening example of the effect of the labour market on employment standards. Existing contractors were undercut on retendering by those who had calculated their prices on longer hours and lower pay. The remedy actually existed in the Acquired Rights Directive but was not effectively pointed out until Professors Hepple and Byre[92] undertook still inadequately acknowledged research into the failure of UK law properly to implement EC law.

Much more could be added to this account. As Professor Hepple says:

The law has been an important factor favouring employers in the bargaining process and changing union strategy in negotiations, it has been an arm of politics in which alternative notions of law, economic efficiency and social justice have been fought out, it has legitimated an ideology of individualistic self-interest, and it has been a weapon of great importance in disputes such as those in the printing and mining industries in the 1980s.

Those who maintain that social and economic engineering cannot successfully be carried out by the law are right in the sense that this massive revolution was achieved by a combination of law, economic circumstance, propaganda, and sheer determination.[93] As a result the whole foundation of what was once frequently called the law of industrial relations has shifted. Labour law is no longer the law of industrial relations. That law scarcely exists save in a negative, prohibitory sense. Labour law is now a law of individualism monitored, if at all and haphazardly, by the judiciary. The common law is in resurgence. The law of the contract of employment, always a powerful force where law operated, now pervades the whole field of labour relations. Those who resisted the changes of the 1970s and 1980s, partly on the ground that the parties to the employment relationship would come to think only of law and no longer of that relationship, have been shown to be right.

---

[91] See M. Radford and A. Kerr, 'Acquiring Rights' (1997) 60 *MLR* 23.

[92] B. Hepple and A. Byre, *The Application of EEC Labour Law in the United Kingdom* (A report to the Directorate General, Employment, Social Affairs and Education of the European Commission) (London, 1988).

[93] B. Hepple, n. 21 above, 311–12. He points out that Sir Otto Kahn-Freund described as 'superstition' the 'magic belief in the efficacy of the law in shaping human conduct and social relations'. If the belief were justified the Industrial Relations Act 1971 would have had tremendous success.

But labour law itself is increasingly inadequate without consideration of sociology, economics, public law, constitutional law, and
many other subject areas bearing upon the working (and non-
working) environment.

The Way Ahead

If there is to be an effective change of direction only one approach is
possible. The success of deregulation and individualization in the
past eighteen years has been in very large measure due to the
creation of an ideology of such power that its guiding principles
were widely accepted.[94] Professor Hepple positively asserts that
'[a]n alternative strategy needs a clear ideology, one which is
capable of forming the basis for a new social consensus, for without
such a consensus a divided and demoralized Britain will be
incapable of competing successfully in the European and international economies.'[95] Typically, he incorporates in his demand the
very ideology he requires, for it is the ideology of necessary
competitiveness which fuelled the process of deregulation. He
invokes it to support the consensus necessary effectively to change
direction.

Future development of labour law has, of course, both substantive and procedural aspects. Both begin with a debate whether
any new directions should be taken. To the issue of substantive
change the Conservative governments of the past eighteen years
have generally responded with the age-old assumption that
increased regulation means increased cost. The claim is certainly as
old as industrialization in Western Europe. Support from influential industrialists for the first Factories Act and the 1831 Truck
Act undoubtedly existed and was often based on the assumption
that undercutting of costs by smaller competitors would be curbed
by the regulatory imposition of certain standards.[96] Sir Otto Kahn-
Freund put the converse thus:

Protective legislation . . . thus enlarges the worker's freedom, his freedom
from the employer's power of command, or, if you like, his freedom to give

[94] See S. Fredman, 'The New Rights: Labour Law and Ideology in the Thatcher
Years' (1992) 12 *OJLS* 24.   [95] Hepple, n. 21 above, 312.
[96] S. Deakin and F. Wilkinson, 'Rights vs Efficiency? The Economic Base for
Transnational Labour Standards' (1994) 23 *ILJ* 289.

priority to his own and his family's interests over those of his employer. . . . Conversely, to restrain a person's freedom of contract may be necessary to protect his freedom, that is to protect him against oppression which he may otherwise be constrained to impose upon himself through an act of his legally free, and socially unfree, will.[97]

The first question must be whether it is necessary to embark on a programme of substantial development of new rights. The EC has made its position clear although there are several ways of describing it. Its 'socialism' lies in a declaration that the worker is entitled to share in the increasing prosperity it seeks to produce. The power a directive can have has already been commented upon in relation to the Acquired Rights Directive and the then government had good reason to be alarmed at the potentially regulatory effect of the Working Time Directive.[98] Assuming that the United Kingdom remains a member of the EC it will, ultimately, be compelled to accept this source of regulation. Arguably, that source can be expected to supply all the significant forward movement which might reasonably be expected from legislation. How that hypothetical legislation is received and applied, however, will depend on the degree of acceptance of the principle and protective purpose of regulation.

Wherever the momentum for new rights derives from its success depends on recognition that such developments are necessary. It is submitted that a strong case can be made out on many aspects not thought of hitherto as part of employment law. That case rests on acceptance of a general principle. If the worker is to work well he or she needs to feel secure. This, it is submitted ,is the fallacy of the neo-Liberal argument. Even if it is correct to say that deregulation will bring long-term benefits they do not include security. Prosperity

---

[97] Kahn-Freund, n. 2 above, 15–16.

[98] Council Directive 93/104 [1993] OJ L307/18. The government Consultative Document on the implementation of this Dir., issued early in 1997, emphasizes the alternative to bargaining with recognized trade unions by consulting with elected representatives who are likely to be inexpert, inexperienced, ill-informed, and relatively ineffective. Such deactivization of collective bargaining potential is not new. The response to imposition of collective consultation under the Collective Redundancies Directive (75/129, [1975] OJ L48/29) was to adopt the minimum EC requirement of application to redundancies of 20 or more persons, thereby removing some 95% of redundancies from the previous UK consultation requirement. See SI 2587/1995, reg. 3, amending TULR(C)A 1992, s. 188.

deriving from an absence of regulated benefit is precisely the same as prosperity derived from paternalism. Both depend on the continuing prosperity of the source of the benefits. It can be argued that absence of regulation assists the prosperity of that source but by no means does it ensure it. Even if we assume that most employers are paternalistic, an assumption which a week in an industrial tribunal will always dissipate, there is no guarantee that the employer will be in a position to afford the benefits and the protection of security which the worker needs. It has already been said that the root cause of a high proportion of past industrial unrest has been insecurity. An insecure workforce, therefore, will not, in the long term, produce the prosperity on which the benefits of deregulation depend.

Some aspects of the need for protective regulation cannot be brushed out of sight. Admirable as was the Goode Report on pension provision as a holding operation, it is suggested that it will be, or already has been, overtaken by the speed with which governments throughout the EC are abandoning the concept of the state providing anything approaching adequate financial provision following retirement. At the present time, however, almost one quarter of the working population has no pension provision other than that of the State. Of the 5.5 million who have personal pensions some 4.5 million last year made contributions which would yield less than £2,000 per year. Forty per cent of all employees have no employer's pension scheme. In another dimension, a woman taking the average four-year break to have, and care for, children is likely to suffer a 30 per cent reduction of entitlement compared to a woman taking no such break. Despite the guarantee of terminal and surrender value there is no continuing right to private pension provision. As the apparent security of state provision is withdrawn the worker will expect it to be replaced by private provision. It would appear a matter of history, experience, common sense, and even legal logic that the individualism of the contract of employment will not do so. At present, however, not even that source of rights governs the provision of occupational pensions which rest upon the voluntary continuation of the trust established by the employer and of which the employer is the beneficiary, and, frequently, the majority of the trustees. It is a simple enough step, given the will to take it, to impose a statutory obligation upon employers to make pension provision to specified minimum standards, as is the case in Holland.[99] Costs rise and our products become less competitive, but it is questionable whether a justifiable cost of maintaining competitiveness is streets filled with ageing beggars. Nor is it clear that the worker in general can be said to benefit if many workers avoid joining them.

One of the most frequently remarked developments of the past twenty years is the increase in part-time and casual employment. Like so many changes considered by government as desirable the phenomenon is often given a more acceptable name, of which 'flexibility' is the most common. In much of continental Europe the development is actively encouraged. A survey of five countries in 1989[100] revealed that seven times as many managers thought it made their companies more competitive than took the opposite view. The ability it gives to management to cope with peaks and troughs of demand is obvious. Governments welcome it as a means of reducing the apparent rate of unemployment. There is, therefore, little chance of reversing the trend, even if that were to be considered in the overall interest of workers. Indeed the principal pressure is to take steps to increase opportunities for part-time working, as for instance by better nursery provision. The EC has responded by moves to equalize the rights of part- and full-time workers. But in the United Kingdom part-time employment generally has a low status and is relatively poorly remunerated. Most part-timers consider they have little chance of promotion. It follows, also, that many part-time and casual workers move in and out of employment never escaping poverty. In the United Kingdom the common law has gone a stage further by casting doubt on the status as employees of many workers involved in this development and its associated types such as home- and tele-working. In sum, part-time employment continues, in the United Kingdom, to be a major means of deskilling and dilution of labour standards. If these forms of work are with us to stay the case for regulation to equalize and protect part-timers is clear. It is a case to which the EC has begun to respond. The United Kingdom may be dragged in its wake but does not appear to accept the justification of such protective regulation. One could develop a long list of such social and

---

[99] See *Dietz* v. *Stichting Thuisorg Rotterdam* [1996] IRLR 692.
[100] New forms of work and activity: representative survey of enterprises— European Foundation for the Improvement of Living and Working Conditions.

economic needs. The need to develop training programmes to equip workers to retain employment in an era of rapidly developing technology and an absence of jobs for life is only one of the most obvious.

Such examples of the need for regulation to maintain standards could be multiplied many times. How best is that provision to be made? Supporters of deregulation and reliance on market forces must, ultimately, rely on the individual contract of employment. We have already seen how extensive this reliance has become. It is, in turn, encouraging market developments which increase insecurity. There is, for instance, much less tendency for employers to apply standard terms to the whole workforce. That means that those 'weak' in one respect or another suffer. But the control the employer has over the formulation of the contract must mean that the interests of both weak and strong are subordinate to the interests of the business. Academically, it is tempting to suggest that the evidence briefly examined earlier in this article indicates that reasonably benevolent common law courts could develop sufficient protection of contractual rights. They cannot do so. Quite apart from the sporadic nature of such judicial protection, and the fact that it can be traced to a very small number of judges, all the development of implied terms since 1971 has provided instruction to those employers who wish to heed it as to how the contract may be revised to exclude the protection particular decisions have afforded. Only lawyers grow richer advising where the loopholes lie in such defined areas of protection. Whilst the express term prevails and employers are free to devise the express term the contract will grant only the rights that the employer is prepared to concede. The situation is not as hopeless as that logical deduction would suggest, since employers continue to demonstrate an historical reluctance to impose express terms. But suppose for a moment that this is most probably because there is no great economic incentive to do so. Then imagine a situation in which statutory redundancy compensation ceases to be inadequate even for the worker with some job prospects, let alone for the worker over the age of 50 with little chance of securing permanent employment again. Imagine, further, the removal of the ridiculous limit on compensation for unfair dismissal, one of the aspects of which is set at half average weekly earnings. Deregulation, incidentally, ought to involve the increase of both these items to market levels. Ask then whether the future of labour law can scarcely rely on *ex gratia* concessions by the goodwill of the employer alone.

There is much more to be said for a combination of legislative regulation and sympathetic judicial construction as a means of effective protection. An older generation of labour lawyers will not have forgotten that Phillips J saved the Equal Pay Act, and indeed much more of anti-discrimination law, from the impotence with which such equivocal concepts as 'like work' threatened it. The careful reasoning of Lord Oliver's judgment in *Litster* v. *Forth Dry Dock and Engineering Co. Ltd.*[101] rescued the Transfer of Undertakings (Protection of Employment) Regulations 1981[102] from the contemptuous disregard engendered by the simple device of dismissing the workforce an hour before the nominal documented time for transfer of the undertaking and, instead, established those regulations as the single most effective legislative protection to appear in labour law since 1978. It is scarcely necessary to point out the scope offered by judicial interpretation[103] nor the risk that it will have a restrictive, rather than an enabling, effect.[104] History also demonstrates that legislative regulation does not always produce the result intended.[105]

If general protective measures are to be developed much will have

---

[101] [1989] ICR 341.   [102] SI 1981 No. 1794.

[103] Not all such adventures take hold upon the law. In *Bass Leisure Ltd.* v. *Thomas* [1994] IRLR 104, e.g., Judge Hicks sought to reverse the well established conclusion that the reference in the Redundancy Payments Act 1965 to 'place of employment' indicated the full range of mobility permitted by an express mobility clause in a contract of employment. He distinguished the contractual definition of the place where the employee worked from such a wider mobility. Such a change would produce an enormous increase in the situations in which employees were entitled to claim to be redundant but it is unlikely that it can withstand the fact that the employee would still be under a contractual obligation to move. As the decision in *Evans* v. *Elemeta Holdings Ltd.* (n. 81, above) reveals even the influence of a decision of Browne-Wilkinson J is not proof of lasting effect.

[104] The history of restrictive judicial interpretation of s. 14 of the Factories Act 1961 and its predecessors, was a major reason for removing health and safety protection from the influence of reported decisions.

[105] The effect may, on occasion, be far greater than was intended, as use made of the Wages Act 1986, s. 1 demonstrates. On the other hand what is now the Employment Rights Act 1996, s. 1, was obviously designed to provide the employee with useful knowledge of the content of the contract of employment, but has more often furnished the employee with an instrument whereby he is able to confirm his initiation of that content or the effect of an initially unilateral variation of that contract.

to be done by legislation rendered immune from contractual dilution. But legislation has inherent limits. One is clear. Whilst it is tempting to suggest that if the historical reliance on collective industrial relations to maintain employment standards has been destroyed the historical absence of a Labour Code should be made good, few with experience of similar attempts at sweeping social engineering in this field would advocate the effectiveness of a development likely to be seen as both alien, radical, and cast in generalized statements. Legislation is also rigid and incapable of adaptation to individual needs, and so its protection is only relative and often inadequate.

One example of the fallibility of all the preceding types of protection will suffice, since it is obvious that it can, and will, be repeated many times in the future. Thirteen hundred employees at the Halewood plant of the Ford Motor Company in January 1997 had contracts of employment. They were 'protected' by legislative redundancy rights both individually and by way of collective consultation. It is not clear whether they lost their jobs because of poor productivity or because an aging plant would cost too much to retool or, very simply, because it is much cheaper and easier in this country to deal with redundancy rights.[106] Whatever the reason, neither in the short or the long term were they protected when the prosperity was diverted elsewhere.

It is submitted that only collective regulation achieved by negotiation between employers and worker representatives is sufficiently flexible to adapt itself to the conflicting interests of an industrial situation in which the sources of paternalism have run out. Collective bargaining possesses a far higher degree of flexibility to adapt to particular circumstances than does legislation. Its express intention is in this country usually much less clear but, paradoxically, interpretation by further negotiation is far more reliable. Its understanding of the problem to be resolved is inevitably clearer. Its ultimate result is, by definition, likely to be acceptable to both sides. In the late 1960s the Royal Commission

---

[106] *Independent*, 5 Feb. 1997 reported that confidential management documents revealed that a major consideration had been the saving of £45 million in making British, rather than German, workers redundant. It was calculated that there would be an increase in labour costs as between Britain and Germany between 1998 and 2001 of $27.3million, offset by this saving.

rightly saw local bargaining as the most effective regulator of the employment relationship.[107] By the late 1970s it was seen as unacceptably restrictive of productivity. It, and its operators, have been held responsible for the relatively poor economic performance of the United Kingdom throughout most of the second half of the century despite the obvious deduction that if that was so management must be equally responsible. Its ultimate effectiveness has been seen to depend upon the effectiveness of industrial action, and where it continues to exist today it is a far less potent weapon than it was mainly by reason of a combination of legal sanction and general job insecurity, which makes it difficult to induce workers to risk such industrial action. An atmosphere has been created in which collective bargaining is frequently insufficiently effective in modifying managerial initiative. The prevailing ideology has had its effect. There is an increasing tendency either to reject collective regulation entirely or to shade it off into consultation.

Not surprisingly, therefore, the Institute of Employment Rights has produced a blueprint for reform which would substantially remove legal sanctions from industrial action whilst increasing the power of labour organizations to seek recognition by employers.[108] But how is this ideological revolution to be made acceptable? Surely not by a return to withdrawal of the law, once more leaving establishment of standards to the unregulated interplay of organized capital and organized labour. That would be to invite precisely the backlash which destroyed the experiments of the 1970s, for we have to accept that the Thatcherite ideology is now as firmly entrenched as traditional pluralism had been before that time. It seems unlikely that any government would consciously restore trade unions to the position of power they had in the late 1970s. Governments which strove to cope with the economic effects of frequent industrial action are unlikely to permit its relatively unregulated return. In any event no such radical return to the past is

---

[107] If, in the light of earlier comments about the ability of trade unions nationally to deliver wage restraint in the context of effective local wage bargaining, the answer must be that that cannot, and should not, be the function of trade unions. Trade unions should be consulted by government. Bargaining with government is not their proper function.

[108] Institute of Employment Rights, *The Guide to Working Life* (ed. K. Ewing) (London, 1996). The section of this report on limitation of the right to strike, for example, contains no suggestion of any significant limitation.

practicable. Whilst suggesting that the blueprint is impractical, it must be accepted that it is based on recognition of the need to reintroduce the effectiveness of the only reliable method of maintaining labour standards. One must answer, therefore, the question how a new era of co-operative collective industrial relations might take hold in a new ideological atmosphere.

There are plenty of alternative theories to that which says that productivity is best enhanced by deregulation and the unchecked operation of market forces. In January 1997, for instance, Portland Cement announced the completion of a five-year agreement based on acceptance of the fact that more was to be expected of a motivated workforce than of an insecure and disgruntled group of individuals. In such an atmosphere, as Professor Hepple points out,[109] Sir Otto Kahn-Freund's concepts of the auxillary and the regulatory functions of labour law may be allowed to take their proper place, whilst the restrictive function, dominant since the mid-1980s, is cut back to allow effective representation of labour. He designates much of the area of necessary new provision already exemplified in this article as a fourth 'integrative' function. All these elements, clearly, could be operated in the threefold system of legislation, judicial interpretation, and, in the case of contract, control, and collective standard-making envisaged previously in this section of this article. So far, so good. Most commentators seem to stop at about this point with some high-sounding statements of objective, such as the establishment of equality for all with labour law as the guardian of human rights in employment; a touch, here and there, on the rules imposing an impossible individualism on trade unions. This lack of substantive proposals is a wise precaution since it avoids discussion of some of the most difficult areas of dispute. It will, however, be necessary to embark upon such detail at some stage, and an attempt will now be made to begin to do so.

Tactically it might seem most acceptable that auxillary machinery should first be put in place, allowing collective action to develop around it. The individualizing effect of industrial tribunals must be paralleled by a similar collective arbiter. Whether or not the Central Arbitration Committee is given a new lease of life is immaterial so long as collective jurisdictions are established. Most obviously, it is

---

[109] (1995) 24 *ILJ* at 321.

submitted, there should be a mechanism whereby the standards set by employers who are passing on benefits to their workforce may be applied to prevent others undercutting those standards. It does not need great perception to see that fear of such undercutting will act as a brake upon negotiation. A limited system of extension of collective agreements has worked successfully in this country under the Fair Wages Resolution and Schedule 11 of the Employment Protection Act 1975. A more extensive system works well in other countries. Such a system cannot itself be inflationary, which was the principal reason given for its abolition. Only an imbalance between those operating such a system can produce such an effect. If collective agreement is agreement on equal terms, rather than on the basis of management capitulation to the strike weapon, as it frequently was in the 1960s and 1970s, there is no reason why it should not be recognized as the real source of agreed standards, replacing the imbalance of the individual contract. The development of compulsory arbitration as an auxiliary mechanism to replace strikes has been mooted. But compulsory arbitration needs full and careful study. It can, for instance, have a gravely detrimental effect on settlement by inducing one party or the other to defer agreement to the arbitrator. It will also, in many cases either defer or even exacerbate the dispute to a later outbreak. Finally, it is distinctly reminiscent of the radical change of direction which has failed in the past. Statistics are, of course, not comparable, but it may be asked whether a country in which the official machinery handles around 150 cases of arbitration a year is likely to operate widespread compulsory arbitration effectively.

There are, additionally a considerable number of employment disputes which are actually better dealt with collectively. A very good example is provided by the repeal of section 3 of the Equal Pay Act 1970 and its replacement by section 6 of the Sex Discrimination Act 1986, at the behest, incidentally, of the European Commission. The first had conferred upon trade unions the right to seek rectification of discriminatory collective agreements. Although severely restricted by the Divisional Court[110] trade unions were prepared to resort to this jurisdiction, which is rather more than can be said of an individual employee threatened

---

[110] See particularly *R. v. Central Arbitration Committee, ex p. Hy-Mac Ltd.* [1979] IRLR 461.

with equalizing downwards if her claim succeeds. Revival of both these jurisdictions would demonstrate faith in collective agreement as a provider of employment standards. Re-establishment of the power to extend collective agreements; inderogability as Professor Lord Wedderburn would put it,[111] is, therefore, a step to the introduction of the new ideology to which Professor Hepple refers. A collective jurisdiction in general would do much to restore the ideology of acceptance of the role of trade unions in employment protection whilst also providing some of the much sought alternative to industrial action.

Much else could be done to re-establish this ideology and significantly advance the cause of co-operation, and even equality. The grant of socially useful collective rights to information and consultation is an obvious example. No clearer example exists of the fact that it has not been policy to establish co-operation, rather than subordination, than the fact that, when required to grant to all employees a right of consultation on impending redundancy, the UK government, petulantly reverting to its minimum obligation under the Collective Redundancies Directive,[112] eliminated 95 per cent of such situations by excluding all cases where fewer than twenty employees are involved.[113]

This raises one of those problems previously referred to as a deterrent to such specific discussion. That question is how wide the collective net is to be cast. The tendency to seize upon *ad hoc* representation as an alternative to representation by experienced officials of established trade unions is an obvious means of preserving the principle of voluntary negotiation. But voluntary recognition does not so much assume the unacceptability of trade unions as the absence of necessity for negotiation or consultation with the workforce. If the ideology is to change that necessity must be accepted. The choice is then between discussion with experienced negotiators backed up with central services of training, information, and advice, and representatives who may or may not have acquired experience but are isolated from such support. The reason an employer might choose the latter is obvious. If his

---

[111] Lord Wedderburn, 'Inderogability, Collective Agreements, and Community Law' (1992) 21 *ILJ* 245.
[112] Council Dir. 75/129 [1975] OJ L48/29.
[113] SI 2587/1995, reg. 3, amending TULR(C)A 1992, s. 188.

workforce prefer the former then denial of their freedom of choice will undo all the objectives of a new ideology.

I have said nothing about removal of restrictions on the right to strike. I have probably sufficiently indicated my belief that many of them should remain. As I have previously said,[114] the extent to which the old ideology as an instrument of political campaigning has invaded labour law is clearly demonstrated by indications that, despite the abolition of the Department of Employment, government will never regard the process of restriction of collective rights as completed until those rights are totally abolished. Professor Hepple[115] indicates a popular preference for retention of some of the 1980s restrictions such as the requirement of a strike ballot. It is unlikely that he intends to suggest that even this should be retained in a form so restrictive, bureaucratic, and expensive as to make compliance difficult. It is absurd to suggest equal bargaining if labour has little real chance of deploying its economic weapon in response to those of the employer. It seems right to view with some scepticism the value of 'consultation', which is all one can expect between employer and trade union in such circumstances. A thorough review and recasting of these restrictions in the spirit of the new ideology is necessary. The establishment of a balance of power is now, as it has been in the past, the most difficult task facing the legislature in the field of employment. It is a problem which is not resolved by abandoning that balance. At the end of the century no area of law is more in need of change than is labour law. The issue is nothing less than the survival of labour law as an effective protection of the worker.

---

[114] See n. 41.   [115] N. 21 above, 321.

ROMAN LAW IN THE MIDDLE OF ITS THIRD MILLENNIUM

Andrew Lewis

I

The problem faced by one offering a Roman law lecture in a *Current Legal Problems* series is not, primarily, that of choosing a topic which sits comfortably within the overall theme of the series; on this occasion at least, the more specific brief of addressing the state of the subject at the end of this century affords a relatively straightforward solution. The difficulty first in importance is of finding a register in which to address a diverse audience: one composed not only of those who are well acquainted with the subject, and who will be looking for some considerable, if not substantial, contribution to learning, but also of those who are either neophytes or well-wishers, whose commitment to the occasion may be greater than their knowledge of the field and whom any detailed argument runs the risk of bemusing if not of alienating altogether.

My solution, imperfect though it may be, is to take a grand, though probably uncontroversial, theme and suggest some undoubtedly controversial corollaries of it sufficient to engage the attention (though not necessarily the support) of my Romanist colleagues, and then to proceed to justify and illustrate it with material which, though probably all too familiar to these, may afford some degree of interest to those who will be more attracted by this than the methodological concerns of Romanists. To ensure that all have an interest in the argument throughout the lecture I shall adopt the following sequence: first addressing the general theme to which I have referred, then proceeding to a fairly long sequence of illustration concluding with my, I hope, controversial deductions for the future of my subject.

II

It is a commonplace to say that there have been two lives of Roman law. The first life of Roman law is that which begins with the local law of a small city-state in Italy sometime in the early part of the first millennium BC—the Romans' own traditional date for the foundation of their city was 754 BC—and ends with the grand codification of Roman law as the law of an empire still stretching in the mind over the whole Mediterranean world under the emperor Justinian in 534 AD. By comparison with what follows there is little enough that can usefully be said about the earliest period until the compilation of the Twelve Tables, the code of practice which in Maine's pithy phrase marked the beginning, as Justinian's codification marked the end, of Roman law. Maine's apothegm is one of those quotations so dear to the minds of examiners that it is something of a shock actually to come across it in print.[1] If the Twelve Tables indicate a point of irreducible impenetrability at one end of the period, the codification of Justinian is a somewhat less obvious place to pause. We do not regard the French codification of 1804 as the end, or the beginning, of French legal history, though the event has an unsettling effect upon the distribution of effort amongst French legal historians. Justinian saw his work, more strictly the work he inspired, as a continuation of a tradition rather than a new beginning: it was certainly not for him the end of anything. Yet from our perspective nothing could be clearer than that the act of codification effected a complete change of legal culture. Thitherto the law of the Romans had been fundamentally a matter of tradition, *mos maiorum*—the path of the ancestors; henceforward it would be the will of the emperor who enacted the codification and forbade any further reference to the authorities of the past.

There are two further, extrinsic, factors which reinforce this perspective. At the time of the codification in the 530s the Roman empire was undergoing a period of expansion: Justinian's armies under Belisarius embarked upon a successful reconquest of North

---

[1] H. Maine, *Ancient Law* (London, 1861), 1.

Africa, Italy, and southern Spain which had for more than a century been under control of various Germanic tribes, albeit operating through the medium of Roman local government. This recrudescence of Roman power was shortlived and was to crumble almost entirely in the face of Islam in the seventh century. The consequence was to shut the Roman empire increasingly into a monoglot Greek world, that which we call the Byzantine empire. Greek language and culture had been an important, if not dominating, influence upon Roman law since the time of Constantine, the founder of Constantinople. One of the unresolvable puzzles surrounding the sixth century codification of Roman law in Latin in a largely Greek-speaking world is how long the tradition of learning and practising law in Latin would have survived in a renovated Roman empire if the armies of Islam had not intervened. In Justinian's own time an extensive Greek commentary, effectively a crib, on the introductory *Institutes* was produced by one of Justinian's own compilers to assist the Greek student with no Latin to get a start on the material. Its author Theophilus will surely have expected his pupils to develop enough Latin eventually to read Papinian, one of the pithier stylists among the classical jurists. His successors in later Greek centuries abandoned the struggle and composed translations and glosses, *scholia*, on Justinian's texts which were eventually, in the tenth century, published as the *Basilica*.[2] Prior to this the actual legislative force of Justinian's codification had been replaced by the somewhat simplified, if more practical, *Ecloga*.[3] Western culture's fascination with the ancient Greeks never extended to the world of their medieval successors, so that the history of Byzantine law from Justinian to the fall of Constantinople in 1453 nearly a millennium later is perceived in the West, if at all, as a sort of appendix, an object of little known practical value. This neglect is unfortunate not only on its own terms, as it is apparent from the occasional use made of this material in modern scholarship that it has much to

---

[2] H. J. Scheltema and N. van der Wal (eds.), *Basilicorum libri LX*, (Groningen, 1953–88).

[3] On the *Ecloga ton nomon* see N. van der Wal and H. J. A. Lokin, *Historiae iuris graeco-romani delineatio* (Groningen, 1985), 75 and D. Simon, 'Legislation Both a World Order and a Legal Order' in A. E. Laiou and D. Simon, *Law and Society in Byzantium: Ninth–Twelfth Centuries* (Dumbarton Oaks, DC, 1994). The text is edited by L. Burgmann, *Ecloga. Das Gesetzbuch Leons III und Konstantinos V* (Frankfurt-am-Main, 1983).

favoured. His view is contrasted with that of *plerique*—most everybody—who hold that it does not become ours until we have seized it. Gaius himself thinks this latter the truer view for much can happen (*possunt*) to prevent our taking it. When Justinian's compilers came to write an introductory institutional text of their own—Justinian's *Institutes*—they borrowed much material from Gaius's two earlier works. When it came to acquisition of property in animals they lifted almost entire this discussion of Gaius from the *Res cottidiana*. Perhaps surprisingly Trebatius's name is suppressed: the *Institutes* having *quibusdam* (certain persons) thinking what Gaius tells us Trebatius thought, and others (*alii*) as holding the view Gaius attributes to most people. This gives the impression that Trebatius's opinion was perhaps more widely held than we could deduce from Gaius's original. We do not know what access the compilers had to other classical discussions of this point. Any which existed would have been suppressed and we can have no knowledge of it. The generalization of Trebatius's view in the *Institutes* might be some recognition of the presence of other supportive opinions. The failure to make a similar alteration in the *Digest* passage is one, rather weak, further argument in favour of a conservative attitude towards interpolations. There is, however, another and more cynical explanation for the change. As we have seen, the conclusion of Gaius's account in the *Digest* is that he sides with the majority against Trebatius: 'this', he says, 'is the truer view'. In the *Institutes* this is strengthened considerably: 'we' (this is the imperial plural speaking) 'confirm this latter view for much *invariably* happens (*solent*) to prevent your taking it'. By presenting the earlier opinions as more evenly balanced than they perhaps were, the compilers give Justinian the opportunity to pose here, as frequently elsewhere, as the resolver of classical disputes, the imposer of harmony upon dissonance.

Trebatius' opinion did not finally succeed in convincing his successors and the impractical implications of his conclusions make us wonder why they should ever have seemed attractive. There is much moral force behind his ruling even though the mode of expression, via the analysis in terms of possession, makes it ultimately unsatisfactory. The Roman lawyers were conscious, in their customary and uncodified system, of the need to ground their opinions on what was both morally and practically acceptable: as the system developed in detail during the last century of the

Republic solutions which reflected the practicalities of the procedural system won out over those which were cast in merely moral terms. It was this which eventually led to Trebatius's solution falling into disfavour. Nevertheless it retained sufficient credibility to be cited as an extreme position right down until the sixth century. Surviving until then it entered the mainstream of the Roman law tradition.

In the eighteenth-century United States there were significant libraries of civilian learning. The second president of the United States, John Adams, started out in life as a self-taught lawyer. His reading, as we know from his diary, included Justinian's *Institutes* in Vinnius's edition and Wood.[31] Even his English learning began with Cowell's *Institute* 'in imitation of Justinian'. His diary contains noted extracts from *Institutes* passages, including *J.Inst.* 2.1.12, the passage immediately prior to that containing the discussion of Trebatius's opinion about game.[32] Some years later an opportunity arose for Adams to put this learning into practice.

The English Admiralty courts had long used civilian procedure and learning. In England before 1857 their practitioners were not members of the Bar but the civilians of Doctor's Commons, possessed of a degree in Civil law from one of the Universities. In the Vice-Admiralty courts which were established in English colonies throughout the world following the passing of the Navigation Acts 1696, need dictated a more flexible policy of admission, though the procedure and principles were still in theory civilian. The Vice-Admiralty court in Massachusetts was established at this time, previously maritime matters arising there had been dealt with by the common law jurisdictions. It did not prove popular, save for the litigation of claims for seamen's wages, probably because of its close association with the resented administration of the customs.[33] Procedure seems to have followed that set out in the standard Admiralty text, Francis Clerke's *Praxis Curiae Admiralitatibus Angliae*, a copy of the 1727 edition of

---

[31] Adams' early reading is revealed in his diaries: J. Adams, *Earliest Diary of John Adams* (ed. L. H. Butterfield) (Cambridge, Mass., 1966).

[32] *Ibid.* 53–9.

[33] L. Kinvin Wroth, 'The Massachusetts Vice-Admiralty Court in G. Billias (ed.), *Law & Authority in Colonial America: Selected Essays* (Barre, Mass., 1965), and cf. the same author's article, 'The Massachusetts Vice Admiralty Court and the Federal Admiralty Jurisdiction', in (1962) 6 *American Journal of Legal History*, 250, 347.

which, now in the Harvard Law Library, may once have belonged
to Adams. The language of the court had however always been
English, a change only made in England in 1733.[34]

In 1766 a whaling case, *Doane* v. *Gage*, came before the court.
What motivated the plaintiff to sue there is uncertain, as previous
claims of a similar cast, involving the same plaintiff, had been
determined in common law courts. Adams was counsel for the
plaintiff, Captain Doane, and the initial choice of forum may be
presumed to be his. The facts of the matter were relatively simple
and of a sort apparently familiar in whaling practice. As readers of
Melville's *Moby Dick* will recall, in the days of sail whaling was
carried out in small craft, launched from a mother ship, which
would be rowed close up to a surfaced whale for the harpooner to
sink his harpoon or iron into the animal. It was rare for this to kill:
the whale would run for long distances and maybe receive more
strikes before becoming sufficiently exhausted to allow itself to be
slaughtered. The harpooner in one of Doane's boats struck a whale
which immediately sounded, taking line with him. On resurfacing
the whale was struck by a second harpoon cast from another boat
by its commander himself, a Captain Gage. At some point, about
which there was conflicting evidence, Doane's line ceased to be
attached to the whale. Gage then took up the whale, slaughtered it
and sold the proceeds in the usual way. A custom of the sea was
proved whereby a whale belonged to the ship which first
harpooned it, so long as its line remained attached. In the words of
Herman Melville in *Moby Dick*: 'A Fast-fish belongs to the party
fast to it. A Loose-fish is fair game'. The question between the
parties was simply whether Doane's line was still attached when
Gage's harpoon struck. If so, the whale was Doane's: if not, Gage's.

Although no substantial record of the admiralty proceedings
appears to survive, a mass of witness depositions are preserved in
the Suffolk, Massachusetts, County records. These written depositions were taken before local magistrates, in broad accordance with

---

[34] See Burrell's Reports 243: the Restoration of the monarch in 1660 seems to
have taken second place in the minds of the Admiralty clerks to that of Latin: 'Primo
die mensis Augusti Anno Domini millesimo et sexcentesimo anno scilicet jubileeo
non solum linguae Latinae feliciter restitutae sed et Illustrissimi principis Caroli
Secundi a populo suo diu per proditores depulsi, nunc miranda Dei providentia
restaurati'.

the civilian practice which largely excluded oral testimony at the trial. These can be supplemented by the extensive notes taken by Adams and his assistant. It emerges from the best of the evidence led by Adams that, although Doane's boat was the first to strike and although it kept up with the whale until after Gage's iron went home, there was no clear demonstration that Doane's boat was actually 'fast' to the whale during this period. By the whaling custom Doane would have to show that this was certainly the case in order to succeed.

Adams, perhaps remembering his early study, dug out both the *Institutes* and *Digest* version of the passage and copied them into his case notes.[35] As it happened, and perhaps not surprisingly, the custom of the sea accords with the view adopted by Justinian and, perhaps, the majority of the classical jurists: you only retain ownership of wild animals whilst you are so to speak attached to them. Though that attachment may be artificially extended there comes a point when your loss of possession signals your loss of title. In fact the whalers' rule is both practical and conservative and accords with the *ius commune*.

Why did Adams plead the case initially in the Admiralty court? He knew presumably that the procedure and practice there were civilian in inspiration and may have acquired the copy of Clerke's *Praxis* for the purpose: this appears to have been his first Admiralty case though he had others subsequently. What did he hope to gain? It emerges from the evidence given in the case that the whaling custom reported by Melville was well known in Massachusetts. Much similar litigation was brought before the common law courts and decided on the basis of this custom. Adams may have been hoping that an appeal to Roman law, in the shape of Trebatius's argument, would be more effective in the civilian than the common law forum. Trebatius's authority would support an argument that once Doane's boat struck the whale it was his so long as he was in chase of it, irrespective of whether he remained fast to it. He cannot have sustained this hope for long. As we have seen, Justinian's resolution of the problem in the *Institutes*, dismissing Trebatius, accords with the whaling custom and it may therefore have been an

---

[35] L. Kinvin Wroth and H. B. Zobel (eds.), *Legal Papers of John Adams*, 3 vols. (Cambridge, Mass., 1965), Case no 43, vol. II, 73.

eventual realization of the futility of his position that drove Adams
to accept arbitration.[36]

My purpose in citing this rather exotic piece of Revived Roman
learning is to demonstrate the extent to which even common
lawyers, admittedly in quasi-civilian tribunals, could be influenced
by the practical consequences of Roman learning. The ease with
which John Adams considered a Roman solution to his client's
problem indicates the extent to which Roman law remained
potentially authoritative during the eighteenth century and even in
America. Our interest on both these examples, Trebatius's original
problem and Adams' attempted exploitation of it, is an historical
one.

V

What, then, is the present status of Roman law and of the Roman
legal tradition? It follows from my earlier willingness to entertain
the notion of overlapping periodization that I might be satisfied
with an answer that placed us within, though perhaps towards the
end, of the second period of Revived Roman law, as well as
squarely within the period of what I have inelegantly called
Historical Roman law. I want to suggest that we are no longer
within the tradition of Revived Roman law. This is controversial,
though perhaps not very.

---

[36] The account of Adams' handling of *Doane* v. *Gage* by D. R. Coquillette
'Justinian in Braintree: John Adams, Civilian Learning, and Legal Elitism, 1758–
1775' in *Law in Colonial Massachusetts 1630–1800*, Publications of the Colonial
Society of Massachusetts, Vol. 62 (Boston, 1984), 359, where I first encountered the
issue, is problematic. In particular the passage at 384 where Coquillette represents
Adams'

> 'key point—rather contrary to the whalers' custom—was that once a wild
> animal was acquired by possession (presumably by being hit with his client's
> harpoon) that "Property acquired by Possession does not cease with the Loss of
> Possession".This point comes direct from Grotius'

is misleading at best. I agree with Coquillette that Adams may have tried to run such
an argument, but if he did so it must have been on the basis of Trebatius's solution,
as I have suggested above. Once Doane's boat struck the whale it was his so long as
he was in chase of it, irrespective of whether he was fast to it. Adams cannot have
derived this from Grotius who, in the passage cited *in extenso* in Adams' papers
from *The Rights of War and Peace* (London, 1738), 'B.2 chap. 8 sect. 3' shows that
this is simply not applicable to animals: ' "The Roman lawyers say we lose our
Property in Wild Beasts as soon as ever they recover their natural liberty. But in all
other Things, the Property acquired by Possession does not cease with the Loss of
Possession." '

There are few legal systems which retain Roman law—in the form of the *ius commune*—as a direct source of law. San Marino in Italy and Andorra are two such. Peter Stein showed in his Thomas lecture four years ago how far the tradition was still a living force in the law of the Channel Islands, and the same author has written a study of the present state of the *ius commune* tradition as it is contained in the judgments of the court of San Marino.[37] I was myself a few years ago involved on the margins of a case in Andorra when a friend of our then head of Department wrote for advice concerning an attempt to evict him from his house there. He experienced difficulty in obtaining any useful advice locally. I drafted some remarks including citations from the *Digest* title 19.2 on letting and hiring and was gratified a little later to receive notification from the correspondent that he had successfully argued his own case and that the court had adopted the opinion of Labeo![38]

But, with due apologies to any Channel Islanders or Sammarinese present, these are little more than fossils. The mainstream continental European systems are only exiguously connected to the *ius commune* since codification. To see the current practical state of the Roman law tradition we must turn to those major *ius commune* jurisdictions which have not codified. There are two significant ones: South Africa and Scotland.

The present state of the Roman-Dutch system in South Africa is magnificently presented in a recent volume entitled *Southern Cross* produced from the Law School at the University of Cape Town and published by Oxford University Press last autumn.[39] In their introduction, the editors, Reinhard Zimmermann and Danie Visser, summarize the history of influences on the development of South African law. Isolated from the codification of law in continental Europe during the Napoleonic period by its conquest by Britain,

---

[37] P. Stein, 'The Crime of Fraud in the Uncodified Civil Law' (1993) 46 *CLP* 135; 'Civil Law Reports and the Case of San Marino' in O. Behrends, M. Diesselhorst, and W. E. Voss (eds.), *Römisches Recht in der europäischen Tradition: Symposion aus Anlass des 75 Geburtstag von Franz Wieacker.* (Ebelsbach, 1985), 323, reprinted in P. Stein, *The Character and Influence of the Roman Civil Law*, n. 13 above, 115.

[38] I regret not having kept some documentary record of my opinion, but I believe it to have involved citation of D.19.2.28 (Labeo *lib 4 posteriora epit.Iavoleno*).

[39] R. Zimmermann and D. Visser, *Southern Cross: Civil law and Common Law in South Africa* (Oxford, 1996).

this former Dutch colony retained much of the substantive *ius commune* whilst accommodating this to an essentially common law procedural system. One of the more striking developments was an indigenous law of trusts, drawing upon English ideas but adapting them to a civilian climate.[40] Zimmermann and Visser choose in their introduction to stress the combination of the two main intellectual tools for developing South African law in the past 200 years: the individual judicial opinion characteristic of the common law tradition on the one hand and the writings of jurists in accordance with the civilian pattern on the other. However just as the political and social revolution of the 1990s have brought about linguistic change, privileging some eleven African languages alongside Afrikaans and English—it is commonplace to have a major sporting fixture commentated on on television in a sequential range of languages—just so the challenge for South African law in the next century is the absorbing of a variety of local African customary usages into the mainstream of the legal system. Besides this the traditional debate over which of two imported European traditions is the more eminent appears an irrelevance.

The position of Roman law in Scotland is canvassed in a recent volume of the Stair Society edited by Robin Evans-Jones[41] and was also the main theme of a conference held last summer to celebrate 500 years of Roman law teaching at the University of Aberdeen. In a powerful contribution to the Stair Society volume, given orally at Aberdeen, the then Lord Advocate delivered some strong remarks on those who chose to regard Roman law as a living tool for the development of Scots law.[42] His premise, amply documented, was that aside from any questions of desirability, modern Scottish practitioners whether at the bar or on the bench lacked the technical skills, both of language and knowledge, to do justice to the tradition.[43] Now that the then Lord Advocate has, in the person of our chair, become Lord President of the Court of Session, we can

---

[40] See T. Honoré, 'Trust', chap. 26 in *ibid.*, 849.

[41] R. Evans-Jones (ed.), *The Civil Law Tradition in Scotland* (Stair Society Supplementary vol. 2, Edinburgh, 1995).

[42] A. Rodger, 'Roman Law Comes to Partick' in *ibid.* 198.

[43] 'It is hard to avoid the impression that the judges were not entirely at ease in dealing with the Roman law materials and, although this is harder to detect from the pages of the report, it is likely that this applied to counsel. It certainly applies to the *Session Cases* reporter who was plainly unfamiliar with the material and as a result

expect that attention will be paid to his extra-judicial expression of opinion on this matter.

Despite the enthusiasm of law students for Roman law, of which I had personal experience during my visit to Cape Town last September, it must be wondered whether the practitioners in South Africa are in any better case. In a contribution to the Stair Society volume, dedicated to the place of Roman law in South Africa, Zimmermann, whilst stressing the creative possibilities of the tradition, comes to much the same conclusion about the practicalities as Rodger has for Scotland.[44]

VI

I have in this article argued that a proper view of Roman law at the end of the twentieth century is that it is wholly an historical study. The important question which arises from this is where this study can be most effectively centred. This is not, as I see it, primarily a question about legal education—about what law students should or can usefully study or about what good law schools ought to teach.[45] Rather these matters are contingent upon the more significant answer to the question where primary historical research upon Roman law (both in its first and second lives) can best be carried out. Let us briefly compare the position of the historical study of the common law. The revival of the study of English common law in the past forty years has been the work of lawyers,

produced many unfortunate citations': Rodger, n. 28 above, at 210. The case under discussion is *Sloans Dairy* v. *Glasgow Corporation*, 1977 SC 238. Consider further 'The downgrading of the study of Roman law in the universities gives no cause for optimism about the future handling of such issues': Rodger, at 212.

[44] Zimmermann, 'Roman Law in a Mixed Legal System', in Evans-Jones, n. 41 above, 41. At 78 he concludes: 'All in all, I should think that devotion and faithfulness to our civilian heritage cannot be counted by the number of judgements which abound with learned disquisitions on the Roman sources or with elaborate analyses of Bartolus, Donellus, Voet or Stair. Much as we may admire them, such judicial pronouncements appear somewhat odd in the modern world'.

[45] This is emphatically not to ignore the very great importance of this question. Peter Birks has emphasized the past contribution and the continuing importance of the Roman Institutional model for our understanding and classification of law in his chapter 'The Foundation of Legal Rationality in Scotland' in Evans-Jones, n. 41 above, 81; cf. his 'Equity in the Modern Law, An Exercise in Taxonomy' (1996) 26 *UWALR* 1–99 and his forthcoming 'Definition and Division: A Meditation on Institutes 13.3' in P. Birks (ed.), *The Classification of Obligations* (Oxford, 1997).

that of Milsom and Baker being pre-eminent.[46] But historians have
not been far behind, and the work of historians like Brand and
Hyams is indispensable for even the narrowest of juristic pictures to
be drawn.[47] In the USA economic factors have encouraged the
establishment of joint chairs of Law and History occupied by
persons of either background teaching in both schools. The
position of Roman law, at least this side of the Atlantic, is currently
more problematic. Roman law is still seen as the province of
lawyers in law schools despite the fact that it is taught in only very
few. The very presence of skilled practitioners of Roman legal
scholarship in law schools has understandably put the historians
off. The contrast, though by no means an exact one, with the study
of Greek law is striking: nearly all the English work on the history
of Greek law is done by historians, and there is little competition
from the lawyers (the picture is again different in the United
States).[48] We are, perhaps I should say I am, enormously supported
in London by having an ancient historian not only sympathetic to
the study of Roman law and not only active in publishing ancient
texts of Roman law but also very alive to the intellectual tradition
of Roman law which lay behind the sixteenth-century historical
movement.[49]

There is no possibility of legal history, whether of Rome or
elsewhere, becoming the exclusive domain of historians untrained
in law. Legal history, I should have no difficulty in persuading this
audience, is not primarily social history. It is rather a branch of
intellectual history best carried out by those who have some
insights into the dynamics of living legal traditions. Lawyers and
historians are not, or should not be, enemies. It is a striking fact

[46] See their respective general surveys: S. F. C. Milsom, *Historical Foundations of
the Common Law* (London, 1969, 2nd edn. 1981); J. H. Baker, *Introduction to
English Legal History* (London, 1971, 2nd edn. 1978, 3rd edn. 1989).

[47] See e.g. P. Brand, *The Origins of the English Legal Profession* (Oxford, 1992);
P. R. Hyams, *Kings, Lords and Peasants in Medieval England* (Oxford, 1980).

[48] See e.g. S. Todd, *The Shape of Athenian Law* (Oxford, 1993) and the studies
collected in P. Cartledge, P. Millett, and S. Todd (eds.), *Nomos: Essays in Athenian
Law, Politics and Society* (Cambridge, 1990). L. Foxhall and A. D. E. Lewis (eds.),
Justifications not Justice: Greek Law in its Political Context (Oxford, 1996) is only
a partial exception.

[49] See M. H. Crawford *et al.*, *Roman Statutes*, two vols., (Institute of Classical
Studies, London, 1995); M. H. Crawford, 'Bembo giureconsulto?' in A. D. E. Lewis
and D. Ibbetson, *The Roman Law Tradition* (Cambridge, 1994), 98.

that two of the greatest historians of the last century whose work continues to influence their fields, Maitland and Mommsen, were both lawyers. What is required for the tradition of Roman legal history—by which term I most assuredly mean to include Roman law's intellectual history—is closer and more effective co-operation between lawyers and ancient and modern historians. It may be that the resources both of *personnel* and of *matériel* can be located as well in the historical as the legal sphere: the siting of the current Project Volterra for a cataloguing of the legislation of the later imperial period within the UCL History department, but drawing on the skills of Romanists and Roman historians from a wide field, is an example. Only when the future of the study of the subject beyond the current generations of Roman law teachers in law schools is secured can we usefully turn to the equally vital but secondary question of the importance of legal history, whether of Rome or of Europe or a wider world, for the training of lawyers and others. Some straws in the wind include the vivid correspondence in *The Times* a few years ago on the news that Roman law had ceased to be a compulsory subject in the University of Oxford, and the inclusion by that University's Professor of Modern History in his recent history of Europe of a 'capsule' on Roman law which would have benefited from some advice from his legal colleagues.[50] But all this is matter for another lecture.

[50] *The Times*, 18 Oct. 1993; N. Davies, *Europe: A History* (Oxford, 1996), 172.

INTERNATIONAL LAW IN THE PAST HALF CENTURY—AND THE NEXT?

Maurice Mendelson

The first paper on public international law to appear in *Current Legal Problems* was given at UCL in 1947 by the distinguished scholar Albert de la Pradelle.[1] It was delivered and published in French. Some of you will perhaps be relieved to know that I am not going to follow his example.

I intend to confine myself, for the most part, to the period following the establishment of the United Nations a little more than half a century ago, in 1945. More than enough has taken place since then to fill this article, especially when I intend also to say something about how I see the future of the subject.

The past fifty years have seen profound transformations in the composition of international society, both quantitatively and qualitatively. They have also witnessed very significant changes in the law of that society—a very large expansion in the subject matter which international law covers, and in the way that it deals with the distribution of resources and other social values. These changes have been powered by developments in ideology and technology of the most profound importance. The ways that law is made have also undergone some transformations, though not, perhaps, so dramatic. There have also been some developments in the theory of international law, though these seem likely to prove ephemeral, for the most part. Those are the themes that I want to develop in this article, as well as considering whether there has been some

---

[1] 'La place de l'homme dans la construction du droit international', (1948) 1 *CLP* 140.

fundamental change in the nature of international law and society. I shall also attempt a brief glimpse into the future.

Changes in the Composition of International Society

Fifty-one states founded the United Nations. There were some others—mainly the former enemy states—who were not permitted to join at first; but in 1945 the total number of states did not exceed about seventy. Today, there are nearly 200 states in the world. In any small group, almost tripling its size is bound to have an effect on the nature of the social process—the more so if members represent millions, tens of millions, or hundreds of millions of people. But even more important than this quantitative change has been the qualitative one.

The great majority of states in 1945 were representatives of the European form of civilization.[2] Most of them were of a certain size and importance, with a history of independent statehood behind them. All were more or less capitalist, save for the Soviet Union.[3] But all of this has changed. The post-war period was one of virtually uninterrupted decolonization until today, when there are practically no colonies left. In 1960 alone, seventeen states were admitted to the UN, all but one of them[4] African former colonies. The same process took place in Asia and the Pacific. These new members of international society were countries which, typically, had their own form of culture and did not share the values or traditions of those whose yoke they had just thrown off. At the same time, though their societies might be ancient, for the most part they had no tradition of independent statehood. In most cases they were weak in military and economic terms, and in some the population, too, was exiguous.[5] But, because the principle of the

---

[2] This includes the states, notably in North and South America and Australasia, to which it had been exported.

[3] The Byelorussian and Ukrainian Soviet Socialist Republics were also original members of the UN, but they were of course fully part of the USSR. Their separate membership was the result of a political deal to partly offset the influence the United States had over Latin America, and of the United Kingdom over the independent members of the British Commonwealth.   [4] Cyprus.

[5] Attempts in the 1960s and 1970s to restrict diminutive states to associate membership of the UN came to nothing. See M. H. Mendelson, 'Diminutive States in the United Nations', (1972) 21 *ICLQ* 609.

sovereign equality of states had to be respected, at least formally, each was entitled to one vote in the UN General Assembly, in the many other international organizations[6] which were established in the post-war period, and in international treaty-making conferences. Individually weak, for the most part, these 'developing countries'—as they came to be known—quickly realized that they could increase their political influence if they could manage to act and vote together, which they did regularly, and more and more vociferously.[7]

If—understandably—the developing countries did not like the way the earth's resources had been shared out in the past, they found an ideology to hand to support their aspiration for a fairer share of the cake. This was socialism in its various manifestations. By 1955, when a number of ex-enemy states and others were admitted to the UN, Soviet communism had already spread to the countries of central and eastern Europe, to China, to North Korea and North Vietnam, and to one or two other parts of the world. Later on, it obtained a hold in Cuba and—though in modified form—elsewhere. It should not be forgotten, however, that aside from communism, milder forms of socialism were also very much in vogue during the past half-century, and not only in the developing countries. It was, after all, a Labour government which deposited the British ratification of the Charter, and many countries in Western Europe, not to mention the rest of the world, have had socialist governments at some time during the past half century. So the socialist agenda of redistribution and of direct assistance to the poorest was seen by some to be readily transposable to international society.

It has found expression in all sorts of ways. One was the attempt to introduce the so-called 'New International Economic Order', in which those with the know-how and resources would be obliged to transfer technology to developing countries, to submit to nationalization with reduced compensation, to co-operate in price

---

[6] Though some organizations, such as the World Bank and International Monetary Fund, do have a system of weighted voting reflecting (in part) the size of contributions.

[7] It should not be forgotten that some of the older states, such as Ethiopia, Liberia, and the Latin American countries, also belong to the category of developing states; they joined their voices to those of their more recently independent colleagues.

stabilization, and so on.[8] Another manifestation was the 'right to development', and there have been other ambitious schemes. Most came to nothing, but this movement has borne some fruit. For example, in the General Agreement on Tariffs and Trade the previously heretical notion has been accepted of preferential treatment for developing countries. And though it has been watered down[9] recognition in Part XI of the Law of the Sea Convention 1982 that the resources of the deep sea bed are the 'common heritage of mankind', with the proceeds of the international licensing system being used for the benefit of developing countries in particular, is an endorsement in some measure of a communitarian approach. Again, whilst the objectives of the group of international organizations known as the UN Specialized Agencies were originally mainly regulatory and hortatory, from the International Monetary Fund to the World Meteorological Organization, and from the International Labour Organization to the Universal Postal Union, they have increasingly been drawn into providing technical and developmental assistance. Indeed, the United Nations itself no longer just undertakes peace-keeping and provides a forum for multilateral diplomacy: a large part of its budget is devoted to the UN Development Programme and like activities.

This leads me to another way in which what might very loosely be described as a socialist agenda has influenced international relations. In the eighteenth century and much of the nineteenth, the functions of the state were very limited. It had to protect its citizens from attack from without, and from criminals and other wrongdoers within. That was more or less all. So the departments of a typical government were largely confined to an army and navy, a foreign ministry, an interior ministry (mainly to run the police), the courts, and a treasury to pay for them With the advent of the Welfare State, many more activities were seen for the first time, or to a greatly increased degree, to be the business of government. The provision and promotion of education, medical services, transport,

---

[8] See e.g. the Charter of Economic Rights and Duties of States, UN General Assembly res. 3281 (XXIX) of 12 Dec. 1974, 262.

[9] By the euphemistically entitled 'Agreement relating to the Implementation of Part XI of the Law of the Sea Convention . . . 1982': General Assembly res. 48/263 of 28 July 1994, (1994) 33 ILM, 1309.

food, energy, employment, communications, water, industrial and agricultural development, financial protection against the misfortunes of unemployment, sickness, injury, bereavement, or old age, and so on, have become the norm throughout the world. And those who could not afford to pay for these services were given expectations that the state would foot the bill, through taxation which, in virtually all countries, whatever their official ideology, came to be regarded as (partly) an instrument of redistribution. This involvement of the state in more and more areas of human activity is very much a twentieth-century phenomenon—and above all a post-war one; and it is reflected in the horizontal expansion of the areas in which international law has come to involve itself. For international law reflects the interests of governments, and the increasing interdependence of states means that they need international machinery to deal with these many new activities. Usually, this international machinery is embodied in a treaty, and often an intergovernmental organization is established to supervise its continuing implementation and the promotion of the activities concerned. Just as we all have a ministry of health, we have the World Health Organization; aviation officials of different states meet in the International Civil Aviation Organization; trade officials in the World Trade Organization; and so on. They are the bureaucracies of bureaucracies. Before the Second World War there were only a handful of international organizations; today, there are several hundred, and their number is growing.

I am not, I should emphasize, suggesting that socialist ideology as such has been the only, or even the main, cause of these developments. With or without an ideology to justify it, the indigent will always want to change the *status quo*; and Latin American governments, for instance, were resisting what they saw as the unfair claims of the richer and more powerful long before socialism became a force in the world. The collapse of communism is not going to make such aspirations disappear.

It is nevertheless true that political and ideological conflict has been a noticeable feature of the international scene for the whole of the post-war period. In many instances, it has impeded the full development of international law. The conflict was not just between the communist states and the West. In between, most developing states were, to a greater or lesser extent, 'non-aligned', and the prolonged stalemate between the two antagonists left them with a substantial degree of freedom. Thus, the effective international protection of human rights at the global level was for a long time largely frustrated by ideological conflict. Political and ideological rivalry also prevented the UN's collective security machinery from operating properly until the collapse of the Soviet Union changed things, at least temporarily. Soviet objections to the compulsory submission of international disputes to adjudication or arbitration received a sympathetic hearing in the Third World, for various reasons.[10] There are other examples.

Before I leave the subject of the impact on international law of the multiplication and diversification of its traditional and archetypical subjects—states—I must say something more about the emergence of other types of actor.

As already mentioned, the post-war period has seen the creation of a great many intergovernmental organizations. Most of these are endowed with international legal personality, which has led some to overestimate their importance as independent actors on the international stage. Some, no doubt, are very potent legally or politically. European Community law, for example, can overreach national law; and the requirements of the International Monetary Fund have caused many states to adopt policies which they would not otherwise have chosen. But most organizations are of relatively minor importance and *all* of them remain the instrumentalities of states. Governments collectively keep a great deal of control over these bodies, by limiting their objectives, curtailing their powers, retaining a veto over at least their most important decisions, and keeping a tight grip on the purse-strings. Sovereign states are very jealous of admitting others to their exclusive club; and generally speaking, I do not think that intergovernmental organizations should be regarded as subjects of international law of the same order as states.

The post-war period has also seen a considerable increase in the number of *non*-governmental international associations. These link people across the world with common interests in a particular political issue, religion, sport, hobby, trade or profession, and so on. They may act as pressure groups, seeking to influence the conduct of governments internally or in the exercise of their foreign affairs. The effect of most of them on international relations

---

[10] Though today, the USA is significantly cooler about this than in the past.

seems to be relatively small. But some, such as Amnesty International and Greenpeace, can cause a good deal of embarrassment to governments, whilst others, such the Red Cross, Oxfam, and similar aid organizations, play an important part in relieving the suffering caused by natural or—only too often—man-made disasters. But, once again, their formal role in the international legal system is exiguous: with the partial exception of the International Committee of the Red Cross, the norms of international law are not addressed to them, and they play no direct part in creating or applying them.

Turning to corporations, there is no doubt that the larger amongst them can wield a great deal of influence—especially so-called transnational corporations (TNCs) which are typically controlled by a 'parent' company in one state, but have branches or subsidiaries in many different countries. The annual turnover of the biggest fifty of these corporations in 1983, for instance, exceeded the gross national product of all but fifty states.[11] TNCs wield a great deal of influence over the countries they invest in, and also over their 'home' state, whose policies may well be tailored to advance the interests of these large contributors to the national wealth. For instance, attempts were made in the UN, in the 1970s and 1980s in particular, to fetter the power of these bodies, with endeavours to formulate a Code of Conduct on Transnational Corporations,[12] but these have not been successful. So in practice TNCs may seem easily the equals, if not more, of quite a lot of states. But they are not subjects of *international* law; and neither are they, strictly speaking, over-mighty subjects beyond the reach of *domestic* law. They are bound, not just by the law of the 'home' state, but also by that of each country in which they operate, under the ordinary principles of territorial sovereignty. And most host and home countries do try to exercise their powers of regulation. In reality, however, it is far from easy for individual states to monitor, let alone control, the offshore activities of TNCs, and

---

[11] I. Benson and J. Lloyd, *New Technology & Industrial Change* (London, 1983), 77, quoted in Peter Dicken, *Global Shift* (2nd edn., London, 1992), 49. Dicken also observes that 'Between one-fifth and one quarter of total world production in the world's market economies is performed by TNC's', *ibid.* 48.

[12] See e.g. UN Commission on Transnational Corporations, report of 29 May 1984, UN doc. E/C. 10/1984/S/5, (1984) 23 ILM 602. This attempt has still not come to fruition.

concerted action is technically difficult. But up till now the main obstacle has been a lack not so much of legal tools, but of political ones. Developing countries who rely on multinationals as customers or suppliers would be in a much stronger negotiating position if they could maintain a common front and bargain collectively; but so far they have found it virtually impossible to do so. There always seems to be someone who is willing to break rank—perhaps understandably, for the immediate needs are often very pressing.[13]

Working our way down through this list of actors we come, finally, to the individual. For Georg Schwarzenberger, my distinguished predecessor but one in this Chair, the individual was not a subject, but rather an object, of international law.[14] Just as territory was an object of state power, and one of its resources, so were people. Useless to point out also that international law has always had special rules about jurisdiction over pirates, who were regarded as *hostes humani generis*—the enemies of the human race; all this meant was that, whereas on the high seas normally only the flag state had jurisdiction, in the case of pirates everyone had jurisdiction—they were fair game for all states, and so were even more the objects of state power than the rest of us.[15] Even the provisions in the UN Charter and the numerous human rights conventions which have been concluded since 1945 need not fundamentally disturb this type of analysis: after all, we have domestic laws for the protection of endangered species and against cruelty to animals, but this does not make animals legal persons. On the other hand, there is the approach powerfully articulated by Schwarzenberger's arch-rival, Sir Hersch Lauterpacht,[16] and, interestingly enough, by Albert de La Pradelle himself in the first CLP International Law lecture, which he must have given at Schwarzenberger's invitation. He rightly pointed out that the state exists—or should exist—for the benefit of individual humans: it is not an end in itself, and he inveighed against the concentration on the sovereign state, '[le] Prince de Machiavel, Leviathan de Hobbes,

---

[13] The only producer organization to have had any significant success is the Organization of the Petroleum Exporting Countries ('OPEC'), whose members are not generally in such straightened circumstances as the typical developing country. And even here, the success of the cartel has been strictly limited.

[14] G. Schwarzenberger, *International Law* (3rd edn.) (London, 1957), 354.

[15] *Ibid.*, 346–7.

[16] *International Law and Human Rights* (London, 1950).

Dieu de Hegel, surpassé par le *Volk* de Hitler'. He had a good point, of course. Furthermore, much of even classical international law was concerned with conduct of, and towards, individual aliens. For instance, the law of diplomatic privileges and immunities is very much concerned with the position of individual representatives of the state. Much of the law of state responsibility has grown up in response to the maltreatment of individuals. A good deal of the law of the sea concerns the freedoms of merchant ships and fishing boats, both of course generally operated by people or companies for their own benefit, not as state organs. A large part of the laws of war—the *ius in bello*[17]—concerns the treatment of individuals, be they non-combatant civilians, prisoners of war, or the sick and wounded. Nevertheless, the bearers of rights and obligations in these and all other matters are essentially states, not the individuals themselves. In particular, individuals and corporations could not, in classical international law, bring claims through the diplomatic channel or before international courts and tribunals. The fact that the *function* or *purpose* of the state is the benefit of individual human beings does not invalidate the analytical point that the subjects of international law—those who make and apply the rules, and those to whom they are directed—are for the most part states, not individuals.

To some extent, this position has changed during the past half century. There are now international tribunals before which individuals and corporations can bring claims against states. In the case of investment and similar disputes we have, for example, the Iran–United States Claims Tribunal and the *ad hoc tribunals* established under the ægis of the Convention on the Settlement of Investment Disputes between States and Nationals of Other States.[18] Under some human rights conventions—the European, for example—people can bring applications to special courts or quasi-judicial bodies. And of course individuals and companies also have access to the European Court of Justice in Luxembourg, which is in a sense an international tribunal, even though much of its work and jurisprudence is *sui generis*. So, to a limited extent (and normally only by specific treaty) individuals may indeed be regarded as

---

[17] To be contrasted with the *ius ad bellum*, which attempts to regulate when states are entitled to go to war or otherwise employ armed force.

[18] Washington, 18 Mar. 1965, 575 UNTS 159.

bearers of rights and duties in their own person. But what really matters, much more than the rather sterile theoretical question whether or to what extent this makes them subjects of international law, is whether their rights are properly protected. The results over the past half century have been rather mixed.

Before 1945, there was hardly any international law on the protection of human rights. There were some fairly modest provisions in the League of Nations Mandates, and some of the states which had been defeated in the First World War, or had come into being following that conflict, had been obliged to accept treaty obligations in relation to minorities. And that was almost all. Today, there are literally dozens of conventions, some global and some regional, dealing with such matters as civil and political rights, economic, social, and cultural rights, the rights of women and children, trade union freedoms, refugees, the prohibition of genocide, torture, and so forth. Plus, of course, the treaties seeking to impose humanitarian treatment in time of war, though these have a somewhat longer pedigree. Numerous bodies have been established to try and supervise compliance with these obligations, voluminous reports are issued, and mountains of paper emerge from Geneva, Strasbourg, and other places. I do not want to belittle the value of these instruments: they have had some effect. But at the same time—and this is one of the cruel paradoxes of my subject— this century has seen the inhumanity of man towards man on a scale probably unprecedented in human history. I think this is in large part due to a terrible synergy between ideology and technology, which has enabled us to dehumanize our victims and to torture and destroy them in greater numbers than ever before.

Of course, people have always feared and hated foreigners abroad, and the stranger within their gates: the injunction to love thy neighbour as thyself has rarely been applied in practice to those who look, cook, or pray differently from ourselves. But ideology has added fuel to the flames. It has not always been thus. In the eighteenth century, wars were mainly fought for territory and plunder, and there were some in which literally no-one was killed. But just as once Christians burnt each other alive for the good of their immortal souls and to save others from the contagion of heresy, so in our own time millions and millions of people have been subjected to torture, to enslavement, and to mass destruction in order to save, if not their souls, then at any rate those of others, from pollution by capitalism, communism, or other isms. Seen from the point of view of those doing the torturing or the killing, this is understandable: if someone is possessed by the Devil, it is your moral duty to do whatever is necessary to exorcise the foul Fiend.

What has also helped the atrocities of this century to surpass those of our forefathers is technology. Technology enabled Hitler to industrialize genocide in a way that previous tyrants could not have dreamed of; technology enabled Stalin's secret police to enslave and spy on millions. Technology, like ideology, also helps us to distance ourselves from the sufferings of our victims. As an American airman in the Vietnam War is reputed to have said, 'I would never dream of going up to a little girl in the street and setting her on fire; but from two miles up, napalm just looks pretty.'

The Impact of Technology

Having said something about the significance of the quantitative and qualitative changes which have occurred in the composition of international society, and about the impact of ideological change and political conflict, I have now come on to what has been an equal, or perhaps even a more important, force for change in international society: the development of technology of all sorts. Of course, technological development is not something which started in the last fifty years; it began with the emergence of *homo sapiens*, if not before. And even the Industrial Revolution dates back nearly 200 years. But it is a striking feature of technological change in modern times that it has been taking place at an every-increasing rate, and the developments which have occurred during this century, and particularly in the last fifty years, have transformed, and will continue to transform, international relations and law.

Whole new fields of international law have come about in response to scientific developments. International air law is no older than the invention of heavier-than-air craft and the realization, at the outbreak of the First World War, of the military threat they represented. Again, you will not find anything in Grotius, or indeed writers up to about the 1960s, about the regime of outer space or the abyssal plains of the deep sea-bed, for the simple reason that they were not previously within reach and it would have been wholly academic, in the pejorative sense of that term, to write about them.[19] Similarly, it was only in the past half-century or so that people began to bother about the delimitation of the continental shelf; they had previously known it was there, but it was only after the Second World War that it became commercially and technically feasible to drill in it for oil and gas. The law relating to the peaceful—and other—uses of atomic energy is yet another example.

In some cases, new branches of international law have grown up, not so much because the activity itself was new, but because its increased scale has resulted in problems not previously perceived. The modernist faith was that, with the advance of science and technology, human suffering would be alleviated and a new era of health and welfare for all would be ushered in. We are beginning to realize that this is not necessarily the case. On the contrary, more science and more technology have been the cause of some of our most serious problems. The damage done to our air by the combustion of hydrocarbons, and to our water by pesticides and industrial effluent, have led to the development of international environmental law. Similarly, though people have always used rivers for irrigation and drinking water and as sewers, the increasing demands on such resources have led to the development of a body of law relating to the non-navigational uses of international waterways.

In yet other cases it is not so much a question of new branches of law emerging, as of existing branches being radically transformed by technological developments. In his *Mare Liberum* of 1609, Grotius gave various reasons for rejecting the pretensions of some states to sovereignty over huge tracts of the sea. One was the fact that it was physically impossible for a warship to stay on station, with the result that states could control the seas only within the range of cannon shot from the shore—not more than three miles at that time. The invention of steamships and the development of artillery made that idea somewhat outmoded. Again, he argued that in general there was no need for states to claim exclusive fishing rights in adjacent waters, because the fish of the sea were an abundant and inexhaustible resource. Today, what with sonar,

---

[19] Manganese nodules had in fact been brought up from the deep sea-bed 100 years earlier in a scientific expedition, but it was only in the 1960s that it was first thought possible to exploit them commercially.

radar, and other devices, huge fishing boats dragging nets many miles long, factory ships capable of freezing the fish and remaining at sea for many months on end, and so on, there are no longer enough fish for all: indeed, activities of this sort can totally destroy a fishery. This has resulted, not only in an extension of the breadth of the territorial sea, but also in the creation of the 200-mile exclusive economic zone.[20] Other examples could easily be identified.

Not all branches of international law have responded to changes in technology, however. Take the law relating to the right of states to use force, for instance—the *ius ad bellum*. Article 51 of the UN Charter refers to a state's right to use force in self-defence 'if an armed attack occurs'. The phrase is redolent of the tank battles of the Second World War. In a sense, it has been said, the Charter was out of date before the ink had dried on it: seven weeks after it was signed, the first nuclear bomb was dropped on Hiroshima.[21] The past half-century has come to know not only atomic weapons, but intercontinental ballistic missiles, large-scale defoliants, hostage-taking by terrorists, cross-border guerrilla warfare, civil wars which were largely superpower conflicts in disguise, and so on—features of modern 'civilization' wholly or largely unknown to previous generations.[22]

The Sources of International Law

The development of technology, and in particular the technology of mass-production and of communications, has affected international law in even more profound ways. Before the Second World War, the number of people from, say, this country who went abroad every year could have been counted in their thousands. Now, literally, in their millions. The same pattern is repeated world-wide, save that the travel is not always for recreational or business purposes: many more refugees, too, travel than ever

---

[20] Its breadth, strictly, is less than 200 miles, for out of this total has to be taken the breadth of the territorial sea—usually 12 nautical miles.

[21] On 6 Aug. 1945.

[22] I am not suggesting that the Charter would be unworkable if applied by states in good faith; simply that it does not expressly provide for many of our current forms of the use of force. Subsequent instruments have achieved but little in that regard.

before. Similarly, the quantity and value of goods which flow from one country to another have increased hugely. Improved methods of transport have also meant that armed forces and weapons can be transported across international boundaries with ever-increasing rapidity, which has transformed warfare. Money, too, can be and is transferred across international frontiers in larger and larger quantities, faster and faster. All of this, and similar developments, have made states ever more interdependent. This interdependence has in turn resulted in an enormous growth in the *quantity* of international law that is made.[23] If one examines Parry's *Consolidated Treaty Series*[24] one discovers that in 1900 131 treaties were concluded. By 1939, virtually the end of the *League of Nations Treaty Series*, this had increased to 185.[25] The *United Nations Treaty Series* is not up to date, but in the volumes for 1983[26] the number had increased to 1,125. Moreover, even these striking figures conceal the full extent of the development. More and bigger *multinational* treaties have been concluded. A bilateral treaty obviously binds only two states. But a treaty to which fifty States are party creates 1,225 bilateral links, and one between 180 states produces 16,110.[27]

Turning to customary law, although in quite a few cases it has been supplanted by treaties[28]—one thinks, for instance, of diplomatic and consular relations, the law of the sea, the *ius ad bellum* and international humanitarian law—there are quite a few areas

---

[23] But, contrary to the predictions of 'functionalists' like David Mitrany, *A Working Peace System* (Chicago, Ill., 1966), this interdependence does not necessarily reduce international conflict. On the contrary, the more you depend on others for imported food or raw materials, the greater the temptation to intervene if they do not do what you want. And the smaller the world becomes strategically, the further out states—or, at least, powerful ones—tend to move their security frontiers.

[24] Dobbs Ferry, NY, 1969–86.   [25] Vols. 194–9.

[26] Vols. 1298–1345. In 1994 there were 927.

[27] Furthermore, some international organizations created by such conventions have the power to make regulations which are not registered as treaties and so do not appear in these statistics: not just the European Community, but the International Civil Aviation Organization, the World Health Organization, and so on—not to mention staff regulations and other internal rules of all organizations. So the corpus of treaty-based law is considerably greater than the corpus of treaties.

[28] Notwithstanding the finding of the International Court of Justice in the *Case Concerning Military and Paramilitary Activities in and against Nicaragua (Merits)* [1986] ICJ Rep. 3, that the customary international law relating to non-intervention and to the use of force had survived the adoption of the UN Charter, for most practical purposes treaty law supersedes customary rules.

where it remains alive and well, and new rules are still being created by this process. Although technological developments have made treaty-making more necessary and more easy than ever before, the communications revolution means that the process of informal state interaction which creates customary law has also become easier, though doctrine has only just begun to take on board the implications of this fact.

Advances in communications also mean that representatives of all states in the world can meet regularly in international organizations, most notably in the General Assembly of the United Nations, where they all have an equal vote. From the annual meetings of that body there emerges a veritable torrent of resolutions. The legally binding force of these resolutions has been questioned, not least by those who have been outvoted; and it is certainly true that, in the current state of international relations, governments have not yet agreed to the creation of a world legislature. But, at the very least, such resolutions have the potential to influence the way that the law develops, and the closer the resolution approaches unanimity, the greater that influence can be. Maybe, in the not very distant future, electronic communications will mean that government representatives will not even need to be physically present at the General Assembly or other international conferences in order to express their views and their votes.

Turning to what has been described as a law-determining source of international law, there has also been a considerable increase in international adjudication in the past half century. The International Court of Justice in The Hague has continued the work of its predecessor—the unfortunately named Permanent Court of International Justice—but in addition to this we have other, regional international courts dealing with human rights and with economic relations, respectively. Although there is no *stare decisis* in international law, the precedents these bodies have created have had an important influence over the evolution of the law.[29]

Yet another development relating to the sources of international law in the past half century has been the acceptance, since the late 1960s, of the notion of *ius cogens* —in other words, peremptory rules of international public policy which cannot be derogated from

---

[29] The work of international arbitral tribunals should not be ignored; but they were also a feature of the pevious half century.

by treaty.[30] But important though this might be from a theoretical point of view, so far it has had no practical significance.

On the other hand, international law's growing influence on domestic law is very striking. When I first started reading the law reports in *The Times*, it was rare indeed to find one which involved international law. Now I hardly exaggerate when I say that they appear daily. Even if one leaves aside the impact of European Community law—for when international law is at its most successful, it ceases to be regarded as international law—one regularly finds reports in which English courts have had to take into account such treaties as the Geneva Convention Relating to the Status of Refugees 1951,[31] the Hague Convention on the abduction of children,[32] the European Convention of Human Rights,[33] and so on.[34] Customary international law, too, comes before the domestic courts from time to time, though I cannot resist quoting an observation of Donaldson LJ (as he then was) in *Buttes Oil Co. v. Hammer (No. 3)*[35]: 'Such problems [of maritime delimitation] are the staple diet of distinguished international jurists . . . but have rarely if ever before been visited upon an unsuspecting, and probably unappreciative, English common jury.' But this growing involvement in domestic law is inevitable: just as in many other areas of national life, in law too we increasingly need to co-operate with other states in order to further our national objectives, and the medium for this co-operation is international law.

International Legal Theory

All of these profound changes in international law have not been matched by great developments in its theory. By the time the UN was founded, positivism had long supplanted the natural law

---

[30] See the Vienna Convention on the Law of Treaties 1969, 1155 *UNTS* 331, Arts. 43 and 64.

[31] 189 *UNTS* 150, as amended by the Protocol Relating to the Status of Refugees 1969, 606 *UNTS* 267.

[32] Convention on the Civil Aspects of International Child Abduction (1986), 66 *UKTS* Cm 33.		[33] 213 *UNTS* 221.

[34] This is all the more remarkable when one reflect that (unlike many other countries) treaties are strictly not part of the law of the land until they have been formally transformed into our law by Parliament—and not all of them have been, most notably the European Convention on Human Rights.

[35] [1980] 3 WLR 668, 685.

approach; and this is still the case. General Marxist legal theory no doubt offered some useful insights into the relations between law and society; but for the most part communist international legal theory was the handmaiden of the ever-changing policies of the Soviet State, and it has suffered the same fate. In the United States, the policy-oriented approach developed at the Yale Law School by Myres McDougal and his associates[36] has shown signs of falling into a similar trap, the beneficiary here being US foreign policy. The work of Richard Falk has shown that this is not necessarily inherent in the theory,[37] and he has used it to develop a very radical left-wing agenda. But by doing so he has pointed up some of the deeper faults of the approach. Above all, even if we could all agree on the things everyone is said to value, such as well-being, skill, affection, wealth, and so forth—all of the things which conduce, in McDougal's phrase, to 'human dignity'—we would profoundly disagree on the relative importance to be accorded to these various goals, and probably even more on the means to attain them.[38]

More recently, there has emerged, in the United States in particular, the critical legal studies movement.[39] Like most theories of law, there is of course something in it. But probably the most fundamental defects of this approach are, first, that its adherents seem to adopt a methodology whose premise is that something can only be black or white, not appreciating that there are many shades of grey in between; and, secondly, that they seek to replace law by diplomacy, thus depriving society of a very valuable—not to say indispensable—instrument.

Finally, the theory of international law seems to have been very little influenced of late by international relations theory—perhaps

---

[36] See e.g. Myres S. McDougal and Harold D. Lasswell, 'The Indentification and Appraisal of Diverse Systems of Public Order' (1959) 53 *AJIL* 1; Myres S. McDougal, Harold Lasswell, and W. Michael Reisman, 'Theories about International Law: Prologue to a Configurative Jurisprudence' (1958) 8 *Virginia J. of International Law* 188.

[37] e.g. 'New Approaches to the Study of International Law' (1967) 61 *AJIL* 477; 'A New Paradigm for International Legal Studies' (1975) 84 *Yale LJ* 969.

[38] This is also one of the objections which can be levelled against theories of natural law. This is not to say that the policy-oriented approach has not made any useful contribution; it has, for instance, produced some valuable insights by approaching international laws as a *process*.

[39] See especially Martti Koskenniemi, *From Apology to Utopia* (Helsinki, 1989); David Kennedy, *International Legal Stuctures* (Baden-Baden, 1987).

because there is in fact a bewildering multiplicity of theories of international relations.

But maybe the chief reason why there has been no fundamental change in the theory of international law is that, despite its huge quantitative expansion, its extension into new fields, and its greater penetration into domestic law, international relations have not changed all that much so far. The nation state is still king; it is the focus of our allegiance and the most immediate source of power over us. Politicians, and those who elect them, remain motivated almost exclusively by perceptions of the national interest[40] rather than those of humanity. We have not advanced very far from the days of the League of Nations—or, indeed, of the Treaty of Westphalia of 1648.

The Next Half Century?

What, finally, of the next half century? Specifically, is there anything which might *fundamentally* transform the existing system? Some have predicted the decay of the state, which (as we have seen) is the basis of our present system. There are indeed a number of threats to it.

First, there are the pressures leading to the breakdown of states into smaller and smaller components. Briefly, the state has come to be associated with the idea—and often it is little more than a myth—of the 'nation'. If the nation is thought to mean a group of people, occupying a more or less determinate territory, with a common language, culture, and history, then there are many groups within existing states who do or might lay claim to separate nationhood. In this country alone, there are Scottish, Welsh, and Irish nationalist movements; in France the Bretons and the Corsicans; in Spain the Basques and others; in India the Kashmiris, Sikhs, and various other groups; and so on. The break-up of former Yugoslavia and of the Soviet Union are recent examples of the success of such movements; and the attempts to 'sub-Balkanize' Bosnia represent, not just the *reductio ad absurdum*, but *ad genocidam*, of the idea of the nation-state. For if your claim to separate statehood is based on your ethnic identity, you may be tempted to 'ethnically cleanse' those who do not belong to your group. Understandably,

---

[40] Some, of course, are not even that altruistic.

existing states are trying to resist this centrifugal tendency, but there are many places where it could conceivably occur. If it did, a world in which there were, say, 400 states, most of them tiny, would I think be very different one from the one we know today.

On the other hand, there are certain agglomerative tendencies too, as existing states find that they cannot achieve all of their objectives in relative isolation. So we have the European Union, the North American Free Trade Area, Mercosur, and so on. At the moment even the most developed of them, the EU, is no more than a limited confederation for limited purposes. But confederations rarely stay that way: they either break up, or become federal states. Perhaps in fifty years time there will exist only a small number of regional super-states. If this occurred, there might be a modified form of international law operating within each federation,[41] and a different one between the blocs. But such a state of affairs would not be a great novelty for international law: in the nineteenth century, for instance, the law of nations was a system which operated mainly between a small number of Great Powers.

A further threat to the state is said to be posed by technological change, especially in communications. Until recently, the loyalty of the citizens could be largely assured through the control that the authorities could exercise over the sources of information available in books, the press, radio, and television. Now, with satellite communications, the internet, and so on, it is becoming more and more easy for people to find out the truth: and in many countries the truth, and a perception of shared interests with others abroad, may undermine the state's claims to loyalty.

Internationalization, or, some would say, the communications revolution, has also contributed greatly to the globalization of the world economy. If states cannot control the inward and outward flow of goods, currency, and other forms of investment they lose, it is suggested, an important part of what has traditionally been regarded as their power base. We may need to distinguish here between industrialized and developing countries.[42] With the liberalization of capital flows, industrialized countries seem to have

---

[41] Just as public international law still regulates boundary questions between the United States of America, for instance.

[42] The 'newly industrialized countries' of East and South-East Asia are in a category of their own.

lost a great deal of control over their exchange rates, and all that flows from them—not to another type of statal organization, but to offshore funds and the like which have great influence but no policy as such. For essentially they react to momentary situations, often with very serious effects. In the case of international trade, on the other hand, although individual countries have relinquished a good deal of their authority to intergovernmental and supranational bodies, this means that collectively, at least, they still retain a certain measure of control. In any case, it must not be forgotten that much trade still remains purely domestic. And when it comes to investment, again, much of it is domestic, not foreign. So I think that this alleged threat to the industrialized state from globalization, though far from negligible, may be exaggerated. Third World countries may be in a different position—in some respects more vulnerable, in others less so. They are obviously *more* vulnerable to the extent that they have a weak economic base and are dependent on trade, investment, and economic assistance from the outside. Paradoxically, they may be *less* vulnerable so long as the great majority of their citizens are unable, through poverty and lack of communications, to participate in the global system, except very indirectly.

The speed of change in the world today is such that it would be very unwise to predict how things will be fifty years hence. But I cannot see the state disappearing through globalization in the near future.[43] The more so since there seems to be no power structure ready to take its place. Even today, no single state is able to establish a global empire: and I really do not think that Coca-Cola, Shell, or Citibank are ready or anxious to administer individual countries, let alone the world. So it seems that states are likely to be with us for a good while yet, though their functions may change a good deal.

The other thing that could *conceivably* transform international society and its legal system is the increasing realization that all mankind is in the same, very leaky, boat. The dangers which face the survival of civilization or even of our entire species are very real and very imminent. The Cold War may have receded, but there are many tonnes of plutonium and highly enriched uranium left in the

---

[43] Cf. Paul Q. Hirst and & Grahame Thompson, *Globalization in Question: The International Economy & the Possibilities of Governance* (Cambridge, 1996).

world, much of it badly guarded; and more and more states and, possibly, even terrorists are acquiring the technology to make nuclear weapons, each of which requires only a few kilogrammes of either of these minerals. Some responsible scientists think that the danger is even greater now than before the break-up of the Soviet Union. Chemical and bacteriological weapons, too, have been, and probably will continue to be, developed with greater and greater ease, and with more and more deadly effect. Apart from these grave military threats, overpopulation and the pollution and despoliation of our planet create an ever-growing danger of mass starvation and disease. We have so far relied on science and technology to improve the world; but many of these problems are themselves the result of what seemed advances in those disciplines, and there is no guarantee that their practitioners will be able to pull our chestnuts out of the fire.

So far, although states have responded to these threats by a series of treaties and other instruments, their reaction has been woefully inadequate. The problem is that, in a world of sovereign states, only too often the convoy moves at the pace of the slowest ship; and different states, for different reasons which seem good to them, are unwilling to take the drastic measures which could—if we are lucky—avert these catastrophes. It is possible that nations will wake up in time to the collision course that spaceship Earth seems to be on. After all, 'men and nations sometimes behave wisely, once they have exhausted all the other alternatives'.[44] If so, there will probably have to be very radical changes to the way the world is managed and the way the law made. But there again, the past record and the apparent inability of our species to see far enough ahead give cause for considerable pessimism.

Hence, I fear, the question mark at the end of the title of this paper: 'International Law in the Past Half Century—and the Next?'. It is not just that I am necessarily unsure what the next half century holds in store for us. It is also that none of us can be certain that there will be another half century for mankind. This is the challenge which confronts my generation and that of today's students: should we prove unequal to it, it will perhaps be fitting if cockroaches inherit the earth.

---

[44] Abba Eban, 'Prospects for Peace in the Middle East' (David Davies Memorial Institute of International Studies, Annual Memorial Lecture, 1988).

INDEX